PRINCIPLES OF GOVERNMENT CONTRACTS

Seventh Edition

Steven W. Feldman

Attorney Advisor (Ret.),
U.S. Army Engineering and Support Center,
Huntsville, Alabama

CONCISE HORNBOOK SERIES™

COPYRIGHT © 1979, 1990 WEST PUBLISHING CO.
© 2000, 2004 West, a Thomson business
© 2011 Thomson Reuters
© 2016 LEG, Inc. d/b/a West Academic
© 2020 LEG, Inc. d/b/a West Academic
      444 Cedar Street, Suite 700
      St. Paul, MN 55101
      1-877-888-1330

Printed in the United States of America

ISBN: 978-1-68467-940-9

I would like to thank two special persons for their support. First and foremost, to my dear wife, Gayla, for her continuing love and encouragement. She was with me every night (and many days) as I worked on this text. I also express my appreciation to my late wife of 25 years, Ann Feldman, who was a wonderful helpmate during our marriage, even in the final stages of her cancer.

Preface

Contracting with the federal government is an important part of American economic life. The United States spends billions of dollars every year on the procurement of supplies, services, and construction. But government contracting also has unique problems and pitfalls. So, while many companies have become successful by concentrating most of their efforts on doing business with the federal government, either as a prime contractor or subcontractor, others have not fared as well.

This Principles of Government Contracts Concise Hornbook, Seventh Edition, is intended to highlight the essential elements and principles of government contracting regarding both contract formation and contract administration. It provides the reader with a foundation for understanding how government procurement works in formal and informal ways. Ideally, this treatment will enable students and practitioners to become familiar with the fundamentals of government contracting in a relatively short time.

As its title indicates, this text is a "Concise Hornbook," and not a full analysis of all contracting doctrines and procedures. Thomson Reuters has several multi-volume treatises devoted to this subject. Government contracting is a field filled with laws and regulations and countless significant legal decisions and is rife with protests, disputes and litigation. It is also a field in constant flux and has changed in major ways since the publication of the Sixth Edition of this book in 2016. Chapter numbering follows the coverage in the applicable part of the Federal Acquisition Regulation, the guidepost of federal executive branch contracting.

Although the Hornbook's primary audience is the student of federal government procurement, those with contracting experience should also find it of value. The text has been organized to parallel the events that someone would probably experience as a government contractor or as a government contracting official or other procurement professional. For them, the book will serve as a guide to specific areas with which they may be unfamiliar and as a useful reference in those areas where they are already knowledgeable.*

Steven W. Feldman

April 2020

---

* This text was written by Mr. Feldman in his personal capacity and the views expressed do not represent those of any federal agency.

Summary of Contents

Table of Contents

PART III. CONTRACTING METHODS
AND CONTRACT TYPES

PART IV. SOCIOECONOMIC PROGRAMS

PART V. GENERAL CONTRACTING REQUIREMENTS

PRINCIPLES OF GOVERNMENT CONTRACTS

Seventh Edition

Part I

GENERAL

Chapter 1

FEDERAL ACQUISITION
REGULATIONS SYSTEM

Analysis

A. REGULATIONS ISSUED UNDER
THE BASIC STATUTES

§ 1.1   In General

Congress plays a fundamental role in federal procurement. Under Article I, section 9, clause 7 of the United States Constitution, Congress is the ultimate source of funds for federal government contracts. As an outgrowth of its constitutional procurement powers, Congress may enact statutes that prescribe the substantive and procedural policies of federal contracting.

After World War II, Congress enacted the Armed Services Procurement Act of 1947, which applies to the military agencies, the Coast Guard and the National Aeronautics and Space Administration, and the Federal Property and Administrative Services Act of 1949, which controls the civilian executive agencies, except as provided by law. These Acts, as amended, together with voluminous implementing regulations, comprise most of the

3

procedures governing the Federal procurement system. These enactments directly affect federal procurement or can less directly control the field. Examples of the latter category are those laws implementing socioeconomic policies, such as the Small Business Act, which promotes use of small business concerns or the Miller Act, which requires certain construction contractors to carry performance and payment bonds.

Some statutes may subordinate federal acquisition to state law. On the other hand, the supremacy clause of the Constitution, Article VI, clause 2, requires that federal statutes, regulations with the force of law, and the federal "common law"—case law legal principles— rather than conflicting state or local law, determine the parties' rights and obligations under a federal contract when a substantial federal interest would be adversely affected by state or local law application.

Another key aspect of the congressional impact on federal procurement is the Government Accountability Office (GAO), headed by the Comptroller General. In the procurement field, the GAO's chief role is to conduct audits of the effectiveness and efficiency of government operations and to decide, after the request of a federal agency or an interested party, the propriety of contract solicitations, the cancellation of solicitations, and awards and proposed awards. These latter administrative challenges are known as "bid protests" and the case law coming from the GAO has great weight with both the courts and federal agencies.

The judicial branch also plays an important role primarily through the decisions of the United States Court of Federal Claims, which has jurisdiction under the Tucker Act to consider bid protests by interested private parties. The Court of Federal Claims also has jurisdiction under the Contract Disputes Act to adjudicate contract claims by either the government or the contractor that have become contract disputes. The United States Court of Appeals for the Federal Circuit is the Court of Federal Claims' immediate appellate authority. The United States Supreme Court only rarely will decide a procurement action, usually one of national importance.

The Executive Branch is the third major player, primarily though the actions of the federal agency purchasing activities, the Office of Federal Procurement Policy, the Defense Acquisition Regulations Council, the Civilian Agency Acquisition Council, and the agency boards of contract appeals, the latter deciding contract disputes. The President frequently issues executive orders that can impact government contracting as well.

§ 1.2   The Federal Acquisition Regulation

Effective April 1, 1984, the Federal Acquisition Regulation (FAR) was established for the codification and publication of uniform policies and procedures for acquisition by all executive agencies, unless excluded. The System consists of the FAR (which is called "the primary document") and agency acquisition regulations that implement or supplement the FAR.

FAR clauses and provisions are incorporated in covered federal solicitations and contracts either in full text (where there is a fill-in) or more commonly by reference. Clauses and provisions included by reference have the same force and effect as those FAR terms included in full text. The FAR is available at http://farsite.hill.af.mil/.

The FAR is codified as Chapter 1 of Title 48 of the Code of Federal Regulations and contains 52 parts categorized in eight Subchapters: (A) General; (B) Competition and Acquisition Planning; (C) Contracting Methods and Contract Types; (D) Socioeconomic Programs; (E) General Contracting Requirements; (F) Special Categories of Contracting; (G) Contract Management; and (H) Clauses and Forms. This Hornbook shall generally follow the FAR sequence in treating the subject matter of government contract law.

The Office of Federal Procurement Policy in the Executive Branch has created the Federal Acquisition Regulatory Council to oversee the coordination of executive branch-wide procurement policy. The two councils within this body—namely, the Defense Acquisition Regulations Council (DAR Council) and the Civilian Agency Acquisition Council (CAA Council)—jointly prepare, issue and maintain the FAR and are subject to its being "in accordance with the requirements of the Office of Federal Procurement Policy Act."

The FAR System is prepared, issued, maintained, and "prescribed," jointly by the Secretary of Defense, the Administrators of General Services and the National Aeronautics and Space Administration under their several statutory authorities. Except where expressly excluded, the FAR applies to all "acquisitions." The quoted concept means "the acquiring by contract with appropriated funds of supplies or services (including construction) by and for the use of the Federal Government through purchase or lease." Thus, the FAR by its terms applies to services, supplies and construction but does not apply to procurements using non-appropriated funds or to the sale of government property. Furthermore, it applies to the purchase of new and old items, i.e., to the supplies or services "already in existence" or which "must be created, developed, demonstrated, and evaluated."

The "statement of guiding principles for the Federal Acquisition System" tells participants in the acquisition process "to work together as a team" and not only (a) to "exercise personal initiative and sound business judgment;" but also (b) that they "may assume" if a "specific strategy is not addressed in the FAR, nor prohibited by law (statute or case law), Executive order or other regulation" that the strategy is a permissible exercise of authority.

The FAR demonstrates a new overriding policy. That direction is for the Federal Acquisition System to deliver on a timely basis the best value product or service to the customer, while maintaining the public's trust and fulfilling public policy objectives.

In contrast to the wide discretion granted to the acquisition team to innovate, controls on deviations to the FAR policies are tightly administered. One variety of a deviation is any policy, practice, or procedure "inconsistent with the FAR." Another variety is the issuance of any policy or procedure that has not been properly incorporated into agency acquisition regulations. Contracting officials must obtain higher level approval for one time or class based deviations. Section § 1.6 discusses this topic in greater detail.

§ 1.3   Revisions to the FAR

A possible impediment to the efficient promulgation of new or revised regulations exists as a result of the separation between the military and civilian councils, discussed above. Revisions to the FAR are prepared and issued through the coordinated action of these two councils. The chairperson of the CAA Council is the representative of the Administrator of General Services. The other members of this council are "one each representative from the (1) Departments of Agriculture, Commerce, Energy, Health and Human Services, Housing and Urban Development, Interior, Labor, and Transportation, and (2) Environmental Protection Agency, Small Business Administration, and Department of Veterans Affairs and the Social Security Administration."

The Director of the DAR Council is the representative of the Secretary of Defense. The operation of the DAR Council is as prescribed by the Secretary of Defense. Membership includes representatives of the military Departments, the Defense Logistics Agency, and the National Aeronautics and Space Administration. Each Council has cognizance over specified parts or subparts of FAR and is responsible for agreeing on all revisions with the other Council; submitting to the FAR Secretariat information; and publicizing in the Federal Register of a notice soliciting comments on a proposed revision to the FAR.

All comments received in response to a notice of proposed revisions must be considered. Each Council must arrange for public meetings; prepare any final revision in the appropriate FAR format and language; and submit any final revision to the FAR Secretariat for publication in the Federal Register and printing for distribution. Notice of a proposed regulation and a comment period must be published in the Federal Register. Unsolicited recommendations for revisions for meeting certain criteria may also be considered and public meetings may be held.

Unless otherwise specified, the general rule is that FAR changes apply to solicitations issued on or after the effective date of the change. For solicitations issued before the effective date of the FAR revision, Contracting Officers may include the revision, provided that the contract award will occur on or after the effective date of the revision. At their discretion, Contracting Officers may include FAR changes in any existing contract with consideration going to the contractor.

Federal Acquisition Circulars (FACs) updating portions of the FAR are made quickly available from GSA's website. Both suggested and actual revisions in portions of the FAR have normally come from several sources. Discussion of the recent revisions will be made in this volume. They were mostly derived from the Office of Federal Procurement Policy (OFPP).

§ 1.4   The Force of Procurement Regulations— the *Christian* Doctrine

Regulations published in the Federal Register and the Code of Federal Regulations have the force and effect of law, i.e., they are binding on Federal agencies and the general public. Such publication gives legal notice of their contents to all who may be affected thereby.

Where the primary intended beneficiary of a procurement regulation is the Government, a private party cannot complain about the Government's failure to comply, even if the private party would derive some incidental benefit from Government compliance.

The *Christian* doctrine affects contracts in those instances where the government has failed to follow mandatory regulations. The case of *G.L. Christian & Associates v. United States,* 312 F.2d 418 (Ct. Cl. 1963), concerned a contract that did not include a clause required by a regulation, i.e., the standard termination for convenience clause. In holding that the particular clause must be read into the contract by operation of law, the former Court of Claims (predecessor to the Federal Circuit) ruled that required contract clauses can be deemed included in a validly awarded contract as a matter of law, even if physically absent.

The rationale for this doctrine is that the Contracting Officer has no authority to contract except in accordance with the regulation which has the force and effect of law. Furthermore, the only regulations governing the legality of a contract are generally those that were in existence at the time the contract was awarded. A court must "reasonably be able to conclude that the grant of authority contemplates the regulations issued."

As clarified by later decisions, the *Christian* doctrine holds that a mandatory contract clause that expresses a significant or deeply ingrained strand of public procurement policy is considered to be included in a contract by operation of law. The *Christian* doctrine does not result in the automatic incorporation of non-mandatory clauses.

Continuous use of the word "shall" found in many FAR clauses indicates that its drafters were cognizant of the *Christian* Doctrine and anticipated its being applied to errors of inadvertent omission on the part of a Contracting Officer. However, in 1996 a board of contract appeals case, *Computing Application Software Tech.*, ASBCA No. 47554, 96-1 BCA ¶ 28,204, the ASBCA refused to hold that an omitted mandatory NASA FAR Supplement property clause must be incorporated into a contract. This decision illustrates that the *Christian* doctrine is not self-defining. It grants courts and boards discretion on the malleable concept of what constitutes a "deeply ingrained strand of public procurement policy." Notably, *Christian* applies only to missing clauses from a contract, and not to provisions missing from a solicitation.

A few decisions seem to apply a more lenient standard on whether missing FAR clauses will apply under *Christian*. For example, a Court of Federal Claims decision has ruled that when a contract subject to the FAR incorporates improper terms of the FAR, the correct provisions of the FAR will control.

§ 1.5   FAR Implementation and Supplementation

The FAR is subject to further implementation by the procuring agencies where they follow their procedures and the process for FAR supplementation. Where published in the Federal Register and codified in the Code of Federal Regulations, these agency level policies similarly have the force and effect of law.

The FAR itself specifically provides that "an agency head may issue or authorize the issuance of agency acquisition regulations that implement or supplement the FAR." ("Supplementary material" means that there is no counterpart in the FAR.) These regulations are for the military departments and defense agencies, NASA, and the civilian agencies other than NASA. The latter civilian agency regulations are "issued by the heads of those agencies subject to the overall authority of the Administrator of General Services or any independent authority the agency may have."

Such implementing or supplementing regulations incorporate, together with the FAR, agency-wide policies, procedures, contract clauses, and solicitation provisions that govern the contracting process. In addition, they control the relationship between the agencies, including any of its suborganizations, and contractors or prospective contractors and must be published in the Federal Register (as required by the Federal Register Act) and codified (under an assigned chapter in Title 48, Code of Federal Regulations). They are parallel to the FAR in format, arrangement, and numbering system.

An agency's acquisition regulations "shall not unnecessarily repeat, paraphrase, or otherwise restate material contained in the FAR or higher-level agency acquisition regulations; or (except as required by law or as provided in FAR Subpart 1.4) conflict or be inconsistent with FAR content" unless an agency's statutes specifically require such an inconsistency. Yet, these lower level regulations are often very detailed (and rarely challenged as being unauthorized).

§ 1.6   FAR Deviations

The making of "deviations" from the FAR is a practice of conducting procurement actions of any kind and at any stage of the acquisition process that is "inconsistent with the FAR." The term also includes "the omission of any prescribed solicitation provision or contract clause," as well as the use of any such provision or clause with modified or alternate language that is not authorized by the FAR. The FAR states that deviations from the FAR may be granted when necessary to meet the specific needs and requirements of each agency. Part of the justification for this authority to deviate is to permit "the development and testing of new techniques and methods of acquisition."

An "individual deviation" affects only one contract action and must be approved by the agency head or an authorized delegee. If the deviation is to affect more than one contract action and is to be used on a permanent basis, it is called a "class deviation" and the agency then "should propose an appropriate FAR revision to cover the matter."

The use of the word "should" raises the questions of (a) how long an agency may wait before submitting the deviation proposal, and (b) how long an agency may continue to use a "class deviation" after submission to the FAR Secretariat while awaiting a possible revision of the FAR. The term "may" is defined in the FAR definitions section as "permissive," with the exception that where the words "No person may ..." appear in the regulation, then no person is authorized, required, or permitted to do the act described. The word "should" in the definitions section means "an expected course of action or policy that is to be followed unless inappropriate for a particular circumstance."

A deviation from the FAR is authorized when it is required to comply with a treaty (a government to government agreement). However, a deviation cannot be authorized if it has become inconsistent with FAR coverage based on a law enacted after the execution of the treaty.

§ 1.7   Other Procurement Policies and Directives

In addition to the FAR, other official policies and directives may impact federal contracting: Executive Orders; Office of Management and Budget (OMB) Circulars; Office of Federal Procurement Policy Letters; and various other military and civilian regulations, directives, manuals, and orders. The agencies also may issue particular instructions for its personnel in conducting an acquisition.

Generally, the procurement adjudicators will not consider legal challenges based merely on violations of internal agency policies. Thus, the GAO has declined to do so because its statutory jurisdiction only extends to asserted violations of procurement statutes or regulations. Similarly, the federal courts have held that internal agency procurement policies do not contain implied private rights of action for a party to enforce their provisions.

Absent a statute or regulation incorporating such internal guidance, the adjudicators usually view these policies as only managerial tools to aid in procurements, and any violations are to be redressed by agency officials. These internal regulations and procedures stem from 5 U.S.C.A. § 301, a "housekeeping" statute allowing agency heads to govern internal departmental affairs. The only exception is that if the solicitation states that the agency will be bound by an internal agency policy, then the agency must comply with the term during the source selection phase or be subject to protest for a violation.

B. CONTRACTING AUTHORITY AND RESPONSIBILITIES

§ 1.8   Authority to Represent the Government— the Contracting Officer

The person executing or terminating a contract on behalf of the government is called a "Contracting Officer." The term includes authorized representatives of the Contracting Officer acting within the limits of their authority delegated by the Contracting Officer. Thus, several individuals may represent the public body in the capacity of Contracting Officers. For example, a "termination Contracting Officer" (TCO) is only authorized to settle terminated contracts while a single Contracting Officer may be responsible for duties in this area as well as many others.

Today, agency heads are authorized to delegate micro-purchase authority, i.e., $3,500 or below, except for construction subject to the Wage Rate Requirements Construction (formerly known as the Davis Bacon Act), where the threshold is $2,000 and except for services subject to the Service Contract Labor Standards (formerly known as the Service Contract Act), where the threshold is $2,500). Statute may affect these thresholds in described instances.

Agency heads may also "assign contracting functions and responsibilities from one agency to another" as well as create "joint or combined offices" to exercise acquisition functions and responsibilities.

Contracting Officers have unique authority to bind the government after ensuring that all requirements of law, executive orders, regulations and all other applicable procedures, including clearances and approvals, have been met. Such officials receive instructions regarding the limits of their authority. If they are without authority, payments under a contract will generally be refused because contracting officer power is limited to binding the government "only to the extent of the authority delegated to them." As stated above, Contracting Officers receive from the appointing authority instructions in writing regarding the limits of their authority.

Only a limited number of high-level agency officials are designated Contracting Officers solely by virtue of their position. Otherwise, Contracting Officers also are allowed wide latitude to exercise business judgment and are responsible for ensuring "compliance with the terms of the contract, and safeguarding the interests of the United States in its contractual relationships" and they must ensure that "contractors receive impartial, fair, and equitable treatment."

Sometimes, the government will seek to escape a bargain on the theory that the Contracting Officer exceeded his or her authority by making a poor business judgment. Some cases state that the Contracting Officer's obligation to protect the government's business interests does not immunize the agency from improvident agreements. But the Contracting Officer is prohibited from exceeding statutory or regulatory restrictions.

To counteract a Contracting Officer's tendency to over-enhance his reputation as one who can "get along with" a contractor, a Contracting Officer in many instances should not make many decisions alone. The FAR provides that this official must "request and consider the advice of specialists in audit, law, engineering, transportation, and other fields, as appropriate." However, these persons are advisors only and are without contractual authority to bind the government.

As a result of the acquisition streamlining reforms of the 1990's, Government agencies may delegate micro-purchase authority to employees and members of the Armed Forces who are not Contracting Officers. Micro-purchases do not require any provisions or clauses, with certain exceptions. The Government-wide commercial purchase card is the preferred method to purchase and pay for micro-purchases.

The Government-wide commercial purchase card may be used to make micro-purchases, place task or delivery orders, or make payments when the contractor has agreed to accept payment by that means. Although the micro-purchase threshold and use of government purchase cards revolutionized government contracting, some persons have expressed concern about the lack of effective oversight. Indeed, the GAO has periodically issued reports criticizing agencies for abuses in this area.

For the rules on simplified purchases, see Chapter 13.

§ 1.9   Government Agents and Actual Authority

In a government of delegated powers, no activity may be undertaken by a government employee except pursuant to such power. Accordingly, persons in the private sector are bound by operation of law to have knowledge of the limitations of the particular government employee's authority, in negotiating a government contract, in order to meet or, if necessary, to counter the actions of the government.

A major concern in the negotiation of a government contract is the principle that a private party's lack of knowledge of the government employee's actual authority is normally not reason enough to hold the government liable if such authority is absent. Unlike dealings between private parties, a person is charged with knowledge of the extent of the actual authority of the government's contracting agent because no agent of the government can hold himself out to have any authority not sanctioned by law. Apparent authority is not sufficient to bind the government employee's agency. It is presumed that one can always ascertain the extent of the employee's authority. By contrast, the government may freely invoke the doctrine of apparent authority when dealing with agents of a contractor.

Actual authority is not always express; it may be implied. Boards and courts will examine the totality of the circumstances to determine whether a reasonable person would have considered the agent's actions to be an integral part of the agent's specifically assigned duties. Put another way, the government agent has implied authority to take those actions that are reasonably and naturally incidental to his express authority. It must be emphasized that the question of authority differs from whether the agreement was merely improvident—boards and courts have rejected a government defense on this basis.

The requirement of actual authority is illustrated by the decision of the United States Supreme Court in *Federal Crop Insurance Corp. v. Merrill,* 332 U.S. 380, 68 S. Ct. 1, 92 L. Ed. 10 (1947). A government corporation created under the Crop Insurance Act was vested with the authority to insure crops against loss. In spite of regulations issued by the corporation prohibiting reseeding, the plaintiff, who had applied for crop insurance, reseeded after his crop was destroyed by drought. Further, this action was apparently done with the knowledge and consent of an agent of the government corporation.

When the government refused to pay for his loss, the plaintiff sued in a state court and recovered. In these state proceedings, the Idaho Supreme Court held that the knowledge and consent of an agent of a private insurance company, under circumstances identical or similar to this case, would bind a private insurance company in addition to binding the government corporation.

The government appealed and the United States Supreme Court reversed the decision of the Idaho Supreme Court. The Supreme Court granted judgment for the government on the grounds that the regulations specifically prohibited insurance of the wheat that was reseeded and such regulations duly published in the Federal Register are binding, regardless of a plaintiff's lack of actual knowledge thereof. The Court noted that:

> Whatever the form in which the government functions, anyone entering into an arrangement with the government takes the risk of having accurately ascertained that he who purports to act for the government stays within the bounds of his authority.

Although the dissent argued that it was absurd to require farmers to take cognizance of such regulations, the majority held that "not even the temptations of a hard case can elude the clear meaning of the regulations." The rationale that the Court used is that a government of delegated powers goes to the Federal constitution and the authority of all Contracting Officers is limited.

Although a contractor may be able to recover costs based on implied-in-fact contract to pay for such costs, there can be no recovery if the Contracting Officer lacked the requisite authority to bind the government and the Government refuses to ratify (discussed in § 1.10 below). Further, lack of proper delegation of authority may deprive a plaintiff of any compensation. Thus, the United States Court of Appeals for the Federal Circuit held in *CACI, Inc. v. Stone,* 990 F.2d 1233 (Fed. Cir. 1993), that the Army's failure to obtain a delegation of procurement authority (under a now-superseded statute) for the purchase of information technology resources resulted in a contract being declared void, i.e., a nullity. Other cases, however, say the contract in such circumstances is only voidable, i.e., capable of being approved after the fact by an authorized person.

§ 1.10   Apparent Authority, Estoppel and Ratification

(a) Apparent Authority

Although government and private contracts are similar, when a contract is executed by a government official or employee without authority to do so, or if funds have not been appropriated by the Congress for a contract so executed, it has generally been held that the agreement does not bind the government. A leading case is *The Floyd Acceptances,* 74 U.S. 666, 19 L. Ed. 169 (1868), in which the Supreme Court held that the United States was not bound by bills of exchange accepted by government agents where the bills constituted advance payments that were prohibited by statute. The Court stated:

> We have no officers in this government, from the President down to the most subordinate agent, who does not hold office under the law, with prescribed duties and limited authority.

In a government contract, the Contracting Officer authority differs from the agent of a private corporation in that the doctrine of apparent authority is normally inapplicable.

(b) Estoppel

Where a contract is made on an unauthorized basis, the U.S. Supreme Court has strongly indicated that payment thereon cannot be made on the grounds of an estoppel against the United States. "Equitable estoppel" is a legal doctrine that precludes a party from raising an otherwise available defense or claim because that party is guilty of some improper conduct in relation to the instant legal action.

The traditional elements of equitable estoppel are: (1) the party to be estopped must know the facts; (2) that party must intent that his conduct is to be acted on or must so act that the party asserting the estoppel has a right to believe it is so intended; (3) the party asserting the estoppel must be ignorant of the true facts; and (4) the party asserting the estoppel must rely on the other party's conduct to his detriment. Modern courts have since elaborated upon this doctrine by requiring a higher level of government misconduct as will be discussed below).

The Supreme Court in 1981 confirmed the doctrines pertaining to the necessity of authority (in the *Merrill* case) and the general inapplicability of estoppel against the United States in *Schweiker v. Hansen,* 450 U.S. 785, 101 S. Ct. 1468, 67 L.Ed.2d 685 (1981). There, the Respondent was erroneously told by a Social Security representative that she was not eligible for certain benefits. In reliance thereon she failed to file an application as required by statute and regulation.

Later she did receive a district court ruling for retroactive benefits on the ground of estoppel against the United States. The court of appeals affirmed below and stated "misinformation provided by a government official combined with a showing of misconduct (even if it does not rise to the level of a violation of a legally binding rule) should be sufficient to require estoppel." The Supreme Court reversed, claiming it "has never decided what type of conduct by a government employee will estop (i.e., preclude) the government from insisting upon compliance with valid regulations." The Court suggested that approval might occur where "estoppel [does] not threaten the public fisc as estoppel does here."

More recent cases have addressed the possible availability of equitable estoppel against the Government. For example, in 1990, the Supreme Court in *Office of Personnel Management v. Richmond,* 496 U.S. 414, 110 S. Ct. 2465, 110 L.Ed.2d 387 (1990), held that equitable estoppel cannot form the basis for a monetary claim against the United States contrary to statute; this was because of a constitutional rule requiring disbursements from the treasury only by congressional authorization. Notwithstanding this decision, the United States Court of Appeals for the Federal Circuit held in *Burnside-Ott Aviation Training Center, Inc. v. United States*, 985 F.2d 1574 (Fed. Cir. 1993), that equitable estoppel has not been foreclosed as a possible theory for recovery on a contract claim.

The decisions further indicate that the equitable estoppel doctrine is disfavored, mandates proof of serious injustice, and requires courts to exhibit the utmost caution and restraint. Another view in the circuit courts is that a party seeking to estop the Government must prove the agency's affirmative misconduct. Indeed, every court of appeals adds this misconduct element to the traditional test in theory for equitable estoppel, which goes beyond the government agent's simple negligence or misrepresentation.

(c) *Ratification*

Courts and boards have often taken on the responsibility of determining whether ratification, i.e., after the fact approval, has occurred. If it has not occurred (that is, if the government agent with such authority has not ratified unauthorized acts), then courts have held that they "are powerless to do it for him."

In the past, some common law principles of ratification have been applied to Contracting Officers with respect to actions by government employees who did not have authority to bind the government. By definition, the ratifying officials themselves must have the authority to take the original unsupported action.

In 1988, the FAR finally provided for formal ratification of "unauthorized commitments"—namely, "an agreement that is not binding solely because the Government representative who made it lacked the authority to enter into that agreement on behalf of the Government. This person is the head of the contracting activity, unless a higher level official is designated by the agency, and he or she may ratify an unauthorized commitment. The FAR permits delegation of ratification authority from the head of the agency to the chief of the local contracting office. Based on the FAR, these transactions can occur under progressively lower monetary ceilings the further down the delegation, but this authority may only be exercised under strict criteria. Therefore, ratification might occur where supplies or services have been provided to and accepted by the government, or the government otherwise has obtained or will obtain a benefit resulting from performance of the unauthorized commitment.

The price for a valid ratification must have been determined as "fair and reasonable." The funds must have been available at the time the authorized commitment was made. FAR 1.602–3 requires legal advice to be obtained in cases that are not ratifiable and (erroneously) states that agencies should process unauthorized commitments instead of referring such actions to the Government Accountability Office (GAO) for resolution—the mistake in the regulation is the GAO by statute no longer has claims resolution authority. The regulation further advises that unauthorized commitments that would involve claims subject to resolution under the Contract Disputes Act of 1978 "should be processed" in accordance with Disputes and Appeals (see Chapter 33).

Notwithstanding the FAR's formal ratification process, courts and boards of contract appeals continue to allow informal ratification of unauthorized actions. According to the decisions, the agency's failure to follow the FAR's ratification procedures does not preclude a tribunal's findings of ratification. For an informal ratification to occur, (a) the ratifying official must have had actual or constructive knowledge of the unauthorized action, and (b) there must be a demonstrated acceptance of the unauthorized action by the ratifying official.

Informal ratification also can occur through "institutional ratification," which exists when a government agency accepts benefits followed by a promise of payment by the agency or approval of payment by a senior agency official with authority to obtain reimbursement for the one providing the benefits. Query whether courts and boards should allow informal ratification where the intent of the FAR is to limit ratification to the regulatory criteria.

§ 1.11   Illegal Contracts

(a) In General

Contracting officials lack authority to waive the statutory and mandatory regulatory rules for procurement, except as authorized by law. Although some decisions (and even some statutes) state without qualification that a contract executed in violation of statute or regulation is illegal and unenforceable, such is not the prevailing view under most cases.

The majority of cases hold that if a government officer awards a contract in violation of statute or regulation, the agreement will be void where the illegality is plain or palpable under the circumstances, that is, the deviation is egregious or obvious to the awardee (and regardless of any competitive prejudice to another offeror). Where the contractor did not contribute to and was not on direct notice of a mistake before award, the award is not clearly illegal and the resulting contract is not void. Examples of void contracts are those that have a disability from their inception, such as those executed in contravention of the anti-kickback laws, the conflict of interest statutes, and the statutes on the availability of appropriations. The awardee's good faith conduct, however, will ordinarily preclude a finding of voidness.

As just indicated, the legality question is case-specific. A statutory or regulatory violation may be plain or palpable in one circumstance, but not in another. If a reasonable doubt exists, the court or board should find the contract legally enforceable rather than void if the agreement is otherwise not subject to challenge. The reasoning here is that voiding a contract for illegality is not a favored approach because courts and boards should strive to preserve contractual validity/stability and to employ the presumption that the parties intended a binding transaction.

After the government's cancellation of a void agreement, the private party has no right to compensation for goods or services previously provided if the illegality stemmed from that party's fraudulent or criminal conduct. The government also may seek recoupment of payments previously made. The rationale for this harsh rule of forfeiture is to deter tainted contracts, and is supported by 28 U.S.C.A. § 2514 (applicable only to the Court of Federal Claims), which directs the forfeiture of a claim against the government infected by fraud or criminality. However, in *Laguna Constr. Co. v. Carter*, 828 F.3d 1364 (Fed. Cir. 2016); 58 GC ¶ 264, the Federal Circuit allowed agencies to achieve the same type of forfeiture allowed at the Court of Federal Claims through the doctrine of prior breach.

If the statutory infraction does not relate to the party's misconduct, then the entity may recover *quantum meruit* (the reasonable value of services) or *quantum valebant* (the reasonable value of goods and materials) for conforming services or goods the government accepted before any rescission. The contractor here is not compensated under the contract, but rather under a separate implied-in-fact contract.

(b) Anti-Deficiency Act

The Anti-Deficiency Act, 31 U.S.C.A. § 1341, prohibits contracts purporting to bind the government beyond the obligational characteristics of the appropriation. Under the Act, and except as otherwise provided by law, an officer or employee of the United States Government or of the District of Columbia may not: (1) make or authorize an expenditure or obligation *exceeding an amount* available in an appropriation or fund for the expenditure or obligation; or (2) involve either government in a contract or obligation for the payment of money *in advance of* an appropriation is made unless authorized by law.

Violations can occur in a wide variety of factual circumstances, such as: (1) recording an obligation in excess of available appropriations; (2) making payments against an exhausted or insufficient appropriation; (3) making a firm commitment for a multiyear contract absent compliance with the multiyear contracting procedures; and (4) committing the government to contingent or unlimited liability. An example in the latter category is an indemnification agreement to make good on a contractor's losses absent statutory authority.

In sum, the Act serves to restrict the use of appropriations only to the purposes for the particular fiscal year that they are authorized. The Act has criminal penalties for knowing and willful violations, and law and regulation requires the reporting of the improper obligation through channels all the way to the president and Congress, and the possibility of administrative penalties against the involved employees. A possible Anti-Deficiency Act violation will be present at the instant the improper obligation occurs, and not when actual payment is scheduled (or when the problem is discovered).

C. DETERMINATIONS AND FINDINGS

§ 1.12   In General

The regulations state that for certain contract actions, a Determination and Findings (D & F) is required. These consist of written approval by an authorized official that is required by statute or regulation. The "determination" is a conclusion or decision supported by the "findings." The findings are statements of fact or rationale essential to support the determination and it covers each requirement of the statute or regulation.

Each D & F must set forth facts and circumstances that clearly and convincingly justify the specific determination being made. Examples of a contract action requiring a D & F are where the Contracting Officer uses a time and materials contract or where the contracting activity on behalf of another government agency provides services or supplies under an interagency arrangement pursuant to the Economy Act.

These approvals may also be granted for classes of contract actions for the same or related supplies or services. Both individual and class D & F's may provide for flexibility in their application, such as reasonable variations in estimated quantities or prices. If a D & F is superseded by another D & F, then that action shall not render invalid any action already taken under the original D & F. Further, a modification of the D & F does not require cancellation of a solicitation where the D & F, as modified, supports the contract action.

Chapter 2

DEFINITIONS OF WORDS AND TERMS

Analysis

§ 2.1   In General

---

§ 2.1   In General

The definition section of the Federal Acquisition Regulation (FAR), Part 2, sets forth the meanings of many terms that are used throughout the regulation; this meaning prevails unless a different definition appears elsewhere or the context "clearly requires a different meaning." Two of these definitions ("Head of Agency," and "Contracting Office") are included in a "Definitions Clause" to be included in all significant solicitations and contracts. More definitions are being found to be commonly used in the regulation. For example, in July, 1996, the regulators transferred to Part 2 the definitions pertaining to micro-purchases and simplified acquisition procedures.

Definitions in FAR Part 2 apply to the entire regulation unless specifically defined in another part, subpart, section, provision, or clause. Words or terms defined in a specific part, when used in one of those places have that meaning when used in that part, subpart, section, provision, or clause. The Index section of the FAR contains a comprehensive listing of all definitions in all sections. Thus, for example, "administrative change" appears in the FAR part on contract modifications (Part 43). Significant changes in these definitions may occur from time to time. For example, when "signature" was modified to include electronic symbols in 1995 and where the regulators provided comprehensive definitions of a "commercial item" and "electronic commerce."

The overwhelming majority of terms appear in the particular parts of the FAR without indicating another Part. Some terms found elsewhere become among those set forth in Part 2. For example, the definitions of "bid sample" and "descriptive literature" were moved from FAR Part 14 to FAR 2.101 because the definitions apply to more than one FAR part (i.e., Parts 14 and 25). Regulations supplementing the FAR also may define terms; for example, the Department of

Defense FAR Supplement gives the meaning of "Contracting Officer's Representative" and "tiered evaluation of offers."

FAR uses the word "shall" extensively. This term has an "imperative" meaning and is to be contrasted with "should," which means an "expected course of action or policy that is to be followed unless inappropriate for a particular course of action." An example of "shall" in the regulation is that agencies "shall" impose and collect civil penalties pursuant to the Program Fraud and Civil Remedies Act. An example of a "should" is that the files for firm fixed price contracts above the simplified acquisition threshold should be closed within six months after the date on which the Contracting Officer received evidence of physical completion.

The FAR system is not all-inclusive on the meaning of the procurement concepts. In construing solicitations and contracts, courts, boards, and GAO commonly employ standard dictionaries as a guide.

Chapter 3

IMPROPER BUSINESS PRACTICES AND PERSONAL CONFLICTS OF INTEREST

Analysis

§ 3.1   Ethics in Contracting

In an attempt to assure that government business be conducted in a manner above reproach and with impartiality, certain statutes have been enacted and regulations promulgated. For example, the regulations state that "as a rule, no government employee may solicit or accept, directly or indirectly, any gratuity, gift, favor, entertainment, loan, or anything of monetary value from anyone who has or is seeking to obtain government business with the employee's agency . . . ". The words "as a rule" themselves denote that the words which follow are not necessarily to be taken automatically, and the paragraph ends by specifying that "certain limited exceptions are authorized in agency regulations." This approach is designed to emphasize the use of other parts of the regulation.

Numerous statutes and regulations cover ethics in government contracting. Emphasizing the steady flow of False Claims Act court decisions, this Chapter will analyze some of the more important restrictions on government and industry personnel.

§ 3.2   Procurement Integrity

What is commonly called the "Procurement Integrity Act" was amended by Congress in 1996 to overhaul the rules regulating the relationship between government employees involved in the procurement process and contractors competing for government contracts. The Act imposes broad restrictions on the conduct of government procurement officials and their contractor counterparts and represents an intensive effort on the part of Congress "to correct the seedy trade of favors and information" and thus restore the public's confidence in the procurement process. The Act and its implementing regulations target both improper conflicts of interest and the improper disclosure or receipt of procurement information.

The Procurement Integrity Act imposes restrictions on the acceptance of employment by former agency officials from government contractors and on employment contacts between agency officials and government contractors. Specifically, designated agency officials involved in a procurement more than $10 million may not accept compensation from the contractor as an employee or consultant of the contractor for one year. No prohibition exists against accepting compensation from a division or affiliate of the contractor that does not produce the same or similar products or services. In addition, if an agency official, who is personally and substantially involved in a competitive agency procurement in excess of the simplified acquisition threshold, contacts or is contacted by a bidder or offeror on that procurement regarding nonfederal employment for the official, the agency official must report the contact to the agency and promptly reject the employment opportunity or disqualify himself from further participation in the procurement.

Individuals or companies that violate the conflict-of-interest provisions of the Procurement Integrity Act face substantial administrative and civil penalties. The criminal penalties provided by the Act apply only to violations of the Act's prohibitions on disclosing or obtaining procurement information.

The Procurement Integrity Act circumscribes the disclosure or receipt of procurement information and defines the scope of the proper exchange of information between agency officials and contractors during the procurement process. The Act prohibits current or former federal officials (or those acting on their behalf or advising the agency) from, "other than as provided by law," "knowingly" disclosing—or a "person" (such as a contractor, or individual, or other business entity) from knowingly obtaining—"contractor bid or proposal information or source selection information before the award of a federal agency procurement contract to which the information relates."

A "federal agency procurement" is defined as a procurement using competitive procedures (and is subject to dollar thresholds for covered contracts as indicated above). "Contractor bid or proposal information" is information submitted to a federal agency in connection with a bid or proposal (including cost or pricing data, indirect costs and direct labor rates, proprietary information, etc.), and "source selection information" is information not previously made available to the public that is prepared for use by a federal agency in evaluating a bid or proposal.

Violations of the procurement information provisions of the Procurement Integrity Act carry criminal, civil, and administrative sanctions. In addition, the government may take actions to cancel the procurement, rescind the contract, or initiate suspension or debarment proceedings against the contractor.

In a separate statute, a DOD official covered by the requirements of Pub. L. No. 110–181 (a "covered DOD official") who, within 2 years after leaving DOD service, expects to receive compensation from a DOD contractor, shall, prior to accepting such compensation, request a written opinion from the appropriate DOD ethics counselor regarding the applicability of post-employment restrictions to activities that the official may undertake on behalf of a contractor. A DOD contractor may not knowingly provide compensation to a covered DOD official within two years after the official leaves DOD service unless the contractor first determines that the official has received, or has requested at least 30 days prior to receiving compensation from the contractor, the requisite post-employment ethics opinion. A standard Department of Defense Federal Acquisition Regulation Supplement clause implements these requirements.

If a DOD contractor knowingly fails to comply with the above requirements, administrative and contractual actions may be taken, including cancellation of a procurement, rescission of a contract, or initiation of suspension or debarment proceedings.

§ 3.3   Anti-Kickback Act

The ongoing federal campaign against fraud, waste, and abuse in the contracting process has focused primarily on prime contractors and their dealings with the federal government. As part of this trend, in 1986, Congress passed the Anti-Kickback Act to revitalize efforts to control "kickbacks"—commercial bribes—paid by subcontractors, vendors, and suppliers to prime contractors, other subcontractors, or their representatives in return for favorable contractual treatment.

The Anti-Kickback Act injected new life into a pre-existing anti-kickback statute that had been characterized as "extraordinarily ambiguous" and filled with "loopholes, limitations, and relics of a bygone contracting era that has not kept pace with changes in contracting practices." A result of the 1986 Act, there has been more vigorous criminal and civil policing of both prime contractors and subcontractors.

The Anti-Kickback Act expressly bans three categories or types of conduct. It forbids any individual or business entity from: (1) providing, attempting to provide, or offering to provide any kickback; (2) soliciting, accepting, or attempting to accept any kickback. and (3) including (directly or indirectly) the amount of any prohibited kickback in the price charged by a subcontractor to a prime contractor or higher-tier subcontractor, or in the price charged by the prime contractor to the government. Violations of the Act also can support a qui tam action under the False Claims Act.

The term "kickback" is defined as "any money, fee, commission, credit, gift, gratuity, thing of value, or compensation of any kind which is provided, directly or indirectly," to any prime or subcontractor or their employees "for the purpose of improperly obtaining or rewarding favorable treatment in connection with a prime contract or in connection with a subcontract relating to a prime contract." The terms "money," "credit," and "thing of value" were intended to expand the definition of a "kickback" to allow the government to prosecute more violators under the Act by making it clear that the Act reaches all forms of payment.

The Anti-Kickback Act extends to any type of government contract (although most violations occur in the context of construction projects) and prohibits offers and attempts to provide kickbacks as well as executed kickbacks. The Act also places obligations on contractors and subcontractors to report, in writing, suspected violations of kickback laws to the government, and the procurement regulations require prime contractors on large contracts to establish and follow "reasonable procedures" designed to prevent and detect violations of the Act.

The Act provides for criminal, civil, and administrative penalties. "Knowing and willful" violations of the Anti-Kickback Act are criminal offenses. The Contracting Officer may also offset the amount of the kickback paid against any amounts owed by the government under the contract to which the kickback relates. Employers may be vicariously liable for double damages under the Anti-Kickback Act. The Act does not, however, grant a defendant a right of indemnification or contribution from third parties.

§ 3.4   Buying-In

"Buying-in" occurs when a proposer submits an offer below its anticipated costs with the intent to recover any losses on an inappropriate basis from the government thereafter. Thus, a buy-in can occur when a vendor submits a below cost offer expecting to increase the contract amount after award through unnecessary or excessively priced change orders. In another example, a buy-in can occur when the below cost offeror expects to recoup its losses by receiving follow-on contracts at artificially high prices.

Buy-ins can decrease competition and cause poor contract performance. Contracting officials must take appropriate action to ensure that the below cost awardee does not seek to "get well" with change orders or follow-on contracts. The GAO has held that this preventive approach is the sole policy of the buy-in procurement regulations.

The government can minimize the opportunity for buy-ins by soliciting offers with a price commitment that covers as much of the agency's program needs as practicable. Available techniques in this regard can include multiyear contracting (with prices only submitted for the total multiyear quantity) or priced options that together with firm contract quantities will equal the program requirement. The FAR mentions other safeguards against buy-ins, such as amortization of nonrecurring costs.

The Comptroller General has considered numerous protests that an award to a below cost or buy-in offeror would restrict full and open competition. Such challenges have arisen regarding both firm fixed price and cost reimbursement contracts.

A firm fixed price contract is not subject to adjustment based on the contractor's cost experience during performance and places no obligation on the contracting agency to pay more than the contract price (except as allowed by remedy-granting clauses, such as the Changes clause). Therefore, the GAO has held that, without more, the submission of a below cost or low profit offer in this context is not an illegal buy-in and provides no basis for challenging or withholding an award of a firm fixed price contract to a responsible prospective contractor. Moreover, various valid reasons can justify a below cost offer for a firm fixed price contract, such as the desire to keep a plant running, to best its competitors, to retain a group of employees or to establish a new market.

The Comptroller General also has reviewed protests concerning buy-ins for a proposed cost reimbursement contract. In this context, an alleged buy-in furnishes no basis to challenge an award when the agency knows the realistic estimated costs of contractor performance before award and makes the award based on that knowledge. Thus, a below cost offer for a cost reimbursement contract (or for that matter a firm fixed price contract) is not legally objectionable per se so long as the Contracting Officer finds the offeror responsible.

§ 3.5   Conflicts of Interest and Former and Current Government Employees

A conflict of interest violation can occur when the particular person's violation is known to or condoned by his or her superiors, and a prime contractor representing the United States will be governed by the same standards as allowed by law. Examples of the criminal statutes in this area include those targeting bribery; accepting compensation in matters affecting government; acting as agent for another against interests of United States; having a financial interest in a government matter wherein the employee has substantial personal participation; and accepting salary supplementation from private sources for performance of government duties. The courts have held that they may set aside a government contract if the award is tainted by a conflict of interest.

(a) Former Employees

Regarding former employees, some of the applicable statutes, executive orders, and regulations strike a balance between the individual's right to make a living versus the government's need to prevent conflicts of interest by a government employee who might favor a firm he or she thinks may offer rewards after his or her separation from public service. Other rules seek to deter either "influence peddling" or a former employee's exertion of undue influence with agency personnel. In sum, these provisions create a code of ethics for former federal personnel to ensure their undivided loyalty as government employees.

Titles 10 and 18 of the United States Code contain most of the post-employment restrictions. In an example of a felony conflict of interest provision, one statute states that no "former government employee" (as defined by law and regulation) after terminating government employment may knowingly act as agent or attorney for, or otherwise represent any other person in any informal or formal appearance before, or with the intent to influence, make any oral or written communication on behalf of any other person: (1) to the United States, (2) in connection with any particular government matter involving a specific party; and (3) in which matter such employee participated personally and substantially as a government employee.

In GAO bid protests, disappointed offerors increasingly have contended that a proposed awardee should be excluded from the competition (or an award terminated) because a present or former government official has violated a conflict of interest statute or regulation. Generally, the GAO will consider such allegations, but only to decide whether the present or former employee's actions resulted in prejudice for, or on behalf of, the awardee.

The Comptroller General generally refuses to decide whether the former executive branch employee has violated these laws or regulations, because the Comptroller General claims a lack of authority to render formal opinions concerning the conduct of employees of other government agencies. Therefore, the Comptroller General has said such questions must be resolved by the agency, the Department of Justice, and the courts.

In a 1989 case, *Damron Corp.*, Comp. Gen. Dec. B-232721, 89-1 ¶ 113, the GAO summarized the standard of review regarding former employees:

> When a conflict of interest is alleged, our role within the context of a bid protest is to determine whether any action of the former government employee resulted in prejudice for or on behalf of the awardee. The mere fact that a former government employee is subsequently employed by a company that was awarded a contract by the employee's former agency is an insufficient basis to challenge the award where there is no evidence that the former employee influenced the award. Further, there must be hard facts and not mere suspicion or innuendo that a conflict of interest exists before a firm may be excluded from a competition on this basis.

The protester has the burden of affirmatively proving its case. Therefore, the GAO will not conduct an investigation for the purpose of establishing the truth of a protester's speculative statements. Similarly, a firm's mere employment of a former government official who is familiar with the type of work required, but who is not privy to the proposals or to other inside information, does not establish any unfair competitive advantage for that firm.

(b) Current Employees

Consistent with its general view, the GAO in a bid protest will not determine whether a current government employee has violated one of these conflict of interest statutes or regulations. The GAO's review generally will focus on whether the individual involved in the alleged improper conduct exerted improper influence in the procurement on behalf of the awardee or if the firm obtained any improper competitive advantage through the employee. Thus, a conflict of interest violation is not automatic grounds for disqualifying an offeror from further consideration, except where a statute or regulation so requires.

Similarly, a government employee's violation of agency standards of conduct regulation regarding a particular firm is not automatic grounds for disqualifying that firm. On the other hand, the GAO has sustained protests (and even recommended contract termination) where a government official wrongfully disclosed procurement-sensitive information about one offeror to another such offeror during an acquisition, regardless of whether the disclosure gave the firm an actual competitive advantage. In this setting, the GAO has dispensed with the normal requirement for competitive prejudice to uphold a bid protest because the propriety of the award must also be judged on whether the integrity of the competitive system has been compromised by allowing the award to remain undisturbed.

The procuring agency has the initial responsibility for determining whether a competing offeror has a conflict of interest. When the agency's decision is based on credible evidence and not on mere suspicion or innuendo, contracting officials may reasonably exclude a firm from further consideration or take lesser corrective action to protect the integrity of the procurement system. The agency may even take such corrective action when (1) no statute or regulation specifically covers the problem at hand, and (2) the solicitation has not given advance notice of such grounds for rejection. FAR provides the regulatory authority for taking this action to safeguard the government's interests.

As indicated above, even if no *actual* conflict of interest can be shown, a procuring agency may reasonably decide to disqualify a firm or to take other corrective action based on some reasonably *apparent* conflict of interest. Here, "hard facts" (and not mere suspicion, innuendo, or theoretical or remote concerns) must reasonably support the agency's judgment that the likelihood exists of an actual conflict of interest.

Generally, an offeror rejected for these reasons is not being excluded for lack of responsibility but is excluded to ensure the integrity of the competitive process. Similarly, when the agency decides to allow an offeror to compete in the face of conflict of interest allegations or indications, the GAO will only determine whether the agency acted reasonably. The perpetrator's alleged intention to benefit the government is irrelevant and does not alter the result of an actual or reasonably apparent unfair competitive advantage or disadvantage accruing to an offeror.

§ 3.6 Contractor Responsibility to Avoid Improper Business Practices

The Close the Contractor Fraud Loophole Act of 2008 requires timely notification by federal contractors of violations of certain federal laws or overpayments in connection with the award or performance of covered contracts or subcontracts, including those performed outside the United States and those for commercial items.

"Covered contract" means "any contract in an amount greater than $5,000,000 and more than 120 days in duration." FAR now requires government contractors and subcontractors to report to the Government whenever they have "credible evidence" of certain criminal violations, a violation of the civil False Claims Act, or a "significant overpayment" in connection with the award, performance, or close-out of a government contract or subcontract.

The mandatory disclosure rule has three parts. First, it requires mandatory disclosure to the agency's Office of the Inspector General (IG) and the cognizant Contracting Officer when the contractor, in connection with the contract incorporating the clause, has credible evidence that a principal, employee, agent, or subcontractor has committed (1) a violation of federal criminal law involving fraud, conflict of interest, bribery, or gratuity violations found in Title 18 of the United States Code, or (2) a violation of the civil False Claims Act. Second, the standard "Contractor Code of Business Ethics and Conduct" FAR clause requires contractors to establish and maintain an internal control system that includes timely disclosure to the agency IG and Contracting Officer when the contractor, in connection with the award, performance, or closeout of *any* government contract performed by the contractor or its subcontractors, has credible evidence that a principal, employee, agent, or subcontractor has committed a violation of one of the specified federal criminal laws or civil False Claims Act. Third, the rule adds the knowing failure to disclose credible evidence of specific crimes, false claims and significant overpayments as a new cause for suspension or debarment.

As with disclosures under the internal control system, the disclosure obligation imposed by the suspension/debarment rule applies to violations in connection with any Government contract or subcontract, and therefore includes violations occurring before the new rule took effect on December 12, 2008.

§ 3.7 Voiding and Rescinding Contracts

The FAR has a subpart (3.7) to implement a statute and Executive Order which prescribes procedures for exercising discretionary authority to declare void and rescind contracts in relation to which there has been "a final conviction for bribery, conflict of interest, disclosure or receipt of contractor bid or proposal information or source selection information in exchange for a thing of value or to give anyone a competitive advantage in the award of a Federal agency procurement contract, or similar misconduct." Administrative remedies may apply, authorizing the voiding or rescission of such contracts and recommending the initiation of suspension or debarment proceedings (see Chapter 9).

"Final conviction" for purposes of this remedy includes a plea of *nolo contendere*, for which sentence has been imposed. Such final convictions must be reported to the agency head or his designee, who may issue a notice of the proposed action to declare void and rescind the contract by certified mail. The contractor then has 30 days to submit pertinent information and an opportunity to be heard if "no inquiry shall be made regarding the validity of the conviction." If a decision is made to declare void and rescind the contract, it must reflect consideration of the fair value of any tangible benefits received and retained by the agency and state the amount due and the property to be returned to the agency. This decision is not a claim within the meaning of the Contract Disputes Act of 1978 (CDA) (see Chapter 33).

§ 3.8   Fraud, Whistleblowers and the Civil False Claims Act

The civil False Claims Act, as amended in 1986, permits the government to recover treble damages and penalties from any person (or company) who submits a false claim to a federal agency, which infraction can include a private contractor managing a state construction project.

Damages trebled under the Civil False Claims Act are limited to the difference between the market value of the products the Government actually received and the market value of what the Government should have received under its contract(s) with a defendant. The Government is not entitled to damages equal to three times the full amount paid under any contract "tainted" by illegality. Similarly, if the civil penalties are grossly disproportionate to the gravity of defendant's offense, the award could be an excessive fine prohibited by the Eighth Amendment.

A person may be liable under the Civil False Claims Act, as amended by the Fraud Enforcement and Recovery Act of 2009, if he—

(A) knowingly presents, or causes to be presented, a false or fraudulent claim for payment or approval;

(B) knowingly makes, uses, or causes to be made or used, a false record or statement material to a false or fraudulent claim;

(C) conspires to commit a violation of subparagraph (A), (B), (D), (E), (F), or (G);

(D) has possession, custody, or control of property or money used, or to be used, by the Government and knowingly delivers, or causes to be delivered, less than all of that money or property;

(E) is authorized to make or deliver a document certifying receipt of property used, or to be used, by the Government and, intending to defraud the Government, makes or delivers the receipt without completely knowing that the information on the receipt is true;

(F) knowingly buys, or receives as a pledge of an obligation or debt, public property from an officer or employee of the Government, or a member of the Armed Forces, who lawfully may not sell or pledge property; or

(G) knowingly makes, uses, or causes to be made or used, a false record or statement material to an obligation to pay or transmit money or property to the Government, or knowingly conceals or knowingly and improperly avoids or decreases an obligation to pay or transmit money or property to the Government.

Under the civil False Claims Act, the government must show a violation by "a preponderance of the evidence." This burden of proof applies to all essential elements of a civil false claims violation, including proof of damages. The Act does not, however, allow a defendant a right of indemnification or contribution from third parties.

(a) The "Knowledge" Requirement

The civil False Claims Act defines the terms "knowingly" as used in the Act. A person acts "knowingly" if he has actual knowledge of the information or acts in deliberate ignorance (or in reckless disregard) of the truth or falsity of the information. The term has been held to include "an aggravated form of gross negligence" or "gross negligence plus." In construing this requirement, the courts have said that the evidence must demonstrate guilty knowledge or a purpose on the part of the defendant to cheat the government, or knowledge or guilty intent. Note, however, that no proof of specific intent (as in the sense of the criminal law) to defraud the government is required.

Under the 2009 revisions to the False Claims Act, it no longer matters whether the submitter of the record or statement intends that the Government rely on it where deciding to pay a claim or whether the submitter knows that Government funds are involved. It matters only whether the record or statement has a natural tendency to influence, or be capable of influencing, the payment or receipt of money or property.

Innocent mistakes or negligence in submitting a claim are not violations under the Act. Nevertheless, even where a contractor submits a payment voucher to the government in the correct, fixed amount, if the required work has not been completely performed, contrary to the representation in the request for payment, the voucher constitutes presentation of a false claim. The revised False Claims Act deletes the former requirement that the claim be "presented" to an officer, agent or employee of the United States, although this circumstance may still support false claims liability.

Contract interpretation issues—and whether an incorrect, but reasonable interpretation can constitute a false claim—have also been considered by several courts. In one case—involving an interpretation of a number of provisions of the Cost Accounting Standards—the court said that while the question of reasonable interpretation could have an impact on the contractor's intent, the key issue here was whether the claim was "false." This point is determined by examining whether the contractor's representations were accurate in light of applicable law. In another case involving the interpretation of regulations, the court looked at all of the relevant facts and concluded that no intent to defraud the government was present. In yet another case, the court focused on whether the contractor believed in its interpretation of the contract terms without the court's making a detailed analysis of the contract language.

The contractor's reasonable interpretation of an ambiguous regulation precludes a finding of scienter absent authoritative guidance warning the defendant away from its interpretation. However, a contractor would not necessarily be shielded from False Claims Act liability based on the contactor's assertion the agency knew the contractor's proposed costs were inaccurate.

(b) Definition of a "Claim"

The term "claim" under the Fraud Enforcement and Recovery Act of 2009 (FERA), means any request or demand, whether under a contract or otherwise, for money or property and whether the United States has title to the money or property that is presented to an officer, employee, or agent of the United States or that is made to a contractor, grantee, or other recipient, if the money or property is to be spent or used on the Government's behalf or to advance a Government program or interest.

The qualification to this last variation is if the United States Government provides or has provided any portion of the money or property requested or demanded or will reimburse such contractor, grantee, or other recipient for any portion of the money or property which is requested or demanded. Lastly, the term "claim" does not include requests or demands for money or property that the Government has paid to an individual as compensation for Federal employment or as an income subsidy with no restrictions on that individual's use of the money or property.

Assume the prime contractor had initially made false statements regarding the need for award of a subcontract and certified the lack of a conflict of interest with the subcontractor. Even though the prime's actual claim for payment to the government for the subcontractor's services was not literally "false," each claim had been submitted under a subcontract that was fraudulently approved by the government, thereby making the claims for payment "false" under the Act. Similarly, a False Claims Act violation can occur where the contractor had obtained a contract, not by submitting false information to the government, but by submitting the information in a deceptive way.

A "false claim" can be present with the submission of preliminary paperwork, even if a subsequent claim for payment is truthful, whereas a claim will not be "false" when there was no evidence that the contractor's request for compensation was invalid. Similarly, a mere scheme to defraud is not adequate proof of a "false claim." Indeed, even a false certification may not suffice for a "false claim" where the firm making the certification was otherwise contractually entitled to the government funds. Conclusory allegations of false certifications of compliance with statutory, regulatory, or contractual provisions do not give rise to a false claim for payment unless payment is conditioned on compliance.

Another possible basis for a "false claim" is that materially false statements in a proposal inducing the agency to enter a contract can violate the False Claims Act where the contractor submits invoices for payment under the contract. False estimates, defined to include fraudulent underbidding in which the offer is not what the defendant actually intends to charge, can be a source of liability under the False Claims Act, assuming that the other elements of a claim are met. Another common variety of a false claim is the submission of false payroll certifications required by the Wage Rate Requirements statute (formerly called the Davis-Bacon Act).

The Fraud Enforcement and Recovery Act of 2009 (FERA) eliminates the intent requirement from the Supreme Court's decision in *Allison Engine Co. v. United States ex rel. Sanders*, 553 U.S. 662,

128 S. Ct. 2123, 170 L.Ed.2d 1030 (2008), which limited False Claims Act liability to fraudulent statements that were designed to get false claims paid or approved by the Government. Another key FERA changes include a materiality requirement, which means having a natural tendency to influence, or be capable of influencing, the payment or receipt of money or property. Other FERA revisions are an expansion of the conspiracy section, new liability for overpayment, an expanded definition of "obligation," new protections against retaliation against the reporting individual, and authority for civil investigative demands.

The most-frequently litigated False Claim Act issue in recent years is whether the claimant has made an implied false certification sufficient to show legal falsity. In *Universal Health Servs., Inc. v. United States ex rel. Escobar*, 136 S. Ct. 1989, 195 L.Ed.2d 348 (2016), a case concerning a medical provider's alleged violations of medical licensing and supervising regulations, the United States Supreme Court considered whether noncompliance with a material precondition of payment, even if that precondition is not expressly designated as such, is sufficient to state a viable FCA claim.

The Court unanimously held that the implied false certification theory could, under certain circumstances, provide a basis for False Claims Act liability where two conditions are satisfied: first, the claim does not merely request payment but also makes specific representations about the goods or services provided; and second, the defendant's failure to disclose noncompliance with material statutory, regulatory, or contractual requirements makes those representations misleading half-truths.

The False Claims Act also provides for "reverse false claims" actions, although this theory is not frequently used. These claims are called "reverse" false claims because the false statement or record is intended to "conceal, avoid, or decrease an obligation" to pay money to the government as opposed to support a monetary claim against the government. The revised Act expands reverse False Claims Act liability either to knowingly conceal or to knowingly and improperly avoid or decrease an obligation to pay. Thus, the new provision does not require the submission of any false record or statement; the act of simple concealment or even merely avoiding the obligation to pay back funds can qualify.

A prerequisite to "reverse" actions is that the pertinent obligation must have arisen before the person charged made or used the false statement. For example, allegations that a contractor improperly identified new government aircraft equipment as "old" to lower the purchase price were held sufficient to support a reverse false claims action because the contractor was expressly obligated by its contract to account for the full value of any government property.

(c) Penalties

The penalties for violation of the civil False Claims Act may include the assessment of significant damages and fines. The government may recover (1) a fine of between $5,000 and $10,000 for each false claim (or $5,500 and $11,000 for violations occurring after September 29, 1999), (2) an amount equal to three times the amount of damages the government sustained because of the false claim, plus (3) the costs to the government of prosecution. The government may use sampling and extrapolation to establish both liability and damages under the False Claims Act.

Because penalties are imposed for each false claim presented, violation of the civil False Claims Act can lead to large fines that have, at times, been criticized as "unreasonable or excessive." Because damages under the False Claims Act "are essentially punitive in nature," lower federal courts have left open the possibility that damage awards under the statute can violate the constitutional prohibition against excessive fines. To this end, The Department of Defense has issued a Defense Federal Acquisition Regulation Supplement final rule to double to $50 million the FAR 44.302(a) threshold for contractor purchasing system reviews (CPSRs). According to DOD, the change allows DOD to focus its personnel and resources on "other essential priorities and missions of greater contractual risk, while reducing regulatory impact on contractors." See 84 Fed. Reg. 72247 (Dec. 31, 2019). Competitive firm-fixed-price contracts, competitive fixed-price contracts with economic price adjustment and commercial item contracts do not violate the Constitution's Eighth Amendment regarding excessive fines.

The Act attempts to encourage violators to cooperate in the investigation by providing for a reduced penalty of not more than two times the amount of damages sustained by the government if, before the commencement of any criminal, civil, or administrative action, the alleged violator (a) furnishes to the government all information that person has about the violation (within 30 days of receiving the information), (b) cooperates fully with any government investigation, and (c) did not have actual knowledge of the existence of an investigation into the alleged violation.

(d) "Qui Tam" Provisions

"Qui tam" provisions have been part of the civil False Claims Act since its original passage. These provisions allow private individuals—sometimes informally called "whistleblowers"—to initiate civil false claims lawsuits on behalf of themselves and the government and to keep a share of the government's recovery. The government may take over prosecution of the action if it wishes to do so. The law was invigorated by the 1986 amendments to the False Claims Act "to encourage any individual knowing of government fraud to bring that information forward" by making such lawsuits more attractive and lucrative to a plaintiff.

(e) Qui Tam Relators

When a private party files a *qui tam* suit in the name of the government, the lawsuit is said to be brought "on relation of" the private party. Hence, the private party is referred to as the "relator." Relators may be natural persons or artificial entities such as corporations. Most *qui tam* suits are filed by disgruntled or even terminated employees against their former employers. Some *qui tam* relators, however, have continued working for their employers even after filing suits against them.

A law firm, a nonprofit organization, government employees, and an in-house attorney are among those that have filed suits pursuant to the *qui tam* provisions of the civil False Claims Act. The Act bars copycat *qui tam* actions, but a jurisdictionally defective action does not count in determining the first party to file.

The Act also protects employee relators from retaliation (for example, discharge, demotion, or harassment) by their employers for filing *qui tam* suits. The revised False Claims Act extends whistle blower protections to contractors and agents. A retaliation claim is a private action that is separate from any associated "qui tam" claim. Employee severance agreements releasing potential retaliation claims under the *qui tam* provisions of the Act are permissible. The statute no longer protects, however, all lawful acts taken by the by the individual in furtherance of a *qui tam* action. Instead, it protects only those lawful acts in furtherance of other efforts to stop one or more violations of the civil False Claims Act.

(f) Qui Tam Limitations

The False Claims Act sets forth several jurisdictional limitations in *qui tam* suits. For example, the Act precludes (a) suits between members of the military, (b) suits against government officials based on information already known to the government, and (c) suits based on allegations that are the subject of a civil suit to which the government is a party. In addition, where a *qui tam* action is based on publicly disclosed information, the relator must be an "original source" of the information.

Information may be "publicly disclosed" in hearings, reports, audits, investigations, or the news media. A company voluntarily and confidentially disclosing illegal activity to the government may not shield itself from False Claims Act liability on the theory that the voluntary confidential information constitutes a "public disclosure." The False Claims Act precludes an action based on information contained in a publicly disclosed state or local administrative report, unless the United States or an "original source" brings the action.

Numerous cases analyze the "public disclosure" bar to a qui tam action whereby the relator cannot recover a monetary award for certain information already in the public domain. Some fine distinctions exist in this area. An e-mail exchange between a federal employee and a state employee was not a "public disclosure" for purposes of the False Claims Act's public disclosure bar. By contrast, a company voluntarily and confidentially disclosing illegal activity to the government may not shield itself from False Claims Act liability on the theory that the voluntary confidential disclosure constitutes a "public disclosure." The defendant's disclosure of information to an agency inspector general did not trigger the public disclosure bar of the False Claims Act because (1) the information must be placed in the public domain to constitute a public disclosure, and (2) the disclosure was not otherwise sufficient for application.

Where a relator's qui tam action under the False Claims Act was based on public information of which the relator was not an original source, and it is thus foreclosed by the FCA's public disclosure bar. The distribution of state and federal government reports to state and federal agencies does constitute public disclosure for purposes of the False Claims Act; and where an element of a claim under the False Claims Act was not publicly disclosed, the public disclosure bar does not bar a qui tam action.

Congress has significantly changed the False Claims Act's 31 U.S.C.A § 3730's public disclosure bar by narrowing its scope. A disclosure will be considered public only if it occurred in a federal criminal, civil or administrative hearing in which the U.S. government or its agent was a participant in the proceeding, or if the disclosure was made in a federal hearing, audit, report, or investigation. The revised statute effectively moots the U.S. Supreme Court's decision in *Graham County Soil & Water Conservation Dist. v. United States ex rel. Wilson*, 559 U.S. 280, 110 S. Ct. 1396, 176 L.Ed.2d 225 (2010), which ruled that the Act's reference to "administrative" reports include federal and state and local disclosures.

The amendment also eliminates the requirement that the relator has direct knowledge of the claim." Original source" means an individual who has direct and independent knowledge of the information and has voluntarily provided the information to the government before filing the *qui tam* action. In one case, for example, an Administrative Contracting Officer was found not to qualify as an original source because disclosures to the government about the defendant's alleged fraud were an obligation of his job and therefore deemed not "voluntary."

A number of courts have dismissed *qui tam* suits by government auditors under the same rationale. Other decisions hold that a federal auditor, even one whose job it is to investigate fraud, has standing to bring a qui tam lawsuit under the False Claims Act based on evidence uncovered during the course of his employment The original source need only have direct knowledge of the underlying facts, not direct knowledge of the alleged false claims.

Some relators have run afoul of the original source rule where the information that formed the basis of their *qui tam* actions was obtained through a Freedom of Information Act (FOIA) request to the government and was therefore considered information that had already been publicly disclosed. FOIA information, however, is not considered to have been publicly disclosed until it is received by the requester. The mere fact that a government agency has assembled and duplicated records, or noted the absence of records, in responding to a FOIA request does not by itself render the material produced in an administrative report or investigation within the False Claims Act's jurisdictional bar.

Resolving a split within the federal circuits, the United States. Supreme Court has held that materials the agency produces in response to a FOIA request are administrative reports or investigations under the False Claims Act's public disclosure bar, 31 U.S.C.A. § 3730(e)(4)(A). *Schindler Elevator Corp. v. United States ex rel. Kirk*, 563 U.S. 401, 131 S. Ct. 1885, 179 L.Ed.2d 825 (2011).

(g) Qui Tam Procedures

Procedures for initiating a *qui tam* action are detailed and specific. The relator's failure to comply with the statutory procedural requirements can result in dismissal of the action. A general release may bar a relator from bringing a qui tam suit under the False Claims Act if the federal interest in enforcing settlements outweighs the interest in preventing harm to federal policy.

The action is initiated by the relator's filing a complaint in the name of the United States under seal. One potential pitfall is the complaint must specifically identify the particular claim, in keeping with the heightened standards for pleading fraud. For purposes of the False Claims Act's first-to-file rule, however, a first-filed complaint need not necessarily meet heightened pleading requirements for fraud under Federal Rule of Civil Procedure 9(b) to bar later-filed complaints. Another potential pitfall is the relator may not maintain a pro se *qui tam* action under the False Claims Act; he or she must have a lawyer. The relator must provide the complaint, together with substantially all material evidence, to the government.

Until recently, the Circuit courts had split on whether the first to file bar's application lasts only while the earlier-filed suit remains pending or in perpetuity. In *Kellogg Brown & Root v. United States ex rel. Carter*, 575 U.S. 650, 135 S. Ct. 1970, 191 L.Ed.2d 899 (2015), the Court affirmed the Fourth Circuit's holding that the bar is only temporary and no longer bars a related action once the first-filed suit has been dismissed or resolved.

The complaint remains under seal for at least 60 days while the government determines whether it will take over prosecution of the matter or decline to prosecute. In *State Farm Fire & Cas. Co. v. United States ex rel. Rigsby*, 137 S. Ct. 436, 196 L.Ed.2d 340 (2016), the Court held that a violation of the False Claims Act seal provision does not require dismissal of a qui tam complaint in every case.

If the government declines to intervene, the relator has the right to continue the prosecution of the action, subject to a number of limitations. The government may—if it shows good cause—intervene later in the proceedings. Under FERA, the government's complaint in intervention or amendment to a relator's complaint now relates back to the date of the original complaint.

If the government assumes primary responsibility for the case, it may limit the relator's participation and may settle or dismiss the case without the relator's concurrence provided that the government's actions are determined to be fair by the court. The *qui tam* statute provides that the government may dismiss an action over the objections of the relator if the relator was notified by the government of the filing of the motion to dismiss and if the court provided the relator with an opportunity for a hearing on the motion. However, where the government does not intervene and the relator proceeds alone, the case may be dismissed by the relator only if the government concurs in writing.

An ongoing question (and a split among the federal circuits) concerning the constitutionality of *qui tam* actions in which the government opts not to participate was partially resolved by the Supreme Court in *Vermont Agency of Natural Resources v. United States ex rel. Stevens,* 529 U.S. 765, 120 S. Ct. 1858, 146 L.Ed.2d 836 (2000), when it concluded that relators, as "assignees" of the government, have the requisite standing under Article III of the

Constitution to sue on the government's behalf, even in cases where the government has chosen not to intervene.

At the same time, the Supreme Court put to rest several other controversial issues when it held that states are not proper defendants under the False Claims Act, but held in *Cook County, Ill. v. United States ex rel. Chandler*, 538 U.S. 119, 123 S. Ct. 1239, 155 L.Ed.2d 247 (2003), that municipal corporations are "persons" amenable to *qui tam* actions under the Act. But the Supreme Court has not completely closed the door on possible constitutional challenges to the statute's qui tam provisions, and some lower court decisions have held that *qui tam* suits do not violate the "Appointments" and "Take Care" clauses of Article II of the Constitution.

(h) Qui Tam Recovery

If the government prosecutes the action and is successful, the relator receives between 15% and 25% of any proceeds of the action or settlement, depending on the relator's contributions to prosecution of the action, plus an amount for reasonable expenses, attorney fees, and costs. If the government does not proceed with the action and the relator proceeds alone to trial or settlement, it receives between 25% and 30% of the proceeds of the action or settlement, plus an amount for reasonable expenses, attorney's fees, and costs. Any award of legal fees is paid to the relator's lawyer rather than to the relator.

The court may reduce a relator's reward if it finds that the relator planned and initiated the False Claims Act violation. If the relator is convicted of criminal conduct arising out of its role in violating the Act, the relator must be dismissed from the civil action and may not receive any proceeds.

The United States Court of Appeals for the Fifth Circuit has held that the Government has absolute veto power over voluntary dismissals in False Claims Act qui tam actions even when the Government had declined to intervene. *Searcy v. Philips Electronics North America Corp.*, 117 F.3d 154 (5th Cir. 1997).

(i) Other Whistleblower Statutes

Other whistleblower protections protect government personnel. The Whistleblower Protection Act of 1989 prohibits Federal agencies from taking adverse personnel actions against civil servants for disclosures of legal violations or "gross mismanagement, a gross waste of funds, an abuse of authority, or a substantial and specific danger to public health or safety."

DOD has adopted a final rule amending the DFARS to implement statutory amendments to whistleblower protections for contractor and subcontractor employees. In the final rule, DOD inserted a statement in § 203.900 indicating that DFARS subpart 203.9 is to be used in lieu of FAR subpart 3.9. DFARS contractor whistleblower policies are based on 10 U.S.C.A. § 2409, which is no longer implemented in the FAR.

§ 3.9   The Major Fraud Act

The Major Fraud Act of 1988 created a new crime called "major fraud against the United States." This crime covers any government prime contractor (or subcontractor or supplier) who knowingly executes (or attempts to execute) any scheme to defraud the government (or to obtain money or property from the government by false or fraudulent pretenses, representations, or promises) in any procurement of property or services over $1 million. Even if a subcontract is well below the $1 million threshold, a subcontractor is subject to the Act if its prime contract exceeds $1 million.

The Major Fraud Act also contains "whistleblower" protections and rewards. If a contractor discharges, demotes, suspends, threatens, harasses, or otherwise discriminates against an employee who (a) assists in a prosecution under the statute and (b) was not a participant in the unlawful activity that is the subject of the prosecution, the employee can file suit to obtain any relief needed to make him "whole" (including twice the amount of his back pay and any special damages, including litigation costs and reasonable attorney fees). The Attorney General may also pay up to $250,000 to whistleblowers who furnish information relating to a possible prosecution for a major fraud.

Chapter 4

ADMINISTRATIVE MATTERS

Analysis

§ 4.1   In General

Administration of contracts in a general sense covers all matters treated in this Hornbook. The Federal Acquisition Regulation (FAR), however, has limited one part solely to prescribing policies and procedures relating to the administrative aspects of contract execution, distribution, reporting, retention, and files. These minimum administrative guidelines are for files made uniform among all agencies of the government, which constitutes an improvement by itself.

§ 4.2   Signatures of Contracting Officer and Contractor

Only a Contracting Officer can sign contracts, including contract modifications, on behalf of the United States. Further, his or her name and official title must be "typed, stamped, or printed on the contract."

In addition, he or she has the duty to ensure that the "signer(s) have authority to bind the contractor." In this connection, a contract with an individual must be signed by that individual. A contract with an individual doing business as a firm must be signed by that individual, and the signature must be followed by the individual's typed, stamped, or printed name and the words, "an individual doing business as _____."

In the case of partnerships, a contract must be signed in the partnership name. Before signing for the government, the Contracting Officer must obtain a list of all partners and ensure that the individual(s) signing for the partnership "have authority to bind the partnership." A contract with a corporation is signed in the corporate name, followed by the word "by" and the signature and title of the person authorized to sign. Special rules govern signatures by joint ventures as stated in FAR 4.102(d). The regulations prescribe that a Contracting Officer ensures that the person signing for the corporation "has authority to bind the corporation." Normally this action is accomplished by having the corporate secretary certify that the corporate officer who signed in fact held that office at the time he signed; the secretary will also stamp the corporate seal on top of (or after) his certification.

Each signed or reproduced copy of the signed contract or modification that is intended to have the same force and effect as the signed original was formerly required to be marked "DUPLICATE ORIGINAL." Once signed by both parties, Contracting Officers must distribute copies of contracts or modifications within ten working days. However, where approval of a contract is not binding until written approval at a level higher than that of the Contracting Officer, the contract must so provide, and presumably final distribution will await written approval by the higher level.

The government must ascertain the authority of the signor and requires often-illegible script be followed by the typed or printed name that can be read. In the case of a corporation, where the contract involves a significant amount, it is commonplace for the signature of the corporate officer to be certified by corporate secretary after execution. This is because the board of directors could have modified or eliminated that officer's authority on the eve of the date the contract was executed. The Contracting Officer normally signs the contract after it has been signed by the contractor.

On June 30, 2000, the President digitally signed into law the Electronic Signatures in Global and National Commerce Act. "E-sign," as the Act is known, provides for acceptance of digital signatures in commercial contracts, and allows the public and private sectors to maintain and supply most business records in electronic form. A digital signature uses secured codes and identifying markers, rather than handwriting, to ascertain the identity of the signer. In 1996, the Comptroller General held in *National Inst. of Standards & Tec.*, Comp. Gen. Dec. B-245714, 96-2 CPD ¶ 225 that digital signatures meeting the Digital Signature Standard promulgated by the National Institute of Standards and Technology can constitute evidence of a binding agreement.

The term "signature" in the definitions section of the FAR means the "discrete, verifiable symbol of an individual which, when affixed to a writing with the knowledge and consent of the individual, indicates a present intention to authenticate the writing." This action can include electronic symbols. The term "in writing" means any worded or numbered expression that can be read, reproduced, and later communicated, and includes electronically transmitted and stored information.

Cybersecurity for contractor and government information system has taken on increased importance in recent years. See, e.g., FAR subpart 4.1901, Basic Safeguarding of Covered Contractor Information Systems; DFARS Subpart 204.73—Safeguarding Covered Defense Information and Cyber Incident Reporting; and DFARS 252.204–7008 Compliance with Safeguarding Covered Defense Information Controls.

§ 4.3　　Paper Documents

When electronic commerce methods are not being used, a contractor should submit paper documents to the Government relating to an acquisition printed or copied double-sided on recycled paper whenever practicable. If the contractor cannot print or copy double-sided, it should print or copy single-sided on recycled paper.

§ 4.4　　Safeguarding Classified Information

Information may be classified by agencies pursuant to Executive Order. For example, the National Industrial Security Program established a program to safeguard Federal Government classified information that is released to contractors, licensees, and grantees of the United States government. During review of proposed solicitations, access to classified information may be needed by offerors or by a contractor during contract performance; the prescribed procedures must be followed and a special contract clause inserted. A huge number of persons have access to classified data, and the information has not always been well protected.

§ 4.5　　Contract Reporting, Record Retention and Closeout

The Federal Procurement Data System (FPDS) collects data on contracts from government agencies. It then disseminates statistical data to provide a basis for submitting a special report to the President, the Congress, the Government Accountability Office, executive agencies, and the general public. This process provides a means of measuring and assessing the impact of contracting on the economy and the extent to which small business concerns and small disadvantaged business concerns are sharing in contracts. It also provides data for other policy and management control purposes. A clause entitled "Data Universal Numbering System (DUNS)

Number" must be placed in solicitations that are expected to result in a requirement for the generation of a Federal Procurement Data System (FPDS)—Individual Contract. All contract actions over the micro-purchase threshold must be reported to FPDS-NG as individual contract actions after September 30, 2004. The FPDS website, https://www.fpds.gov, provides instructions for submitting data.

In general, contractors must retain records in order to make them available for administration, audit requirements of the contracting agencies, and inspection by the Comptroller General for a period of 3 years after final payment. Certain clauses may require record retention for a longer or shorter period of time. The Audit Clauses used in sealed bid or negotiated procurements require retention of records "until 3 years after any resulting final payment termination settlement," and those pertaining to disputes or litigation must be kept until "such appeals, litigation, or claims are disposed of." These clauses are required to be inserted in all subcontracts over the simplified acquisition threshold (see Chapter 13).

Financial and cost accounting records, including pay administration records, must be retained for four years. Labor cost distribution cards and petty cash records need be held for only two years. The regulation sets forth many examples of the contents of contract files, including purchase requests, acquisition planning information, solicitation documents, request for authority to negotiate, determination and findings, evidence of availability of funds, synopsis of proposed acquisition as published in the SAM.gov and the list of sources solicited.

Regulatory procedures are given for the close-out of files, which will not take place if a contract is in litigation or under appeal, or in the case of a termination, where all termination actions have not been completed. A schedule is set forth for the disposal of contract files which varies according to the documents from six months (for expediting records) until six years and three months after final payment (for signed originals of Determination and Findings and for other documents). Except in the case of litigation or termination, files for contracts using simplified acquisition procedures should be considered closed when the Contracting Officer receives evidence of receipt of property and final payment. Other files for firm-fixed-price contracts should be closed within 6 months after the date on which the Contracting Officer receives evidence of physical completion. Files for all other contracts should be closed within 20 months of the month in which the Contracting Officer receives such evidence, but for files requiring settlement of indirect cost rates should be closed within 36 months of the month in which the Contracting Officer receives that evidence.

The FAR further permits contractors to satisfy the record retention requirements by duplicating or storing records in electronic form "unless they contain significant information not shown on the record copy." Original paper records need not be retained or submitted for audit purposes, so long as the contractor is able, with respect to the electronic record, to: (1) establish procedures ensuring the integrity of the record, (2) provide timely and convenient access through indexing, and (3) retain the original document for one year after imaging to permit validation of the imaging system. Information maintained on a computer must be retained "on a reliable medium" that must not be overwritten for the time periods prescribed for the retention of paper records.

§ 4.6 Electronic Commerce in Contracting

The FAR requires agencies to use electronic commerce "whenever practicable or cost-effective." It further provides that the "use of terms commonly associated with paper transactions (*e.g.,* 'copy,' 'document,' 'page,' 'printed,' 'sealed envelope,' and 'stamped') shall not be interpreted to restrict the use of electronic commerce."

Agencies have broad discretion to select the hardware and software they will use for conducting e-commerce, provided the selected systems, technologies and procedures: (1) are uniform throughout each agency to the maximum extent practical; (2) are implemented only after considering the use of existing infrastructures; (3) facilitate access by small, small disadvantaged, veteran owned, HUBZone, service disabled, and women-owned small business concerns; (4) provide widespread public notice of acquisition opportunities through a "single, Government-wide point of entry" and a means of responding to notices or solicitations electronically; and (5) comply with nationally and internationally recognized standards that broaden interoperability and ease the electronic interchange of information. Additionally, before using e-commerce methods, agencies must ensure their systems are capable of providing appropriate authenticity and confidentiality measures "commensurate with the risk and magnitude of the harm" that may arise from the loss, misuse or modification of electronic information.

§ 4.7 System for Award Management

The System for Award Management (SAM) database to increases visibility of vendor sources (including their geographical locations) for specific supplies and services; and establishes a common source of vendor data for the Government.

Prospective contractors must be registered in the SAM database prior to award of a contract or agreement, with some exceptions, such as (but not limited to) (1) purchases under the micro-purchase threshold that use a Government-wide commercial purchase card as both the purchasing and payment mechanism, as opposed to using the purchase card for payment only and (2) classified contracts when registration in the SAM database, or use of SAM data, could compromise the safeguarding of classified information or national security. Unless the acquisition is exempt, the contracting officer shall verify that the prospective contractor is registered in the SAM database be awarding a contract or agreement.

If the contracting officer, when awarding a contract or agreement, determines that a prospective contractor is not registered in the SAM database and an exception to the registration requirements for the award does not apply, the contracting officer shall, if the needs of the requiring activity allow for a delay, make award after the apparently successful offeror has registered in the SAM database. The contracting officer shall advise the offeror of the number of days it will be allowed to become registered. If the offeror does not become registered by the required date, the contracting officer shall award to the next otherwise successful registered offeror following the same procedures.

GSA is transitioning from its long-term, exclusive reliance on the (Dun & Bradstreet (D&B-based) Data Universal Numbering System (DUNS) as the Unique Entity Identifier (UEI) for contractor identification and registration in the System for Award Management (SAM). Contractors (and prospective contractors) will now self-identify using SAM Managed Identifiers (SAMMIs), with Ernst & Young initially providing the validation services. See, generally, https://servicetoamericamedals.org/about/. Developments In Brief: GSA Begins Transition from DUNS Numbers to SAMMI, 61 GC ¶ 93(a); https://www.gsa.gov/about-us/newsroom/news-releases/gsa-announces-award-for-entity-validation-services; see also, Done with DUNS, https://gsa.federalschedules.com/blog/done-with-duns/.

Chapter 5

PUBLICIZING CONTRACT ACTIONS

Analysis

§ 5.1   Dissemination of Information

With various exceptions (such as emergency procurements or those involving classified matter or perishable goods), information on proposed contract actions in amounts expected to exceed $25,000 must be disseminated to affected industries. The term "contract action" includes all actions regulating in a "contract" as defined by the Federal Acquisition Regulation (FAR), including actions for additional supplies outside the existing contract scope, but excluding actions that are within the scope and under the terms of the existing contract, such as actions properly made under the "Changes" clause.

This dissemination of opportunities to contract is accomplished by transmitting a brief synopsis to the Governmentwide Point of Entry ("GPE"). Until very recently, the Federal Business Opportunities website ("FedBizOpps") has been designated the GPE for federal procurement opportunities, replacing the *Commerce Business Daily* as the primary source for information on competitive opportunities. In early FY 2020, Federal Business Opportunities, or FedBizOpps.gov, was decommissioned in favor of beta.SAM.gov, and later became the Contract Opportunities section of SAM.gov, which delivers more precise results for number, keyword and location searches using new filters.

Notice of proposed contract actions expected to exceed $15,000 but not to exceed $25,000 must be publicly displayed by the Contracting Officer or electronically posted for at least ten days or until after quotations have been opened, whichever is later. The notice must include a statement that all responsible sources may submit a response, which, if timely received, will be considered by the agency. However, the Contracting Officer need not comply with these display requirements when oral solicitations are used or when access to a notice of proposed contract action and solicitation are provided through the SAM.gov and the notice permits the public to respond to the solicitation electronically.

§ 5.2   Synopses of Proposed Contract Actions

(a) In General

For acquisitions of supplies and services, other than those covered by the exceptions and certain special situations, the Contracting Officer must transmit a notice to the government point of entry (GPE) for each proposed contract action expected to exceed $25,000 and may transmit this notice for any mount when advantageous to the Government. The GPE may be accessed via the Internet at SAM.gov. The primary purposes of the notice are to improve small business access to acquisition information and enhance competition by identifying contracting and subcontracting opportunities.

The regulations contain fifteen exceptions to the synopsizing requirement, for example, the synopsis cannot be worded to avoid compromising the national security; unusual and compelling urgency; actions expressly authorized or required by a statute to be made through another Government agency; and orders issued under an indefinite delivery contract.

(b) Publicizing and Response Times

Whenever agencies are required to publicize notice of proposed contract actions, all publicizing and response times are calculated based on the date of publication. The publication date is the date the notice appears on SAM.gov. Generally, the notice must be published at least 15 days before issuance of a solicitation or a proposed contract action the Government intends to solicit and negotiate with only one source, commonly called a "sole source" procurement. For acquisitions of commercial items (see Chapter 12), the Contracting Officer may establish a shorter period for issuance of the solicitation; or use the combined synopsis and solicitation procedure.

The Contracting Officer must establish a solicitation response time that will afford potential offerors a reasonable opportunity to respond to each proposed contract action, (including actions where the notice of proposed contract action and solicitation information is accessible through the SAM.gov), in an amount estimated to be greater than $25,000, but not greater than the simplified acquisition threshold; or each contract action for the acquisition of commercial items in an amount estimated to be greater than $25,000. The

Contracting Officer should consider the circumstances of the individual acquisition, such as the complexity, commerciality, availability, and urgency, when establishing the solicitation response time.

Except for the acquisition of commercial items, agencies shall allow at least a 30-day response time for receipt of bids or proposals from the date of issuance of a solicitation if the proposed contract action is expected to exceed the simplified acquisition threshold. Similarly, agencies shall allow at least a 30 day response time from the date of publication of a proper notice of intent to contract for architect-engineer services or before issuance of an order under a basic ordering agreement or similar arrangement if the proposed contract action is expected to exceed the simplified acquisition threshold. A different time period, 45 days, applies to the receipt of bids or proposals from the date of publication of the notice for proposed research and development contract actions expected to exceed the simplified acquisition threshold.

Unless they have evidence to the contrary, Contracting Officers may presume the notice was published one day after transmission to SAM.gov. This presumption does not negate the mandatory waiting or response times specified above. Upon learning that a particular notice has not in fact been published within the presumed timeframes, Contracting Officers should consider whether the date for receipt of offers can be extended or whether circumstances have become sufficiently compelling to justify proceeding with the proposed contract action under the urgent and compelling circumstances exception to notice publication.

(c) Legal Consequences

There are various legal consequences from publication of the SAM.gov notice and its predecessors (i.e., the Commerce Business Daily and FedBizOpps notice), including the constructive notice doctrine; comparison to solicitations; and misclassification or misdescription of notices.

Although a defective SAM.gov notice can render the entire procurement defective, the publication of a materially correct SAM.gov notice places all potential offerors (including an incumbent contractor) on "constructive notice"—knowledge imputed as a matter of law—of the solicitation and its contents. Moreover, publication of a SAM.gov synopsis obligates interested firms to make a reasonable effort to obtain a copy of any resulting solicitation. If a protester fails in this obligation or fails to challenge the basis of the synopsized action in timely fashion, the GAO will deny or dismiss the protest.

On the other hand, a SAM.gov notice is not a solicitation of proposals and does not lock the agency into the advertised features. Similarly, the SAM.gov notice does not create a formal competition among responding firms. As compared with an RFP, the SAM.gov generally is not subject to any statutory or regulatory requirement to disclose the anticipated evaluation factors or the basis for award. The Comptroller General also has held that if a conflict exists between what is now the SAM.gov notice and the resulting RFP, the solicitation will control.

One issue sometimes facing the procurement agencies is whether it should amend the SAM.gov after issuance of the solicitation. For example, if the agency amends the solicitation's delivery schedule the day after it releases the RFP, must the agency also amend the schedule announced in the SAM.gov? Although the FAR has no specific guidance on this point, the answer lies in the essential nature of the SAM.gov synopsis. If the solicitation change is so material that the current synopsis would no longer enable interested firms to make an informed business judgment on participation in the procurement, then the agency should amend the notice, if practicable. As just indicated, however, no legal requirement mandates such a revised SAM.gov notice, and the agency's failure to do so could not be grounds for protest. On the other hand, FAR prohibits notice of RFP cancellation or indefinite suspension of contract actions in the SAM.gov.

Occasionally, agencies will misclassify or misdescribe the requirement in the SAM.gov. When will such an error be grounds for protest if a firm claims that it overlooked the procurement and was thereby unable to compete?

With the passage of the Competition in Contracting Act (CICA), the Comptroller General has overruled his decisions predating this law. Although the agency has reasonable judgment in classifying proposed procurements in the SAM.gov, the GAO now holds that an agency's failure to synopsize pending procurements in the SAM.gov in a manner reasonably expected to provide potential offerors with actual notice of the pending procurement would violate CICA's demand for full and open competition. If the misclassification or misdescription prejudices even one responsible source from competing, the GAO will sustain such a firm's timely challenge to the solicitation or the award, notwithstanding the agency's good faith attempt to publicize the procurement.

"Prejudice" in this sense means that the SAM.gov deficiency was material and that the prospective offeror had no knowledge or reason to know of the pending acquisition and its essential elements. On the other hand, even if the agency has published a misleading or misclassified SAM.gov announcement, if the offeror has submitted a timely proposal under the RFP and was not otherwise prejudiced, there are no grounds for complaint. In accordance with the GAO's bid protest regulations, the Comptroller General's recommended remedy can be as drastic as termination of the improper award or cancellation of the solicitation.

(d) Special Situations

Frequently an agency can do in-house work where it is less costly than if it were contracted out. In this connection it is important to be cognizant of restrictions in the regulations requiring cost comparisons between contractor and government performance. However, as noted above the Contracting Officer cannot arrive at a conclusion that there are no commercial sources capable of providing the required supplies or services until publicizing the requirement.

Other special situations include where Contracting Officers decide to transmit SAM.gov notices for procurement matters such as business fairs, long range procurement estimates, prebid or preproposal conferences, meetings, and the availability of draft solicitations or draft specifications for review.

(e) Publicizing Subcontract Opportunities

In instances where significant subcontracting opportunities exist, the names and addresses of prospective offerors are published in the SAM.gov with the suggestion that small business firms or others interested in subcontracting opportunities in connection with the acquisition make direct contract with firm(s) listed. Prime contractors and subcontractors are to be encouraged to use the SAM.gov to publicize subcontracting opportunities stemming from their government business. Accordingly, where a contract or subcontract exceeding the simplified acquisition threshold is likely to result in award of subcontracts, a notice may be used to seek competition for qualified HUBZone, small business, small, disadvantaged, service disabled, veteran owned, and women-owned small business concerns.

§ 5.3   Synopses of Contract Awards

Generally, Contracting Officers must synopsize through the SAM.gov awards exceeding $25,000 that are covered by the World Trade Organization Government Procurement Agreement or a Free Trade Agreement. Similarly, the agency must publicize prime contract awards likely to result in the award of any subcontracts. However, the dollar threshold is not a prohibition against publicizing an award of a smaller amount when publicizing would be advantageous to industry or to the Government.

Some exceptions exist to the above requirements. For example, a notice is not required under if the notice would disclose the executive agency's needs and the disclosure of such needs would compromise the national security.

§ 5.4 Announcement of Contract Awards

Contracting Officers shall make information available on awards over $4 million (unless another dollar amount is specified in agency acquisition regulations) in sufficient time for the agency concerned to announce it by 5 p.m. Washington, DC, time on the day of award. Agencies shall not release information on awards before this time. Contracts excluded from this reporting requirement include, for example, those placed with the Small Business Administration under section 8(a) of the Small Business Act. Agencies may also release information on contract awards to the local press or other media with some limitations.

§ 5.5 Release of Procurement Information

Although Contracting Officers may make available maximum information to the public, agencies must maintain a high level of business security to preserve the integrity of the acquisition process. Thus, all Government personnel who participate directly or indirectly in any stage of the acquisition cycle must not release information received in confidence from an offeror, exempt under the Freedom of Information Act or the Privacy Act or that would provide undue or discriminatory advantage to private or personal interests.

In recent policy change, agencies must post in SAM.gov the agency website justifications for use of other than full and open competition, minus contractor proprietary information or information exempt under the Freedom of Information Act or the Privacy Act.

Chapter 6

COMPETITION REQUIREMENTS

Analysis

§ 6.1   In General

The Competition in Contracting Act of 1984 (CICA) states that executive agencies must acquire property and services "in the most timely and efficient manner." In this regard, the procurement statutes and regulations in general require agencies to use "full and open competition," which is consistent with a longstanding competition preference. The last quoted term means that all responsible sources are permitted to compete with respect to a contract action. At the same time, CICA and the FAR contain numerous exclusions and exceptions to the general requirement for full and open competition, as this Chapter will explain below.

Despite the statutory preference for competition, the purpose of a competitive procurement is not to ensure that all offerors face the same odds in seeking government contracts or that the government must equalize the competitive position of all potential contractors. No offeror has a right to the award of a government contract, but only the right to a fair competition. The GAO has stated that CICA's requirement to increase the use of full and open competition is primarily a means to an end—that of "fulfilling the government's requirements at the lowest reasonable cost considering the nature of the property or services procured." For this reason, the GAO has frequently commented that the propriety of a particular procurement is not judged by whether every potential contractor is included in the competition. Furthermore, the statutes and regulations recognize that unrestricted competition sometimes can be impracticable, unnecessary, or outweighed by other public policies.

Implementing CICA, the Federal Acquisition Regulation (FAR) defines the competition requirements for agency "acquisitions" (which concept would exclude such matters simplified purchases, contracts authorized by statute, and contract modifications within the scope and under the terms of an existing contract). CICA applies to all executive agencies, except as provided by law. Thus, to name one statutory exception, if the agency uses non-appropriated funds to make the purchase, the CICA competition rules are inapplicable, although agency regulations commonly impose parallel standards.

In accordance with CICA, FAR creates three classes of competition: full and open competition, full and open competition after exclusion of sources, and other than full and open competition. The agency's compliance with CICA is subject to both administrative and judicial review.

The CICA requirement for full and open competition permeates all aspects of the formation process, and not just the source selection phase. Thus, CICA allows agencies to include solicitation terms restrictive of competition, but only when necessary to meet the government's minimum requirements.

§ 6.2   Use of Competitive Procedures

The procuring agencies must use sound judgment in selecting the competitive procedure or combination of procedures best suited to the circumstances, except that an agency may not contract with another government agency to avoid the FAR competition requirements. Various competitive procedures are available for use in fulfilling the requirement for full and open competition.

Contracting Officers shall solicit sealed bids if (1) time permits the solicitation, submission, and evaluation of sealed bids; (2) the award will be made on the basis of price and other price-related factors; (3) it is not necessary to conduct discussions with the responding offerors about their bids; and (4) there is reasonable expectation of receiving more than one sealed bid.

Otherwise, the agency may request competitive proposals if sealed bids are not appropriate under the four part test. A combination of competitive procedures can also be appropriate. Thus, if sealed bids are not appropriate, Contracting Officers may use any combination of competitive procedures, for example, two-step sealed bidding (see Chapter 14). Despite the statutory primacy of sealed bidding, however, an argument can be made that the present day practice and preference for negotiated procurement has all but made sealed bidding a second, not a first, choice of federal procuring activities.

Other competitive procedures exist to meet the full and open competition mandate. Selection of sources for architect-engineer contracts in accordance with the provisions of the Brooks Act and FAR (see Chapter 36) is a competitive procedure. Competitive selection for basic and applied research activity and that part of development not related to the development of a specific system or hardware can be a competitive procedure under prescribed conditions. These circumstances are if award results from either (a) a broad agency announcement that is general in nature identifying areas of research interest, including criteria for selecting proposals, and soliciting the participation of all offerors capable of satisfying the Government's needs or (2) a peer of scientific review (see Chapter 35). Lastly, use of multiple award schedules issued under the procedures established by the Administrator of General Services consistent with the requirement of statute for the multiple award schedule program of the General Services Administration is a competitive procedure (see Chapter 8).

§ 6.3   Full and Open Competition After Exclusion of Sources

In two situations, the statutes and regulations authorize procuring agencies to exclude certain sources from otherwise fully competitive acquisitions. Put another way, once the agency uses this limited power to exclude one or more potential sources, the remaining vendors in these situations will compete under conventional full and open competition procedures.

In the first instance, the agency under the Competition in Contracting Act (CICA) and FAR may exclude a particular source to establish or maintain alternative sources for supplies or services. The head of the agency (or an authorized designee) may authorize the exclusion when the action would:

1.   Increase or maintain competition and likely result in reduced overall costs for the actual or anticipated acquisition;

2.   Be in the interest of national defense, in that there would be a source available in case of national emergency or industrial mobilization;

3.   Be in the interest of national defense, in that it would establish or maintain an essential engineering, research or development capability to be provided by nonprofit institutions or a federally funded research and development center;

4.   Ensure the continuous availability of a reliable source of supplies or services;

5.   Satisfy projected needs based on a history of high demand; or

6.   Satisfy a critical need for medical, safety or emergency supplies.

This authority is used to exclude one source. FAR further requires the agency head or a designee invoking this procedure to execute a Determination and Finding (D & F) on a case by case basis. The GAO will question an award under this authority only when the record clearly establishes that the agency abused its discretion.

In the second instance, the agency under CICA and FAR may "set aside"—restrict—the procurement to allow only small business concerns to compete. Such set-asides can include contract actions under the Small Business Innovation Research Program pursuant to Pub. L. No. 97–219. No requirement exists for a D & F justifying these set-asides. Chapter 19 discusses this program in detail.

§ 6.4   Other Statutory Exceptions Providing for Contracting Without Full and Open Competition

(a) In General

In implementing the Competition in Contracting Act (CICA), FAR provides seven possible circumstances for other than full and open competition:

1.   Only one or a limited number of responsible sources and no other supplies or services will satisfy agency requirements;

2.   Unusual and compelling urgency;

3.   Industrial mobilization, or engineering, developmental or research capability;

4.   International agreement;

5.   Authorized or required by statute;

6.   National security; and

7.   The public interest.

Except as allowed by law, agencies may not limit competition, regardless of their good motives. Contracting without providing for full and open competition (or full and open competition after exclusion of sources) violates CICA, unless permitted by one of the statutory and regulatory exceptions. Under CICA and FAR, other than full and open competition cannot be justified, however, by the requiring activity's lack of advance planning or by concerns that funds may not later be available for the supplies or services. Even when an agency properly limits competition, FAR still requires the government to solicit as many offers as practicable under the circumstances.

(b) Only One Responsible Source

Under the FAR an agency need not obtain full and open competition when only one responsible source can satisfy agency requirements for supplies or services and no other type of supplies or services will be acceptable. In the Department of Defense (DOD), the National Aeronautics and Space Administration (NASA) and the Coast Guard, this FAR exception will be equally applicable when a "limited" number of responsible sources can meet the agency's needs and no other supplies or services will be acceptable. Similarly, FAR provides that an acquisition that uses a brand name description or other proprietary description to specify a particular brand name, product, or feature of a particular product peculiar to one manufacturer does not provide for full and open competition, regardless of the number of sources solicited.

The rationale for allowing a sole source or limited source acquisition (hereinafter "sole source") is that the government's needs must not be compromised simply to achieve competition. Because these sole source or limited source procurements are anti-competitive, however, they are generally disfavored. With one exception, agencies may not use this exemption when any other exemption to full and open competition is appropriate. The exception is that agencies must use this authority in preference to the "public interest" exemption of the FAR when both could be applicable. Agency regulations may impose even greater limits on the use of this authority.

Contracting officials must support the use of a sole source procurement by (1) executing a detailed written justification, (2) obtaining higher level agency approvals for certain large dollar awards, (3) publishing a SAM.gov notice and considering any responses, and (4) proceeding either with a competitive or noncompetitive procurement as justified by the circumstances.

Agencies have a duty to give full and honest consideration to the vendor responses to the SAM.gov notice. In one case, GAO held that the agency violated FAR 1.102(b)(3), 1.102–2(c)(3) and 3.101–1 by failing to treat the vendor fairly and honestly in connection with a sole-source solicitation when it invited responses to the proposed action but did not intend to consider them. Agencies also must post on SAM.gov the written justification, noted above, within fourteen days, with some exceptions. The Court of Federal Claims has held that the government's deliberate delay in posting the justification in the hopes of avoiding a protest was arbitrary and capricious and a violation of the FAR duty of fair dealing with prospective contractors.

Sole source acquisitions occur only when the agency limits the field of competition to one vendor. By contrast, if the agency issues a Request for Proposals (RFP) allowing all responsible vendors to compete, but only one offeror responds, such procurements generally will not be a sole source acquisition. The agency in this situation has sought full and open competition, irrespective of the single response.

Similarly, if the agency after review of initial proposals sets a competitive range of one firm, this action alone does not equate to a sole source procurement. One exception does exist to these principles, however, and that is where the agency issues a de facto sole source RFP in the form of a competitive solicitation. The GAO will deny a challenge to the agency action when, despite the single offer, evidence existed that other viable offerors could have responded.

One common area of de facto sole source procurements is a non-competitive modification to an existing contract. A modification will trigger CICA competition requirements for a new acquisition where a material difference exists between the modified contract and the contract that was originally awarded. A broad scope of work can support a wider range of contract changes without violating the competition rules.

With the enactment of CICA, Congress has plainly stated that sole source awards may be made only when "truly necessary" and "properly justified." The GAO has said: "Under a sole source acquisition, the agency should only procure its actual needs that cannot await an anticipated competitive environment."

Based on this public policy, the following circumstances will *never* support a sole source acquisition under the FAR: administrative convenience; the simple preference of agency officials for particular products or services; the belief that competition is unnecessary because one prospective offeror has a commanding price or technical advantage over its competitors; one vendor's greater familiarity with the supplies or services being acquired or the firm's prior experience which the agency believes will ease contract performance; the superior or ideal nature of the vendor's product or service as compared with other acceptable items; the fact that a firm has threatened the agency with litigation; the agency's lack of advance planning; or agency concerns that funds will not later be available for the acquisition.

The procurement regulations and case law do recognize a number of *possible* justifications for sole source acquisitions. Frequently, one or more of these rationales can support a particular sole source arrangement. Whether the agency has a reasonable or rational basis for invoking these theories is determined on a case-specific basis. Some potential sole source situations include that the source:

1.   Submits an unsolicited research proposal that:

A.   Describes a unique or innovative concept or that demonstrates a unique capability to provide the particular research services;

B.   Offers a concept or service not otherwise available to the government; and

C.   Does not resemble the substance of a pending competitive acquisition.

2.   The source has previously developed or produced a major system or highly specialized equipment (or major components), and award to any other source under a follow-on contract would likely create either:

A.   Substantial duplication of cost that the government could not expect to recover through competition; or

B.   Unacceptable delays in meeting agency requirements.

3.   The source has rights in data, patents, or secret processes, or the control of basic raw materials, such that the supplies or services are available only from that source;

4.   The source provides utility services (e.g., electricity, gas, or water) that are available only from that source;

5.   The source provides spare parts and replacement items and the agency head has determined in accordance with the agency's standardization program that only the specified makes and models of technical equipment will satisfy the agency's needs for additional units or replacement items, and only one source is available;

6.   The source provides the only products that are necessarily compatible or interchangeable with existing equipment;

7.   The source is the only supplier whose product or service does not create unacceptable technical risks;

8.   The source is the only supplier that can meet the agency's legitimate need to acquire items on a "total package" basis as opposed to a break-out of the requirement into separate competitive acquisitions;

9.   The source provides unique supplies or services for the agency's minimum needs;

10. The source is the only vendor available because the agency lacks sufficient information in time to develop technical specifications for a competitive procurement; and

11. The source is an incumbent contractor and an out of scope contract extension is the only means to ensure that the required services are provided without interruption.

In a protest, the GAO will "closely scrutinize" sole source procurements. The Comptroller General has stated repeatedly: "In sum, excepting those noncompetitive situations which arise from a lack of advance procurement planning, a sole source award is justified only where the agency reasonably concludes that only one known source can meet the government's needs within the required time."

(c) Unusual and Compelling Urgency

FAR permits agencies to limit the number of potential offers when there is an "unusual and compelling urgency." This authority is available when the particular emergency does not permit full and open competition and a delay in making the award will cause serious injury, financial or otherwise, to the government. As with sole source purchases, urgency acquisitions cannot be justified based on mere administrative expediency or convenience, the simple preference of agency officials, or any basis other than bona fide exigency.

Even when a true urgency exists, contracting officials may not rely upon this authority when the emergency was the result of either the requiring activity's lack of advance planning or concerns about the availability of funds. The exigency must be real and imminent, and not theoretical or speculative. The agency's position becomes less reasonable with an unexplained delay between either (1) the initiation of the acquisition and the execution of the award, or (2) the award date and the delivery schedule.

The Defense Federal Acquisition Regulation Supplement (DFARS) provides an illustrative, nonexclusive list of circumstances that could possibly justify a purchase based on unusual and compelling urgency within the Department of Defense (DOD). These substantive rationales would appear equally valid for the other Executive Branch agencies. According to DFARS, these situations are:

(1) Supplies, services, or construction needed at once because of fire, flood, explosion, or other disaster;

(2) Essential equipment for, or repair to, a ship when such equipment repair is needed at once to enable the ship to be seaworthy;

(3) Essential equipment for, or repair to, the operational mission of an aircraft;

(4) Construction needed at once to preserve a structure or its contents from damage;

(5) Essential equipment or repair needed at once to preclude impairment of launch capabilities or mission performance of missiles or missile support equipment; and

(6) Purchases of certain high priority electronic warfare equipment.

All such purchases will be judged on the circumstances existing at the time of the acquisition. The propriety of a sole source procurement must be determined on a case-specific basis. Also, the agency's particular explanation will be subject to "close scrutiny" before procurement adjudicators like the GAO, except that procurements for direct support for military operations or matters concerning human life and safety will receive greater deference.

The Contracting Officer must support an urgency award using the same FAR justification and approval procedures as is required for a sole source procurement but with one important exception. Here, the Contracting Officer may execute the justification and obtain the requisite approval a "reasonable time" *after* award when compliance beforehand would unduly delay the acquisition and thereby increase the prospect of serious injury to the government.

This authority, of course, is not a "blank check" to execute the justification and approval after award, but to do so only when the time involved with processing these documents would exacerbate the particular emergency. Another distinction between urgency and sole source procurements is that the emergency will exempt the agency from publicizing the acquisition in the SAM.gov.

The procurement statutes, regulations, and decisional law all stress that agencies using this FAR authority must solicit as many offers as practicable under the circumstances. "Practicability" in this sense will depend on the time available to evaluate proposals, the nature of the supplies or services, and the information reasonably available to the agency concerning the number of qualified vendors able to submit timely proposals.

While contracting officials must maximize competition when using the FAR urgency authority, the agency also may properly reject an offer from a vendor which is merely potentially able to meet the government's needs. The GAO has said: "An agency using the urgency exception may restrict competition to the firms it reasonably believes can perform the work properly and promptly, and we will object to the agency's determination only where the decision lacks a reasonable basis."

In a related issue, protesters will sometimes argue that the requiring agency improperly created its own emergency because of a lack of advance planning Although agencies must engage in advance procurement planning, no requirement exists for error-free planning. The GAO will sustain a protest on this basis only where the lack of planning is attributable to the agency's culpable fault or negligence. Thus, urgency can still be present when the procuring activity was reasonably unaware of the impending problems and it otherwise diligently processed the acquisition.

The urgency rationale will only be valid for those aspects of the procurement within the actual scope of the exigency. Thus, for example, emergency purchases must have as limited a duration as possible and should rarely include options. In any event, the duration may not exceed one year unless the head of the agency (or a delegee) determines that "exceptional circumstances" are present. Similarly, the quantity of items or services must be limited to the scope of the exigency.

(d) Industrial Mobilization; Experimental Development; Research Work; Public Interest; National Security; or Expert Services in Litigation

Regarding the next category, FAR has three exceptions to full and open competition. The first is the "industrial mobilization" exception; the agency may use other than full and open competition procedures in awarding a contract to a particular source or sources when such action is necessary to maintain a facility, producer, manufacturer or other supplier available in case of a national emergency or to achieve industrial mobilization.

The second exception is the "essential facilities" exception; the government may use noncompetitive procedures when necessary to establish or maintain an essential engineering, research or developmental capability to be provided by an educational or other nonprofit institution or a federally funded research and development center.

The third exception concerns the provision of expert or neutral person to assist in anticipated litigation or disputes. The last variety stems from the Federal Acquisition Streamlining Act and covers any trial, hearing or proceeding before any court, administrative tribunal, or agency, irrespective of whether the expert testifies. Similarly, the agency may contract with persons like mediators or arbitrators, such as those commonly used in alternative disputes procedures.

In using these authorities, contracting officials must comply with the standard justification and approval procedures. Although

FAR exempts the agency from publicizing these procurements in the SAM.gov the agency must still seek as many offers as practicable when relying on this exemption. Also, the government may not employ these procedures based on the requiring agency's lack of advance planning or concerns over the availability of funds.

These FAR exemptions must be distinguished from where the agency provides for full and open competition after exclusion of sources. In the former context, the agency deliberately limits the field of competition to one or more selected firms. In the latter situation, the agency excludes a particular source in the interests of national defense, and the remaining vendors compete under the usual full and open competition procedures.

(e) International Agreements

Under the Competition in Contracting Act (CICA) and FAR, a procurement can be exempt from full and open competition as allowed by international agreement. One example is a treaty between the United States and a foreign government that specifies or limits the sources to be solicited in a contract to be performed in foreign territory. The most common application of this authority is a procurement under the Department of Defense's (DOD's) Foreign Military Sale (FMS) program.

The basis of the FMS program is the Arms Export Control Act, as amended. This law authorizes the DOD to enter into contracts with private sources for purpose of resale to foreign countries or international organizations. Generally, the DOD acts as an agent or trustee for the foreign government when DOD conducts these acquisitions. DOD officials will use the foreign government's funds— which may include funds loaned by the United States—that have been properly deposited in the FMS trust fund account in the United States Department of Treasury.

Because federal contracting officials act only as representatives in these transactions, the procurement statutes and regulations governing appropriated fund acquisitions will apply to FMS sales only as specifically provided. To allow a regulatory basis for administrative implementation and dispute resolution, DFARS 225.7300 provides: "This Subpart contains policies and procedures for acquisitions for foreign military sales (FMS) under the Arms Export Control Act." Thus, the GAO bid protest forum is available to disappointed offerors.

Contracting officials must conduct acquisitions for FMS customers under the usual full and open competition procedures, except as requested otherwise by the FMS customer. When the foreign country requires that the product be obtained from a particular firm as specified in a Letter of Offer and Acceptance or other written direction (such as a country-to-country agreement), the Contracting Officer must honor the limit on competition so long as the written directive meets the requirements of FAR. Under DFARS, these restrictions may include sole source prime contracts and subcontracts. No SAM.gov announcement is required for such restricted FMS acquisitions, although the agency (except for DOD, the National Aeronautics and Space Administration (NASA), and the Coast Guard) must satisfy the standard FAR justification and approval provisions.

(f) Authorized or Required by Statute

FAR lists some statutory programs that qualify for a noncompetitive procurement, Federal Prison Industries; Qualified Nonprofit Agencies for the Blind or other Severely Disabled; Government Printing and Binding; and sole source (but not competitive) acquisitions under the "8(a)" Program (see Chapter 19). Another example of a statute in the latter category is the Buy Indian Act, which authorizes the Secretary of the Interior to contract with Indian-owned firms to the extent practicable.

With some exceptions, the agency must support a FAR purchase on this authority by satisfying the FAR justification and approval procedures. Note further that if the particular statute authorizes, but does not require its use, the agency would still be entitled to rely on this exemption from the general requirement for full and open competition.

(g) National Security

Under the Competition in Contracting Act (CICA) and FAR, full and open competition is not required when disclosure of the agency's needs would compromise the national security. As explained in CICA's legislative history, the intent of this exception is to permit the use of noncompetitive procedures where the general publication or dissemination of the agency's needs would jeopardize the national security.

That the acquisition is classified or that the contractor will require access to classified data, without more, does not justify application of this authority. If the agency already has publicly disclosed its needs, then the agency may not rely on this exception, although it would seem plain that unauthorized disclosures should require a different result. It is questionable how enforceable this rule is in practice, and how many agencies would actually endanger (or compound the endangerment of) valid national security interests because of a prior improper disclosure of classified information.

Contracts awarded under this exception must comply with the FAR written justification and approval procedures. Although no SAM.gov synopsis is necessary, agencies relying on this authority are still required to solicit as many sources as practicable. Thus, a security classification does not automatically justify a sole source award, and classified procurements should be competed among all vendors having the proper clearance.

(h) Public Interest

The Competition in Contracting Act (CICA) and FAR state that full and open competition is not necessary when the agency head determines that the public interest mandates otherwise for a particular procurement. According to FAR, agencies may use the public interest exception only when no other FAR exemption applies. The various heads of the agencies listed—Defense, Army, Navy, Transportation (for the Coast Guard), and the National Aeronautics and Space Administration (NASA)—must execute a written Determination and Finding (D & F) on a nondelegable basis. The head of the agency may require the Contracting Officer to prepare a justification to support a public interest acquisition. The agency must notify Congress of the determination not less than 30 days before the award.

The GAO has held that when the agency head makes such a public interest determination, this discretionary decision is immune from review, except on limited procedural grounds. The Comptroller General indicated that a public interest procurement would be invalid where the agency violated the "report and wait" provision of the regulation, discussed above. Another possible ground for protest would be where the agency head improperly purports to delegate this authority.

§ 6.5   Competition Advocates

Another innovation that became law upon enactment of the Competition in Contracting Act is the requirement that the head of an executive agency designate another employee called a "competition advocate for the agency and each contracting activity of the agency."

He or she must be in a position other than that of the agency's senior procurement executive, and not be assigned any duties or responsibilities that are inconsistent with his duties. His or her job is to challenge barriers to and promote full and open competition by spotting competitive opportunities in the acquisition of supplies and services by the agency. He or she reviews the contracting operations of the agency and identifies and reports to the agency senior procurement executive opportunities and actions taken to achieve full and open competition in the contracting operations of the agency, as well as any condition or action that has the effect of unnecessarily restricting competition in the contract actions of the agency. The ombudsman process is not, however, a substitute for the formal protest process.

Normally the competition advocate should be provided "with staff or assistance (e.g., specialists in engineering, technical operations, contract administration, financial management, supply management, and utilization of small and disadvantaged business concerns), as may be necessary to carry out his or her responsibilities." Not being a line officer, he or she can only make recommendations to the senior procurement executive of the agency. He or she also may make suggestions for plans for increasing competition as well as a system of personal and organizational accountability for competition, which may include the use of recognition and awards to motivate program managers, Contracting Officers, and others in authority to promote competition in acquisition.

Part II

ACQUISITION PLANNING

Chapter 7

ACQUISITION PLANS

Analysis

§ 7.1   Advance Procurement Planning

As provided by law and regulation, agencies must use advance procurement planning to open the procurement process to all capable firms. Implementing the Competition in Contracting Act (CICA), the Federal Acquisition Regulation (FAR) requires the use of acquisition planning "[t]o ensure that the government meets its needs in the most effective, economical and timely manner." Proper acquisition planning occurs before, and not after, the agency issues the solicitation. The program manager or similar agency official has overall responsibility for acquisition planning.

Government outsourcing and privatization is currently under a moratorium. See https://digital.library.unt.edu/ark:/67531/metadc 820847/m1/2. On a related issue, DOD has issued an interim rule amending the DFARS to implement a section of the National Defense Authorization Act on private-sector notification of insourcing actions. The interim rule revises DFARS § 237.102–79 to establish procedures for the timely notification of any contractor who performs a function that DOD plans to convert to performance by DOD civilian employees. 78 Fed. Reg. 65218 (Oct. 31, 2013).

Advance procurement planning has two key concepts: "acquisition planning" and "market research" (also called market surveys). Acquisition planning under FAR refers to when agency acquisition personnel coordinate and integrate their efforts through a comprehensive plan to meet the agency's needs. The development of an overall strategy is critical for sound acquisition planning. Market research under the FAR refers to a testing of the marketplace to determine the existence of qualified sources for the government's requirement (as opposed to an assessment of the cost/benefits of contracting). These methods can be as informal as agency telephone contacts with government or private sources knowledgeable about potential contractors to the more formal sources-sought announcements in sources such as Contract Opportunities in SAM.gov.

Congress's chief concern in mandating acquisition planning was to forestall the agencies' improper use of noncompetitive procurements. In one such dubious practice, many agencies pre-CICA were entering into noncompetitive contracts based primarily on concerns over the availability of expiring end of year funds. These compressed lead times also frequently resulted in unduly restrictive specifications or other solicitation deficiencies that precluded effective competition. Another instance of inadequate planning would be agency negligence in making a timely award and the agency resolves the issue by the device of citing the sole source or urgency rationales CICA now provides that in "no case" may an agency enter into a contract without providing for full and open competition simply because of the lack of advance planning or concerns related to the amount of funds available to the agency for procurement functions.

Although FAR emphasizes the use of acquisition planning for the development of specifications and purchase descriptions, the requirement for acquisition planning permeates all aspects of the formation cycle. As stated in the regulations, this planning shall integrate the efforts of all personnel responsible for significant aspects of the acquisition. The acquisition planning team members include contracting, fiscal, legal, and technical agency personnel. The same regulation further instructs contracting activities to commence their acquisition planning as soon as the agency identifies its requirement, and preferably well in advance of the fiscal year for which the contract award is necessary.

In this manner, the agency will avoid any concerns over the availability of year end funds. Similarly, some individual agency regulations stress the importance of sufficient acquisition lead time and prudent preparation of acquisition strategy, and other regulations require that the acquisition plan accompany any proposed justification for the use of other than full and open competition. Thus, urgency is not necessarily an excuse for not preparing an acquisition plan, except as permitted by law or regulation, although the emergency could still legitimately reduce the level of detail in the plan.

CICA requires advance procurement planning, but the law does not require that the planning be successful. It is also true that an agency will not necessarily be guilty of inadequate planning because it encountered unexpected delays, unforeseeable changed conditions, or ineffective communication between the requiring activity and the contracting office, or where the delay is attributable to good faith efforts to encourage competition.

On the other hand, the GAO will not be bound by the agency's self-serving statements in its acquisition memoranda that it has engaged in adequate planning. The agency need only make and the record must show reasonable or substantial efforts in this regard. Thus, a protest based on unsuccessful procurement planning will be sustained only with proof of deliberate agency inaction or the agency's culpable fault or negligence.

§ 7.2   Acquisition Plans

Under the FAR, the agency head or a designee must issue policies and procedures for acquisition plans. Depending on the agency and the dollar value of the acquisition, the plan may or may not be required to be in writing. As an acquisition becomes more complex and costly, however, agency regulations will require the planning process to become more detailed and formalized. Urgency is not a basis for non-preparation of an acquisition plan, although the agency head or a designee may authorize procedures for waiving requirements of detail and formality, as necessary, for compressed delivery schedules because of such exigencies. Both the defense and nondefense contracting agencies have established policies for acquisition plan content.

Agency regulations may impose additional procedures. The Department of Defense (DOD) in DFARS has stated that the formal acquisition planning procedures in FAR are mandatory for the more complex and costly military procurements. These procedures may be adapted for use in the purchase of other supplies or services.

Under the special DOD rules, DFARS provides that agencies must prepare a written plan for acquisitions for "development" as defined in FAR 35.001 when (1) the total cost of all contracts for the acquisition program is estimated at $10 million or more; (2) an acquisition for production or services has a total cost of all contracts for the acquisition program is estimated at $50 million or more for all years or $25 million or more for any fiscal year; or (3) the agency deems it appropriate for any other acquisition considered appropriate by the department or agency.

FAR prescribes the content of required written acquisition plans. The plan must identify milestones for decisions along with the technical, business, management and other significant considerations that will control the procurement. In preparing the acquisition plan, the agency planner must address certain background matters and objectives together with plans of action. Examples of "background matters and objectives" are: statement of need, any life cycle cost considerations, and the technical, cost, or schedule risks. Examples of "plans of action" are: prospective sources of supplies or services, how competition will be sought, promoted, and sustained during the acquisition and the anticipated source selection processes.

The agency regulations implementing FAR sometimes require greater detail in acquisition plan content. For example, in the Department of Defense (DOD), in developing an acquisition plan, agency officials shall take into account the requirement for scheduling and conducting a higher level peer review.

As indicated above, the contracting activity usually submits its acquisition plans for very large dollar purchases to a higher level departmental authority. These implementing regulations also sometimes provide that the acquisition plan is to be approved before the issuance of any related solicitation documents or even publication of the SAM.gov notice. The non-DOD agencies generally follow acquisition plan policies similar to those of their DOD counterparts.

§ 7.3   Bundling

In its broadest sense, "bundling" means the consolidation of one or more requirements into a single solicitation. An example would be where the agency purchases information technology equipment along with maintenance on those systems. The benefits of bundling (economies of scale, reduced administrative costs, improved reliability) and its drawbacks (possible elimination of small-business offerors due to size, dollar value, or geographical dispersion of work; increased dependence on particular products or suppliers; and tendency to reduce competition) are well known and have been the subject of continued controversy.

This first type of bundling is governed by the competition rules of the Competition in Contracting Act (CICA). Specifically, CICA generally requires that solicitations include specifications which permit full and open competition and contain restrictive provisions and conditions only to the extent necessary to satisfy the needs of the agency. Because procurements conducted on a bundled or total package basis can unduly restrict competition, GAO may sustain a challenge to the use of such an approach where it is not necessary to satisfy the agency's needs.

The reach of the restrictions against total package or bundled procurements in CICA is broader than the limits on the second type of bundling under the Small Business Act. In 1997, Congress instructed agencies to avoid "unnecessary and unjustified bundling of contract requirements" that could preclude the participation of small businesses as prime contractors in the procurement.

"Bundling" in this sense is defined as a consolidation into a single contract of two or more procurement requirements that were previously solicited as separate, smaller contracts; for instance, the consolidation of all information technology equipment or service requirements of two or more military installations that previously had been purchased under two different contracts. In fact, this form of bundling is prohibited unless a procuring agency can demonstrate that (a) it will provide "measurable substantial benefits" that are critical to the agency's mission success, and (b) there will be maximum practicable participation by small business. *See InSap Services, Inc.*, B-417596.2, 2019 CPD ¶ 343 (excellent summary of bundling rules).

§ 7.4   Equipment Lease or Purchase

Agencies may acquire equipment by either lease or purchase. FAR states that agencies must make this determination on a case-by-case evaluation of comparative costs and "other factors." Examples of these other factors include net purchase price, transportation and installation costs, and maintenance costs.

Generally, the purchase method is appropriate when the equipment will be used beyond the point at which cumulative leasing costs will exceed the purchase costs. Indeed, federal policy favors purchase, rather than lease, of property on the ground that ownership usually is more economical in the long run. The lease method will be proper when otherwise advantageous to the government. Some agencies require contracting activities to document the contract file accordingly.

If the agency uses the procurement method of a lease with an option to purchase, the contract shall state the purchase price or provide a formula which shows how the purchase price will be established at the time of purchase. Agencies may request assistance from the General Services Administration in making equipment lease or purchase decisions.

§ 7.5   Inherently Governmental Functions

Contracts for services shall not be used for the performance of inherently governmental functions. Agency decisions which determine whether a function is or is not an inherently governmental function may be reviewed and modified by appropriate Office of Management and Budget officials. The FAR lists numerous—but not all inclusive—examples of functions considered to be inherently governmental functions or which shall be treated as such. Among these functions are:

1. The direct conduct of criminal investigations;

2.   The control of prosecutions and performance of adjudicatory functions other than those relating to arbitration or other methods of alternative dispute resolution;

3.   The command of military forces, especially the leadership of military personnel who are members of the combat, combat support, or combat service support role;

4.   The conduct of foreign relations and the determination of foreign policy;

5.   The determination of agency policy, such as determining the content and application of regulations, among other things;

6.   The determination of Federal program priorities for budget requests;

7.   The direction and control of Federal employees;

8.   The direction and control of intelligence and counter-intelligence operations;

9.   The selection or non-selection of individuals for Federal Government employment, including the interviewing of individuals for employment; and

10. The approval of position descriptions and performance standards for Federal employees.

Special guidance exists for federal procurement activities with respect to prime contracts. Some covered instances in this category include, among other matters, participating as a voting member on any source selection boards, approving any contractual documents, to include documents defining requirements, incentive plans, evaluation criteria; and awarding contracts.

The FAR has examples of functions generally not considered to be inherently governmental functions. FAR further cautions that certain services and actions that are not considered to be inherently governmental functions may approach being in that category because of the nature of the function, the manner in which the contractor performs the contract, or the manner in which the Government administers contractor performance. This list of potentially proper circumstances is not all inclusive and references activities such as the following:

1.   Services that involve or relate to budget preparation, including workload modeling, fact finding, efficiency studies, and should-cost analyses;

2.   Services that involve or relate to reorganization and planning activities;

3.   Services that involve or relate to analysis, feasibility studies, and strategy options to be used by agency personnel in developing policy;

4.   Services that involve or relate to the development of regulations;

5.   Services that involve or relate to the evaluation of another contractor's performance;

6.   Services in support of acquisition planning;

7.   Contractors providing assistance in contract management (such as where the contractor might influence official evaluations of other contractors);

8.   Contractors providing technical evaluation of contract proposals;

9.   Contractors providing assistance in the development of statements of work; and

10.   Contractors providing information regarding agency policies or regulations, such as attending conferences on behalf of an agency, conducting community relations campaigns, or conducting agency training courses.

Agency implementation of the FAR requirements include procedures requiring the agency head or designated lower level officials to provide the Contracting Officer, concurrent with transmittal of the statement of work (or any modification thereof), a written determination that none of the functions to be performed are inherently governmental. This assessment should place emphasis on the degree to which conditions and facts restrict the discretionary authority, decision-making responsibility, or accountability of Government officials using contractor services or work products. Disagreements regarding the determination will be resolved in accordance with agency procedures before issuance of a solicitation.

The general prohibition on inherently governmental functions is closely related to the general proscription against personal services contracts. A "personal services" contract is defined by the FAR as a contract that, by its express terms or as administered, makes the contractor personnel appear to be (actually or in effect) government employees, as opposed to independent contractors. Implementing § 831 of the National Defense Authorization Act for Fiscal Year 2009, revised DFARS parts 211 and 237 (1) require that statements of work or performance work statements clearly distinguish between Government employees and contractor employees, and (2) ensure that procedures are adopted to prevent contracts from being awarded or administered as unauthorized personal services contracts.

In keeping with increased government concerns about the relations between government personnel and contractors providing agency support services, a final FAR rule requires contractors that have employees performing acquisition functions strongly associated with inherently governmental functions to identify and prevent personal conflicts of interest for such employees.

Chapter 8

REQUIRED OR AUTHORIZED SOURCES OF SUPPLIES AND SERVICES

Analysis

§ 8.1   In General

Government agencies are required or authorized to obtain supplies and services from or through certain designated sources where possible and where not otherwise provided by law. Such sources include agency inventories, Federal Prison Industries, Inc., the Committee for Purchase from the Blind and Other Severely Disabled, and in the agency's discretion, Federal Supply Schedules.

Except as required by law or regulation, agencies shall satisfy requirements for supplies and services from or through the sources and publications listed below in descending order of priority.

For supplies, the priority is—

1.   Agency inventories;

2.   Excess from other agencies;

3.   Federal Prison Industries, Inc.;

4.   Supplies which are on the Procurement List maintained by the Committee for Purchase From People Who Are Blind or Severely Disabled;

5.   Wholesale supply sources, such as stock programs of the General Services Administration, the Defense Logistics Agency, the Department of Veterans Affairs, and military inventory control points;

6.   Federal Supply Schedules; and

7.   Commercial sources (including educational and nonprofit institutions).

For services, the priority is—

1.   Services which are on the Procurement List maintained by the Committee for Purchase From People Who Are Blind or Severely Disabled;

2.   Federal Supply Schedules (FSS); and

3.   Federal Prison Industries, Inc. or commercial sources (including educational and nonprofit institutions).

The GAO has said that while the list of required sources found in the FAR places FSS contracts above commercial sources in priority, it does not require an agency to order from the FSS. Further, although an agency's placement of an FSS order indicates that the agency has concluded that the order represents the best value, FAR does not establish a presumption that all FSS contractors represent the best value, such that the agency would be required to purchase from an FSS contractor.

§ 8.2   Ordering from Federal Supply Schedules

(a) General Policy

The Federal Supply Schedule (FSS) program, which is directed and managed by the General Services Administration (GSA), provides federal agencies with simplified contracting procedures for obtaining commonly used supplies and services at prices associated with the economies of volume buying. FSS purchases are subject to the FAR and GSA's special regulations.

Typically, two contracting agencies are involved in FSS procurements. The schedule contracting office will award the basic schedule contract. The GSA usually is the schedule contracting office, although the GSA may delegate this authority to other agencies. The second procurement activity is the agency ordering office, which will issue delivery order (supplies) or task order (services) against the basic schedule contract. This procuring activity can be any federal agency, to include any executive agency or even judicial or legislative agencies as permitted by law and regulation. In a recent development, Pub. L. No. 111–263 permits state and local governments and the American National Red Cross to purchase goods and services from the GSA Federal Supply Schedules in certain circumstances.

The General Services Administration is consolidating the 24 schedules in its Multiple Award Schedules program into a single schedule for products and services to make it easier for federal, state and local government customers to use. See interact.gsa.gov/blog/save-date-federal-marketplace-initiative-fmp-industry-day-0.

(b) Multiple Award Schedules

Multiple award schedules encompass contracts made with more than one supplier for comparable supplies or services at the same or different prices for delivery to the same geographic area. Although contracts under multiple award schedules do not create an immediate obligation on the agency to issue orders to the contractor, these schedules enable federal agencies to place orders directly with commercial firms under blanket terms and conditions previously negotiated by the General Services Administration (GSA) (or a delegated agency) when it awarded the original schedule contract.

The purpose of multiple award schedule procurement is to decrease agency open market purchases by making commercial items available where it is impractical to draft adequate specifications for sealed bid or negotiated procurements, or where selectivity in choosing among multiple available contractors is necessary for agencies ordering from the supply schedule to meet their varying needs.

The GSA's published policy is that multiple award schedule procurement practices should conform with usual commercial practice to the extent practicable and that these procedures will be fair to all parties, consistent with cost effectiveness.

A multiple award schedule solicitation typically will have as broad an item description as practicable so that a number of contractors can offer a wide range of comparable items for agency use. The reason for this rule is that it is extremely difficult to draft specifications that will meet the needs of many agencies, so these specifications must of necessity be broad.

All responsible firms may submit offers in response to a solicitation for multiple award schedule contracts, although the GSA or an agency (like the Department of Veterans Affairs) with delegated procurement authority has reasonable discretion under the Request for Proposals (RFP) ground rules on how many contracts will be awarded. Generally, the GSA (or a delegatee agency) will award a multiple award schedule to any vendor that offers price discounts comparable to those offered by other vendors.

An award under a multiple award schedule procurement results in the placement of the awardee on the appropriate schedule contract. In placing orders against the basic contract, the agency's ordering office must use either information in the GSA's automated information database, or contractor catalogs and price lists with the schedules. These references must contain the necessary information regarding items descriptions, prices and discounts, order limitations, and delivery.

As stated in the FAR, the schedule contracting agency may discontinue a firm's participation on the schedule, so long as the procuring activity abides by any interagency agreements and coordinates the action with the GSA's Federal Supply Service. The regulation does not state the reasons the agency may employ in taking this action, however, and so it may be assumed that agency has broad discretion, consistent with the general rule against arbitrary or unfair agency action.

Several instances where termination of a contractor's participation in the GSA program could be proper would when the item was obsolete, discontinued by the manufacturer, transferred to another schedule, to be provided through another method of supply, was similar to an item available from stock, or was unsafe, required a special license, or was a luxury item.

(c) General Competition Policies

The FAR states that, with some exceptions, the following FAR policies are inapplicable to the placement of orders against the schedules: Part 13 (on simplified acquisition), Part 14 (on sealed bidding), Part 15 (on negotiated procurement) and Part 19 (on small business programs).

The exceptions to the above statement are (1) blanket purchase agreements (BPA) under FAR Part 13 must be consistent with the applicable schedule contract, (2) the Contracting Officer shall provide a copy of the proposed solicitation package to the SBA procurement center representative or local SBA representative 30 days in advance for a "bundled" requirement as defined in the FAR, and (3) the placement of orders against schedule contracts allows the agency to obtain credit for meeting its small business goals. Therefore, when correctly establishing a BPA or placing an FSS order, individual ordering agencies "shall not" seek competition outside the schedules or synopsize the requirement.

A "blanket purchase agreement" is a simplified method for filling anticipated repetitive needs for supplies or services whereby the agency establishing "charge accounts" with qualified sources. The important point here is that a BPA is an agreement and not a contract that the parties establish to facilitate the issuance of future orders (which are individual contract actions).

In *Amray, Inc.,* Comp. Gen. Dec. B-238682, 90-1 CPD ¶ 480, 69 Comp. Gen. 456 (1990), the Government Accountability Office (GAO) explained the application of the Competition in Contracting Act (CICA) competition policies to FSS orders under a multiple award schedules:

CICA ... defines the term 'competitive procedures' to include [General Services Administration] multiple award schedule program procedures, if program participation has been open to all responsible sources, and orders and contracts under such procedures result in the lowest overall cost meeting government needs. Under CICA, where the item contained in the FSS contracts have been subject to competitive procedures to ensure that any order placed under the FSS will result in the lowest overall cost to the Government, CICA permits agencies to purchase from FSS contracts [without further competition].

Where competition occurs through Request for Quotation (RFQ) procedures, which is mandatory for services requiring a statement of work, the RFQ may (but is not required to) be posted to GSA's electronic RFQ system, e-Buy. Otherwise, the ordering activity shall provide the RFQ (including the statement of work and evaluation criteria) to at least three schedule contractors that offer services that will meet the agency's needs. The ordering activity should request that contractors submit firm-fixed prices to perform the services identified in the statement of work. The FAR imposes additional competition rules for GSA task or delivery orders parallel to the statutory and regulatory rules for task (for services) or delivery (for supplies) orders for multiple award contracts under FAR subpart 16.5 (see Chapter 16).

When the agency seeks to issue orders exceeding the simplified acquisition threshold or when establishing a BPA above this threshold, the ordering activity, along with meeting other regulatory requirements shall provide the RFQ (including the statement of work and evaluation criteria) to additional schedule contractors that offer services that will meet the needs of the ordering activity. When determining the appropriate number of additional schedule contractors, the ordering activity may consider various factors, including but not limited to the complexity, scope and estimated value of the requirement and the market search results. The agency also must seek price reductions (but no requirement exists for vendors to provide such discounts). The ordering activity shall provide the RFQ (including the statement of work and the evaluation criteria) to any schedule contractor who requests a copy of it.

(d) Agency Restrictions on Competition

An ordering activity under FAR 8.405 must justify its action when restricting consideration of schedule contractors to fewer than the number required by the regulations or when restricting consideration to an item peculiar to one manufacturer, such as a particular brand name, product, or feature of a product peculiar to one manufacturer. The policies and procedures in many respects mirror those under the FAR's larger dollar rules for only one or a limited number of responsible source.

Examples of circumstances that may justify restriction to a limited source FSS procurement are when only one source is capable of responding to the requirement because of the unique or specialized nature of the work or where the new work is a logical follow-on to an original FSS order, provided the agency placed the original order in accordance with applicable, fully competitive FSS ordering procedures. FAR contains the justification requirements for limiting competition and the justification approvals.

(e) Open Market Rules

If the agency announces its intention to order from an FSS contractor, the general rule is that all items are required to be within the scope of the FSS contract of the vendor or, if not prohibited by the solicitation, its subcontractors' FSS contracts. The general rule extends to where the vendor has unpublished rates that the GSA has yet to approve as being fair and reasonable.

The GAO agrees with the United States Court of Federal Claims that agencies generally may not combine FSS and open market items, i.e., non-FSS items, in the same order. These decisions reason that where the agency combines such procurements, it must independently satisfy applicable acquisition regulations for such purchases, such as the FAR rules on simplified buys.

Some qualifications exist to the above rules. For administrative convenience, an ordering activity may add items not on the FSS, i.e., open market items to FSS Blanket Purchase Agreements (BPAs) or an individual task or delivery order as prescribed in the FAR. Thus, for example, combining FSS and non-FSS items can be proper where the ordering activity Contracting Officer has determined that the non-FSS item prices are fair and reasonable and the items are clearly labeled on the order as items not on the FSS. On the other hand, where an agency solicits quotations from vendors for purchase from the FSS, the issuance of a purchase order to a vendor whose quotation includes non-FSS items priced above the micro-purchase threshold is improper.

Because agencies ordinarily uses simplified-type purchase procedures in conducting a competition among multiple award FSS vendors, such as the use of a Request for Quotations (RFQ), the Comptroller General has held that these acquisitions are not subject to the usual FAR Part 15 source selection procedures, such as the requirement for submission of revised final proposals by a common cutoff date. On the other hand, the GAO has generally required fair and equal competition among FSS vendors; for example, the Comptroller General has required agencies to issue solicitation amendments to all firms remaining in the competition.

The rule against deviating from commercial terms under FAR Part 12 applies to FSS buys under FAR subpart 8.4.

(f) FSS Solicitation Policies

FAR 8.405 establishes ordering procedures for supplies, and for services not requiring a statement of work. Under the regulation, ordering activities shall use the procedures of this subsection when ordering supplies, and when ordering services that are listed in the schedules contracts at a fixed price for the performance of a specific task where a statement of work is not required (e.g., installation, maintenance, and repair).

For orders at or below the micro-purchase threshold, ordering activities may place orders with any FSS contractor that can meet the agency's needs. Although not required to solicit from a specific number of schedule contractors, ordering activities in this situation should attempt to distribute orders among contractors. When an order contains brand name specifications, the Contracting Officer shall post the RFQ along with the required justification or documentation required.

For orders exceeding the micro-purchase threshold but not exceeding the simplified acquisition threshold, ordering activities shall place orders with the schedule contractor that can provide the supply or service that represents the best value. Before placing an order, an ordering activity shall consider reasonably available information about the supply or service offered under Multiple Award Schedule contracts by surveying at least three schedule contractors through the GSA Advantage! on-line shopping service, or by reviewing the catalogs or pricelists of at least three schedule contractors.

FAR further establishes the ordering procedures for services requiring a statement of work. Ordering activities shall use the procedures in the regulation when ordering services priced at hourly rates as established by the schedule contracts. The applicable services will be identified in the Federal Supply Schedule publications and the contractor's pricelists.

All Statements of Work under the FAR shall include the work to be performed; the location of work; period of performance; deliverable schedule; applicable performance standards; and any special requirements (e.g., security clearances, travel, vendor special knowledge). To the maximum extent practicable, agency requirements shall follow performance-based statements of work (see Chapter 11).

Special procedures exist when the order contains brand name specifications. Under the FAR, with limited exceptions, the ordering activity shall post certain information along with the RFQ to e-Buy (http://www.ebuy.gsa.gov). For proposed orders exceeding $25,000, but not exceeding the simplified acquisition threshold, the agency shall meet the regulatory procedures for documentation of the restriction. For proposed orders exceeding the simplified acquisition threshold, the agency shall post to Contract Opportunities of SAM.gov the extensive justification and approval required by FAR. In this last respect, the agency's documentation will closely track the justification and approval for limited source procurements as prescribed by FAR's standard dollar purchases.

Where used, RFQs should fully convey the agency's requirement to the FSS vendors so that they can compete on an equal basis. The quotations are not offers subject to government acceptance or rejection, but will simply be informational responses that indicate the products the vendors would propose to meet the government's needs along with the prices of those products and related services. Thus, the agency will disseminate an RFQ with a view toward issuing an order under a FSS (with the evaluation based on the FSS contracts) but not for obtaining independent offers subject to price negotiation.

The agency in issuing a proper RFQ also should clearly indicate that only FSS items are being sought, so as to avoid misleading non-FSS firms seeking to do business with the agency. The standard for RFQ cancellation will be determined under the usual rules for solicitation cancellation.

(g) FSS Technical Evaluation Principles

FAR incorporates a number of principles on the evaluation of quotations for a FSS order. When ordering supplies, and for services not requiring a statement of work, ordering offices shall place orders with the schedule contractor that can provide the supply or service of the "best value." In addition to price, the ordering activity may consider, among other factors, the following matters:

1.   Past performance;

2.   Special features of the supply or service required for effective program performance;

3.   Trade-in considerations;

4.   Probable life of the item selected as compared with that of a comparable item;

5.   Warranty considerations;

6.   Maintenance availability;

7.   Environmental and energy efficiency considerations; and

8.   Delivery terms.

As indicated by the regulation, this list is not exclusive. Therefore, it would appear permissible for the agency to rely on compatibility with existing equipment or systems as the rationale for selecting a higher priced product. The agency may award to a better overall value higher-priced FSS vendor even when the RFQ indicated the award would be made to the vendor offering the lowest price. On the other hand, the agency should not devise an RFQ that allows award to a higher priced source where the RFQ inappropriately includes a requirement in excess of the agency's actual needs.

When the agency acquires services requiring a statement of work, and the order will be at, or below, the micro-purchase threshold, ordering activities may place orders with any FSS contractor that can meet the agency's needs. The ordering activity should attempt to distribute orders among contractors. When the agency will issue an order exceeding the micro-purchase threshold, but not exceeding the simplified acquisition threshold, the ordering activity shall evaluate all responses received using the evaluation criteria provided to the schedule contractors. The agency must place the order, or establish a blanket purchase agreement (BPA), with the schedule contractor that represents the "best value" as defined in FAR.

After applying the announced best value considerations, the ordering activity when proceeding under FAR shall document—

1.   The schedule contracts considered, noting the contractor from which the service was purchased;

2.   A description of the service purchased;

3.   The amount paid;

4.   The evaluation methodology used in selecting the contractor to receive the order;

5.   The rationale for any tradeoffs in making the selection;

6.   The price reasonableness determination required by paragraph (d) of this subsection; and

7.   The rationale for using other than—

(i)   A firm-fixed price order; or

(ii) A performance-based order.

Ordering activities should provide timely notification to unsuccessful offerors. If an unsuccessful offeror requests information on an award that was based on factors other than price alone, a brief explanation of the basis for the award decision shall be provided.

GAO decisions provide further guidance to contracting officials on the evaluation of quotations issued in response to an RFQ. The evaluation of quotations for items listed on a multiple award Federal Supply Schedule (FSS) should be based on the firms' FSS contracts. In reviewing a competition among FSS vendors, the Government Accountability Office (GAO) has said that the determination of the agency's minimum needs and which products on the schedule meet those needs is properly the agency's responsibility. The reason is that agency officials are in the best position to know the agency's minimum needs, because they are the most familiar with the conditions under which supplies and services have been used in the past and will be used in the future.

The GAO in a protest will not substitute its judgment for the agency's but will review the agency's evaluation to ensure that the decision has a reasonable basis, is consistent with the solicitation and the applicable statutes and regulations and does not evidence bad faith. The GAO also has indicated that FSS procurements will be subject to protest when the record shows that the awardee fraudulently obtained the award. These issues must be distinguished from whether the FSS contractor will perform in accordance with the contract, which the GAO has said is a matter of contract administration and outside the GAO's bid protest jurisdiction.

(h) Determining Low Overall Cost

Pricing issues are important for FSS buys. According to FAR, supplies offered on the schedule are listed at fixed prices. Services on the schedule are priced either at hourly rates, or at a fixed price for performance of a specific task (e.g., installation, maintenance, and repair). GSA has already determined the prices of supplies and fixed-price services, and rates for services offered at hourly rates, under schedule contracts to be fair and reasonable.

Therefore, ordering activities are not required to make a separate determination of fair and reasonable pricing, except for a price evaluation as required by FAR when using order procedures for services that require a statement of work. In this regard, the ordering activity is responsible for considering the level of effort and the mix of labor proposed to perform a specific task being ordered and for determining the total price being reasonable.

A DOD class deviation to FAR 8.404(d) requires DOD ordering activity COs to make their own determination of fair and reasonable pricing for individual orders, blanket purchase agreements and orders under BPAs using the proposal analysis techniques in FAR Part 15.

When the ordering activity has placed an order against a schedule contract using the FAR procedures, the ordering activity necessarily has concluded that the order represents the "best value" (as defined in FAR) and results in the lowest overall cost alternative (considering price, special features, administrative costs, etc.) to meet the Government's needs. Although GSA has already negotiated fair and reasonable pricing, ordering activities may seek additional discounts before placing an order.

As just indicated, although the multiple award schedule often will contain the rules for competition amongst the vendors, it is also essential under statute, regulation and Government Accountability Office (GAO) case law that federal agencies procure from a multiple award schedule contractor offering the "best value" at the "lowest overall cost." The Comptroller General has said: "[O]nce the procuring agency determines its minimum needs, it is required to procure from the lowest priced supplier on the schedule, unless it makes an appropriate justification for purchase from a higher priced supplier." The only possible overriding consideration, as stated in FAR, is that when two vendors offer items meeting the ordering office's needs at the same price, the ordering office should give preference to the items of small business concerns.

(i) Price Reductions

Although the Comptroller General has said that the price evaluation must be based on the vendor's Federal Supply Schedule (FSS) contract prices, the Comptroller General also has said that this determination must include the agency's actual knowledge of any contractor-offered price reductions. Absent actual notice of the price reduction, the contracting agency need not consider the price reduction in determining the low price.

As indicated in the preceding paragraph, a schedule contractor sometimes will propose a price lower than its listed price (or even propose no cost for an item), but this practice is not improper per se or grounds for protest. The reason is that the regulations prescribe the inclusion of a GSA price reduction clause, in all multiple award FSS contracts. This clause covers the following points:

1.   Before the award of a contract, the Contracting Officer and the offeror will agree upon (a) the customer or category of customers which will be the basis of award, and (b) the government's price or discount relationship to the identified customer(s). The parties must maintain this relationship during the life of the contract; any change in the contractor's commercial pricing or discount arrangement applicable to the identified customer(s) which disturbs this relationship entitles the government to a price reduction;

2.   During the contract term, the Contractor must report to the agency all price reductions to the customer(s) that were the basis of award, along with an appropriate explanation;

3.   Price reductions shall apply to purchases under the contract if, after the date negotiations conclude, the contractor does one of several described actions, such as revising the commercial catalog or price list upon which the contract award was predicated to reduce prices;

4.   The contractor must offer the price reductions to the government with the same effective date, and for the same time period, as extended to the commercial customer (or category of customers);

5.   Price reductions are prohibited for certain sales, such as to Federal agencies or to commercial customers under firm, fixed-price definite quantity contracts with specified delivery in excess of the maximum order threshold specified in this contract;

6.   The contractor may offer the Contracting Officer a voluntary government-wide price reduction at any time during the contract period;

7.   The contractor shall notify the Contracting Officer of any price reduction subject to GSA clause as soon as possible, but not later than 15 calendar days after the effective date; and

8.   The contract must be modified to reflect any price reduction which becomes applicable in accordance with the clause.

In the ordering procedures for supplies, and for services not requiring a statement of work, FAR further addresses price reductions. Each schedule contract has a maximum order threshold established on a SIN (Special Item Number)-by-SIN basis. Although the agency may seek a price reduction at any time, this threshold represents the point where, given the dollar value of the potential order, the ordering activity shall seek a price reduction. In addition to following the procedures in FAR and before placing an order that exceeds the maximum order threshold or establishing a BPA, ordering activities shall—

1.   Review (except when the order contains brand name specifications) the pricelists of additional schedule contractors; the agency can use the GSA Advantage! on-line shopping service to facilitate this review;

2.   Based upon the initial evaluation, seek price reductions from the schedule contractor(s) considered to offer the best value; and

3.   After seeking price reductions, place the order with the schedule contractor that provides the best value. If further price reductions are not offered, an order may still be placed.

Another FAR policy provides that in addition to seeking price reductions before placing an order exceeding the maximum order threshold, or along with the annual BPA review, the agency may have other reasons to request a price reduction. For example, ordering activities should seek a price reduction when the supply or service is available elsewhere at a lower price, or when establishing a BPA to fill recurring requirements.

The potential volume of orders under BPAs, regardless of the size of individual orders, offers agencies the opportunity to secure greater discounts. Schedule contractors are not required to pass on to all schedule users a price reduction extended only to an individual ordering activity for a specific order. Consequently, all contractors under a multiple award schedule must have the same opportunity to submit price reductions to promote their competitive opportunities in future procurements.

In the case of a voluntary government-wide price reduction, this reduction will be effective under the GSA clause (and an award thereon valid) without regard to prior General Services Administration (GSA) acceptance. This result comports with prior case law, wherein the Comptroller General held that the contractor may offer (and the government may accept) a general price reduction under the clause at any time and by any method without notice to or prior or subsequent approval by GSA or a delegee agency.

The only current contractual requirement regarding these reductions is for the contractor to notify the GSA Contracting Officer within 15 calendar days after the effective date. Additionally, the Comptroller General has recognized that the agency is not obligated to inform one schedule contractor about another's proposed price reductions, since this practice would constitute an unfair competition technique.

(j)   Contract Administration Responsibilities

In placing orders against schedules, agencies ordinarily shall use Optional Form 347, an agency-prescribed form, such as the

Department of Defense (DOD) Form 1155, Order for Supplies or Services, or an established electronic communications format. FAR describes in detail the procedures for placing orders. Implementing agency regulations also may permit orders to be placed orally if the order is within the FAR's simplified purchase threshold and the contractor agrees to furnish a delivery ticket for each shipment under the order.

The schedule contracting agency may perform inspection of the supplies, unless the consignee takes on this responsibility. If the Federal Supply Schedule (FSS) contractor provides delinquent performance, the ordering office may either terminate the order for default or take other appropriate corrective actions. The FAR procedures for default termination are spelled out in detail. Similarly, the ordering office may perform a termination for convenience of an order. In a recent FAR change, ordering officers have jurisdiction to issue final decisions on disputes under FSS orders, whereas the schedule Contracting Officer has that authority for disputes under the basic schedule contract.

Chapter 9

CONTRACTOR QUALIFICATIONS

Analysis

A.   RESPONSIBLE PROSPECTIVE CONTRACTORS

§ 9.1   In General

The agency may award contracts only to "responsible" prospective contractors. Responsibility is concerned with the firm's capabilities and how the firm will accomplish the contract, which ability may be evidenced at any time before award.

Responsibility decisions are necessarily predictive in nature regarding the firm's future capability to perform; therefore, the agencies are not limited to evidence of the firm's existing resources. The Federal Acquisition Regulation (FAR) further requires the prospective contractor to affirmatively establish its responsibility and that contracting officials generally may make no purchase unless the government makes an affirmative determination of contractor responsibility. Put another way, a contract cannot be properly awarded if the Contracting Officer anticipates a default.

Perhaps the primary reason why prospective contractor responsibility is so important is that experience has shown that contracting officials have a tendency to place undue importance on making the award to the firm submitting the lowest priced evaluated offer. Too often, these improvident decisions have led to a subsequent default, late deliveries, or other unsatisfactory performance that can increase the agency's contractual or administrative costs. Thus, it can be seen why FAR emphasizes that the prospective contractor must affirmatively demonstrate its responsibility including, when applicable, the responsibility of its prospective subcontractors.

Sometimes a close question exists on whether a solicitation requirement is a matter of proposal acceptability or offeror responsibility. One good example is where the solicitation requests information on the firm's designated place of performance; ordinarily, this issue is a matter of responsibility, although it can be a matter of offer acceptability when the government has a material need for performance at a certain location.

In negotiated procurements, the rules may be stated as follows. If the point is included in the RFP's evaluation criteria, it concerns technical acceptability primarily (as well as general responsibility). If the point is listed in the specifications or other contract requirements but not in the RFP's evaluation criteria, then the point will concern proposal acceptability if the solicitation requires documentation on this issue and if the point deals with the offeror's promise to meet a material RFP term. The point will pertain to responsibility exclusively if it is not in the technical evaluation criteria and deals with the offeror's abilities or capacities and is not a contractual performance obligation. This analysis holds true regardless of how the RFP characterizes its own terms. Chapter 14 covers the responsibility/responsiveness question in sealed bidding.

§ 9.2   Responsibility Criteria

A responsible contractor is an entity that meets the FAR standards as well as any special standards, which are also called "definitive responsibility criteria" as set forth in the solicitation. The general standards include:

1.   Adequate financial resources to perform the contract (or the ability to obtain them);

2.   The ability to comply with the required or proposed delivery or performance schedule, taking into account the firm's existing commercial and governmental business commitments;

3.   A satisfactory performance record;

4.   A satisfactory record of integrity and business ethics;

5. The necessary organization, experience, accounting, and operational controls and technical skills to perform the contract (or the ability to obtain them);

6. The necessary production, construction, and technical equipment and facilities (or the ability to obtain them); and

7. Eligibility to receive the award under applicable laws and regulations.

Several sections in FAR describe the above general standards in greater detail.

With respect to the prospective contractor's ability to obtain the required resources regarding financing, organization, personnel, etc., the Contracting Officer will generally require acceptable evidence of the firm's ability in these areas. Assuming that the contractor or its proposed subcontractors lack these capabilities on their own account, the firm in question generally must substantiate either a commitment or explicit arrangement that will exist at the time of contract award.

Generally, the contractor assumes the risk of assuring adequate financing to perform the work, except where the contractor can show that financing was denied because of government wrongdoing. If, however, the agency failed to consider sufficiently current information and thereby failed to make a proper and timely responsibility determination regarding the awardee, this failure will be grounds for protest by a competing firm that is an interested party.

With respect to the firm's prior performance record, the Contracting Officer must presume that a prospective contractor is non-responsible when the firm is or has recently been "seriously deficient in contract performance" (such as the failure to apply sufficient tenacity and perseverance). The rule here is that these deficiencies may arise from either prior commercial or government contracts.

This regulatory presumption will be overcome only when the Contracting Officer determines that the circumstances were properly beyond the contractor's control or that the contractor since has taken appropriate corrective action. In making this decision, the Contracting Officer must consider the number of prior contracts involved, the extent of the relevant deficiencies, and any prior noncompliance with a subcontracting plan required by the FAR when the instant solicitation also requires such a plan. A prospective contractor generally shall not be deemed responsible or non-responsible, however, based solely on the lack of relevant performance history.

Frequently, an offeror will have affiliated concerns, that is, one concern controls, or possesses the power to control, another concern. To what extent may the agency consider the responsibility of related entities in judging the prospective contractor's qualifications? FAR provides that affiliated concerns are normally deemed separate entities in determining whether the offeror that is to perform the contract is responsible.

Notwithstanding this doctrine, the FAR requires the Contracting Officer to consider the affiliate's past performance and integrity when these matters may adversely affect the prospective contractor's responsibility. Similarly, the agency may reasonably consider the experience of a parent corporation in considering the subsidiary's responsibility. The Comptroller General has emphasized, however, that affiliation per se does not provide a proper basis for a non-responsibility decision.

Sometimes the affiliation will be based on a joint venture, i.e., an association of persons or firms, with an intent, by way of contract, to engage in and carry out a single business venture for joint profit for which purpose they combine their efforts, property, money, skill, and knowledge. In this situation, the agency may reasonably impute one joint venturer's resources, capabilities, and facilities to the other. The GAO further has recognized that certain qualifications of individual members of a joint venture properly may be considered in evaluating the overall responsibility of the joint venture.

Another issue of frequent importance is whether an awardee's proposed subcontractors—who generally are not in privity with the government—meet the FAR responsibility standards. Ordinarily, the prospective prime contractor must determine the responsibility of its prospective subcontractors, except that the agency must independently assess whether such firms are debarred, ineligible, or suspended. Exceptions to the general rule are where the agency needs to exercise its discretion to determine the subcontractor's responsibility directly, such as where the contract involves urgent requirements, or when a prospective contract involves substantial subcontracting.

If the agency considers a subcontractor non-responsible under the FAR, this finding can affect the prospective prime contractor's responsibility. Conversely, a subcontractor's credentials can overcome concerns about a prime contractor's weaknesses. GAO has said that even assuming that the problems under the contracts were caused solely by the subcontractors, these subcontractors' actions under the relevant contracts properly could be considered by the Contracting Officer in determining the prime contractor's responsibility.

It must always be remembered that social and economic values frequently drive procurement policy. A good example in the responsibility arena is that FAR prohibits award of contracts to any foreign incorporated entity that is treated as an inverted domestic corporation, i.e., a foreign entity formed to acquire the assets of a United States corporation, 80 percent or more of the stock of the foreign entity is owned by former shareholders of the United States corporation, and the foreign entity does not have substantial business activities in the foreign country.

§ 9.3   Information Regarding Responsibility

The Contracting Officer must possess or obtain sufficient information to be satisfied that the prospective contractor meets the FAR standards. Ordinarily, the Contracting Officer should request this information promptly after receipt of offers regarding the firms in range for award. Because the agency is entitled to make its determination on the basis of facts on hand immediately before award, this decision will not necessarily be affected by changes the firm makes after award.

Information regarding a firm's responsibility may be provided or changed at any time before award, although the agency is not required to wait until the last minute on its responsibility decision. Determinations regarding contractor responsibility should be based on the most current information available and should be obtained as close as possible to the time of the decision.

On the other hand, the contracting agency is not limited to the most current information available on the firm, but should also consider older, but recent, probative information to make an intelligent judgment on the firm's capabilities. Furthermore, any evidence considered with respect to responsibility should be "substantial, credible and objective," although the relative quality of that evidence is committed to administrative discretion. In this last respect, procurement officials have broad discretion in deciding whether they have sufficient information to make their responsibility assessments, but should reconsider these determinations when a material change occurs in a principal factor on which the decision was based. According to the FAR, the Contracting Officer should use the following sources of information to support determinations of responsibility or nonresponsibility (but is not mandated to use any particular resource except for #1 below):

1.   The System for Award Management (SAM) Exclusions (formerly the web-based Excluded Parties List System);

2.   Records and experience data, including verifiable information from sources such as personnel within the local contracting office;

3. The prospective contractor itself;

4. Pre-award survey reports;

5. The Federal Awardee Performance and Integrity System lists findings of liability related to federal contracts, including findings from criminal, civil and administrative proceedings; and

6. All other relevant sources, such as publications, suppliers, subcontractors and commercial and government customers of the firm. Contracting agencies routinely use these reports in evaluating contractor responsibility.

The agency violates no law or regulation by seeking relevant information about the firm from persons within the procuring agency. In making this judgment, the Contracting Officer also may reasonably consider the qualifications of an offeror's proposed subcontractor, of a predecessor or parent firm, or of the instant corporation's principal officer; the experience of the contractor's employees with other firms; or the contractor's own references. The contractor's unwillingness or inability to provide relevant information also is pertinent to the final decision. Although a Contracting Officer has significant discretion in determining what experience is relevant in making a responsibility determination, he may not mislead a contractor regarding the nature of his inquiry and later rely on the fact that the contractor failed to provide critical information.

As indicated above, the agency may continue to accept information regarding an offeror's responsibility up until the award. On the other hand, an offeror has the duty to timely and clearly establish that it has the capability to perform the contract. Accordingly, the agency is not required to delay awards indefinitely until an offeror cures the causes of its non-responsibility. The agency also may set a reasonable cutoff date for receipt of information relating to offeror responsibility. It bears emphasis, however, that the contracting agency has no general statutory or regulatory duty to discuss a prospective contractor's responsibility with that firm before the agency makes its responsibility determination.

In sum, the Contracting Officer's responsibility decision should be based on all available information (but he or she is not bound automatically by any one piece of information except as required by law or regulation). To assure that all government agencies makes purchases from responsible firms, FAR requires contracting offices and cognizant contract administration offices to promptly exchange relevant information whenever they become aware of circumstances casting doubt on a contractor's ability to perform contracts successfully.

§ 9.4　　Pre-Award Surveys

As indicated above, one method of gathering information about prospective contractors can be the pre-award survey. A "pre-award survey" is an evaluation by a surveying activity of a prospective contractor's ability to perform a proposed contract, and involves matters such as financial resources, experience, facilities, and performance record. A "surveying activity" is the cognizant contract administration office or another organization designated by the agency to conduct pre-award surveys.

Usually, where the agency decides to use this technique, the agency will conduct this survey only for the firm in line for award; there is no useful purpose in most cases in reviewing the responsibility of an offeror to whom the agency will not make the award. On the other hand, the GAO has recognized that the agency may conduct a pre-award survey for offerors not in line for award and may even request a pre-award survey before the evaluation of proposals is complete to save time.

These surveys are normally required when the information on hand or readily available to the Contracting Officer is insufficient to make a determination regarding responsibility. For most agencies in most procurements, these surveys are not necessary because the agency's market research will reveal the prospective contractors' responsibility. These surveys also are labor intensive and tend to delay awards, which increase the cost and time for processing procurements.

Subject to agency regulations, the Contracting Officer has broad discretion on whether to use this technique, the extent of the investigation, and the degree of reliance to be placed on the report. Accordingly, the Comptroller General has said that: (1) a pre-award survey is not a legal prerequisite for an affirmative finding of responsibility; (2) a favorable pre-award survey does not compel a finding of offeror responsibility; and (3) GAO will not review the agency's determination not to use a pre-award survey absent proof that the agency acted fraudulently, in bad faith, or failed to apply definitive responsibility criteria. Indeed, as indicated above, the Comptroller General has said that various valid reasons could explain the agency's decision not to conduct a pre-award survey.

If the survey discloses the contractor's prior unsatisfactory performance, the team must specify in its report the extent to which the contractor plans to take (or has taken) corrective action. The absence of evidence that the failure to meet contractual requirements was not the prime contractor's fault is not necessarily evidence of satisfactory performance. The report shall document any persistent pattern of the firm's need for costly and burdensome government assistance that was not contractually required.

§ 9.5   Determinations and Documentation

The Contracting Officer's signing of the contract necessarily amounts to a determination that the awardee is responsible regarding that contract. The agency has no FAR obligation to make specific findings and rationale to support a responsibility decision; the CO's signature alone will suffice. Agencies are nonetheless well-advised to explain in at least adequate detail why the firm is qualified to perform the contact. On the other hand, the Contracting Officer is required to include in the contract file those documents and reports supporting a determination of responsibility.

When the agency rejects an offeror otherwise in line for award because the firm is deemed non-responsible, the Contracting Officer must make a formal written determination for the file explaining the basis for the non-responsibility decision. Again, agencies are well advised to prepare a carefully researched and documented statement for why the offeror apparently in line for award is being denied the contact. As stated in the regulation, special referral procedures involving the Small Business Administration do exist, however, for when the Contracting Officer believes that a small business concern submitting the offer in line for award is non-responsible.

§ 9.6   Challenge to Determination of Responsibility

Numerous disappointed offerors have alleged that the Contracting Officer erred in approving the awardee's responsibility. The Comptroller General has said that, generally, the determination of a prospective contractor's responsibility rests within the broad discretion of the Contracting Officer who, in making that decision, must of necessity rely on his or her business judgment.

Under the GAO's protest regulations, the GAO will review this decision where (1) the protest alleges that definitive responsibility criteria in the solicitation were not met, (2) possible fraud or bad faith on the part of procurement officials, or (3) the evidence raises serious concerns that in reaching a particular responsibility determination, the Contracting Officer unreasonably failed to consider available relevant information or otherwise violated statute or regulation.

In this last regard, the GAO frequently has reviewed allegations that the awardee is non-responsible. For example, GAO has considered protest allegations that an agency failed to carefully consider that a contractor committed fraud, that principals of a contractor had criminal convictions, or that a contractor engaged in improper financial practices and improperly reported earnings. GAO also has sustained a protest regarding the awardee's affirmative responsibility because the contracting officer lacked the facts necessary to make an informed decision about the specific allegations of fraudulent activity. In contrast, GAO will not review unsupported allegations of illegal action, such as mere assertions of insider trading. Lastly, GAO will not consider allegations concerning financial issues confronting a contractor, such as cash on hand and declining net worth or poor business or financial performance or the allegation that principals of the firm planned to violate a non-competition agreement.

The protester has the burden of establishing that the agency improperly approved the awardee's affirmative responsibility; the GAO will not conduct independent investigations under its regulations to establish a protester's case. An agency's affirmative responsibility determination will be flawed, and subject to protest, when the agency was generally aware of allegations of misconduct against the awardee, but did not consider specific available and relevant information about the awardee's record of integrity and business ethics.

GAO also has held that a firm should not automatically be considered non-responsible simply because:

1.   It is a first time offeror;

2.   It is undergoing bankruptcy;

3.   The firm has a negative net worth;

4.   The firm or its personnel have been convicted of a crime;

5.   A criminal indictment or civil action for damages is pending against the firm or its personnel;

6.   The firm has federal tax liens against its facility;

7.   The agency has defaulted on a recent prior contract(s);

8.   The firm is a "broker;"

9.   The firm is allegedly seeking to "buy in" to the contract; and

10.   The firm's proposal contains an alleged patent infringement.

§ 9.7   Definitive Responsibility Criteria

The preceding section mentioned that firms may challenge affirmative determinations of responsibility based on the awardee's failure to meet definitive responsibility criteria. Both FAR and the decisional law recognize the concept of "definitive responsibility criteria" (also called special responsibility standards), which factors are in addition to (and distinguishable from) the FAR's general responsibility criteria.

The above-quoted term refers to specific, objective, and mandatory solicitation standards established by the agency that must be documented in the offer and that measure an offeror's ability to perform the contract, as stated in certain qualitative or quantitative requirements. These criteria also are distinct from an RFP's technical evaluation criteria, the proposal preparation instructions, and the offeror's performance obligations in the proposed contract.

Put another way, a definitive responsibility criterion is a precondition for award established in the solicitation as part of the selection process, but that does not affect the acceptability of a bid in sealed bidding or the relative rating of offerors in a negotiated procurement. These standards place the competing firms on notice that the class of prospective contractors is limited to those whose offers can document the ability to meet the applicable standards.

When the agency rejects an offer because the proposer has failed to meet a definitive responsibility criterion, the agency is rejecting the firm on responsibility grounds and not because the offer is unacceptable. Subcontractor qualifications are not permitted to cure a proposed prime contractor's shortcomings on this issue where the RFP permits consideration of just proposed prime contractor credentials.

An example of definitive responsibility criteria would be where an RFP for instructional services in a specific type of electrical engineering requires the awardee—outside the award evaluation criteria—to provide (and for the offeror to document) three instructors who have masters degrees with five years' experience in the specific type of electrical engineering. This requirement fits the definition, because the RFP here states the specific and objective standards for evaluation.

In a protest, the GAO would review the reasonableness of the agency's judgments in the same way it would assess the agency's technical evaluation of proposals. On the other hand, if the same RFP required instructors who are "qualified electrical engineers," this statement would not satisfy the definition, because it contains no objective criteria for evaluation (although the contractor's ability to furnish such personnel is encompassed by the Contracting Officer's subjective responsibility decision).

The GAO has held that the agency may not waive definitive responsibility criteria specifically and purposefully included in an RFP. The reason is that such a waiver is misleading and prejudicial both to the offerors that met the requirement and to any prospective offerors that did not participate in the competition because of the expressed requirement. When the agency decides before award that the RFP contains an unnecessary definitive criterion of responsibility, the proper course of action is for the agency to cancel the solicitation (or to amend the RFP as practicable).

§ 9.8　Challenge to Determination of Non-Responsibility

As indicated above, the determination of a prospective contractor's responsibility is the duty of the Contracting Officer, who has wide discretion in exercising his or her business judgment. Therefore, the GAO will not question a non-responsibility decision unless the protester meets its burden of proof of showing agency bad faith or the lack of any reasonable basis for the decision. If the agency proffers one valid reason for its non-responsibility decision, the validity of any other reasons will become academic in a GAO bid protest.

In establishing agency bad faith regarding a negative responsibility decision, the protester must do more than disagree with the Contracting Officer's determination of non-responsibility or allege that the agency has failed to gather sufficient information. Contracting officials are strongly presumed to act in good faith; to make a showing otherwise, the protester must demonstrate by virtually irrefutable proof that the Contracting Officer had a specific and malicious intent to injure the protester.

A Contracting Officer should base a determination of non-responsibility upon current evidence of record, including any pre-award survey information compiled. To be reasonable, the agency's non-responsibility decision must reflect a reasoned judgment based on the investigation and evaluation of the evidence available at the time the decision is made. The sufficiency of the information needed to assure an agency that the firm will meet (or not meet) its contractual obligations is a matter of administrative discretion, although the agency may not declare a firm non-responsible solely on the allegations of a competing firm.

The agency's non-responsibility decision will not necessarily be erroneous because the agency relied in part on invalid or unsupported information. Instead, the GAO will overturn such a decision only when the record as a whole shows that the agency's decision was unreasonable or unsupported in "material respects." Further, even if the firm's responsibility record is generally satisfactory, the agency may reasonably decide that the firm's material shortcomings in just one responsibility area can suffice for a non-responsibility finding and proposal rejection.

In reviewing the sufficiency of the evidence, the Comptroller General has said that a current pre-award survey report either detailing performance deficiencies in recent contracts or including a criminal investigating agency's report of misconduct may satisfy this requirement. In the latter instance, an official criminal investigative report which raises a serious doubt about a firm's integrity can form the basis for a non-responsibility decision even in the absence of an independent procuring agency investigation and regardless of whether the report results in a criminal conviction.

If the protest centers on a technical dispute, the protester's mere disagreement with the agency's conclusion will not suffice to satisfy its burden of proof. Also, a firm is not automatically entitled to a finding of responsibility because other procuring agencies have recently found the firm to be responsible after a pre-award survey or otherwise or even because the same Contracting Officer (or agency) earlier had found the same firm responsible under a different procurement.

Frequently, the agency will deem a firm non-responsible because of a poor performance record. Under the FAR, the circumstances surrounding an offeror's prior performance should be considered as one of several factors relevant to the firm's responsibility. Thus, the mere fact of a contractor's earlier unsatisfactory performance or a prior default termination does not necessarily establish a lack of responsibility, although both are proper matters for the contracting agency's consideration. An agency may properly rely upon its reasonable perception of a contractor's inadequate performance record even where the contractor disputes the agency's position.

Similarly, a firm's recent satisfactory contractual performance does not necessarily establish a firm's current responsibility, because the relevant factor is the firm's overall performance record. In making these judgments, the Contracting Officer must take into consideration the FAR's rebuttable presumption that a prospective contractor that recently has been seriously deficient in contract performance must be presumed non-responsible, unless the agency determines that the circumstances were properly beyond the firm's control or that the firm has taken appropriate corrective action.

B. DEBARMENT, SUSPENSION AND INELIGIBILITY

§ 9.9   Debarment and Suspension

Because the FAR sets forth specific procedures for imposing and challenging a suspension or debarment decision, GAO is not the appropriate forum for challenging the agency's decision. Therefore, GAO no longer considers protests against these decisions. On the other hand, the Court of Federal Claims, which has a broader grant of statutory jurisdiction, will entertain protests involving a challenge against a debarment or a suspension. See *IMCO, Inc. v. United States*, 97 F.3d 1422 (Fed. Cir. 1996). United States district courts also have jurisdiction to consider the propriety of such proceedings. See *United States v. Glymph*, 96 F.3d 722 (4th Cir. 1996).

To ensure full and open competition, federal policy is that contracting agencies are to solicit offers from, award contracts to, and consent to subcontract only with, responsible contractors. In limited cases, the agency may exclude an individual or other legal entity from contracting with executive branch activities by applying the remedy of debarment or suspension. As explained more fully below, "debarment" is a total exclusion of a contractor from government contracting for a specified term, and "suspension" is a temporary exclusion from government contracting for a specified term pending the completion of other proceedings.

It bears emphasis that the government may impose these remedies only to protect the government's legitimate business interests, i.e., to protect it against non-responsible contractors and not to punish the particular individual or other entity. Thus, it can be seen that the key consideration in those cases is the contractor's present and likely future responsibility, i.e., its honesty and integrity as well as its ability to perform the contract. "Present responsibility" in this sense refers to the contractor itself, not its employees or other company personnel personally responsible for past misdeeds.

If the agency does inadvertently award a contract to a debarred or suspended contractor, the award will be void if the ineligibility is imposed by statute and voidable at the agency's election if imposed by regulation. To ensure that debarment and suspension serve these remedial objectives, the regulations impose various due process protections for the affected person or firm before the action may be taken.

In certain instances, and as permitted by statute and regulation, the agency may preclude a firm from receiving a type of contract or a class of contracts without employing debarment or suspension proceedings. Thus, when a firm is in the Small Business Administration's (SBA's) 8(a) program (see Chapter 19), but no longer qualifies under the applicable size standards, the agency may hold the company's awards in abeyance, and the agency may prohibit the firm from further participation in the program after an SBA administrative hearing.

The GAO has said that such exclusions do not amount to a debarment or a suspension, because debarment and suspension refer to a complete exclusion from contracting with a government agency, which is not true for firms disqualified from (or not allowed to participate in) the 8(a) program in a single procurement or class of procurements.

A FAR solicitation provision requires information from an offeror in contracts expected to exceed the simplified acquisition threshold (see Chapter 13) certifying its status on debarment, suspension, proposed debarment, and related responsibility issues. A standard contract clause protects the government's interests when a contractor subcontracts with contractors debarred, suspended, or proposed for debarment in solicitations and contracts where the contract value exceeds $35,000.

The firm's failure to complete the above provision justifies possible rejection on responsibility grounds, as opposed to the grounds of technical unacceptability. As just indicated, the purpose of the certification is to assist the Contracting Officer in assessing the firm's responsibility. If the firm makes a misstatement in the certification, proposal rejection is warranted when (1) the certification was made in bad faith, or (2) the misstatement materially influenced the agency's responsibility determination.

New provisions in the Department of Defense Procedures, Guidance and Information 209.406–3 revise the information an agency should submit when referring a contractor for suspension or debarment and change the decision-making procedures for suspension and debarment officials from discretionary to mandatory.

§ 9.10   Debarment

"Debarment" means action taken by a debarring official under to exclude a contractor from government contracting and government approved subcontracting for a reasonable, specified period. The "debarring official" is the agency head or a designee authorized to impose debarment. A "contractor" is an individual or any other legal entity that submits an offer for, or is awarded, or reasonably may be expected to submit offers for, or be awarded, a government contract or a subcontract under a government contract. In addition, a person or firm is a "contractor" when it conducts business with the government as an agent or representative of another contractor or when the firm is a subcontractor under a prime contract for which the government must give consent to the award.

The agency should initiate debarment proceedings as soon as practicable if debarment is the intended remedy. FAR authorizes the debarring official to debar a contractor for any of the described causes using the FAR procedures described below. The existence of cause for debarment does not automatically require the debarring official to issue an adverse decision to the contractor; the official must exercise sound discretion, consider the seriousness of the contractor's acts or omissions and analyze any circumstances favoring the person or entity.

In any action in which the proposed debarment is not based on a conviction or a civil judgment, the cause for debarment must be established by a preponderance of the evidence. Under the FAR, the debarring official may debar a contractor for any of the following causes:

1. Conviction of, or civil judgment for:

a. Commission of fraud or a criminal offense in connection with obtaining, attempting to obtain, or performing a public contract or subcontract;

b. Violation of federal or state antitrust statutes relating to the submission of offers;

c. Commission of embezzlement, theft, forgery, bribery, falsification or destruction of records, making false statements, tax evasion, or receiving stolen property; or

d. Commission of any other offense indicating a lack of business integrity or business honesty that seriously and directly affects the present responsibility of a government contractor or subcontractor.

2. Violation of the terms of a government contract or subcontract so serious as to justify debarment, such as:

a. Willful failure to perform in accordance with the terms of one or more contracts; or

b. A history of failure to perform, or of unsatisfactory performance of, one or more contracts.

3. Violations of the Drug Free Workplace Act of 1988 as indicated by:

a. The offeror's submission of a false certificate;

b. The contractor's failure to comply with its certification; or

c.   Such a number of contractor employees having been convicted of violations of criminal drug statutes occurring in the workplace, as to indicate that the contractor has failed to make a good-faith effort to provide a drug free workplace.

4.   Any other cause of so serious or compelling a nature that it affects the present responsibility of a government contractor or subcontractor.

FAR provides that a debarring official may debar a contractor, based on a determination by the Attorney General, or a designee, that the contractor has violated the Immigration and Nationality Act employment provisions of Executive Order 12989, i.e., the firm has hired illegal aliens. The government may extend the debarment for an additional year if the Attorney General or a designee determines that the contractor is still in violation of the Act.

FAR describes the debarment procedures. First, the agency will promptly investigate, report, and refer a proper case to the debarring official in accordance with agency procedures. The agency is required to establish procedures governing the debarment decision making process that are as informal as practicable, consistent with fundamental fairness. These procedures must afford the contractor, and any named affiliates, notice of the proposed debarment and an opportunity to submit information and argument in opposition to debarment. The procedures for notice of proposals to debar are listed in the regulation.

If the debarment is not based on a conviction or civil judgment, and the contractor's case in opposition raised a genuine dispute over facts material to the proposed debarment, the agency must also permit the contractor to make a personal appearance with counsel before the appropriate agency official, to present witnesses, to confront any person the agency presents, and to obtain a transcript of the proceedings.

The debarring official's decision must be based on the record; an additional procedure exists under the FAR for referring disputed material facts to another agency official for adjudication, and this official's findings of fact must be accepted by the debarring official unless that official specifically deems them arbitrary and capricious or clearly erroneous.

According to the FAR, if the debarring official decides to impose debarment, the contractor (and any involved affiliates) will be given prompt notice of the decision along with the reasons therefor, the period of debarment (including effective dates), and advice that the debarment is effective throughout the executive branch of the government (unless the head of the agency or a designee makes an exception). If the official decides that debarment is not appropriate, an appropriate notification is required.

The debarring official must impose a period of debarment consistent with the seriousness of the cause(s). The debarred contractor (or a contractor proposed for debarment) will then be listed in the System for Award Management (SAM) Exclusions which will include those firms debarred, proposed for debarment, suspended, or otherwise declared ineligible.

Generally, the debarment period may not exceed three years, although debarment for violations of the Drug Free Workplace Act may be for a period up to five years. The debarring official may reduce the period or extent of debarment for good cause shown, such as a bona fide change in the entity's ownership. The debarring official also may extend the debarment for an additional period when necessary to protect the public interest, in accordance with the FAR procedures. A key limitation here is that the debarring official may not extend the original debarment based solely on the facts and circumstances justifying the original debarment.

FAR recognizes that a corporation cannot act except through its agents and employees. Under this regulation, when an officer, director, shareholder, partner, employee, or other individual associated with a contractor has committed fraudulent, criminal, or other seriously improper conduct, this conduct may be imputed to the contractor proposed for debarment when it occurred in connection with the individual's performance of his duties for or on behalf of the contractor, or with the contractor's knowledge, approval, or acquiescence.

Similarly, the same misconduct by a contractor may be imputed to an individual associated with the contractor who participated in, knew of, or had reason to know of, the contractor's conduct. If the conduct is imputable as just described, then the contractor or an individual may be debarred under the FAR procedures. It bears emphasis, however, that a debarment of a corporation does not automatically dictate the debarment of a corporate employee or officer and vice versa.

(a) Other Debarment Procedures

Numerous statutes, regulations, and executive orders have provisions for exclusion from federal contracting for described violations. These proceedings are not necessarily governed by the FAR processes. Thus, the well-known 40 U.S.C.A. chapter 31, subchapter IV, Wage Rate Requirements (Construction) 41 U.S.C.A. 1903, formerly known as the Davis Bacon Act, which provides in part for minimum wage requirements for covered construction contracts (see Chapter 19), requires that persons or firms who have committed substantial intentional violations of the act, as demonstrated by bad faith or gross carelessness, be debarred from government contracting. Other examples of statutes having similar debarment or ineligibility procedures are 41 U.S.C.A. chapter 67, Service Contract Labor Standards, formerly known as the Service Contract Act), the Equal Employment Opportunity Act (and executive orders thereunder), the Buy American Act, the Federal Water Pollution Control Act, and the Clean Air Act. Courts have inferred debarment remedies from some statutes of this nature where express debarment terms are not included.

(b) "De Facto" Debarments

An agency may not debar, or otherwise declare or treat as ineligible, a firm without satisfying the procedural due process protections of the applicable statutes and regulations. Without following the pertinent procedures, the agency may not lawfully exclude a firm from contracting by refusing to make an award to that firm for an indefinite time, by making repeated determinations of non-responsibility, or even by making a single determination of non-responsibility if it is part of a long-term disqualification effort. The case law refers to such improper exclusions as "de facto" (in fact) or "constructive" debarments.

A de facto debarment does not occur when the government's actions have no immediate effect on the firm's present or future intent or ability to do government business. Notwithstanding the above rules and regulations, a few decisions do recognize an emergency exception for excluding a firm from government contracting for a limited time without notice or a hearing when the action is based on national security considerations. On the other hand, the agency may not avoid applying the due process requirements by calling an action an "abeyance" or a "temporary declaration of ineligibility," or similar designations, or by complying with the governing rules after the fact.

Another example of an improper de facto debarment is when the agency in more than one procurement excludes a firm from award because of a lack of integrity without giving the firm prompt notice of the charges and an opportunity to present opposing evidence before adverse action is taken. The point to be emphasized for this category of cases is that there must be a government defamation of the firm's reputation which has an immediate and tangible effect on the firm's ability to do business. These due process requirements will not be applicable, however, if the rejection decision is based on such factors as a lack of facilities or a lack of demonstrated ability as opposed to a lack of integrity.

Usually, when an agency deprives a contractor of an award in a single procurement, no basis exists for a finding of a de facto debarment unless specific facts warrant this conclusion. This rule is based on the principle that a finding of non-responsibility pertains only to the contract in question and does not bar the firm from competing for future contracts and receiving awards if it is otherwise qualified.

(c) Debarment and Contract Formation

When a contractor is debarred or if the agency has proposed a contractor for debarment, the agency may not solicit offers from, award contracts to, or consent to subcontract with the person or firm, pending the debarment decision, unless the agency head or a designee determines that a compelling reason exists to do so.

Agencies commonly receive proposals from debarred firms, firms that are proposed for debarment, or firms that are otherwise ineligible for award. According to FAR, proposals, quotations, or offers received from any contractor listed in the System for Award Management (SAM) Exclusions may not be evaluated for award or included in the competitive range, nor may discussions be conducted with a listed offeror during a period of ineligibility, unless the agency head or a designee makes a special determination of compelling circumstances.

If the period of ineligibility expires or terminates prior to award, the Contracting Officer may, but is not required to, consider such proposals, quotations, or offers. The same rules apply to firms declared ineligible under the FAR or to firms conducting business with the government as agents or representatives of other contractors debarred or otherwise ineligible. To effectuate these policies, the FAR further provides that, after the Contracting Officer receives proposals, he or she must check the SAM.gov Exclusions.

Generally, FAR permits continuation of current contracts or subcontracts with a debarred contractor, unless the appropriate agency official determines otherwise. Consistent with this rule, the FAR provides that unless the agency head makes a written determination finding a compelling reason, ordering activities shall not place orders exceeding the guaranteed minimum under an indefinite quantity contract, nor place orders under Federal Supply Schedule contracts, blanket purchase agreements, or basic ordering agreements; nor add new work, exercise options, or otherwise extend the duration of current contracts or orders.

§ 9.11   Suspension

"Suspension" means action taken by a suspending official to disqualify a contractor temporarily from government contracting and government-approved subcontracting. When an agency suspends a contractor or subcontractor, the action will be effective throughout the government's executive branch, unless an acquiring agency head or a designee states in writing a compelling reason justifying continued business dealing between the agency and the contractor.

The agency should initiate suspension procedures as early as practicable when suspension is the intended remedy. Suspension is a "serious action" that may only be imposed with adequate evidence, pending the completion of investigatory or legal proceedings, when immediate protection is needed for the government's interests. Thus, for example, if a firm has been indicted for a criminal offense, such as bribery, in attempting to obtain a government contract, the agency may invoke the suspension remedy pending the completion of the criminal investigation and the trial. A suspended firm usually (but not automatically) will later be debarred in accordance with the FAR.

When a firm is suspended, all divisions or other organizational elements of the firm will be covered, unless the suspension official's decision is limited to specific divisions, organizational elements, or commodities. Affiliates of the firm may be suspended if they are specifically named in the decision and if the affiliate had prior written notice of the suspension and an opportunity to respond. At the same time, affiliates should be suspended only as necessary in the exercise of sound discretion considering the public interest.

FAR lists the causes for suspension. They resemble the grounds for debarment with several exceptions; for example, a serious violation of a contract is not specifically identified as a cause for suspension. Another important distinction is the standard of proof. Because of the differing interests at stake, FAR permits suspension upon "adequate evidence," which is less than the "preponderance of evidence" required for debarment under the FAR.

The quantum of evidence necessary for suspension is analogous to the probable cause necessary for issuing a search warrant or binding over a suspect at a preliminary hearing in a criminal case. As with debarment, however, the focus will be on whether the firm is "presently responsible" in light of the grounds substantiated against the contractor. In this regard, the suspension decision is prospective and does not affect any prior affirmative findings of responsibility concerning that firm.

The FAR procedures for suspension are analogous to the FAR procedures for debarment. The FAR emphasizes that the agency is to use an informal decision making process that is consistent with fundamental fairness. Suspension is a temporary measure pending the completion of an investigation and any ensuing legal proceedings, unless the suspension official terminates the measure sooner. The suspended contractor will be included in the SAM Exclusions.

If the agency does not initiate legal proceedings within 12 months of the date of the suspension notice, the suspension will terminate automatically unless a Department of Justice Assistant Attorney General requests an extension. Upon such a request, the suspension may continue for another six months (although the suspension may not extend beyond this period). The scope of the suspension must be same as that for a debarment.

(a) "De Facto" Suspension

The same rules apply for de facto suspension as apply for de facto debarment. Thus, an offeror may be suspended from competing for government contracts only under the administrative due process requirements of the regulation.

(b) Suspension and Contract Formation

Generally, FAR permits continuation of current contracts or subcontracts with a suspended contractor, unless the appropriate agency official determines otherwise. Consistent with this rule, the FAR provides that unless the agency head makes a written determination finding a compelling reason, ordering activities shall not place orders exceeding the guaranteed minimum under an indefinite quantity contract, nor place orders under Federal Supply Schedule contracts, blanket purchase agreements, or basic ordering agreements; nor add new work, exercise options, or otherwise extend the duration of current contracts or orders.

C. ORGANIZATIONAL CONFLICTS OF INTEREST

§ 9.12   In General

An "organizational conflict of interest (OCI)" under FAR means that because of other activities or relationships with other persons, a person is unable or potentially unable to render impartial assistance or advice to the government, or the person's objectivity in performing the contract work is or might be otherwise impaired, or a person has an unfair competitive advantage. FAR further states that an organizational conflict of interest may result when the circumstances create an actual or potential conflict of interest on an instant contract or when the nature of the work performed on the instant contract creates an actual or potential conflict of interest on a future acquisition.

Many cases hold that an inference or suspicion is insufficient to establish an OCI. For example, in *Turner Construction v. United States*, 645 F.3d 1377 (Fed. Cir. 2011), the Federal Circuit acknowledged that the "hard facts" need not show an actual conflict. A potential conflict based on specific facts is sufficient, but a finding of a potential conflict cannot be supported by an inference based on suspicion and innuendo. A significant potential OCI of one joint venture partner, however, will be imputed to the joint venture as a whole.

When before the award of the contract, the protester knew or should have known the information underlying an OCI concerning a competitor but failed to raise the OCI before the award, the protest will be untimely. In fact where an offeror has grounds to believe that the solicitation itself creates a significant possibility of an OCI, such as where this offeror knows before the closing date for offers that a competitor with a significant OCI will submit a proposal, and the agency confirms this fact beforehand, a protest against this second offeror's participation must filed before the closing date of the RFP.

According to FAR, an agency must withhold a contract award when a significant organizational conflict of interest cannot be avoided, neutralized, or mitigated. For example, unequal access to information may be mitigated by (among other security measures) creating firewalls within the organization to ensure that competitive information is walled off from potentially tainted contract employees preparing a proposal for a later contract. The regulation requires the Contracting Officer to notify the contractor before withholding the contract, to give the reasons for the proposed withholding, and to allow the contractor a reasonable opportunity to respond. The GAO has held that failing to give the contractor this opportunity is a procedural informality that will not affect an otherwise valid determination. Exchanges regarding OCI issues before award amount to responsibility inquiries and not discussions.

The dangers of organizational conflicts of interest are:

1.   The undermining of public confidence in the fairness of the procurement system;

2.   The possibility that the government will receive biased advice on the instant contract performance; and

3.   The possibility that the firm could obtain an unfair advantage in follow-on competitive acquisitions, i.e., the first contract places the

contractor in a position where the agency might favor the firm's own products or services in future purchases.

In counteracting such significant conflicts, agency contracting officials should act as early as possible in the acquisition process and should seek the advice of agency experts, such as legal counsel. On the other hand, even when such a conflict exists, special circumstances consistent with the government's best interests may dictate that the firm be allowed to compete for a contract nevertheless. In this regard, FAR provides that the contracting activity may apply to the head of the agency or a designee for a waiver of a general rule or procedure.

The most serious consequence of a significant organizational conflict of interest is that the agency may prohibit a firm having such a conflict from competing for a contract. The agency may disqualify a firm from so competing even when the firm's prior contract, or the instant solicitation, does not give the firm notice of this possibility. Moreover, the agency may apply a variety of other restrictions to a firm's activities, even when not explicitly provided for in statute or regulation, when the needs of the agency in a particular procurement reasonably require such a restriction.

It is grounds for protest that the agency mitigation efforts were inadequate with regard to a significant organizational conflict of interest problem presented by the awardee. Nonetheless, when a Contracting Officer takes steps to alleviate a conflict as required under the FAR, the GAO will not overturn the contracting agency's determination unless it is shown to be unreasonable. A protest will be untimely, however, where the solicitation was issued on an unrestricted basis, the protester was aware of facts giving rise to the potential for a significant conflict of interest for a competitor, the protester had been advised by the agency that it considers the potential offeror eligible for award, but where the protester waited until after the closing date to challenge the particular offeror's awardee's eligibility for the award.

§ 9.13   FAR Standards

Before issuing an RFP for a contract that involves a significant potential organizational conflict of interest which might exist, the Contracting Officer must recommend to a higher-level official a course of action for resolving any conflict. This course of action must include the Contracting Officer's written analysis of the recommended course of action, a draft solicitation provision to preclude any such problems, and (as appropriate) a contract clause. A non-significant potential conflict, however, does not require such a written analysis.

According to the FAR, the solicitation's proposed clause must specify the nature and duration of the proposed restraint. Once the higher-level official approves the Contracting Officer's recommendations, the Contracting Officer must include the approved provision and clause in the RFP, the contract, or both, must consider any additional information disclosed during the pre-award process, and must resolve any such organizational conflict of interest consistent with higher-level agency approval or other direction.

By definition, the rules on including appropriate RFP and contract provisions and clauses will be invoked only when the agency recognizes the potential for a conflict. Thus, it bears emphasis that the contracting agency may properly disqualify a firm from the competition (or take other corrective action) even when the prior contract or the instant RFP gives no notice of a potential conflict situation.

Organizational conflicts of interest come in three basic varieties.

The first group consists of situations in which a firm has access to nonpublic information as part of its performance of a government contract, and where that information may provide the firm a competitive advantage in a later competitive advantage for a government contract. In these "unequal access to information" cases, the concern is limited to the risk of the firm gaining a competitive advantage; there is no issue of bias. The agency must specifically identify competitively useful, nonpublic information to which the offeror had access.

The second group consists of situations in which a firm, as part of its performance of a government contract, has in some sense set the ground rules for another government contract by, for example, writing the statement of work or the specifications. In these "biased ground rules" cases, the primary concern is whether the firm could skew the competition, whether intentionally or not, in favor of itself. These situations also may involve a concern that the firm, by virtue of its special knowledge of the agency's future requirements, would have an unfair advantage in the competition for these requirements.

The third group of cases comprises instances where a firm's work under one government contract could entail evaluating itself, either through an assessment of performance under another contract or an evaluation of proposals. In these "impaired objectivity" cases, the concern is that the firm's ability to render impartial advice to the government could appear to be undermined by its relationship with the entity whose work product is being evaluated.

Chapter 10

MARKET RESEARCH

Analysis

§ 10.1   Market Research

---

§ 10.1   Market Research

Implementing statute, the Federal Acquisition Regulation (FAR) prescribes the policies and procedures for conducting market research to arrive at the most suitable approach for acquiring, distributing and supporting supplies and services.

The regulation mandates that agencies conduct market research appropriate to the circumstances before developing new requirements or soliciting offers exceeding the simplified acquisition threshold (see Chapter 13). Planning is needed even below this threshold when adequate information is not available and the circumstances justify the cost. Agencies use the results of market research to determine if sources are available to meet their needs, especially any sources providing commercial or non-developmental items.

FAR states the procedures for market research. According to the regulation, acquisitions must begin with a description of the government's needs stated in terms sufficient to conduct market research, especially with respect to commercial or non-developmental items. The actual process of market research involves the gathering of information specific to the item being acquired, and should include such information as: the type of source that can satisfy the requirement (commercial v. noncommercial); the requirements of any laws or regulations unique to the item being procured; and the size and status of potential sources.

The extent of market research is within the agency's discretion and is dependent upon such factors as urgency, estimated cost, complexity, and past experience. Proper techniques for conducting market research vary, and may include such procedures as: querying government data bases; obtaining source lists of similar items from other contracting activities or trade associations; and reviewing catalogs and other generally available product literature.

In keeping with the federal policy giving increased emphasis to commercial or non-developmental item purchasing, FAR states that if the market research indicates that commercial or non-developmental items might not be available to suit agency needs, the agency must reevaluate the need and determine if it can be restated to permit commercial or non-developmental item purchases.

If the market research indicates that commercial item purchasing is feasible, then the agency under FAR must use the commercial item procedures to conduct the acquisition. If the market research indicates that commercial item purchasing is not feasible, then the agency may not use the commercial item mechanism and shall state in the SAM.gov notice that it will not use commercial item processes.

As stated in FAR, agencies are encouraged—but not required—to document their market research activity, commensurate with the size and complexity of the acquisition. Of course, the absence of a written document requirement does not excuse the agency from performing these efforts in fact. At bottom, the government's acquisition planning efforts should stem in large measure from the agency's market research efforts. No legal bar exists against the same contracting officials who will be conducting the procurement from engaging in market research.

A protest against a solicitation's failure to use commercial products based on poor acquisition planning or inadequate market research must establish that better planning might have resulted in a less restrictive or more commercial-friendly solicitation. A protester alleging a lack of market research for a non-competitive sole source procurement must establish prejudice.

Chapter 11

DESCRIBING AGENCY NEEDS

Analysis

§ 11.1   In General

The requirement description may identify the need in terms of function, performance, or design, subject to agency needs and the available market. As mandated by the Competition in Contracting Act (CICA) and Federal Acquisition Regulation (FAR), agencies must state their needs—whenever practicable—in functional or performance terms as opposed to design requirements. Similarly, the GAO has held that agencies may not use design requirements when performance or functional descriptions would be satisfactory. A violation of the above rules is grounds for protest when the solicitation unnecessarily restricts competition.

As explained below, functional, performance, and design requirement descriptions all have their advantages and disadvantages.

A *functional* requirement (recognized by CICA) describes the work to be performed in terms of end purpose or the government's ultimate objective rather than the way in which the work is to be performed. In this manner, functional descriptions allow a broad range of supplies or services to qualify. On the other hand, because functional descriptions contain relatively few objective criteria, they are the most subject to challenge as being ambiguous, indefinite, or unduly risky. The use of these broad descriptions also can be disadvantageous to the agency in that (1) the government must sometimes devote significant effort to drafting these requirements and evaluating the proposals, and (2) vendors are given leeway to propose costly offers.

A *performance* requirement (also recognized by CICA) sets forth an objective or standard to be achieved, and the successful offeror is expected to exercise ingenuity in achieving that objective or standard of performance. In these descriptions, the design requirements, measurements, and other specific details are not stated nor are they considered important, so long as the contractor meets the performance requirement. The sole qualification to this statement is that, under CICA, performance specifications also must inform prospective offerors of the range of acceptable characteristics or of the minimum acceptable standards.

Because performance requirements will combine elements of functional and design descriptions to a greater or lesser extent, they can have the advantages or disadvantages of both in a particular procurement. With performance specifications, the contractor accepts general responsibility for the design, engineering, and achievement of the performance requirements, although the government retains the right of final inspection and approval or rejection.

Design requirements (also recognized by CICA) set forth characteristics such as precise measurements, tolerances, materials, in-process and finished product tests, quality control, inspection requirements, or any other specific features for the end product. Stated another way, design specifications are explicit, unquestionable specifications which tell the contractor exactly how the contract is to be performed and that no deviation therefrom is permissible.

Such technical requirements, when stated in clear and precise terms, are presumed to be essential to the needs of the government. While contracts containing such requirements frequently require that the product pass a performance test or standard, these matters do not convert the requirement description into a performance requirement. The government will be liable for design and design-related omissions, errors, and deficiencies in these specifications. These descriptions are the most prone to challenge as preventing full and open competition because they are the most objective and inflexible of the three requirement descriptions.

To meet its needs, the government frequently combines functional, performance, and design features in its requirement descriptions. Combining these features in one requirement description also can be necessary to ensure full and open competition. For example, the agency could neither adequately convey its needs nor maximize competition for an extremely complex and precisely engineered item—such as a missile system—without including any design features.

§ 11.2   Other Policies

Social or economic policies may affect the agency's requirement descriptions. FAR contains increased emphasis on environmental, conservation, and occupational concerns in the drafting of product descriptions and other solicitation requirements.

First, FAR states that agencies shall consider energy efficiency in the procurement of products and services, to include consideration of these factors in the preparation of drawings, specifications, and other product descriptions.

Second, FAR states the government's policy to acquire, in a cost effective manner, items composed of the highest percentage of recovered materials practicable consistent with maintaining a satisfactory level of competition without adversely affecting performance requirements or exposing suppliers' employees to undue hazards from the recovered materials.

Additionally, FAR contains guidance on contracting for environmentally preferable and energy efficient products and services, prescribes instructions concerning ozone depleting substances and covers toxic chemical release reporting (the latter being inapplicable to acquisition of commercial items or contractor facilities outside the United States).

FAR provides for "performance based" service contracting. The quoted term means "structuring all aspects of an acquisition around the purpose of the work to be performed as opposed to either the manner by which the work is to be performed or broad and imprecise statements of work." Accordingly, the quoted term includes the following: (1) the use of a performance work statement, (2) the agency describes its requirements in terms of results required rather than the method of performing the work; (3) the agency provides for measurable performance standards in such areas as quality, timeliness, and quantity; and (4) performance incentives corresponding to the contractual performance standards, where appropriate.

As stated in FAR, agencies must use performance-based contracting to the maximum practicable extent for acquisition of services, including those acquired under supply contracts, with some exceptions. Some exceptions are for architect engineer services utility services, and incidental services to supply contracts.

§ 11.3   Brand Name or Equal

For many years, agencies have employed the minimum acceptable product description by the identification of a requirement by use of a brand name followed by the words "or equal." A proper brand name or equal product description provides for full and open competition, and refers to supply, but not service, procurements. The agency may use this technique in either negotiated or sealed bid procurements.

FAR provides detailed guidance on this technique. FAR necessarily requires the agencies in most cases to identify the brand name product by the commercial name and make or model number or other appropriate nomenclature by which the manufacturer, producer, or distributor offers the product for sale. The solicitation should reference all known acceptable brand name products, as feasible.

When the agency uses this type of product description, it must allow prospective contractors to offer an "equal" product if that product will meet the government's needs in essentially the same manner as the brand name product (which could include products not actually in existence at the time of proposal submission). The GAO has recognized that government contracting officials, and not potential offerors, are generally in the best position to select appropriate brand name or equal product descriptions.

The brand name or equal product description should clearly set forth the "salient features"—those physical, functional or other characteristics of the brand name product that the agency considers essential for its needs. In a brand name or equal acquisition, the solicitation's failure to list proper or sufficient salient characteristics is an improper restriction on competition that ordinarily requires cancellation or amendment of the solicitation (although an award under such a defective product description could sometimes be valid when there is no competitive prejudice and the government's needs will be satisfied). Similarly, a brand name or equal solicitation is defective if it states salient features which are not in fact features of the brand name item.

The solicitation's brand name or equal product description should include the standard solicitation provision that sets forth the solicitation's ground rules for determining acceptable products. Unless the offeror clearly indicates in the offer that the product being offered is an "equal" product, the Contracting Officer will consider the offer as offering the brand name item referenced in the solicitation. If the vendor offers the brand name product without exception, its offer need not demonstrate compliance with the stated salient characteristics. A Contracting Officer may award a contract to a vendor presenting an "equal" item when the alternative is equivalent in all material respects to the brand name item, and when the award meets the solicitation's ground rules for the procurement.

The Comptroller General has held that when the salient characteristics of a brand name or equal product description are listed in terms of specific performance standards or design features, the "equal" product must meet these requirements precisely. Further, a brand name or equal solicitation describing various aspects of a particular firm's approach as salient characteristics is not to be interpreted as expressing only a functional requirement. On the contrary, technical requirements, stated in clear and precise terms, are presumed to be material to the needs of the government. Even when negotiated procurement techniques are used, offerors have the right to assume that such material requirements will be enforced and, on that basis, to anticipate the scope of competition for award.

Conversely, where the salient characteristics state features in general terms as opposed to precise design or functional requirements, items offered as equal need not meet the characteristics exactly as the brand name item does. The item need only be substantially equivalent in function to the brand name item.

§ 11.4   Brand Name Only

Brand name only product descriptions, i.e., a solicitation's description of a particular vendor's product, can be proper or improper. If the agency purports to use a brand name or equal product description, but omits the salient physical, functional or other characteristics of the referenced product (or omits an equivalent statement), the solicitation will be defective in stating a brand name or equally product description. A brand name only description can be appropriate when the agency meets the requirements for justifying other than full and open competition as prescribed by FAR. Thus, if the product description requires that brand name components be delivered as part of a system, then the brand name restriction can be sustained where the requirement meets the government's minimum needs and where the acquisition is justified in accordance with FAR. Otherwise, FAR provides that an acquisition that uses a brand name description or other product description to specify a particular brand name, product, or feature of a product, peculiar to one manufacturer, does not provide for full and open competition, regardless of the number of sources solicited.

Of course, where such descriptions are otherwise proper, an aggrieved vendor may still challenge the brand name only description as being unduly restrictive of competition, notwithstanding the agency's compliance with the brand name (or brand name or equal product description) with the procedures of FAR or other statues and regulations. When the agency properly uses the "brand name only" technique, no requirement exists for the solicitation to identify any salient characteristics.

A common misconception among government and industry personnel alike is that a solicitation with a brand name only product description permits award only to firms proposing that particular product. To the contrary, the GAO has said (somewhat counter intuitively) that the issuance of solicitation specifying only a particular brand name item does not preclude award to a firm offering an equivalent product. The only qualification is that in construction contracting where standard clause, FAR 52.236–5(a) states that reference to a brand name product description actually means equal products can also be acceptable.

Although the above GAO doctrine does have the effect of broadening competition, this line of GAO decisions is questionable because it is inherently open-ended on whether offerors can furnish equivalent items. Similarly, these cases omit the view in other GAO decisions that such a procurement may function as a brand name or equal acquisition only when the government's needs will be satisfied and no other offeror will be prejudiced by such a purchase description.

Except in construction contracting, most vendors unaware of these GAO decisions would naturally assume that only the brand name items are acceptable and would propose accordingly, thereby losing a possible competitive advantage if they have an alternate that would meet the agency's true (but unexpressed) needs. Accordingly, the Comptroller General should overrule this line of authority.

§ 11.5   Determining Agency Needs

The determination of the government's minimum needs for a particular acquisition and the best method of accommodating them are primarily the responsibility of the contracting agencies. As the GAO repeatedly has recognized, government procurement officials are generally in the best position to know the government's minimum needs, because agency personnel are the ones most familiar with the conditions and experience under which supplies, equipment, or services have been acquired in the past and how they are to be used in the future. The GAO has said: "We give more credence to those persons charged with the responsibility for making such discretionary judgments than we give to the opinions of vendors which have not clearly demonstrated greater knowledge of the government's internal operations."

The agency's technical choices also merit "great weight," except when based on mere preference or ease of administration. No legal requirement exists that the agency's requirement descriptions be determined by exhaustive studies to establish them with finite accuracy. Consequently, the GAO will not question an agency's determination of its minimum needs in a requirement description unless there is a clear showing that the determination was arbitrary or otherwise unreasonable.

Where a solicitation overstates the government's minimum needs, or the agency decides after receipt of offers that its needs may be met by less restrictive alternatives, the best interests of the government require that no award be made under that solicitation. In negotiated procurements, an RFP amendment (and a round of Final Proposal Revisions) or RFP cancellation would be the appropriate course depending on the circumstances.

§ 11.6   Restrictiveness

The adoption of any solicitation specification or requirement necessarily restricts competition to some extent; thus, "a decision to purchase an electronic pocket calculator excludes . . . the abacus." Similarly, the GAO and the former General Services Administration Board of Contract Appeals (GSBCA) had recognized that whether a solicitation requirement may be burdensome or even impossible for a particular firm to meet does not make it objectionable if it accurately reflects the agency's minimum needs. Accordingly, the correct question under the CICA and the FAR under either sealed bid or negotiated procedures is not whether competition has been restricted, but whether it has been *unduly* restricted, because most exclusions of competition are inherently reasonable and incontestable.

Relying on CICA, the GAO has commented: "A solicitation may include restrictive provisions only to the extent necessary to satisfy the needs of the agency or as otherwise authorized by law." In restrictiveness protests, the GAO has said "Where a protester alleges that a requirement is unduly restrictive, we review the record to determine whether the requirement has been justified as necessary to satisfy the agency's minimum needs." In sum, a requirement description will be unduly restrictive when it unnecessarily prevents one or more responsible firms from competing.

This restrictiveness question is determined by information available to the agency at the time the requirement description was created, and not through hindsight. The statutory and regulatory restrictiveness doctrine also potentially applies to solicitation elements other than the technical descriptions of the supplies or services, for example, a requirement for performance and payment bonds in non-construction contracts, liquidated damages provisions, definitive responsibility criteria or free on board provisions.

The GAO will not read a solicitation provision restrictively, unless it is clear from the solicitation that such an interpretation was intended by the agency. In a similar doctrine, the GSBCA has read solicitation requirements in the least restrictive manner possible given the situational context so that the maximum variety of products or services can qualify for award. The GSBCA further has held that where the specifications can carry more than one reasonable interpretation, the Board will interpret the requirement descriptions in the manner which promotes competition. Accordingly, the Board has held that those vendors who fail to seek clarification of even ambiguous solicitation terms are bound by the government's interpretation in a protest, assuming that the interpretation is reasonable and less restrictive.

The restrictiveness issue must be distinguished from several related situations. First, whether an awardee will deliver conforming goods or services is not a restrictiveness question but is a matter of contract administration that the GAO generally will not consider under its Bid Protest Regulations. Second, if an entity unconnected with the government imposes restrictions that can limit competition—such as where one firm will not sell its products to another firm—these limitations will not be imputed to the contracting agency. Third, if the protester simply argues that the agency should use better methods for accomplishing its needs, the GAO will not review this policy question except for possible agency bad faith or fraud. Fourth, a complaint that the requirement descriptions are duplicative or superfluous does not confer grounds for protest unless some prejudice results.

§ 11.7   Restrictiveness—Corollary Principles

The GAO has developed numerous corollary principles for the basic test on restrictive requirement descriptions. A sampling exists below.

1.   The protester bears a "heavy" burden in affirmatively proving undue restrictiveness, which burden becomes even more onerous when the agency seeks to acquire highly technical supplies or services;

2.   If the agency offers multiple defenses for the requirement, the agency will prevail so long as one theory reasonably explains the restriction;

3.   The number of potential or actual offerors does not determine restrictiveness, because other responsible firms could have been excluded, without justification, in violation of the Competition in Contracting Act (CICA). Therefore, a particular offeror's or class of offerors' mere inability to compete—or the simple difficulty or burdensomeness of competing—is legally inconsequential *if* the requirement represents legitimate agency needs;

4.   The agency may use requirement descriptions of a particular size, strength, or material when necessary to ensure adequate performance;

5.   The protester's mere disagreement with the government, even when supported by some expert evidence, will not suffice to meet the burden of proof, and neither will evidence simply that other government users were satisfied with the protester's product or service;

6.   The solicitation may properly state agency requirements to account for both present and future needs when this approach has a rational basis;

7.   The agency may properly state its needs so as to reduce technical risk to the extent deemed practicable;

8.   If the requirements concern services or supplies critical to national defense or to human health or safety, the agency may state its needs to provide for the highest possible reliability or effectiveness. In a similar vein, where a contractor will be performing critical or dangerous work, the solicitation may require that contractor personnel have experience in the same work setting;

9.   Requirement descriptions need not be cast so as to compensate for a particular offeror's competitive disadvantage, so long as the advantage or disadvantage accruing to a prospective contractor is not the result of preferential or other unfair government action;

10. The government has no obligation to purchase technologically advanced equipment if less sophisticated equipment will meet its actual needs at a lower cost or risk; and

11. A contracting agency's responsibility for determining its actual needs includes determining the type and amount of testing necessary to ensure product compliance with specifications.

Several GAO doctrines on restrictive requirement descriptions require more in-depth treatment.

Frequently, protesters will contend that the agency unduly restricted competition by procuring its needs on a "total package" basis in a single procurement, as opposed to a breakout of the requirement into separate procurements. In this situation—which also can arise when the agency makes a single award under a solicitation permitting multiple awards—the GAO has upheld total package procurements when the agency has reasonably concluded that this approach meets its minimum needs.

For instance, the GAO has rejected challenges to a total package acquisition when a single contractor was needed to ensure the effective coordination and integration of interrelated tasks, or where procurement by means of separate acquisitions involved undue technical risk or would defeat a requirement for interchangeability and compatibility. Additionally, recognizing that an agency's minimum requirements include the need to procure services and supplies on the most cost effective basis, the GAO has found that the possibilities of achieving economies of scale or avoiding the unnecessary duplication of costs may justify a total package approach.

Ultimately, the decision to procure on a total package basis or to break out divisible portions of the total requirement for separate awards is a matter generally within the discretion of the contracting agency. The GAO will not disturb this decision absent a clear showing that the agency's determination lacks a reasonable basis (such as when the agency decides the issue based on mere administrative convenience).

Protests may also be based on the contention that the requirement description is not restrictive enough, and permits too much competition, and that this approach could compromise the agency's needs or otherwise prove counterproductive for the government. One variation of this theme is where the protester contends that a solicitation amendment has improperly relaxed the requirement description so as to expand the field of competition.

Absent agency fraud, bad faith or willful misconduct, or a specific statute or regulation that clearly requires an agency to tailor its requirement description in a particular way, protests that a solicitation is insufficiently restrictive lack merit because the GAO has nothing to enforce. The Comptroller General has stated: "Our role in resolving bid protests is to ensure that the statutory requirement for full and open competition in the award of government contracts is met; we therefore will not consider a protest that an agency requires more restrictive specifications to meet its minimum needs." Also, the GAO has recognized that the selection of sufficiently rigorous requirement descriptions is primarily the concern of the agency, which must bear the consequences of inadequate supplies or services.

§ 11.8 Ambiguity and Risk

The requirement descriptions in negotiated acquisitions need not be as precise as those for sealed bid purchases because of the differing nature of these procurement methods. Nonetheless, the agency in a negotiated acquisition must still draft the specifications (and all other solicitation elements) clearly, accurately, and unambiguously. In this manner, the RFP will meet the CICA mandate for full and open competition—the offerors will be able to prepare proposals on a common understanding of the solicitation requirements and not on their own definitions of the agency's needs. Also, the agency's use of properly descriptive requirements relieves offerors from including excessive price contingencies in their proposals and reduces post-award controversies regarding the contractual requirements.

As contrasted with where a requirement description omits a term or condition, a description is "ambiguous" when subject to more than one reasonable interpretation. The requirement description will not be ambiguous, however, simply because of the location of the requirement in the solicitation, a protester's disagreement with the agency's construction, a mere allegation that the requirement descriptions are ambiguous, or the protester's dubious interpretation of clearly stated terms.

While it is not necessary for a finding of an ambiguity that the interpretation of the charging party be the most reasonable one, that party is still required to show that its interpretation is reasonable. To be reasonable, the interpretation must be consistent with the solicitation read as a whole and in a reasonable manner.

The GAO will use the established canons of construction in considering allegations of ambiguous requirement descriptions. As indicated above, the GAO will read a solicitation as a whole, giving effect to all of its provisions where possible. In addition, words and terms will be given their plain meaning where possible under the context, and an agency generally will not be permitted to deny the express terms of its own solicitation. The GAO also will consider all relevant evidence regarding the proper interpretation, including the instant specifications, preclosing correspondence between the government and vendor, site visits, and any other probative information.

Agencies are not required to draft requirement descriptions in such detail as to eliminate completely any risk or to remove every uncertainty from the mind of every prospective offeror. The GAO has said: "[I]t is not practicable to draft specifications that attempt to provide solutions to every imaginable problem that might arise, no matter how unlikely or extreme." Similarly, the solicitation need not be so detailed as to completely eliminate the possibility that the successful contractor will encounter conditions or be required to perform work other than that specified.

Indeed, the agency may issue a solicitation clearly imposing maximum risks upon the contractor and minimum administrative burdens upon the government. To the extent that a solicitation contains some uncertainty, the GAO has said that some risk is inherent in most types of contracts, and that offerors can take any contingencies into account in pricing their offers.

§ 11.9   Delivery or Performance Schedules

The time of delivery or performance is an essential contract element and shall be clearly stated in solicitations. Contracting Officers shall ensure that delivery or performance schedules are realistic and meet the requirements of the acquisition. Schedules that are unnecessarily short or difficult to attain tend to restrict competition, are inconsistent with small business policies, and may result in higher contract prices.

Except when clearly unnecessary, solicitations must inform bidders or offerors of the basis on which their bids or proposals will be evaluated with respect to time of delivery or performance. If timely delivery or performance is unusually important to the Government, liquidated damages clauses may be used and must be used in most DOD construction contracts exceeding $700,000.

When establishing a delivery or performance schedule in a supply or service contract, agencies shall consider factors such as the urgency of need; industry practices; market conditions; transportation time; production time; capabilities of small business concerns; administrative time for obtaining and evaluating offers and for awarding contracts; time for contractors to comply with any conditions precedent to contract performance; and time for the Government to perform its obligations under the contract, such as furnishing Government property.

When scheduling the time for completion of a construction contract, the Contracting Officer shall consider applicable factors such as the nature and complexity of the project; construction seasons involved; the required completion date; the availability of materials and equipment; capacity of the contractor to perform; and use of multiple completion dates. What this last provision means is that in any given contract, separate completion dates may be established for separable items of work. When the agency uses multiple completion dates, the agency must evaluate requests for extension of time with respect to each item. The agency must modify the affected completion dates when appropriate.

§ 11.10 Liquidated Damages

(a) In General

The topic of liquidated damages is intricately connected to the subject of delays in construction contracting. "Liquidated Damages" clauses are only occasionally used in government supply or service contracts, but they are common in construction contracts. Indeed, as stated above, they must be used in most DOD construction contracts exceeding $700,000.

Because they are pre-established in the contract, liquidated damages afford the government an exceedingly valuable remedy in instances where a construction contractor's delay is caused by its own fault. In a way, these damages—because they place a cap on the contractor's liability for delays—also benefit contractors. This section reviews the "Liquidated Damages" clause and its enforceability in construction contracts, as well as the means by which contractors may seek relief when the government asserts its rights under the clause.

According to the FAR, a "Liquidated Damages" clause "should be used only when both (1) the time of delivery or performance is such an important factor in the award of the contract that the government may reasonably expect to suffer damage if the delivery or performance is delinquent, and (2) the extent or amount of such damage would be difficult or impossible to ascertain or prove." Thus, liquidated damages are intended as a substitute for actual damages for late completion or delivery of the contract work.

(b) Measuring the Damages Period

As the language of the "Liquidated Damages-Construction" clause indicates, it requires payment by the contractor of a specific amount to the government for each day that the contractor does not meet the contract's performance schedule. Generally, liquidated damages are assessed starting at the completion date of the contract. The completion date is generally determined by adding the number of calendar days of the performance period to the date on which the contractor acknowledged receipt of the government's "notice to proceed."

The "Liquidated Damages" clause also specifies the duration for the assessment of damages based on the government's rights in connection with termination of the contract for default: (1) if the contractor's right to proceed *is* terminated, "liquidated damages will continue to accrue until the work is completed" (usually by another contractor that would be solicited by the government after the default), and (2) if the contractor's right to proceed is not terminated, liquidated damages accrue "until the work is completed or accepted." Thus, the clause seeks to put the government in as good a position as it would have been in had the delay not occurred.

(c) Liquidated Damages Rate

The FAR liquidated damages policy contains guidelines for Contracting Officers concerning the rates of any liquidated damages assessment. It states as follows:

Liquidated damages are not punitive and are not negative performance incentives. Liquidated damages are used to compensate the government for probable damages. Therefore, the liquidated damages rate must be a reasonable forecast of just compensation for the harm that is caused by late delivery or untimely performance of the particular contract. Use a maximum amount or a maximum period for assessing liquidated damages if these limits reflect the maximum probable damage to the government. Also, the Contracting Officer may use more than the usual liquidated damages rate when the Contracting Officer expects the probable damage to the government to change over the contract period of performance.

Consistent with the above principles, the cases state that the contractor has an "exacting" burden to prove that a liquidated damages clause should be enforceable. To this end, a presumption exists that contractual liquidated damages are reasonable and not unenforceable penalties.

The rate of liquidated damages will be prescribed in the contract as a specific sum for each day of delay. The FAR requires that the rate "should include the estimated daily cost of government inspection and superintendence." It also advises that if the government will suffer other specific losses due to the failure of the contractor to complete the work on time—such as the cost of renting substitute facilities or the continued payment of allowance for living quarters—the per diem rate should include these amounts.

However, where the specific circumstances in which the contract was to be performed made it obvious that no daily inspection and superintendence by the government would be required, liquidated damages based on additional inspection and superintendence expenses for late performance will be held to constitute an unenforceable penalty.

(d) Enforceability

Liquidated damages provisions must meet two criteria to be valid and enforceable: (1) the amount stipulated in the "Liquidated Damages" clause must be a reasonable forecast of the harm that the breach of the contract (the contractor's delay) would cause to the government, and (2) the harm that would result from the breach must be difficult or impossible to estimate. A liquidated damages assessment that does not meet both of these criteria may be viewed as a penalty and therefore unenforceable.

If a "Liquidated Damages" clause is held to be unenforceable, the government may recover its actual damages for breach of contract. The irony here is that if the contractor prevails in challenging overstated liquidated damages, it could be in a worse position if the government files the action for actual damages

On the other hand, the contractor challenging a liquidated damages clause bears the burden of proving the clause unenforceable. That burden is a difficult one, because when damages are uncertain or hard to measure, it naturally follows that it is difficult to conclude that a particular liquidated damages amount or rate is an unreasonable projection. The irony here is that if the contract had understated the liquidated damages rate, the contractor would ultimately have less liability exposure if it loses the challenge.

(e) Reasonableness of the Forecast

In government contracts, the reasonableness of the forecast of liquidated damages is determined by looking at the situation at the time the parties executed the contract rather than at the time of the breach. The stipulated amount must be reasonable in light of the harm the government anticipates in the case of a breach. In other words, the per diem damages rate must not be disproportionate to the actual damages expected in the event of breach, based on the government's knowledge at the time the contract was made.

Liquidated damages may be assessed only when they bear some "reasonable relation to the probable actual damages which the government would suffer from the contractor's breach." For example, if the government did not incur and should not have expected to incur any actual damages, it is unlikely that a board or court would enforce any assessment of liquidated damages. Similarly, a liquidated damages assessment will not be enforced if it includes a penalty increment that the government knew would not be imposed if the project were late.

"Liquidated Damages" clauses have been enforced despite significant discrepancies between the actual and liquidated damages.

The fact that actual damages far exceed or even fall far short of the liquidated amount will not necessarily invalidate an otherwise proper clause. Indeed, in cases where the government incurred no actual damages, if the liquidated damages amount was reasonable at the time that the contract was entered into, the assessment will be upheld. Even liquidated damages that exceed the contract price have been upheld where the rate fixed in the clause was reasonable as of the time the contract was awarded.

(f) Difficulty in Estimating Loss

The second element of the enforceability of a "Liquidated Damages" clause is that the harm to the government from a breach was difficult or impossible to determine accurately at the time the contract was executed.

This question is not frequently at issue when reviewing the validity of liquidated damages assessments, however, probably because it is difficult for the contractor to dispute government testimony that it cannot accurately estimate the amount of actual damages due to delay. Moreover, as a practical matter, if the contractor senses that there is not much difference between actual and liquidated damages, vigorously contesting the government's assessment is probably of minimal value to its case.

(g) Relief from Liquidated Damages

If the "Liquidated Damages" clause is enforceable and the government assesses damages against the contractor, the contractor may nevertheless have ground to seek relief from the assessment. A claim for the remission of liquidated damages cannot be considered part of an original claim for a contract extension, however, where it arose subsequent to the filing of an appeal of the first claim.

§ 11.11 Priorities, Allocations, and Allotments

A special statute has been enacted in order to keep certain defense and energy production programs on schedule and maintain an administrative means of promptly mobilizing the nation's economic resources in the event of war or national emergency.

This law provides that priorities may be used to require contractors to accept and perform "rated orders" (i.e., orders required to be supported with rating and allotment authority) in preference to other orders, and that materials and facilities may be allocated for defense and energy production purposes.

The Office of Industrial Resource Administration, Department of Commerce (DOC) has the responsibility for establishing the basic priorities and allocations rules. This resulted in a series of regulations and orders called the Defense Materials System and the Defense Priorities System.

Any solicitations that will result in the placement of rated orders or Authorized Control Material orders (any delivery order for controlled material as distinct from a product containing controlled material) must have special clauses inserted to appropriately apprise the vendors that the procurement will be subject to priority system. A "rated order" means a prime contract for any product, service or material (including controlled materials) placed by a Delegate Agency under the provisions of the Defense Priorities and Allocations System (DPAS) in support of an authorized program and which requires preferential treatment, and includes subcontracts and purchase orders resulting under such contracts. All rated orders (symbolized by "DO" and "DX") have precedence over unrated orders; DX orders take precedence over DO orders.

§ 11.12 Variations in Quantity

Fixed-price supply and construction contracts may authorize variation in the quantity of required items.

In supply contracts, the variation is stated as a percentage that may be an increase, a decrease, or a combination of both. Unless an agency regulation specifies otherwise, permissible variations may not exceed plus or minus 10%. Quantities delivered in excess of those specified may be retained without compensating the contractor. In supply contracts, the clause is only required to be used where a variation in quantity is authorized. Above $250, the excess quantities may be returned at the contractor's expense or retained and paid for at the unit price.

In construction contracts, an equitable adjustment shall be made upon demand where the variation is estimated and actual quantity exceeds 15%.

Chapter 12

ACQUISITION OF
COMMERCIAL ITEMS

Analysis

§ 12.1   Commercial Item Policy

Implementing FASA, Federal Acquisition Regulation (FAR) Part 12 establishes acquisition policies more closely resembling those of the commercial marketplace where commercial items (i.e., supplies and services) or non-developmental items are available to meet the government's needs.

The benefits of commercial item procurement procedures are a more streamlined process, increased competition, reduced paperwork, enhanced industry participation, and empowerment of federal purchasing personnel. Consistent with these goals, FAR makes numerous laws inapplicable in whole or part to commercial item purchasing.

There has been a torrent of statutory revisions to the rules on commercial item contracting which has created a lag in the enactment of implementing regulations. For example, The John S. McCain National Defense Authorization Act for Fiscal Year 2019 (H.R. 5515), P.L. 115–232, August 13, 2018, included Section 836: Revised Definition of "Commercial Item." Section 836 eliminates the term "commercial item" and, in its place, creates two new terms: "commercial product" and "commercial service." To reflect this change in nomenclature, conforming changes will be made to acquisition statutes throughout the United States Code, including those that apply to both military and civilian agencies.

There is no change, however, in substance with the new categories. The current, multi-part definition of "commercial item" was simply reformulated into two new definitions: one for a "commercial product" and one for a "commercial service." The language used in both the old and new definitions is largely identical.

Congress is aware of the confusing laws and regulations in this area. The John S. McCain National Defense Authorization Act for Fiscal Year 2019 (H.R. 5515), Pub. L. No.115–232, § 839, requires the FAR Council to conduct three separate reviews aimed at reducing the number of regulations applicable to the acquisition of commercial products and services.

§ 12.2   Definitions

Under statute and the FAR, agencies must conduct market research (see Chapter 10) commensurate with the nature, size and complexity of the procurement to determine whether commercial items or non-developmental items are available and can be acquired to meet the agency's requirements. National Defense Authorization Act for Fiscal Year 2020, Pub. L. No. 116–92, § 818. See also FAR Part 10 (similar rules). The aforementioned concepts, "commercial items" and "non-developmental items" have complex definitions in FAR, as explained below. Further, combinations of the various types of commercial items can qualify for the definitions.

Under FAR 2.101, "Commercial item" means—

(1)   Any item, other than real property, that is of a type customarily used by the general public or by non-governmental entities for purposes other than governmental purposes, and—

(i)   Has been sold, leased, or licensed to the general public; or

(ii)   Has been offered for sale, lease, or license to the general public;

(2)   Any item that evolved from an item described in paragraph (1) of this definition through advances in technology or performance and that is not yet available in the commercial marketplace, but will be available in the commercial marketplace in time to satisfy the delivery requirements under a Government solicitation;

(3)   Any item that would satisfy a criterion expressed in paragraphs (1) or (2) of this definition, but for—

(i)   Modifications of a type customarily available in the commercial marketplace; or

(ii)   Minor modifications of a type not customarily available in the commercial marketplace made to meet Federal Government requirements. Minor modifications means modifications that do not significantly alter the nongovernmental function or essential physical characteristics of an item or component, or change the purpose of a process. Factors to be considered in determining whether a modification is minor include the value and size of the modification and the comparative value and size of the final product. Dollar values and percentages may be used as guideposts, but are not conclusive evidence that a modification is minor;

(4) Any combination of items meeting the requirements of paragraphs (1), (2), (3), or (5) of this definition that are of a type customarily combined and sold in combination to the general public;

(5) Installation services, maintenance services, repair services, training services, and other services if—

(i) Such services are procured for support of an item referred to in paragraph (1), (2), (3), or (4) of this definition, regardless of whether such services are provided by the same source or at the same time as the item; and

(ii) The source of such services provides similar services contemporaneously to the general public under terms and conditions similar to those offered to the Federal Government;

(6) Services of a type offered and sold competitively in substantial quantities in the commercial marketplace based on established catalog or market prices for specific tasks performed or specific outcomes to be achieved and under standard commercial terms and conditions. For purposes of these services—

(i) Catalog price means a price included in a catalog, price list, schedule, or other form that is regularly maintained by the manufacturer or vendor, is either published or otherwise available for inspection by customers, and states prices at which sales are currently, or were last, made to a significant number of buyers constituting the general public; and

(ii) Market prices means current prices that are established in the course of ordinary trade between buyers and sellers free to bargain and that can be substantiated through competition or from sources independent of the offerors;

(7) Any item, combination of items, or service referred to in paragraphs (1) through (6) of this definition, notwithstanding the fact that the item, combination of items, or service is transferred between or among separate divisions, subsidiaries, or affiliates of a contractor; or

(8) A nondevelopmental item, if the procuring agency determines the item was developed exclusively at private expense and sold in

substantial quantities, on a competitive basis, to multiple State and local governments or to multiple foreign governments.

Commercially available off-the-shelf (COTS) item—

(1)   Means any item of supply (including construction material) that is—

(i)   A commercial item (as defined in paragraph (1) of the definition in this section);

(ii)   Sold in substantial quantities in the commercial marketplace; and

(iii) Offered to the Government, under a contract or subcontract at any tier, without modification, in the same form in which it is sold in the commercial marketplace; and

(2)   Does not include bulk cargo, as defined in 46 U.S.C.A. § 40102(4), such as agricultural products and petroleum products.

Some controversy exists on whether FAR Part 12 encompasses construction as defined in FAR 2.101. The FAR does not directly answer this question. The Office of Federal Procurement Policy has stated, "Part 12, as currently promulgated, should rarely, if ever, be used for new construction acquisitions or non-routine alteration and repair services." https://www.whitehouse.gov/sites/whitehouse.gov/files/omb/assets/OMB/procurement/far/far_part12.pdf   However, GAO said in *Voith Hydro, Inc.,* Comp. Gen. Dec. B-401244.2, 2009 CPD ¶ 239, that "there are some situations where construction services fall within the definition of commercial items."

§ 12.3   Other Supporting Rules and Procedures

The Department of Defense has an important presumption in this area. In a final DFARS Rule: Procurement of Commercial Items, 83 Fed. Reg. 4431 (Jan. 31, 2018), the DFARS was amended through a final rule, effective January 31, 2018, implementing § 831(a) of the FY 2013 National Defense Authorization Act (NDAA), various provisions of the FY 2016 NDAA, and § 848 of the FY 2018 NDAA regarding commercial items.

Among other changes, the final rule modifies the DFARS by allowing contracting officers to apply a presumption of commerciality to subsequent procurements of items that any DOD component previously treated as commercial. Contracting officers cannot ignore a prior determination unless they obtain a review of the commercial-item determination "by the head of the contracting activity" conducting the procurement.

In a related policy, DFARS 212.272(b) provides that a contracting officer may not enter into a contract above the simplified acquisition threshold for facilities related services, knowledge-based services other than engineering services, medical services, or transportation services that are not commercial services unless the appropriate person specified in DFARS 212.272(b)(2) determines in writing that no commercial services are suitable to meet the agency's needs.

§ 12.4   Special Policies and Requirements

According to FAR, Contracting Officers must use commercial item procedures for the acquisition of supplies or services that so qualify. These policies are to be used, as appropriate, along with the policies and procedures for solicitation, evaluation and award prescribed in FAR for simplified purchases, sealed bidding, and for negotiated procurements. FAR contains limited exceptions, such as for micro-purchases.

If a regulation in another FAR chapter is inconsistent with the commercial item regulations, FAR 12.102(c) says the latter policies take precedence. This regulation creates an interesting anomaly regarding architect engineer services that also qualify as commercial services. The anomaly is that FAR 12.102(b) instructs contracting officials to use FAR parts 13, 14, or 15 for commercial items but the architect engineer service source selection policies say in FAR 36.602–3(c) they take priority over any requirement in FAR parts 13, 14, or 15. Both regulations cannot proclaim that they are the ultimate authority for resolving FAR conflicts. Because statute does not express any intent to effect an actual or implied repeal of the Brooks Act for architect engineer services, the best solution is to combine the procedures and hold that the Brooks Act source selection procedures still apply to commercial item architect engineer services, but that all other FAR commercial item procedures will apply consistent with FAR Part 12.

FAR states the special requirements for acquisition of commercial items. For example, the regulations here reiterate the FAR guidance concerning market research and descriptions of agency needs. GAO has sustained protests where the agency performed inadequate market research to ensure that the solicitation terms were consistent with customary commercial practice. FAR specifies the rules for use of Standard Form 1449, Solicitation/ Contract/Order for Commercial Items, which is a streamlined solicitation and contract format.

FAR further discusses offers in commercial item procurement. Two highlights are that Contracting Officers should allow offerors to make multiple product offerings in response to the solicitation (which will be separate offers), and the agency may allow fewer than 30 days response time for receipt of offers for commercial items.

Other important prescriptions from FAR are:

1.   For acquisitions of commercial items exceeding the simplified acquisition threshold (usually not more than $7 million) ($13 million for acquisitions as described in 13.500(c), such as where the acquisition is for commercial items that, as determined by the head of the agency, are to be used in support of a contingency operation; to facilitate the defense against or recovery from cyber, nuclear, biological, chemical, or radiological attack) including options, contracting activities under FAR 12.203 shall employ the FAR simplified procedures to the maximum practicable extent;

2.   Agencies should (not shall) use past performance as an evaluation factor for award even though FAR also specifies the rules for evaluation of past performance in covered acquisitions unless the Contracting Officer documents the reasons past performance will not be evaluated;

3.   Agencies may use *either* firm fixed price contracts or fixed price contracts with economic price adjustment for acquisition of commercial items *or* time and materials or labor hour contracts (under strict dollar limits and higher level agency review) but *not* any other contract type (including cost reimbursement contracts);

4.   The contract shall rely upon the contractor's existing quality assurance system as a substitute for government inspection and testing, unless customary market practices for the commercial item being acquired include in-process inspection;

5.   The agency must establish price reasonableness using the usual FAR standards;

6.   The Contracting Officer may offer government financing in commercial item purchasing;

7.   The government shall only acquire the technical data and rights in that data customarily provided to the public with a commercial item or process, absent an agency specific statute;

8.   The government shall acquire commercial computer software or commercial computer software documentation under licenses customarily provided to the public, consistent with federal law and agency needs; and

9.   The government should consider other customary commercial practices satisfactory to both parties and not precluded by law or executive order.

FAR states the policies on warranties for commercial item purchasing. A standard contract clause grants the government the implied warranty of merchantability, the implied warranty of fitness for a particular purpose, and the remedies. As for express warranties, FAR states that agencies shall take advantage of commercial warranties, and that the solicitation shall require offerors to provide the government at least the same warranty terms the firm offers to the general public in customary commercial practice, provided the express warranty must meet the government's needs.

§ 12.5   Implementing the Federal Acquisition Streamlining Act

FAR provides that solicitations and contracts for commercial items shall, to the maximum practicable extent, include only those provisions and clauses required to implement law or executive order applicable to commercial items, or that are consistent with customary commercial practice. Consistent with this guidance, the FAR recognizes several streamlined solicitation provisions and clauses, as described below.

First, FAR, provides a single, streamlined set of instructions to be used when soliciting offers for commercial items. Similarly, FAR provides a consolidated list of certifications and representations for acquisition of commercial items. In addition to the mandatory contract clauses, FAR permits discretionary use of FAR provisions and clauses when consistent with FAR policy on tailoring of FAR provisions and clauses for acquisition of commercial items under certain circumstances.

§ 12.6   Streamlined Procedures

FAR allows optional procedures for streamlined evaluation of offers. This regulation still adheres to the rules that offers may only be evaluated on the announced criteria, the winning offer shall be the most advantageous proposer, and that the selection decision must be fully documented. The regulation also contemplates use of best value decision making for most procurements, although other evaluation methodologies can be proper in a given situation.

FAR encourages use of simplified methods for evaluation. In this regard, FAR strongly indicates that for many commercial item buys, the only appropriate evaluation factors are technical capability, price and past performance. The same regulation discourages use of technical subfactors when the solicitation adequately describes the intended use and requires evaluation of past performance under the usual FAR policies. The usual technical evaluation for commercial item purchases would include examination of product literature, product samples (as needed), technical features, and warranty terms.

To reduce acquisition lead time, FAR permits a procedure similar to A-E procurements (see Chapter 36) whereby the agency combines the required SAM.gov notice with the solicitation into a single document. FAR cautions that this technique is only appropriate where the solicitation is relatively simple and lengthy addenda to SF 1449 are not needed. Amendments to the solicitation are accomplished in the same way.

§ 12.7   Agency Supplements and Other Restraints

Agency regulations may supplement the commercial item purchasing policies in FAR Part 12. Thus, in the Department of Defense, the DFARS contains additional guidance on the approval level for tailoring procedures inconsistent with customary commercial practice. The DOD regulation sets forth a list of additional laws inapplicable to commercial items contracts.

The only restraints on these acquisitions are that they must conform with applicable statutes, executive orders, and other regulations. Thus, for example, the agency must abide by the requirements of FAR Part 6 in achieving full and open competition in these purchases. The FAR definition of commercial item focuses on the availability of the item on the marketplace, and not on the manner in which it is provided. Except as required by law or regulation, there is no rigid requirement that an agency purchase commercial items to meet its needs.

§ 12.8   Evaluation of Commercial Items

Until recently, the GAO followed the view that a commercial item specification—which must be clearly stated as such and not left to inference—was a definitive criterion of responsibility. The latter concept is an objective standard established by an agency for a particular procurement that measures an offeror's responsibility to perform the contract (see Chapter 9).

Presently, the GAO holds that a commercial item requirement is like any other specification requirement bearing on the product to be furnished—the offeror must commit itself to meeting the requirement, but its ability to do so falls within the Contracting Officer's subjective determination of responsibility. An offeror's compliance with a mandatory commercial item specification is generally an essential element of a proposal's technical acceptability and cannot be waived for any one offeror. Given the "broad nature" of the commercial availability concept, however, the GAO will not disturb a Contracting Officer's discretionary decision that an offeror has satisfied a commercial item requirement as long as there is evidence to support the agency's determination. The key factor will be whether the offeror makes the item available for sale, lease, or license under the solicitation ground rules and background FAR requirements.

Other procurement adjudicators have provided relief for a violation of these rules. In *Palantir v. United States*, 904 F.3d 980 (Fed. Cir. 2018), the Army failed to satisfy the requirement in 10 U.S.C.A. § 2377 to determine whether a commercial item could meet or be modified to meet the Army's procurement requirements, the U.S. Court of Appeals for the Federal Circuit said in affirming the Court of Federal Claims, which had granted summary judgment to a protester.

Consistent with the FAR requirements, the solicitation frequently will contain particular rules governing commercial items and this language can be key for the commerciality requirement. Thus, when the solicitation clearly requires that an item be commercially available and capable of full performance at time of offer submission, it will not be sufficient that the offeror can meet the requirement after award. Similarly, if the solicitation calls for "commercial items," the GAO will not extend this concept to mean a "commercial system." Commonly associated terms such as "off the shelf" and "in current production" should receive precise definitions in RFPs. Next, if the solicitation calls for a commercially available end item, it is unacceptable for the offeror to provide a system where only the components are commercially available. Acceptance of a noncommercial item will be allowed if the solicitation has a waiver provision.

Chapter 13

SIMPLIFIED ACQUISITION

Analysis

§ 13.1   Simplified Acquisition Overview

In 1994, Congress exempted certain low dollar purchases from the detailed "full and open competition" procedures and other contractor record keeping and certification requirements established by statute. FAR Part 13 covers this topic in depth. The dollar thresholds for simplified acquisitions differ depending on whether (1) the purchase is a micro-purchase, (2) it is for work performed within or without the United States, (3) the work is for construction or services, (4) the work is for commercial items, or (5) the work is for a contingency or national defense project. An occasional complication is that statute controls the thresholds and so a time lag may occur until the regulators catch up with the statutory revisions.

Congress has prescribed the dollar value for simplified acquisitions. Thus, for example, the FY 2018 National Defense Authorization Act, § 805, Pub. L. No. 115–91 (Dec. 12, 2017), increases the general simplified acquisition threshold Government-wide from $150,000 to $250,000. However, at this writing, FAR 2.101 still defines the general simplified threshold as $150,000.

FAR 13.500(a) authorizes the use of simplified procedures for the acquisition of supplies and services in amounts greater than the simplified acquisition threshold but not exceeding $7 million ($13 million for acquisitions as described for commercial items, FAR 13.500(c)), including options, if the contracting officer reasonably expects, based on the nature of the supplies or services sought, and on market research, that offers will include only commercial items.

Under 41 U.S.C.A. § 1903 and FAR 13.500(c), the simplified acquisition procedures authorized in FAR 13.500 may be used for acquisitions that do not exceed $13 million when—

(1) The acquisition is for commercial items that, as determined by the head of the agency, are to be used in support of a contingency operation; to facilitate the defense against or recovery from cyber, nuclear, biological, chemical, or radiological attack; to support a request from the Secretary of State or the Administrator of the United States Agency for International Development to facilitate provision of international disaster assistance; or to support response to an emergency or major disaster, or

(2) The acquisition will be treated as an acquisition of commercial items in accordance with 12.102(f)(1).

The government's overall goal is to use simplified acquisition procedures to the maximum extent practicable for all purchases (including micro-purchases) of supplies or services below the simplified acquisition threshold. There are some exceptions to this policy, for example, where the agency can use a required source of supply, Thus, for example, FAR 8.002(a)(1)(iii) places purchases of supplies from Federal Prison Industries, Inc. as a priority over a FAR 13 procurement.

The socio-economic FAR rules can apply to these low dollar purchases, such as the rules for small business set asides.

§ 13.2   Micro-Purchases

Under FAR 2.101, Micro-purchase threshold means $3,500, except it means (1) For acquisitions of construction subject to 40 U.S.C. chapter 31, subchapter IV, Wage Rate Requirements (Construction), $2,000; and (2) For acquisitions of services subject to 41 U.S.C. chapter 67, Service Contract Labor Standards, $2,500.

Heightened simplified acquisition thresholds exist for contracting in contingency operations and for defense against or recovery from nuclear, biological, chemical or radiological attack. FAR 13.201(g) raises the micro-purchase threshold for such contracts to $20,000 for contracts with performance inside the United States and to $30,000 for contracts abroad. Special micro-purchase thresholds exist in other circumstances.

Purchases under the "micro-purchase threshold" (see FAR 2.101) may be conducted using any of the simplified acquisition procedures in the FAR and with some exceptions do not require the incorporation of provisions or contract clauses. Statute may affect the usual thresholds. The authority to make micro-purchases is often delegated to individuals in the agency who will be using the supplies or services being purchased and many such purchases are made using the "government-wide commercial purchase card."

Micro-purchases may be made without obtaining competitive quotations if the Contracting Officer considers the price reasonable. Furthermore, since the cost of verifying price reasonableness may more than offset any potential savings from detecting instances of overpricing, verification should be conducted only if (a) there is suspicion or information to indicate that the price may not be reasonable or (b) no comparable pricing information is readily available.

§ 13.3   Simplified Acquisition Procedures

FAR 13.106 contains streamlined solicitation, evaluation, and award and documentation procedures. Simplified acquisition procedures can be controlling even where the solicitation does not explicitly reference FAR Part 13, provided that the substance of the procurement places vendors on notice that the agency is employing the simplified acquisition procedure.

§ 13.4   Competition Policies

Although the FAR relieves an agency conducting a simplified acquisition from most of the detailed procedures that apply to sealed bidding and competitive negotiation, the FAR still directs the Contracting Officer to "promote competition to the maximum extent practical to obtain supplies and services from the source whose offer is the most advantageous to the Government."

Contracting Officers are further admonished not to break down requirements into several purchases that are less than the applicable simplified acquisition thresholds merely to use the simplified procedures or to avoid requirements that apply to purchases that exceed those thresholds. In any event, Contracting Officers are instructed to make purchases "in the simplified manner that is most suitable, efficient, and economical based on the circumstances of each acquisition." They are also required to establish deadlines that afford suppliers a reasonable opportunity to respond, consider all quotations or offers that are timely received, and use innovative acquisition approaches whenever practicable.

Contracting Officers also have broad discretion to determine how to solicit quotes or offers and how suppliers should respond (although they must provide potential vendors with adequate information regarding the agency's requirements). For example, solicitations and responses may be written, oral, or by electronic means. In another example, reverse auctions to select the most advantageous source, including public price disclosures, can be proper. A quotation that does not affirmatively agree to meet a material specification or quotation instruction, however, can be technically unacceptable.

Where consistent with fundamental fairness, the agency must follow the same policies normally applicable to larger dollar procurements. Here, the GAO is not adhering to the letter of these non-FAR Part 13 procedures but to their spirit. For example, the GAO has sustained a protest where the agency elected to establish a competitive range and to hold discussions (see Chapter 15) but unfairly and unreasonably excluded the protester from further consideration.

§ 13.5   Price Reasonableness

The Contracting Officer must conclude, prior to making award, that the proposed price is fair and reasonable. If several offers are being considered, this will be accomplished by comparing the competitive offers. If only one response is received, a statement of price reasonableness must be included in the contract file. This statement should be based upon (a) market research, (b) comparison of the proposed price with prices found reasonable on previous purchases, (c) current price lists, catalogs, or advertisements, (d) comparison with similar items in a related industry, (e) the Contracting Officer's personal knowledge of the item being purchased, (f) comparison with an independent government estimate, or (g) any other reasonable basis.

§ 13.6   Purchase Methods

The recommended simplified acquisition purchase methods are (1) government-wide commercial purchase card, (2) purchase orders, and (3) blanket purchase agreements. Each contemplates payment by the government through electronic funds transfer (EFT).

Government-wide commercial purchase cards are authorized for use in making or paying for purchases of supplies, services or construction. Agencies must establish procedures for their use and control. The use of commercial purchase cards is specifically not limited to micro-purchases. On the contrary, agencies are encouraged to use the purchase cards in transactions involving greater dollar amounts where it is appropriate to do so. In August, 2005, the Office of Management and Budget revised Circular No. A-123, Improving the Management of Government Charge Card Programs (available at http://www.omb.gov), so that agencies and federal managers take new measures to ensure the more effective oversight of all government charge card accounts. These measures include such goals as the mitigation of fraud and abuse, reduction of administrative costs and time for paying for goods and services, and to increased informed management decision making.

Purchase orders—issued on a fixed-price basis and specifying a quantity and performance or delivery date—are also authorized for purchasing commercial supplies and services under simplified acquisition procedures. Normally, purchase orders will specify an f.o.b. destination for supplies to be delivered domestically and will include any trade or prompt payment discounts applicable to the transaction. Vendor quotations made in response to a Request for Quotations, the most common method of simplified acquisition leading to a purchase order, are not offers but are merely informational responses that are not subject to government acceptance as would be true for offers in response to a Request for Proposals. Thus, the government will be the offeror and the vendor will be the offeree in this setting.

Unpriced purchase orders (where price is not established at the time of issuance of the order) may only be used when it is impractical to obtain pricing in advance of issuance of the purchase order and the purchase order is for (a) repairs to equipment requiring disassembly to determine the nature and extent of repairs, or (b) material available only from one source and for which cost cannot be readily established, or (c) supplies or services for which prices are known to be competitive but for which exact prices are not known. A realistic monetary limitation, subject to adjustment when the firm price is established, must be placed on each unpriced order.

If a purchase order is terminated before it has been accepted in writing by the contractor, and the contractor agrees with the termination and does not claim that costs were incurred as a result of beginning performance, the purchase order is considered canceled. If the contractor does not accept the cancellation or claims that some costs were incurred as a result of beginning performance, the matter is processed as any other termination action.

Blanket purchasing agreements (BPAs) represent a simplified method of filling anticipated repetitive needs for supplies or services by establishing "charge accounts" with qualified sources of supply. They are intended for use by an organization responsible for providing supplies for its own operations or for other offices, installations, projects, or functions. Such organizations, for example, may be organized supply points, separate independent field activities, or one-person posts.

An agency will violate the FAR competition requirements by issuing blanket purchase agreements for services without opening them to full competition to allow the selection of the initial BPA vendors or the subsequent selection of purchase order awardees.

BPAs may be established where (1) there is a variety of items in a broad class of supplies or services that are generally purchased but the precise items, quantities and delivery requirements are not known in advance and may vary considerably, (2) there is a requirement to provide commercial sources of supply for one or more offices or projects in a given area that do not have or need authority to purchase otherwise, (3) use of BPAs would avoid the need to write numerous purchase orders, and (4) there is no existing requirements contract for the same supply or service that the contracting activity is required to use.

Once it has been determined that use of a BPA is appropriate, the Contracting Officer should consider suppliers whose past performance has shown them to be dependable, who offer quality supplies or services at consistently lower prices, and who have previously provided numerous purchases at or below the simplified acquisition threshold. BPAs may be established with more than one supplier of the same type of item, with a single firm, and with Federal Supply Schedule contractors, if doing so is not inconsistent with the terms of their schedule contracts.

§ 13.7   The Fast Payment Procedures

The government's fast payment procedure allows payment to contractors—under limited conditions—before it verifies that supplies have been received and accepted. Payment is allowed based upon the contractor's submission of an invoice that certifies that (1) delivery has been made to a post office, common carrier, or point of first receipt by the government, and (2) the contractor agrees to correct any deficiencies due to non-receipt, damage in transit, or nonconforming supplies.

Fast payment procedures may be used when (a) individual purchasing instruments do not exceed $30,000 (higher dollar limitations are allowed under certain limited conditions), (b) deliveries are made to facilities where it will be impractical for the government to make timely payment based on evidence of government acceptance, (c) title passes to the government either upon delivery to a post office or carrier or on receipt by the government, (d) the contractor agrees to correct any deficiencies, and (e) the purchasing instrument is a firm-fixed-price contract, a purchase order, or a delivery order for supplies. Finally, a government system must be in place to ensure that there is adequate documentation of contractor performance and identification of contractors having a current history of abusing the procedure.

Part III

CONTRACTING METHODS AND CONTRACT TYPES

Chapter 14

SEALED BIDDING

Analysis

A. REQUIREMENTS OF SEALED BIDDING

§ 14.1   In General

Under the Competition in Contracting Act (CICA), agencies generally are required to procure supplies and services "competitively." The Federal Acquisition Regulation (FAR) sets forth the conditions for when the use of sealed bidding—previously called "formal advertising"—is appropriate to achieve this objective. Contracting Officers must solicit sealed bids if (a) time permits the solicitation, submission, and evaluation of sealed bids, (b) the award will be made on the basis of price and other price-related factors, (c) it is not necessary to conduct discussions with the responding sources about their bids, and (d) there is a reasonable expectation of receiving more than one sealed bid.

Most agencies spend a relatively low (and steadily decreasing) percentage of their procurement dollars each year on sealed-bid acquisitions. The most frequently used categories for sealed bidding are routine construction, renovation or repair of buildings and other structures, noncomplex services, such as janitorial services, and off-the-shelf commercial supply items. If the use of sealed bids is not appropriate under the regulatory criteria, then the agency in acquisitions above the simplified acquisition threshold (see FAR Part 13) must use competitive negotiation (discussed in Chapter 15) as the procurement method. Because circumstances frequently preclude use of sealed bidding under this standard, competitive negotiation is the predominant method of procurement in the executive branch.

The key to purchasing through the use of sealed bids is its formality—it is a tightly regulated system governed by the rigid FAR requirements. Its basic objective is to give all interested parties an opportunity to deal with the government on an equal basis—with the government reaping the benefits of full and open competition. Therefore, little room exists for considering the comparative merits of a particular prospective contractor or of its particular goods or services—award of the contract must be made (if at all) to the responsible bidder who submits the lowest responsive bid under the announced basis for award. In sealed bidding procurements, the court or GAO will take a less deferential view of whether an agency's actions were rational or reasonable than it will in negotiated procurements.

This chapter discusses the basic elements of the sealed-bid procedure, including (1) the agency's Invitation for Bids (IFB), (2) the preparation of a bid by a prospective bidder, (3) the agency's bid-opening procedures, and (4) the rules regarding the consideration of late bids. The chapter also examines the issues of eligibility for award, mistakes in bids, and award of the contract, and provides a brief overview of a hybrid type of sealed bidding and competitive negotiation called two-step sealed bidding.

§ 14.2   The Invitation for Bids

(a) In General

An agency initiates a sealed-bid procurement by preparing and publicizing an IFB. The IFB should contain all the information that a prospective bidder needs to submit a responsive bid, although no requirement exists that the solicitation be so detailed as to eliminate all performance risks and uncertainties. In perhaps the most important term, the IFB must clearly state the basis on which bids will be evaluated for award; the agency must identify all the price related factors, and unannounced considerations are not authorized. IFBs pertain only to sealed bidding under FAR Part 14 and not to Request for Quotations under other FAR authorities. *Crystal Clear Maintenance, Inc.*, B-417482, 2019 CPD ¶ 244.

The term "price related factors" has regulatory interpretation. If such factors exist, they must be included in the solicitation. For example, there may be foreseeable costs or delays to the government resulting from such factors as differences in inspection, locations of supplies, and transportation if bids are requested on f.o.b. origin basis. Transportation costs to the designated points shall be considered in determining the lowest cost to the government; changes may be requested by the bidder in the terms of the invitation for bids, which may be made if the change does not constitute a ground for rejection.

Advantages or disadvantages to the government might result from making more than one award. The contracting officer shall assume, for the purpose of making multiple awards, that $500 would be the administrative cost to the government for issuing and administering each contract awarded under a solicitation. Individual awards are for the items or combinations of items that result in the lowest aggregate cost to the government, including the assumed administrative costs. Factors such as state and local taxes may need to be considered and, if supplies are of foreign origin, then it may be necessary to consider application of the Buy American Act or any other prohibition on foreign purchases.

Typically, the IFB contains standard forms and a number of common, nonstandard, and special provisions relating to a wide variety of subjects, the most notable being the specifications of the contract work. As discussed in Chapter 5, to publicize the IFB, the agency may post notices in public places or media or make it electronically available.

(b) Standard Forms

An IFB is a collection of standard forms that includes the technical requirements or specifications of the procurement, instructions for bidders to follow, certifications to be signed, price charts to be filled in, and both standard and special terms and conditions to be followed. This accumulation of forms is often referred to as a "bid package" and can be more or less complex, depending on the size and nature of the procurement.

For supply and service contracts, IFBs will normally include Standard Form 33, "Solicitation, Offer, and Award" as the first page. If the solicitation is amended, Standard Form 30, "Amendment of Solicitation/Modification of Contract" will be issued. For small dollar purchases using simplified procurement procedures (see FAR Part 13), the agency may use an Optional Form 347, "Order for Supplies or Services," or its own form.

For contracts for commercial items, the FAR provides Standard Form 1449, "Solicitation/Contract/Order for Commercial Items," which includes contract terms and conditions more in accordance with standard commercial practice (see Chapter 12). For construction contracts, there is a far greater variety and number of IFB forms. The precise forms to be used will depend on the estimated price for the particular contract. Most higher-priced contracts will be processed under Standard Form 1442, "Solicitation, Offer, and Award (Construction, Alteration, or Repair)."

(c) Specifications

As discussed in Chapter 11, the specifications set forth in the solicitation provide bidders with a description of the work required to be performed and establish a standard for determining the rights and obligations of the parties. The IFB should set out the most significant physical, functional, or other characteristics (known as the "salient" characteristics) of the product or services that are essential to the government.

If the specifications are ambiguous or contain other defects (for example, an erroneous dimension or an impossible requirement), and if the defects are discovered before bid opening, the Contracting Officer has a responsibility to (a) correct the deficiency by issuing an amendment to the IFB or (b) even cancel the solicitation.

When necessary for evaluation purposes, an IFB may require bidders to submit samples or descriptive literature along with their bids. The FAR, however, limits the use of bid samples to where the acceptability of a particular product cannot be adequately described in the specifications and descriptive literature for which product acceptability cannot be determined.

Delivery dates may be included in the specifications but more often are in the IFB schedule. Normally, they are expressed as maximums. However, under some circumstances, the IFB may specify a desired delivery date and a required date that is later. Only the required date is significant because a bidder gains no advantage in offering to meet a desired delivery date or any other date earlier than the required date. In some solicitations, the delivery date is stated in "days after award" or "days after date of contract." Generally, the date of award or date of contract is set forth in a supply or service contract on the first page. This date starts the performance period.

(d) Pre-Award Amendments

The agency may cancel the IFB before the bid opening when it is clearly in the public interest. If the government's needs change or the IFB is found to be deficient, it should be amended by the CO before the bid opening. Deficiencies can arise, for example, the IFB (a) fails to conform to statutory or regulatory requirements, (b) does not reflect the reasonable needs of the government, (c) no longer meets the needs of the government (because, for example, the government's needs have changed), (d) unduly restricts competition, (e) omits required information (or fails to ask for necessary information), (f) contains erroneous or misleading information, or (g) contains some ambiguity. Oral advice from agency officials that deviates from the written solicitation, however, will not revise the IFB.

If the IFB deficiency is discovered before bid opening, and if the Contracting Officer is put on notice of the deficiency, the solution is relatively simple: the Contracting Officer can amend the IFB to correct the defect and extend the time for submission of bids, if necessary. It is important that a bidder notify the Contracting Officer immediately if it discovers a deficiency because a protest could be untimely where the bidder knew or should have known about the deficiency before the closing time for receipt of bids. Similarly, if an ambiguity is patent, i.e., obvious or glaring, and the bidder fails in its duty to seek clarification from the Contracting Officer before bid submission, the ambiguity will likely be resolved against the successful bidder after award in the event of a dispute over contract interpretation.

(e) Canceling the IFB—Basic Policies

If a deficiency in the procurement is not noted until after bid opening, the problem is considerably more difficult to remedy because it is no longer possible under the sealed bidding regulations for the agency to amend the IFB and proceed with the competition (as would be possible in negotiated acquisitions). Instead, the agency must decide whether to award a contract despite the deficiency or to cancel the IFB and resolicit the requirement.

Public policy generally frowns on IFB cancellation after the bid opening, because by this time all bids have been publicly exposed, which could lead to the original low bidder either to lose its competitive advantage or to walk away from its bid because it regrets the original offer.

Note, too, that not every solicitation defect or deficiency is serious enough to warrant cancellation of the solicitation. An IFB may be canceled after the bid opening only for compelling reasons, such as when the IFB, taken as a whole, can reasonably be interpreted to call for something other than what was intended by the Contracting Officer, or the agency misled a bidder into submitting an unacceptable bid.

Determining whether a compelling reason exists involves the exercise of the contracting agency's judgment; GAO will review such a determination only to ensure that it is reasonable. On the other hand, if through inadvertence a potential supplier was prevented from competing, this fact alone would not constitute a compelling reason for canceling the procurement—particularly on a showing of adequate competition, reasonable prices, and no deliberate or conscious attempt by the agency to preclude the potential supplier from competing. Agency requests for bid extensions are common to keep the bids viable during the time the agency decides whether to cancel the IFB after the bid opening.

When the agency cancels the procurement because the specifications are deficient or no longer represent the government's needs, the contracting agency must be careful to explain to the disappointed bidders that its stated ground is indeed the real reason for canceling the solicitation and not merely a subterfuge to deprive the low bidder of an award—in other words, that any deficiency in the specifications is significant and cannot be corrected by other means. The Contracting Officer has broad discretion in such matters, and a disappointed bidder that wishes to protest the agency's action must substantiate any allegation of abuse with clear evidence.

(f) Canceling the IFB—Other Reasons

Apart from a deficient IFB, the most common grounds for canceling a solicitation after the bid opening are financial: the bids received are unreasonably high or the agency's circumstances have changed and it now lacks the necessary funding.

The prospect of substantial savings to the government justifies rejection of all bids and resolicitation. Small savings are not a sufficient justification. Substantial savings are most likely to surface when (a) a significantly lower bid is unacceptable because it was late, nonresponsive, or from a non-responsible bidder, (b) the price or prices are unreasonable in relation to the government's estimate or to the Contracting Officer's general knowledge of market conditions or prior procurements, or (c) an uncorrectable mistake in bid indicates that the government could have obtained a significantly lower bid.

The determination of whether the savings would be substantial is usually within the discretion of the Contracting Officer. However, a nonbidder's asserted willingness to offer a lower price is not a proper basis for rejection of all bids on the ground that the bids received were unreasonably priced.

Examples of several other less common, but legitimate grounds for rejecting all bids are: (1) a critical need to negotiate a shorter delivery schedule has developed, (2) there was a lack of fair competition, (3) the goods or services are no longer required, or (4). the design specifications are no longer accurate and the agency's needs have changed materially.

An agency may complete an acquisition through negotiation, after the cancellation of an IFB, where all otherwise acceptable bids are unreasonably priced. FAR § 14.404–1(e)(1). The FAR further provides that if an IFB is cancelled because all bids received are at unreasonable prices, an agency may conduct a negotiated procurement without issuing a new solicitation. FAR § 14.404–1(e)(1), (f). Unlike other situations, where the cancellation of an IFB results in the issuance of a new solicitation, the FAR expressly provides that an agency need not issue a new solicitation following a conversion for unreasonable bid prices. Compare FAR § 14.404–1(e)(1) with FAR § 14.404–1(e)(2). Accordingly, here, the agency is completing its acquisition not through the issuance of a new solicitation, but instead, by changing the contracting method, via amendment, under a single solicitation.

The GAO also has said that the conversion from an IFB to a negotiated procurement under one solicitation, alone, does not impact the time for filing a protest based upon alleged improprieties in a solicitation. *Cashman Dredging & Marine Contracting Company, LLC*, B-417213.3, B-417213.4, 2019 CPD ¶ 259.

§ 14.3   Preparing the Bid

A bidder must take extreme care to ensure that its bid is completed in exact compliance with the terms of the IFB. Any material deviation from those terms (even if inadvertent) could result in rejection of the bid as nonresponsive. Moreover, as discussed below, mistakes in bids—particularly those not discovered until after bid opening or contract award—can lead to significant problems and are not always correctable.

(a) Following Instructions in the IFB

To minimize the possibility of bid responsiveness and mistake problems, experienced bidders typically do the following:

1.   Be certain that the entire bid package—including all attachments and amendments—is completed and returned to the procuring agency in accordance with the IFB instructions;

2.   Check (and recheck) all price computations;

3.   Carefully note the due date on the IFB for submission of bids and the location to which bids must be transmitted; and

4.   Make no suggestions or requests for changes in the terms of the IFB that could be construed as amending its terms (and result in submission of a nonresponsive bid).

Most IFBs state (usually on the first page) the total number of pages in the IFB. It is not unusual, especially in complex procurements, for pages or attachments to be inadvertently omitted. Thus, after receiving the solicitation, a bidder should carefully check it to ensure that all pages and all referenced attachments are included. Otherwise, a bidder could fail fully to understand the nature and extent of its obligation, and its bid could be determined nonresponsive if omitted pages or attachments contain material information regarding the solicitation.

Every solicitation contains basic instructions for bid preparation. These instructions are extremely important and should be strictly followed. Generally, to ensure compliance with these instructions, the experienced bidder will:

1.   Carefully read and examine all the provisions of the IFB, including the drawings, specifications, and standard terms and conditions;

2.   Print or type the bidder's name on the schedule and each continuation sheet on which an entry is made;

3.   Initial all erasures or other changes made in the bid;

4.   Include evidence of the authority of any agent who signs the bid;

5.   State each price accurately to avoid the error of misplaced or erroneous decimals and figures;

6.   Commit to meet at least the minimum requirements of the specifications, even though the product the bidder is offering may be superior in a number of respects;

7.   Commit to meet at least the required delivery schedule, even though there may be an agreement to deliver on an earlier date;

8.   Submit the bid in a sealed envelope (unless the agency is accepting bids through electronic commerce or other alternative procedures) with the requisite number of copies (usually an original and two copies); and

9.   Deliver the bid sufficiently before the deadline to the precise place specified in the IFB.

Submissions of multiple bids by the same vendor is not objectionable where it does not give the bidder an unfair advantage and is therefore non-prejudicial to the interests of the government and of the other bidders.

(b) Other Aids to Bidding

In addition to the information and instructions included in the bid package, a bidder may be aided in preparing a bid by (1) seeking clarification from the Contracting Officer of any ambiguities or uncertainties in the specifications, (2) attending prebid conferences—if scheduled by the procuring agency, (3) inspecting the jobsite (site inspections are often scheduled, particularly in construction contracts), and (4) obtaining any government-furnished models or samples that may be made available to assist bidders in understanding the specifications.

Where a prebid conference is held by the government, it is good policy for firms to attend (although attendance is normally not mandatory), take notes, and request minutes of the meeting from the government. Where a site inspection is authorized by the terms of the solicitation, it is important for a bidder to comply because failure to do so will impair the bidder's right to challenge errors or omissions that could have been discovered by a reasonable and timely inspection. The standard rule applied by the agency boards of contract appeals and courts is that bidders are responsible for the knowledge of site conditions to the same extent that they would be had a reasonable site visit been conducted.

(c) Formulation of Prices

After careful review of the bid package, instructions, and any aids outside the package, a bidder is ready to begin preparing a price. The starting point is a production plan. For a supply contract, for example, this will normally involve consideration of (a) what materials, parts, and components must be purchased, (b) which manufacturing or assembly operations will be performed "in-house" and which will be subcontracted, and (c) what production time schedule will be required to meet the contract delivery date. At that point, the bidder normally solicits subcontract pricing information from potential vendors to provide the bidder with fixed and binding prices for the period that the bidder is required to keep its bid to the government open. Thereafter, the bidder will calculate "in-house" production costs and a theoretical price for the products to be furnished.

This theoretical price may be adjusted by a number of practical considerations. One may be an estimate of what competitors are likely to bid, based on their bidding history and their competitive advantages (or disadvantages) due to such factors as prior experience, "in-place" tooling, financial position, and relative transportation costs (i.e., how close their plant is to the delivery point). Another consideration could be the bidder's other work, which may affect the intensity of the bidder's need to get the contract. A third consideration may be production economies that the bidder could achieve through joint production of several items or advance buying for stock.

When entering unit prices—or extended or total prices—on a bid, a bidder must state them accurately and exactly as required by the IFB. For example, a bid could be considered nonresponsive for failure to include (1) an entry in each price "blank" (note that a "0," "n/c," or "no charge" is generally regarded as a price entry), (2) a list of subcontractors to be used on the project (where this is required by the IFB), or (3) a guaranteed maximum shipping weight or shipping dimensions (again, where required by the IFB).

Prompt payment discounts offered by a bidder are not considered by the agency in evaluating bids. However, any discount offered will form a part of the award and will be taken by the government if payment is made within the discount period specified by the bidder. As an alternative to indicating a discount in conjunction with the offer, bidders may prefer to offer discounts on individual invoices.

(d) Acknowledgment of Amendments

As noted earlier, amendments to IFBs before the time and date set for receipt of bids are frequently required to (a) make changes in the contract work, such as quantity of items solicited, the specifications, or the delivery schedule, or (b) correct a defective or ambiguous term. Amendments are available to every firm obtaining a copy of the IFB; the agency typically posts the amendment on the SAM.gov website. Oral amendments are permissible only to extend the bid opening date, in an exigency, but such an extension must be confirmed by a subsequent written amendment.

Bidder instructions provide—and many bid protest decisions make clear—that IFB amendments must be acknowledged by a bidder unless the amendments do not affect price, quantity, quality, or delivery terms by more than a trivial or negligible amount. Oral acknowledgment of amendments will not suffice.

A prospective contractor bears the risk of nonreceipt of IFB amendments where (1) the agency has made a diligent, good faith effort to comply with the statutory and regulatory requirements for distribution of these materials, and the bidder's nonreceipt appears to result from isolated agency errors as opposed to significant deficiencies in the distribution process, and (2) the agency has received sufficient competition to assure reasonable prices, even when the effect of the nonreceipt is to eliminate a potential offeror from the competition.

An example where an offeror failed in this duty of reasonable diligence would be its failure both to register for e-mail notices for solicitation amendments and to check the SAM.gov website regularly for this information. The simplest, safest and best manner of acknowledgment is for the bidder to sign the acknowledgment form immediately and return it to the procuring agency. However, other methods allowed by the solicitation, such as email, are sufficient so long as it is clear that the bidder has accepted the terms of the amended IFB.

(e) Methods of Submission

Bids must be submitted according to the directions in the IFB and must be submitted in time to be received in the agency office designated in the IFB before the time set for opening of bids. Bids are normally mailed or hand-delivered by the bidder or by a commercial carrier.

Bids sent by facsimile (fax) machines will not be considered unless permitted by the IFB. Contracting Officers may authorize the use of faxed bids unless otherwise restricted by agency procedures. In deciding whether to permit the use of faxed bids for a particular procurement, a Contracting Officer is required to consider a number of factors: (a) the anticipated bid size and volume, (b) the urgency of the requirement, (c) the frequency of price changes, (d) the availability, reliability, speed, and capacity of the receiving fax equipment, and (e) the adequacy of administrative procedures and controls for receiving, identifying, recording, and safeguarding faxed bids and ensuring their timely delivery to the bid-opening location. Unless the solicitation authorizes bidders to use a fax machine, a bid or amendment acknowledgment submitted by fax will be rejected as nonresponsive.

Some strict rules apply the submission of bids by facsimile that put maximum risk on bidders. If the bidder chooses to transmit a facsimile bid, the Government will not be responsible for any failure attributable to the transmission or receipt of the facsimile bid including, but not limited to, the following: (1) receipt of garbled or incomplete bid; (2) availability or condition of the receiving facsimile equipment; (3) incompatibility between the sending and receiving equipment; (4) delay in transmission or receipt of bid; (5) failure of the bidder to properly identify the bid, (6) illegibility of the bid; and (7) security of bid data.

The Contracting Officer frequently will authorize use of electronic commerce for submission of bids. In that instance, the IFB must specify the electronic commerce method that bidders may use. The more modern methods of electronic commerce have made facsimile submission of bids far less important than in the past.

(f) Firm Bid Rule

Once a bid is submitted, the bidder may withdraw or modify it at any time before the time set for bid opening. The modification or withdrawal may be by any method authorized by the solicitation. However, under the "firm bid rule," once the bids are opened, they may not be withdrawn or altered (except when there is a cognizable mistake in bid).

The bid remains open for acceptance in the form submitted until expiration of the acceptance period or rejection of the bid. The reason for this rule is clear—if a bidder is permitted to change its bid after other bids have been publicly opened and disclosed, that bidder would have an unfair advantage. Thus, the otherwise successful bidder might seek to rescind its bid before government acceptance if it discovers that it left a considerable amount of money on the table with an excessively high bid. This outcome varies from the commercial rule that an offer made by one potential party to a contract generally may be freely withdrawn at any time prior to acceptance.

B. OPENING OF BIDS AND AWARD OF CONTRACT

§ 14.4   Bid Opening

Bid opening is a strictly regulated and formal process and a key step in protecting the integrity of the bidding system. All bids (except those that are classified) are opened publicly.

The opening should be held at the precise time and place specified in the IFB and, when possible, each bid will be read aloud. The agency then prepares an abstract of the bids, identifying the procurement, the bidders, the bid prices, and other appropriate information required for bid evaluation. After the abstract is prepared, it is certified by the bid-opening officer, and copies of the bids are normally made available for public inspection. When a bid is received late but nevertheless may be considered under an exception for award it need not be publicly opened. However, it should be included in the abstract of bids and made available for inspection.

(a) Initial Handling by the Agency

All bids received before bid opening are required to be kept unopened in a locked box or safe. Even information regarding the number of bids received or the identity of bidders cannot be disclosed prior to opening except to government employees with a "need-to-know." When samples are submitted with bids, they are handled in a similar manner.

Ordinarily, the bidder writes the applicable IFB number on the outside cover of the bid envelope. This identification helps to ensure that the bid is placed in the proper location on the government installation for the opening. If the bid envelope does not, for some reason, adequately identify the IFB, the rules permit opening the envelope in advance by a government employee specifically authorized to do so to identify the IFB. But if a sealed bid is mistakenly opened in advance, it must be resealed and the circumstances reported in writing. If the prematurely opened bid is read aloud before the scheduled bid opening, however, the bid opening should be postponed to allow the bidder time to revise its bid.

Even with appropriate procedures in place, an agency occasionally will lose or misplace a bid. Mere negligence or lack of diligence by the agency in safeguarding bids will not suffice to allow the submission of replacement material for such a bid. The protester must either show a history or problem with the agency losing bids or to establish agency bad faith against the bidder. The occasional negligent loss of an offer by an agency does not entitle the firm submitting it to any relief. Where the bid is later found, it may be considered without compromising the integrity of the competitive system when: (1) the bid was received at the designated installation before the bid opening, (2) it remained under the agency's control until discovered, and (3) it was discovered before the award.

(b) Early or Late Bid Openings

The bid-opening officer decides when the stated time for opening has arrived and has the responsibility to announce it to those persons present. In one case, *Nueva Construction Co., Inc.*, Comp. Gen. Dec. B-270009, 96-1 CPD ¶ 84, the Comptroller General upheld the Contracting Officer's decision to reject as late a bid that was offered seconds after the announcement of the bid opening but during the minute set in the IFB. The Comptroller General reasoned that the controlling factor was not the time on a particular clock but the Contracting Officer's reasonable declaration of the start of bid-opening time.

In making this decision, the Contracting Officer is guided by the Uniform Time Act of 1966, and the Comptroller General has interpreted this statute to mean that the time for receipt of bids is local time, regardless of whether it is referenced as standard time or daylight savings time in the IFB. These rules—even though they tend to be confusing—are strictly enforced, making it extremely important for bidders to note this distinction and to provide for timely submission of bids.

On occasion, bids may be opened early due to a misunderstanding. Where the agency prematurely opens and officially announces one or more bids, the Comptroller General has allowed the award to stand, despite the violation of the announced bid opening time, where the protesting firm suffered no competitive prejudice.

Bids opened after the time scheduled in the IFB, or intentionally postponed, may be carefully considered, even without prior written notice, when such action is deemed to be in the government's best interest and no bidder is prejudiced thereby. For example, a postponement may occur where the Contracting Officer has reason to believe that the bids of an important segment of bidders have been delayed in the mails, or in the communication system specified for transmission of bids, for causes beyond their control and without their fault or negligence, such as a flood, fire, strike or government equipment blackout.

§ 14.5 Late Bids

A recurring problem with sealed-bid procurements is late submission of bids. Generally, a bid—or a bid modification—will not be considered for award unless it is received no later than the precise time specified in the IFB. The rules regarding late bids are strictly applied. Thus, bids that are received a few minutes (or even seconds) later than the bid-opening time announced by the officer in charge are usually deemed inexcusably late and ineligible for award, no matter how advantageous the bid terms.

(a) Exceptions

Although the bid-opening rule is strictly applied, it has a number of exceptions. Under the FAR, a late bid will be considered if it is received before award is made, the Contracting Officer determines that accepting the late bid would not unduly delay the acquisition, and there is "acceptable evidence" that it was received at the government installation designated for receipt of bids and was under the government's control before the time set for the receipt of bids.

The rule varies slightly for bids transmitted through electronic commerce.

In addition, a late modification of an otherwise successful bid that makes its terms more favorable to the government will be considered at any time it is received. Perhaps the most common instance of an inexcusably late bid is where the bidder's failure to address and label its bid package as instructed by the solicitation was the paramount cause of its late arrival to the bid opening location.

In one case, *Selrico Services, Inc.*, Comp. Gen. Dec. B-259709, 95-1 CPD ¶ 224, the bidder was erroneously advised by the agency that its bid had been timely received when, in fact, it arrived a day late. In rejecting the bidder's contention that had it known its bid had not been received it would have submitted another copy in time, the Comptroller General observed that the rule allowing acceptance of a late bid where improper government action was the cause for the delay is to be narrowly interpreted. In any event, said the Comptroller General, the primary cause for delay here was the bidder's carrier, not the government.

If a bid is delivered to the wrong place, it will also normally be rejected. However, a bid will be considered for award despite this rule where improper government action, such as misdirection by government employees, was the paramount cause for the late delivery and consideration of the bid would not compromise the integrity of the competitive bidding system.

By contrast, a protest challenging agency's acceptance of a bid received in the bid opening room after the time set for bid opening was denied where the record showed the bid was received at the government installation's mailroom and was under the government's control before the time set for the receipt of bids. *Athena Construction Group, Inc.*, B-413406, B-413406.2, 2016 CPD ¶ 297.

(b) Faxed or Electronic Bids

As with mailed or hand-carried bids, faxed or electronic bids or modifications (when permitted by the IFB) must be received on time unless they meet the conditions for exceptions for otherwise late bids. Thus, a bid or modification received late in the bidding room may be considered for award if the government was the cause of the delay, for example, through mishandling or incorrect instructions. Note that for faxed bids, the Contracting Officer may request the apparently successful bidder to provide the complete original signed bid after the date set for bid opening.

A bid modification faxed by the bidder to its representative, who then delivered the modification to the agency in person, was acceptable in a solicitation prohibiting faxed bids. The reason is that the hand delivery of a bid modification on facsimile paper is not a transmission by facsimile. In another case, government mishandling of an authorized faxed bid modification permitted its consideration even though it was received late. Similarly, a faxed bid that could not be sent to the designated address because the agency's equipment had run out of ink was properly considered because its lateness was the result of a "chain of events" for which the agency was solely responsible.

As noted earlier, under the FAR, a late bid will be considered if it is received before award is made, the Contracting Officer determines that accepting the late bid would not unduly delay the acquisition, and there is "acceptable evidence" that the bid was received at the government installation designated for receipt of bids and was under the government's control before the time set for the receipt of bids. If the bid was transmitted through an electronic commerce method authorized by the solicitation, the FAR recognizes receipt of the bid "at the initial point of entry to the government infrastructure not later than 5:00 p.m. one working day before the date specified for the receipt of bids" as the equivalent of "acceptable evidence" of bid receipt.

The phrase, "[offers] received at the Government installation," includes electronic submissions received by a Government computer server. Therefore, in the case of an electronic delivery, the government control exception applies where the electronic proposal is received by a government server (or comparable computer) and is under the agency's control prior to the deadline. For additional discussion, see Sarah Carroll, *Conflicting Bid Protest Decisions: The Split Between The Court Of Federal Claims And The Government Accountability Office On Late Emailed Proposals*, 48 Pub. Cont. L.J. 449 (Spring 2019).

§ 14.6   Eligibility for Award

To be eligible for award, a responsible bidder must have submitted the lowest priced, responsive bid, in accordance with the announced basis for award.

It is important to understand the difference between the term "nonresponsive" and the term "non-responsible." A nonresponsive bid is one that fails to represent an unequivocal offer to provide the exact thing called for in the IFB such that acceptance of the bid will bind the contractor in accordance with the solicitation's material terms and conditions. The term non-responsible refers to the bidder's lack of capacity and qualifications to complete the requirements of the contract. In yet another distinction, bid responsiveness differs from contract administration, i.e., whether the successful bidder has performed or will perform in accordance with the contract.

Most protests in sealed bid procurements relate to the alleged non-responsiveness of the low bid, and there are numerous potential settings for this controversy. Additionally, a disappointed bidder may protest a Contracting Officer's non-responsibility decision regarding such a rejected firm where it submitted the low bid. Elsewise, a competing bidder otherwise in line for award may protest the Contracting Officer's affirmative responsibility decision regarding the low bidder (see Chapter 9).

While bid responsiveness is determined as of the date of bid opening, a bidder's responsibility is determined as of the date of contract award. Therefore, it is possible for a bidder who is non-responsible when its bid is submitted to receive the award on the theory that the bidder will become responsible prior to award or in time satisfactorily to perform, for example, by acquiring necessary equipment, facilities, or personnel. Once a nonresponsive bid has been submitted, however, nothing may be done after the bid opening to make it responsive, because post-bid opening explanations or corrections are inadmissible to rectify a nonresponsive bid.

§ 14.7   Responsiveness of Bids

(a) General Policy

To be awardable, a bid must be responsive. A "responsive bid" is one that contains a definite, unqualified offer to meet the material terms of the IFB. In this context, a "material" term is one that goes to the substance of the bid, rather than its form, and where it relates to the price, quantity, quality, or delivery of the items being procured in more than a negligible way when compared to the total cost or scope of the supplies or services being acquired.

A bidder's failure to furnish required information does not necessarily render the bid non-responsive. Thus, for example, an agency improperly rejected a bid as nonresponsive for not providing information related to the solicitation's Buy American Act requirements, where the information was not needed to establish the bid's responsiveness. *Addison Construction Company*, B-416525, B-416525.2, 2018 CPD ¶ 292 (this missing information could be obtained by the agency through its own investigation and would not affect the relative standing of the bidders). The safest course is for a bidder to provide all required information in all instances and in that way it will help eliminate litigation about incomplete bids.

The policies for requiring a responsive bid are to provide a level playing field for the competitors during bid submission and evaluation, to ensure a valid offer and acceptance that forms a binding contract, and to reduce the "toils of ambiguity" when the tribunals must interpret the contract. Maintaining the integrity of the competitive bid process outweighs any cost savings associated with accepting a particular nonresponsive bid.

Merely signing a bid does not make it acceptable. Responsiveness is determined by the bid terms when the offer is opened. If in its bid a bidder attempts to impose conditions that would modify material requirements of the invitation, limit its liability to the government, or limit rights of the government under any contract clause, then the bid will be nonresponsive, as does an unsigned bid. Likewise, a statement in the bid that it is confidential and can only be viewed by agency officials may render the bid nonresponsive. In addition, if a bid guarantee—usually in the form of a bid bond as security that the bidder will not withdraw the bid during a specified period and will execute the contract if awarded—is required, it must be acceptable under the IFB for the bid to be responsive, with limited exceptions. Thus, for example, copies of bid guarantee documents, whether submitted electronically or hand delivered, are insufficient.

Where an invitation for bids required submission of a bid guarantee, an agency reasonably rejected a protester's bid as nonresponsive where the bid bond was defective because it appeared to limit the liability of the corporate surety with respect to excess reprocurement costs in the event of contractor default. *G2G, LLC*, B-416502, 2018 CPD ¶ 328.

In a recent FAR change, the matter of the authenticity and enforceability of a power of attorney accompanying the bid bond is now a matter of responsibility, which can be resolved after the bid opening so long as it occurs before the award decision and is no longer a matter of responsiveness.

Responsiveness issues frequently center on the bidder's product literature, and some finely drawn rules exist in this area. Generally, where descriptive literature solicited and submitted for evaluation purposes contains a reservation of a right to change the specifications, such as a statement that "Specifications are subject to change without notice," the bid is nonresponsive.

The principal exception to the general rule is where it is clear from the face of the bid that the legend was not intended to reserve a right to change the offered product. Another doctrine is that an agency is required to disregard unsolicited descriptive literature unless it is clear from the bid or accompanying papers that the bidder intended to qualify the bid. Where the descriptive literature describes the exact product to be furnished, or is incorporated into the bid, however, there is a sufficient relationship between the bid and the descriptive literature so that it may not be disregarded.

(b) Minor Informalities

The Contracting Officer may waive minor defects or informalities that have no effect (or merely a trivial effect) on price, quantity, quality, or delivery, and that may be corrected without prejudice to other bidders. For example, the FAR states the following minor informalities may be waived: (a) submitting the wrong number of copies of the bid, (b) omitting a handwritten signature in the signature block on the bidding form if the bid in any way has a signature showing the intent of the bidder to be bound, and (c) failing to acknowledge receipt of an amendment if it is clear from the bid or otherwise that the amendment was in fact received. The evidence that would prove this last point and save the offer from rejection is where the bid includes information that could only be found in the unacknowledged amendment.

Other minor informalities that might be acceptable are (1) failing to supply required information concerning the number of employees, (2) violating the sealed envelope requirement, (3) failing to identify the bid envelope in accordance with the IFB instructions, and (4) not furnishing with the bid evidence of the person's authority to sign the bid. In a common scenario, an agency will properly waive the failure to acknowledge an IFB amendment in any way where the amendment was not material because it failed to impose a new legal obligation upon bidders.

(c) Bid Acceptance Period

If the IFB prescribes a minimum time that bids are required to remain firm or irrevocable, a bid offering a shorter time is nonresponsive. If no minimum is stated, the bid acceptance period will be considered to run for a "reasonable amount of time" or there will be an "automatic" bid acceptance period as specified on the bid form unless the bidder inserts a longer or shorter time on the bid form. However, there can be a substantial drawback in offering a shorter time for acceptance.

If the award is not made within the shorter period specified, the bidder may not be allowed to extend its bid acceptance period— because to do so would give the bidder an unfair advantage—i.e., its initial cost exposure would be for a shorter period of time than applicable to bidders offering the full "automatic" time.

(d) Binding Legal Obligation

A bidder, whether an individual, corporation, or partnership, must be legally bound by the bid so that there can be no question regarding the bidder's obligation to perform. Otherwise, a successful bidder could, if it chose, avoid performance after award without liability. Thus, a bidder must be identifiable and existing at the time of bid opening. Note that with respect to a joint venture, the signature of the joint venture's "managing partner" is sufficient to bind the entity, provided the identity of the joint venture is firmly established at the time of award.

Generally, a bid may not be transferred or assigned by one bidder to another after it has been opened. The rationale for this restriction is analogous to that behind the anti-assignment statutes, 41 U.S.C.A. § 6305 and 31 U.S.C.A. § 3727, which prohibit the assignment of government contracts and claims in order, among other considerations, to prevent parties from acquiring a speculative interest and thereafter selling the contract at a profit to bona fide bidders and contractors.

The qualification is that an agency may properly award a contract to a low bidder's successor in interest, for example, where the original bidder, a wholly owned subsidiary of the parent-successor, merged with the parent company after bid opening, and where the assets of the original bidder (apart from this low bid) transferred in the merger are not negligible.

(e) Firm Price

A bid is not responsive unless it offers a firm, definite price as solicited by the IFB—that is, an "approximate" price is unacceptable because the bidder is not bound to a fixed amount. So, too, a bid that is subject to (a) freight rate or other increases, (b) a service charge on overdue accounts, (c) tax increases, or (d) prices charged by suppliers at the time of delivery, would be nonresponsive.

(f) Completeness

As already noted, the bid must address all material portions of the IFB because the bidder's acceptance of the IFB, and the agency's acceptance of the bid, become the parties' contract. However, the required parts of the bid need not all be physically included if they are allowed to be incorporated by reference.

Nonetheless, a bidder takes some risk that if it indicates no charge for an item, the bidder will be held bound, even if the bidder subjectively intended a different outcome. The Comptroller General has concluded that a handwritten dash on one of 28 line items complied with the requirement that entries be made for all line items, equating the dash with a "zero dollars" or "no cost" response that obligated the bidder to perform the work at no cost to the government.

(g) Ambiguities

Bids are commonly open to more than one reasonable interpretation, and such ambiguities frequently pertain to the pricing. (If the bid is subject to only one reasonable interpretation then it is not "ambiguous."). Where an ambiguously priced low bid is not the lowest bid under any reasonable interpretation of the ambiguity, bid rejection is proper. A contracting officer is not required to interpret an ambiguous bid by sequential logical deductions and inferences to make the bid responsive. Because of this rule, it is important that bidders double- and triple-check their figures, the placement of periods or commas, and price extensions.

One danger area for bidders is to include a recommendation or suggestion in the bid or a letter of transmittal. Such "requests" may result in rejection of a bid because frequently it cannot be determined whether they are mere requests that have no material bearing on the bid or if they call into question the bidder's commitment to the material IFB terms. In this regard, a bid "requesting" progress payments can be responsive where the agency reasonably regards a particular request as precatory and not as a condition of acceptance.

Requests, recommendations, and suggestions are most likely to arise in transmittal letters. Therefore, bidders seeking to make a responsive offer should not include letters of transmittal—or any other unsolicited material—when they submit their bids.

(h) Acceptance of Nonresponsive Bids

Statute, the FAR, and the cases commonly forbid the acceptance of a nonresponsive bid to form a contract. Nonetheless, several GAO and court cases approve such awards when the contract meets the agency's needs and no bidder is prejudiced by the acceptance of the bid.

These decisions are better understood as denying a protest because of the lack of competitive prejudice to the complaining firm, rather than creating an exception to the responsiveness policy. Other cases, however, hold that acceptance of a nonresponsive bid is per se prejudicial to the integrity of the competitive system or that the agency lacks authority to accept a nonresponsive bid. These cases leave no room for the competitive prejudice qualification seen in some decisions.

(i) Unbalanced Bids

Unbalanced bidding is a variation on responsiveness. This circumstance occurs when the prices for any line items or subline items are unduly high or low. Thus, despite an acceptable total evaluated price, the price of one or more contract line items is significantly over or understated as indicated by the application of cost or price analysis techniques.

Unbalanced pricing can increase performance risk and could result in the payment of unreasonably high prices. The greatest potential for unbalanced pricing probably exists with startup work (or like requirements) or where base quantities and option quantities are separate line items. The Contracting Officer may reject an unbalanced bid where the offer poses an unacceptable performance risk or price risk to the government.

Unfortunately, the FAR has a competing definition of an "unbalanced" bid that also can result in rejection of the bid as nonresponsive. In this alternative, an unbalanced bid is based on prices significantly less than cost for some work and prices which are significantly overstated in relation to cost for other work, and there is a reasonable doubt that the bid will result in the lowest overall cost to the government even though it may be the low evaluated bid. Such a front loaded bid would be tantamount to allowing an illegal advance payment, i.e., the contractor's getting paid for work that is greatly over-valued (and might never be performed). This definition omits the additional concerns of performance risk as opposed to just pricing issues.

(j) Other Reasons for Bid Rejection

Bids may be rejected for reasons other than non-responsiveness. Most prominently, any bid may be rejected if the price is unreasonably high, which can mean either the overall price or the prices for individual line items. The contracting officer's decision on price reasonableness will stand in a protest absent agency fraud, bad faith, or unreasonable action. A responsive bid that is below cost or with a low profit margin may not be rejected unless the agency finds the low bidder non-responsible, although the agency should be particularly concerned with a possible bidder mistake with an apparent unduly low priced bid.

§ 14.8   Responsibility of Bidders

As discussed in Chapter 9, to be eligible for award, a bidder must be "responsible." While the responsiveness of a bid is determined at the time bids are opened, the responsibility of a prospective contractor is determined by the time of award of the contract. In sum, information which relates to a bidder's apparent ability and capacity to perform the contract—such as a requirement that the prospective contractor must possess a certain operating license or have a certain number of years of equipment or bidder experience—need not be submitted with the bid but may be provided at any time prior to award, even if the solicitation requests the submission of such information with the bid.

The distinction between these two concepts—responsiveness and responsibility—is not always easy to draw. The interpretation of the solicitation advanced by the procuring agency must be carefully considered because that agency is normally in the best position to set forth what was intended.

To illustrate the interpretive challenge of deciding whether an issue is a matter of responsiveness or responsibility, the Comptroller General has drawn a distinction between those requirements which are directed to the manner in which a bidder proposed to satisfy affirmative action goals set forth in the solicitation and requirements that a bidder commit itself to those affirmative action goals. The former is a matter of responsibility and the latter is a matter of responsiveness. Bidders should review an agency's determinations regarding the acceptability of a bid to ensure that an issue of bid responsiveness has not been confused with an issue of contractor responsibility.

§ 14.9   Mistakes in Bids

The bid mistake procedures are not designed to allow bidders to correct judgmental errors or incorrect premises the bidder discovers after the opening of bids, because such a "correction" would enable the bidder to arrive at a bid never intended before the bid opening. Put another way, this practice gives the bidder that made a misjudgment an unfair second bite of the apple to win a contract when all other bidders had only a single blind bid.

A bedrock principle is that the mistake rules may not convert a nonresponsive bid into an acceptable one. The term "mistake in bid" normally means a mistake made in the bid price. A mistake in price may occur, for example, in the placement of a decimal or a comma, the calculation of the price, or the extension of unit prices. It may also refer to errors in other information required by the IFB—for example, the weight and dimensions of the item to be furnished, a certification, or a statement contained in descriptive literature.

(a) Pre-Award Mistakes

Trivial errors that do not have any material effect on the bids or the bidders may be corrected by the Contracting Officer before award.

Before making such correction, the bidder must furnish the Contracting Officer with a verification of the bid intended. Examples of such apparent mistakes are obvious discount errors (e.g., 1%, 10 days; 2%, 20 days; 5%, 30 days) or obvious reversal of "price f.o.b. destination" with "price f.o.b. factory." Similarly, the Contracting Officer may request that a bidder delete a nonmaterial IFB deviation in the bid. It bears emphasis, however, that an agency may not correct or waive a clerical mistake or other minor irregularity and thereby make a nonresponsive bid responsive.

(b) Bid Verification

As part of the pre-award screening of bids, the Contracting Officer is required to look for possible mistakes. If he or she believes there is a mistake in a bid, he has the further duty to seek verification of the bid from the bidder.

The verification request must be sufficiently detailed to put the bidder on notice of the suspected mistake so that the bidder can either assure the Contracting Officer that the bid as confirmed is without error or that, in fact, a mistake has been made. For example, the bidder should be advised, as is appropriate, of (1) the fact that its bid is so much lower than the other bids or the government's estimate that it indicates a possibility of error, (2) important or unusual characteristics of the specifications, (3) changes in requirements from previous purchases of a similar item, or (4) such other data that may put the bidder on notice of the suspected mistake.

Generally, the Contracting Officer will not require the bidder to make an "on the spot" verification. Most agencies will allow the bidder sufficient time to check the bid thoroughly prior to verification. If the bid is adequately verified, the Contracting Officer will consider it as originally submitted. If the bidder alleges it found a mistake after award to another bidder, and seeks correction, the bidder must follow a strict and objective process as stated in FAR 14.407–4.

(c) Other Pre-Award Mistakes

Mistakes other than apparent clerical mistakes that are discovered after opening and prior to award are handled differently. If the bidder (a) requests permission to withdraw its bid because of a mistake, and (b) the evidence reasonably supports the existence of a mistake, the bidder will normally be allowed to withdraw.

However, if there is also clear and convincing evidence of what the bidder actually intended, and if the bid—both as uncorrected and as corrected—is the lowest received, the Contracting Officer has the option—rarely invoked—of simply allowing the bid to be corrected and not allowing its withdrawal. Because of the incipient problems of forcing the bidder into a contract, agencies will rarely use this avenue even where permissible. Under certain circumstances, a bidder may be allowed to withdraw its allegation of a mistake—if the integrity of the competitive bidding system would not be compromised.

If the bidder requests permission to correct a mistake in its bid, and clear and convincing evidence establishes both the existence of a mistake and the bid actually intended, correction will normally be allowed. However, if correction would result in displacing any lower responsive bids, the evidence of the mistake and the bid actually intended must be ascertainable from an examination of the bid and the solicitation (and not from other documents).

Moreover, if the evidence of the mistake is clear and convincing only as to the mistake, but not as to the intended bid, or the evidence reasonably supports the existence of a mistake, but is not clear and convincing, the government retains the option to permit only withdrawal of the bid—not its correction.

Another prerequisite is that where the low bidder alleges a mistake, the bid as corrected generally must not come too close to the next low responsive bid, and the bidder's burden of proof will become more difficult the closer the bid comes to the next lower bid. Thus, even where the exact amount of the intended bid is not certain, a determination to allow correction is reasonable where the intended bid falls within a "narrow range of uncertainty" and would remain low after correction. As part of this process, the correction of a bid may be permitted to reflect the omission of direct costs without any increase for profit where the bidder requests correction in such form and the bid would remain low whether or not the low bid is amended to reflect profit.

FAR 14.407–3 contains extensive guidance on the agency review process for documentation of bidder mistakes disclosed before award. Workpapers are not required as evidence of mistake in bid where other clear and convincing evidence supports the contention that bidder erred. If a bidder fails or refuses to provide evidence to support a suspected or alleged mistake, the Contracting Officer may still consider the bid as submitted, unless (1) the bid amount is so far out of line with the amounts of other bids received or with the amount the agency determines constitutes a reasonable price, or (2) clear indications exist of an error that reasonably justify a conclusion that bid acceptance would be unfair to the bidder or to other bona fide bidders.

When a protester challenges the agency's refusal to allow upward correction of a low bid, or where a competing firm challenges the agency's decision to allow bid correction, the agency determination regarding the existence of clear and convincing evidence is a matter of fact that GAO will not disturb in a protest absent a reasonable basis.

As can be seen from the foregoing discussion, bid correction is available regardless of whether the bidder's negligence caused the mistake. Indeed, the notion of negligence is often inherent with a mistake. At the same time, the bid mistake rules must be stringent, because the competitive system would suffer serious harm if agencies enabled bidders to cure their mistakes through the process of repeatedly resoliciting bids.

(d) Postaward Mistakes

For good reasons, the government is a much more reluctant to grant relief to a bidder that is awarded a contract and then claims a mistake in bid. Considerations of fairness to the other bidders, as well as the basic concept that a contractor should be obligated to live up to the terms of the contract (even if they turn out to be unprofitable), make this doctrine a necessity. But—under narrow circumstances— relief may be granted for mistakes asserted after award.

If the mistake alleged for the first time after award is a mutual mistake (where the government and the bidder have made the same mistake so that the contract does not express the agreement that the parties intended), the contract may be reformed to reflect the true intent of the parties. Four factors must be satisfied by a party seeking reformation of a government contract on ground of mutual mistake: (1) the parties to the contract were mistaken in their belief regarding a fact, (2) that mistaken belief constituted a basic assumption underlying the contract, (3) the mistake had a material effect on the bargain, and (4) the contract did not put the risk of the mistake on the party seeking reformation. This remedy is available only when the information constituting the mistake existed prior to contract award.

If a unilateral mistake—normally based on the bidder's negligence or carelessness in preparing the bid—is alleged, relief in the form of rescission will not be granted unless it can be shown that the Contracting Officer had actual or constructive notice of the probability of error before accepting the bid.

The verification of bids (discussed above)—if properly conducted—minimizes the number of unilateral mistake claims based on constructive Contracting Officer awareness of the mistake. On the other hand, if award is made without adequate verification, despite the presence of an apparent error in the bid (a price far lower than the other prices or the government estimate, for example), the

Contracting Officer will be said to have constructive knowledge of the mistake—that is, even if he did not actually know of the mistake, he should have known of it.

The bidder in this scenario would be entitled to relief on the general theory that a party (in this case the government) cannot "snap up" an offer that it knows (or should know) is too good to be true. If, however, it is the practice in the industry involved to submit high bids without serious expectation of receiving an award (known as "highballing"), the clustering of high bids will not require the Contracting Officer to request verification.

If the bidder can prove that the Contracting Officer was on actual or constructive notice of an error, the contract may either be reformed (to correct the mistaken contract price) or rescinded (to cancel the obligations of both parties). The FAR contains extensive requirements for bidder documentation and agency review of mistakes alleged or disclosed after award. Workpapers are not required as evidence of mistake in bid where other clear and convincing evidence supports the contention that the bidder erred.

§ 14.10 Contract Award

After bid opening, the Contracting Officer normally awards the contract to the lowest responsive responsible bidder whose bid is most advantageous to the United States considering only price and the price-related factors included in the IFB. In the very rare instance where the agency receives two or more bids that are equal in all respects, the FAR contains an order of priority for breaking the tie.

A bidder that believes it has been unjustly eliminated from a competition or improperly denied an award has a variety of arguments to use in protesting the Contracting Officer's actions. These protests can be made in any of several forums: the contracting agency that issued the solicitation, the GAO, or the Court of Federal Claims. The topic of protests is discussed in detail in Chapter 33.

An award is made either by furnishing the successful bidder with an executed award document (the contract) or by furnishing a written or electronic notice of award, if followed as soon as possible by the formal award document. Mailing or furnishing the written award or acceptance of the bid within the time for acceptance specified in the bid shall result in a binding contract without further action by either party.

This standard effectively follows the "mailbox rule" from common law contracts, which holds that written acceptance is effective when dispatched and not necessarily when received. Often, award is simple—for example, for supply and service contracts, the Contracting Officer executes the contract by filling out the bottom of the Standard Form 33, "Solicitation, Offer, and Award."

In some situations, the Contracting Officer may elect to (1) award a contract for a lesser quantity than that stated in the IFB, (2) award more than one contract for the items to be purchased (i.e., split the award), or (3) reject all bids—and then, if the government has a continuing need for the item or items, resolicit.

Award may be made for a lesser quantity of the items or units indicated under any given item unless (a) this is prohibited under the terms of the IFB or (b) the bid is on an all-or-nothing basis. Where the IFB prohibits multiple awards, only an aggregate award will be proper, regardless of the advantages of a possible split award.

If it appears that sufficient funds might not be available for all the desired items in a proposed construction contract, agency regulations may permit solicitations with additive or deductive bid items. In such procurements, the low bidder will be based on the firm that offers the lowest price for the least amount of work on the base bid less all deductive items.

Bidders are well advised to inspect the bids at the bid opening. In that way, they can detect any deviations in the bids of competitors to support a possible protest if the bidder is non-selected. Unsuccessful bidders must be notified within three days (either in writing or by electronic means) that the contract has been awarded unless the procurement is classified. If award is made to someone other than the low bidder, an explanation is necessary. If requested, the Contracting Officer will provide unsuccessful bidders with the name and address of the successful bidder, the contract price, and the location where a copy of the abstract of offers is available for inspection.

An agency's failure to follow these notification procedures generally will not affect the validity of an otherwise properly awarded contract. An exception is where the firm receives tardy notice of its rejection in a small business set aside, the firm was unable to protest by the close of business of the fifth business day after the bid opening and it thereby lost the opportunity to file a timely small business size status protest against the awardee, and the Small Business Administration later determines that the awardee was not a small business concern (see Chapter 19).

C. TWO-STEP SEALED BIDDING

§ 14.11 Two-Step Sealed Bidding

Two-step sealed bidding is a hybrid method of procurement in that is combines competitive negotiation and sealed bidding. The government may use this technique to promote the maximum competition practicable—especially in procurements for complex and technical items—when (a) available specifications are not sufficiently definite or complete for competitive bidding but definite criteria do exist for evaluating technical proposals, (b) there is more than one technically qualified source available and there is sufficient time available to evaluate each source, and (c) a firm-fixed-price or fixed-price contract with economic price adjustment can be awarded.

This method of procurement requires the Contracting Officer to work closely with technical personnel and to rely on their specialized knowledge in determining the requirements of the procurement and the criteria to be used for evaluating proposals. A principal objective of the two-step procedure is to permit the development of a sufficiently descriptive statement of the government's requirements, including the development of a technical data package, so that subsequent procurements may be made by conventional sealed bidding.

(a) Step One: Request for Technical Proposals

Step One is initiated by the issuance of a Request For Technical Proposals (RFTP). Under the FAR, the RFTP must contain certain minimum information, for example, (1) a description of the supplies or services required, (2) the evaluation criteria for selecting the winning technical proposal, (3) instructions not to include prices or price information with the technical proposal, (4) the technical proposal's due date and requirements, (5) a statement of intent to use the two-step method, and (6) a statement that in the second step, only bids based on technical proposals determined to be acceptable will be considered for award.

Each offeror will submit a detailed description of what the offeror proposes to furnish to satisfy the government's need. The technical proposals are evaluated—and frequently revised or modified—during the negotiations and discussions that follow. After negotiations, those offerors who have submitted technical proposals that the government considers acceptable are then invited to participate in Step Two. There is no consideration of cost or price during this first step.

(b) Step Two: Invitation for Bids

In Step Two of the procedure, IFBs are sent to those firms whose proposals were judged to be in the acceptable category. Each acceptable offeror then submits a sealed bid based on its own technical proposal. Then, award—without further discussion, modification, or negotiation—is made to the offeror that submits the lowest price on an acceptable technical proposal.

Agencies have substantial discretion on whether to use two step sealed bidding. With the increased use of negotiated procurement and the general decline in sealed bidding, it is relatively rare to see a two-step sealed bid procurement.

Chapter 15

CONTRACTING BY
NEGOTIATION

Analysis

This chapter examines the rules governing procurement by negotiation, specifically (a) the conditions permitting use of competitive proposals, (b) the government's solicitation, (c) the preparation and submission of proposals, (d) exchanges of information between the government and offerors, (e) discussions (negotiations) between the government and offerors in the "competitive range," (f) the evaluation of offers by the government, and (g) notices and debriefings. It also addresses unsolicited proposals. This chapter covers acquisitions with a value more than the simplified acquisition threshold (see Chapter 13).

A. GENERAL REQUIREMENTS FOR NEGOTIATION

§ 15.1   The Government's Solicitation

(a) The Government's Document

The Uniform Contract Format (UCF) as used in most procurements facilitates preparation of the solicitation and contract, as well as reference to and use of those documents by offerors and contractors. In essence, solicitations to which the uniform contract format applies include the Schedule (Part I, the solicitation or contract form, description of work and price, packaging, inspection and any special requirements), the contract clauses (required by law or regulation or peculiar to the contract called Part II) and a list of attachments or exhibits (called Part III). A final section constitutes representations and instructions (called Part IV) that is retained by the agency and not physically included in the resulting contract. The representations, certifications, and other statements of offerors, commonly called Section K, is to be incorporated into the contract by reference.

A Request for Proposals (RFP) is used in negotiated acquisitions to communicate government requirements to prospective contractors and to solicit proposals. At a minimum, the RFP must describe the government's requirement and the anticipated terms and conditions that will apply to the contract. In this way, the agency will permit offerors to prepare proposals intelligently and thereby allow the government to meet a fundamental principle of government procurement that competition must be conducted on an equal basis, i.e., offerors must be treated equally and with a common basis for the preparation of their proposals.

(b) Standard Forms

Standard forms are used for competitive proposals in much the same way they are used for sealed bids (see Chapter 14). For example, a solicitation for supplies or services to be obtained through competitive proposals may be made—as for a sealed bid procurement—on Standard Form 33. Although the same form is used in both types of procurements, a prospective offeror can easily determine which method of procurement applies by looking at the form to see whether the IFB or RFP square has been checked. The government's procedures for preparation of a Request for Proposals (RFP) are detailed in the Federal Acquisition Regulation (FAR).

(c) *Amendments*

Under the FAR, the Contracting Officer must amend the solicitation when—either before or after the receipt of proposals—the government changes its requirements or terms and conditions. For example, where the chances of the agency's exercising an option decreased significantly from the time the agency issued the solicitation, but the agency failed to amend the RFP accordingly, the GAO has sustained a protest on this ground.

Ordinarily, the agency will issue the amendment on Standard Form 30, but such use is not essential. If the Contracting Officer issues a document to all prospective offerors referencing the solicitation, this document will qualify as amendment, for example, where the Contracting Officer issues the vendor questions and agency answers about the solicitation.

Amendments issued before the date for receipt of proposals must be provided to all parties that received the solicitation. Amendments issued after the proposal submission date must be provided to all offerors that have not been eliminated from the competition. Indeed, most cases in which agencies have run afoul of the FAR on the issuance of amendments have occurred where evaluation requirements were changed without notice. Oral notices of amendments may be used where "time is of the essence" provided the Contracting Officer later formalizes the amendment in writing.

If the Contracting Officer determines that a proposed amendment is so substantial that it exceeds what prospective offerors reasonably could have anticipated, and if additional sources would likely have submitted offers had the substance of the amendment been known to them, the solicitation under FAR must be canceled and a new one issued, regardless of the stage (or nature) of the acquisition.

Questions and answers that the agency provides to offerors do not always modify or amend a solicitation. However, a Contracting Officer's clarifying response to an offeror's question, or other information this official has provided to all offerors, has been found to amend or modify a particular solicitation provision. Again, the FAR contemplate a formal RFP amendment.

As a general rule, agencies may not properly award a contract on a basis that is fundamentally different from the basis upon which the competition for the requirement was held. Thus, in one GAO decision an agency improperly awarded a contract for its actual requirements, which differed significantly from the solicited requirements, when the actual requirements constituted less than 30 percent of the requirements solicited. Where there is a significant change in the government's requirements, the appropriate course of action is for the agency to apprise the offerors of its revised requirements, and afford them an opportunity to submit proposals responsive to those revised requirements prior to the award of a contract, even where a source selection decision has tentatively been made. If the agency awards a contract with the intention to make a post-award contract change to reflect a material change, and modifies the contract accordingly, the modification can be an illegal de facto sole source modification (see § 6.4).

(d) Cancellation

The government may cancel an RFP after the submission of proposals and before award provided this action is in the best interest of the government. Cancellation may be proper even if there have been extensive negotiations with the offerors. Also, with an adequate basis, an agency properly may cancel a solicitation no matter when the information supporting the cancellation first surfaces or should have been known.

RFP cancellation before the award can be based on a variety of circumstances. Some examples are (a) the government's needs change to an extent not contemplated at the time of original solicitation, (b) the government realizes that the procurement method was not properly justified, and (c) a defective specification was included in the solicitation which so seriously affects the procurement that it cannot be cured by amendment.

Generally, the cancellation of an RFP is difficult to challenge because cancellation is a matter of Contracting Officer discretion. Unlike rejection of all bids after bid opening in sealed bid procurements, offers in a negotiated procurement have not been publicly exposed before award. For this reason, no requirement exists for a compelling reason to justify pre-award RFP cancellation as opposed to an IFB cancellation.

In one case where GAO sustained a pre-award protest against an RFP cancellation, an agency's decision to cancel a solicitation and resolicit because of inadequate competition lacked a reasonable basis.

§ 15.2   Timeliness Requirements

The FAR provides that offerors may use any method authorized by the solicitation to submit a proposal, e.g., mail, electronic commerce, or facsimile. If no submission deadline is specified in the solicitation, the deadline is 4:30 p.m. local time for the procuring office on the date that proposals are due. If an emergency or unanticipated event interrupts normal Government processes so that proposals cannot be received at the Government office designated for receipt of proposals by the exact time specified in the solicitation, and urgent Government requirements preclude amendment of the solicitation closing date, the time specified for receipt of proposals will be deemed to be extended to the same time of day specified in the solicitation on the first work day on which normal Government processes resume.

Any proposal, modification or revision that is received at the designated government office after the exact time specified for receipt of proposals is "late" and must not be considered unless (1) it is received before award is made, (2) the Contracting Officer determines that accepting the late proposal submission would not unduly delay the acquisition, and (3) there is acceptable evidence to establish that it was received at the agency facility and was under government control before the time set for receipt of proposals, or it was the only proposal received, or it was transmitted by electronic commerce and was received at the initial point of entry at the agency facility no later than 5 p.m. one working day before the date set for the receipt of proposals. Absent one of these exceptions, a late proposal is tantamount to no proposal at all, which makes the submitter a stranger to the acquisition.

Another exception to the late proposal rule is that a late modification of an otherwise successful proposal that makes its terms more favorable to the government will be considered and accepted at any time it is received. This exception does not allow the offeror to become the most advantageous proposal by reason of the late submission; the offeror already must have this status and be in line for award at that time. By contrast, a timely acknowledgment of an RFP amendment will not cure submission of a late initial proposal.

Even where the government was the partial cause of the late receipt of a proposal material, if the offeror significantly contributed to the submission's untimeliness, the proposal will not be considered. By comparison, a hand-carried proposal that arrives late may be considered if improper government action was the sole or paramount cause for the late submission. Moreover, consideration of this proposal must not compromise the integrity of the competitive procurement process; improper government action in this context is affirmative action that makes it impossible for the offeror to deliver the proposal on time. The government has no obligation, however, to escort commercial couriers to the correct room for proposal delivery.

Acceptable evidence to establish the time of receipt at the government installation includes the time/date stamp of that installation on the proposal wrapper, other documentary evidence of receipt maintained by the installation, or the statements of government personnel. Records of private commercial carriers cannot be the sole evidence that the proper contracting office timely received a submission.

The phrase, "[offers] received at the Government installation," includes electronic submissions received by a Government computer server. Therefore, in the case of an electronic delivery, the government control exception applies where the electronic proposal is received by a government server (or comparable computer) and is under the agency's control prior to the deadline. An agency's rejection of a revised proposal as "late" was unreasonable and inconsistent with the terms of the solicitation where the installation designated for receipt of proposals possessed the protester's revised proposal by the closing time for receipt of revised proposals.

A protester's late submission of an offer was not excused under the FAR Part 12, commercial item provision, FAR 52.212–1(f)(4), for disruption of "normal Government processes" where the disruption occurred at plaintiff's, rather than the receiving agency's, location.

B. SOURCE SELECTION

§ 15.3   Evaluation of Offers

(a) Evaluation Factors

To ensure commonality in the proposal preparation and evaluation processes, the RFP must adequately disclose all the factors and significant subfactors (both price-related and non-price-related) that will be considered in making an award decision and the relative importance of the combined technical factors and price. The evaluation factors represent the key areas of importance and emphasis to be considered in the source selection decision.

As the Comptroller General noted as far back as 1972 in *Arnold & Porter,* Comp. Gen. Dec. B-176223, 1972 CPD ¶ 85, "each offeror has a right to know whether the procurement is intended to achieve a minimum standard at the lowest cost or whether cost is secondary to quality." This statement is based on a key goal of government contracting—competition that is fair and equal.

Under CICA and FAR 15.304(c) price is a mandatory comparative evaluation factor. The law has recently changed. Pub. L. No. 114–328, § 25: Exception to Requirement to Include Cost or Pricing to the Government for Certain Multiple-Award Task or Delivery Order Contracts, amends 10 U.S.C.A. § 2305(a)(3)(C) to provide that, if the head of a covered DOD, NASA or Coast Guard procuring activity agency issues a solicitation for multiple task or delivery order contracts under [10 U.S.C.A. § 2304a(d)(1)(B)] for the same or similar services and intends to make a contract award to each qualifying offeror, then ([1]) cost or price to the Federal Government need not, at the Government's discretion, be considered . . . as an evaluation factor for the contract award." See also 41 U.S.C.A. § 3306(c)(3)(similar rule for civilian executive federal agencies).

If cost or price to the Government is not a comparative evaluation factor, FAR 15.304(e) shall not impose the usual requirement for the agency to disclose "whether all evaluation factors other than cost or price, when combined, are" "(I) significantly more important than cost or price; (II) approximately equal in importance to cost or price; or (III) significantly less important than cost or price." The agency must in all cases still consider whether the price is fair and reasonable even if price is not a comparative evaluation factor.

Where price is an evaluation factor, agency competition goals would be ill-served if offerors were not given any idea of the relative values of technical excellence and price. When a solicitation is silent on the relative weight to be given to price versus technical factors, price and technical considerations will be accorded approximately equal weight and importance.

Heretofore, agencies commonly used the "lowest priced technically acceptable responsible offeror" (LPTA) to represent the best value source selection decision but Congress recently concluded that this method unduly discounts non-price factors and overemphasizes price. Therefore, LPTA now is tightly controlled by statute, Pub. L. No. 114–328, § 822, Pub. L. No. 115–232, § 880, and regulation, 84 Fed. Reg. 50785 (Sept. 26, 2019); 83 Fed. Reg. 62550 (Dec. 4, 2018).

The evaluation factors used depend on the particular circumstances and can be limited or prescribed by statute and regulation. Evaluation factors generally fall into four major categories: technical, management, past performance, and price/cost.

Consistent with law and regulation, contracting officials have broad discretion in selecting evaluation factors for a source selection. It is well settled that a solicitation need not identify each element to be considered by the agency during the course of the evaluation when that consideration is intrinsic to the stated factors. An agency may consider information about the offeror outside the proposals, however, only as allowed by the RFP. Evaluation ratings, such as numerical scores or adjectival assessments, generally are only guides for intelligent decision-making in the procurement process and are not ends in themselves.

In a qualification to the last sentence in the above paragraph, the agency must describe its general approach for evaluating offerors' past performance information.

In any event, all of the solicitation's stated evaluation factors must be considered by the agency evaluators. "It is a fundamental principle in a negotiated procurement that a proposal that fails to conform to a material solicitation requirement is technically unacceptable and cannot form the basis for award."

GAO has considered numerous technical evaluation issues. Thus, for example, an evaluation was improper where the solicitation stated that proposals would be evaluated on the extent to which they exceeded a requirement but proposals that were substantially different on the same issue were still rated the same. A proposal for a government contract may not be rejected for mere clerical errors, when all material information required by solicitation is present. An individual employee's required letter of commitment is a matter of technical acceptability not offeror responsibility; the agency's judgment on offer acceptability must be reasonably based according to RFP submission instructions. An agency will improperly downgrade a proposal for failure to supply information that was not required by the solicitation. The Contracting Officer would improperly and mechanically reject a proposal as technically unacceptable after using an undisclosed government staffing estimate to determine whether the offerors' proposed staffing approaches were adequate.

In still other examples, GAO has found an evaluation unfounded where an agency: inappropriately awarded a contract where the agency knew, prior to award, that the agency's anticipated schedule for issuing task orders differed materially from the schedule in the solicitation; improperly considered the awardee's proposed approach as a benefit that exceeded the solicitation requirements when the RFP said explicitly to the contrary that this specific approach was not a benefit; evaluated quotations unequally under the "geographic coverage" evaluation factor where the agency erroneously failed to conclude that the protester quoted similar geographical information to the geographical information in the incumbent's contract; made a different evaluation of essentially the same proposal approach by two offerors in response to the same solicitation but for a different award without reconciling the differences; treated offerors unequally where the agency credited the awardee's proposal with a strength without similarly crediting the protester's proposal for the same feature; abandoned the solicitation's evaluation scheme, which provided for a qualitative evaluation of proposed personnel, by adopting a review that assessed only whether the proposed personnel met applicable requirements; and improperly evaluated proposals by relying on features not required by the request for proposals to favor the awardee's proposal and to penalize a lower-priced proposal missing such a feature.

Many protests examine subcontracting. The GAO has rejected the assertion that to be consistent with the evaluation of joint ventures and partnerships, small business offerors proposing prime-subcontractor relationships should have previously worked together as a team. The reason is the Government will have privity of contract only with the prime contractor, not the entire prime-subcontractor team. The prime is the company ultimately responsible for the work and it is not unreasonable to consider whether the prime has worked with each subcontractor at some time in the past. *Sevatec, Inc., et al.,* Comp. Gen. Dec. B-413559.3, et al., 2017 CPD ¶ 3.

In reviewing a protest of an agency's evaluation of a proposal, the GAO and the courts will not independently re-evaluate a proposal but will consider whether the evaluation was consistent with the terms of the solicitation and the applicable statutes and regulations. Proposal evaluations should not be based on a simple count of the number of strengths and weaknesses assigned to the offers. A violation of the agency's source selection plan will not usually confer enforceable rights upon a protester, except where the agency made the plan part of the solicitation.

(b) Source Selection Processes

The source selection official is not bound by the conclusions and recommendation of the lower-level evaluators, although he or she is required to consider them. Where the source selection official disagrees with the ratings and recommendations of the evaluators, however, this official's independent evaluation also must be reasonable, consistent with the stated criteria, and adequately documented on why the evaluators were incorrect.

Frequently, agency evaluators will have different subjective judgments on the relative strengths and weaknesses of proposals; therefore, such differences do not prove that the process was flawed or irrational. The overriding concern is whether the final evaluation ratings accurately reflect the relative merits of the offers. Accordingly, a final consensus should emerge, except when the Source Selection Authority overrules the evaluators, but agencies may not determine the existence of a consensus by a mechanical averaging of the individual evaluator ratings.

The source selection documentation will be inadequate when it contains only general conclusions without significant qualitative comparison of the offers. While GAO generally gives little or no weight to evaluations and judgments prepared in the heat of the adversarial process, post protest explanations that provide a detailed rationale for contemporaneous conclusions and that simply fill in previously unrecorded details will generally be considered in the GAO's review of source selection decisions, provided that those explanations are credible and consistent with the contemporaneous record.

Although not an ideal practice, an agency under GAO case law may destroy the rating sheets of the individual evaluators after the evaluators meet to create a consensus rating, provide that the remaining consensus materials support the agency's judgment. By contrast, the Court of Federal Claims in *Pitney Bowes Government Solutions, Inc. v. United States*, 93 Fed. Cl. 327 (2010), has ruled that a Contracting Officer's intentional destruction of rating sheets of individual members of technical evaluation panel violates the FAR's record-keeping provisions.

Apart from the validity of the proposal evaluation, the GAO and the courts will not sustain a protest absent a showing of competitive prejudice, that is, unless the protester demonstrates that, but for the agency's errors, the protestor would have had a substantial chance of receiving an award. In order to demonstrate unfair competitive prejudice from a waiver or relaxation of the terms and conditions of an RFP, a protester must show that it would have altered its proposal to its competitive advantage had it been given the opportunity to respond to the altered requirements.

In an off-shoot of the above principles, the protest tribunals have considered protester allegations that procurement officials were guilty of bias or bad faith in making the source selection. In such instances, a protester must present virtually irrefutable evidence that the official directed his actions with the intent to injure the protester. By contrast, where the record establishes that a government procurement official was biased in favor of one offeror, and was a significant participant in agency activities that culminated in the decisions forming the basis for protest, the need to maintain the integrity of the procurement process requires a protest by an injured offeror be sustained unless compelling evidence shows the protester was not prejudiced.

Frequently, an agency after award may decide it should take corrective action and reconsider the source selection, either on its own accord or in response to a protest. Agencies have broad discretion to do so when they deem it necessary for fair and impartial competition, even if the awardee's price has been (properly) exposed to competitors, such as in a debriefing. Courts and GAO may second-guess the decision where corrective action lacks a rational basis;

thus, for example, a court may place an agency in error for following an irrational GAO recommendation for corrective action.

§ 15.4 Government-Offeror Exchanges of Information—Prior to Competitive Range Determination

The preceding sections in Chapter 15 analyzed application of the evaluation factors; the remainder of this chapter will delve further into agency/offeror pre-award communications and other key elements of the negotiation process.

(a) Presolicitation Exchanges

In planning for a procurement, the FAR encourages "exchanges of information among all interested parties, from the earliest identification of a requirement through receipt of proposals." Among the methods of conducting these exchanges are industry and small business conferences, public hearings, market research, draft solicitations, site visits, and pre-solicitation or pre-proposal conferences.

Although the FAR cautions that "any exchanges of information must be consistent with procurement integrity requirements," the Contracting Officer to this extent may discuss an agency's requirements for the job with just a single firm provided no unfair advantage inures to that firm.

(b) Exchanges Before Submission of Offers

The FAR also encourages information exchanges after release of the solicitation and before submission of offers by way of, among other techniques, preproposal conferences and one-on-one agency/industry exchanges. FAR 15.201(f) cautions, however, that when information "that would be necessary for the preparation of proposals is disclosed to one or more potential offerors, that information shall be made available to the public as soon as practicable . . . to avoid creating an unfair competitive advantage."

(c) Oral Presentations by Offerors

The FAR provides that the government may request oral presentations by offerors to substitute for, or augment, written information. The use of oral presentations for part of a proposal can be effective in streamlining the source selection process, and they may occur at any time in the acquisition process. Oral presentations are subject, however, to the same restrictions as written submissions regarding timing and content.

Because oral presentations are intended to provide an opportunity for dialogue between the parties, pre-recorded videotaped presentations "that lack real time interactive dialogue are not considered oral presentations" although they may be included in offeror submissions when appropriate.

(d) Clarifications After Proposal Submission

"Clarifications" are limited exchanges between the government and offerors that may occur when the government contemplates making a contract award without "discussions" with eligible offerors. If award will be made without conducting discussions, offerors may be given the opportunity to clarify certain aspects of their proposals (for example, the relevance of an offeror's past performance information) or to resolve minor or clerical errors in a proposal. An award may be made without discussions as long as the solicitation announces that the government intends to evaluate proposals and make award without discussions.

While a Contracting Officer (CO) is required by the sealed-bidding procedures of FAR Part 14 to seek clarification of a suspected clerical error, FAR Part 15, which governs the process for competitive negotiations of the type at issue, has led to conflicting decisions at the COFC on whether a CO has discretion over whether to contact an offeror for the clarification of a suspected clerical error.

As a general rule, the opportunity to "clarify" proposal information and correct mistakes does not include the opportunity to revise the offer. Clarifications are not available to cure proposal deficiencies or material omissions or to alter in a material way the technical or cost elements of the proposal. The bedrock rule is that an agency is not required to permit an exchange of information as a "clarification" when the proposed exchange actually would have been "discussions (explained below)." When an agency holds discussions with an offeror for a government contract, the discussions must be held with all offerors remaining under consideration; but there is no such requirement for clarifications. These distinctions are the key features distinguishing clarifications and discussions.

The substance of the communication rather than the label used by the parties controls on whether the exchange of information was clarifications or discussions. In one case, the contracting officer's e-mail was a clarification and not discussions in asking the awardee to confirm that it understood that in a performance-based acquisition it is responsible for meeting the performance objective for the price proposed regardless of approach. Similarly, an awardee's clarification responses about what was not included in the proposal were proper clarifications because they were consistent with, and did not change, the proposal.

Thus, once the government permits an offeror to revise a proposal, the exchanges between the parties become "discussions" and trigger the requirement that the agency must provide all offerors in the competitive range or otherwise still in the running an opportunity to submit revised proposals.

(e) Communications Before Establishment of Competitive Range

"Communications" are exchanges, between the government and offerors, after the receipt of proposals, leading to establishment of the "competitive range" of offerors with which the government intends to conduct "discussions" (negotiations) before awarding the contract. If a competitive range is to be established, these "communications" are limited to (1) offerors whose past performance information is the determining factor preventing them from being placed within the competitive range and (2) offerors whose exclusion from or inclusion in the competitive range is uncertain.

Such precompetitive range communications may address adverse past performance information to which an offeror has not had prior opportunity to respond or may be conducted to enhance government understanding of proposals, allow reasonable interpretation of the proposal, or facilitate the government's evaluation process. Precompetitive range communications may also be used to address issues that must be explored to determine whether a proposal should be placed in the competitive range. They may not be used, however, to cure proposal deficiencies or material omissions, materially alter the technical or cost elements of the proposal, or otherwise revise the proposal. But they may be considered in rating proposals for the purpose of establishing the competitive range.

(f) Award Without Discussions

Normally, in competitive negotiated procurements, the government must conduct written or oral discussions with all offerors in the "competitive range." However, award may be made without discussions on the basis of initial proposals if the solicitation states that the government intends to evaluate proposals and the government in fact makes award without discussions.

An award without discussions can be made only if the offer is accepted as submitted. As mentioned earlier, some extremely limited dialogue with the offeror—referred to as "clarifications" (e.g., discussing the relevance of adverse past performance reports or to correct minor or clerical errors)—may be held. The contemporaneous nature of the actions of the parties—not merely the agency's characterization of the communication—will determine whether discussions have occurred.

The acid test for deciding whether discussions have been held is whether an offeror was provided the opportunity to revise or modify its proposal. In almost all cases, if the government conducts "discussions" with one offeror it must conduct discussions with all offerors in the competitive range.

Almost always, the courts and GAO uphold agency discretionary calls to award on initial proposals (with no discussions) as allowed by the solicitation.

§ 15.5   Competitive Range

As mentioned above, unless award is made without discussions and on the basis of initial proposals, the government must conduct written or oral discussions with all responsible offerors within the remaining offerors in the "competitive range" or otherwise still under consideration.

If the agency plans to conduct discussions, the agency is to establish a competitive range—based on the ratings of each proposal against all evaluation criteria—that is composed of "all of the most highly rated proposals, unless the range is further reduced for purposes of efficiency." If the Contracting Officer determines that the number of highly rated proposals exceeds the number at which an efficient competition can be conducted—a rare occurrence—the Contracting Officer has discretion to "limit the number of proposals in the competitive range to the greatest number that will permit an efficient competition among the most highly rated proposals," provided the solicitation so advised the offerors. Another possible reason for limiting the competitive range would be where a likelihood exists, based on facts and not mere innuendo or suspicion, that the offeror has obtained an unfair advantage.

Offerors excluded or otherwise eliminated from the competitive range must be given prompt written notice that states the basis for the determination and that a proposal revision will not be considered. The offeror also may request a pre-award debriefing.

In determining whether to include a proposal in the competitive range, the Contracting Officer must consider (1) the merits of the technical proposal, (2) its price, and (3) the responsibility of the offeror. The "responsiveness" of the proposal (better stated as "acceptability") is usually not a factor to be considered, because the very point of employing a competitive range is for the agency to allow offerors to remedy proposal weaknesses and deficiencies. An exception is that a firm is not entitled to come within the competitive range is where the offeror absolutely refuses to comply with one of the material requirements of the solicitation.

Reasonableness on the agency's part is the key to determining the proper makeup of the competitive range in a given procurement. The FAR's direction to limit the competitive range to "all of the most highly rated proposals" does not require an agency to retain even a second-ranked proposal if it reasonably concludes that the proposal has no realistic prospect of award. Given the ever present threat of protest, however, most agencies are liberal in this area and will include proposers that might otherwise be deemed marginal for award.

The formulation of discussions and composition of the competitive range is frequently tied to questions regarding the evaluation of the offers. In reviewing an agency's evaluation of proposals and subsequent competitive range determination, a protest adjudicator will not evaluate the proposals anew to make its own determination of the acceptability of offers or their relative merits.

Instead, the forum will examine the record to determine whether the evaluation was fair, reasonable, and consistent with the evaluation criteria and with procurement statutes and regulations. Thus, for example, the exclusion of a protester's offer from the competitive range as technically unacceptable can be unobjectionable where the agency reasonably concluded that the protester's proposal failed to meet the mandatory technical requirements of the RFP.

GAO has upheld a protester's exclusion from the competitive range where the protester's technical approach included essentially no explanation of how the firm would accomplish the solicitation's specific requirements. This circumstance is one example of where an agency is not required to include in the competitive range a proposal that requires major revisions to be made acceptable.

Even if an offer is initially determined to be within the competitive range, it may be excluded from the competition at a later stage of the procurement. Thus, for example, if the offeror was initially included in the competitive range, participated in discussions, and submitted a revised proposal, but the latter proposal raised new concerns about RFP compliance, the agency may still act reasonably in excluding it from further competition for good cause.

§ 15.6 Government-Offeror Exchanges of Information—After Competitive Range Determination

The scope and extent of discussions are a matter of Contracting Officer judgment. This concept can include, "persuasion, alteration of assumptions and positions, give-and-take, and may apply to price, schedule, technical requirements, type of contract, or other terms of a proposed contract."

Generally, the Contracting Officer must discuss with each offeror still being considered for award deficiencies, significant weaknesses, and adverse past performance information to which the offeror has not yet had an opportunity to respond. The Contracting Officer also may discuss other aspects of the offeror's proposal that could, in the opinion of the Contracting Officer, be altered or explained to enhance materially the proposal's potential for award. For example, the Contracting Officer may suggest to an offeror that it has exceeded mandatory minimums (in ways that are not integral to design) and that its proposal would be more competitive if the excesses were removed and the offered price decreased.

During discussions, the government may not engage in conduct that (a) favors one offeror over another, (b) reveals an offeror's "technical solution, including unique technology, innovative and unique uses of commercial items, or any information that would compromise an offeror's intellectual property to another offeror," (c) reveals an offeror's price without that offeror's permission (but the Contracting Officer may inform an offeror that its price is too low or too high and reveal the basis for that conclusion), (d) reveals the names of individuals providing reference information on an offeror's past performance, or (e) knowingly furnishes source selection information in violation of statutory and regulatory procurement integrity requirements.

Different issues regarding discussions can arise in a "lowest-priced, technically-acceptable" procurement, In one GAO case, the agency's conduct of multiple rounds of discussions with the awardee, but not the protester, was proper because the protester had improved its proposal to be rated technically acceptable following the first round of discussions and its standing therefore could not be improved through more negotiations.

The discussion rules have been subject to considerable litigation before the GAO and the courts. The Comptroller General has stated that while an agency must conduct meaningful discussions that lead an offeror into the areas of its proposal requiring amplification or revision, the agency is not required to "spoon-feed" an offeror by discussing each and every item that could be revised or explained to improve its proposal.

Along similar lines, the mere fact that a weakness became a determinative factor in choosing between two closely ranked proposals does not mean that the agency was required to raise the issue during discussions. Under FAR 15.306(d)(3), at a minimum, the agency must discuss deficiencies, significant weaknesses, or adverse past performance information to which the offeror has not yet had the opportunity to respond. Thus, the Contracting Officer need not discuss areas of a proposal that received less than a perfect rating or discuss "all proposed areas where ratings could be improved." Further, Contracting Officer is not obligated to disclose to an offeror the agency's preference for a competitor's alternative approach. Repeated discussions on identified proposal weaknesses are not legally required, although where the agency does hold discussions on a previously discussed issue, the agency must be even handed with all the firms remaining in the competition.

On the other hand, the Comptroller General has found that discussions that failed to raise a methodology issue that the agency had found unacceptable were improper and that an agency's failure to discuss its serious concern about an offeror's plan to manufacture contract items in a new plant also were inappropriate and created grounds for protest.

The agency's failure to hold meaningful discussions in accordance with FAR 15.306(d)(3) is protestable. Misleading discussions involve Government communications that are either incomplete or "incorrect, confusing or ambiguous." Thus, meaningful discussions will be absent where agency did not convey its real concerns with the vendor's submission and the procuring agency may not withhold crucial and advantageous piece of information from one offeror while providing it to another vendor.

With regard to the adequacy of discussions of price, an agency generally does not have an obligation to tell an offeror that its price is high relative to other offers, unless the government believes the price is unreasonable. If the agency believed that the undisclosed government price estimate reflected its minimum requirements, it is required to disclose that fact during discussions. Similarly, the agency's "failure to react" to the protester's erroneous position regarding the solicitation's requirements can mislead the protester and will not constitute meaningful discussions. An agency is not required to advise an offeror of a minor weakness that was not considered in choosing between two closely ranked proposals.

The question of whether an offeror is entitled to comment on adverse past performance data can be a protest issue. Unless the offeror had a prior opportunity to comment, agencies must discuss adverse past performance information with an offeror in the competitive range, even if the offeror is aware that its performance on earlier contracts was not considered outstanding—the failure to do so may create a presumption that prejudice has occurred.

However, the GAO also has concluded that a Contracting Officer is not required to provide an offeror with an opportunity to discuss adverse past performance information when it makes award on initial proposals. Similarly, the Court of Federal Claims held in *Forestry Surveys and Data v. United States*, 44 Fed. Cl. 493 (1999), that an agency may use adverse past performance information without checking with the offeror if the problem has been identified in the offeror's proposal. Somewhat inconsistently, an agency awarding on initial proposals may "clarify" such adverse information under FAR 15.306(a)(2) but this action lies within agency discretion.

§ 15.7   Proposal Revisions

The FAR provides that at the conclusion of discussions, each offeror still in the competitive range must be given an opportunity to submit a final proposal revision (previously called a best and final offer or "BAFO"). The Contracting Officer must establish a common cut-off date sufficient for receipt of the later final proposal revisions.

When requesting final proposal revisions, the Contracting Officer must advise the offerors that (1) the final proposal revisions must be in writing, and (2) the government intends to make award without obtaining further revisions. Pursuant to these procedures, an agency may accept an expired offer without reopening the competition, provided that such an acceptance will not prejudice the competitive system or allow the awardee an unfair advantage.

In one case, an offeror submitted an untimely final proposal revision but argued that the agency could still accept its timely initial proposal. The Court of Federal Claims in *Integrated Business Solutions, Inc. v. United States,* 58 Fed. Cl. 420 (2003), approved the agency's decision to reject the initial proposal where (1) the final offer revision in legal effect revoked the initial proposal, (2) the offeror's authorized representative did not reconfirm the initial proposal, and (3) the final proposal revision failed to address a material post-proposal RFP amendment.

§ 15.8   Contractor Past Performance

Under the FAR, proposal evaluation in negotiated procurements requires an assessment of both the proposal submitted and the offeror's ability to perform the prospective contract successfully. Thus, because performance on past contracts is an indicator of an offeror's ability to perform successfully, offerors' past performance information must be evaluated in all competitive negotiated procurements expected to exceed the simplified acquisition threshold unless the Contracting Officer documents why past performance is not an appropriate evaluation factor, for example, because award will be made to the lowest priced, technically acceptable offer. It bears noting, however, that even when the RFP does not make past performance a proposal selection factor, this point is always a relevant responsibility consideration (see Chapter 9).

When the agency uses past performance as a selection factor, the solicitation must (1) describe the agency's approach for evaluating past performance (including evaluating offerors with no relevant performance history), (2) provide offerors with the opportunity to identify past or current contracts similar to the government requirement, and (3) permit offerors to provide information on problems encountered and corrective actions taken on identified contracts.

The evaluation should take into account "relevant" past performance information regarding an offeror's predecessor companies, key personnel, and major subcontractors, and must consider the currency, relevance, source, and context of the information, and general trends in the contractor's performance. "Relevant" in this context, however, does not mean "identical," consistent with the RFP's evaluation scheme and how the solicitation defined the quoted term.

"Past performance information" may include the contractor's (a) record of conforming to contract requirements and to standards of good workmanship, (b) record of forecasting and controlling costs, (c) adherence to contract schedules, (d) history of reasonable and cooperative behavior and commitment to customer satisfaction, and (e) businesslike concern for the interest of the customer.

Note that if an offeror does not have a record of relevant past performance, or past performance information is otherwise not available, the offeror may not be evaluated favorably or unfavorably on past performance. With respect to an offeror's prior contract default terminations, the Comptroller has concluded that agencies may reasonably consider them, even though they have been appealed and even where they were the subject of a settlement agreement.

Past performance protest issues constitute a major item on GAO's docket. In some recent examples, GAO has sustained protests in this area where: the agency's numerical past performance scoring system unreasonably penalized the protester for submission of supplementary past performance related to less relevant contracts; the agency evaluated two proposals unequally by crediting the awardee for a subcontractor's experience and past performance, but not similarly crediting the protester, which proposed the same subcontractor; an awardee's "unknown" past performance rating was improper where the offeror failed to produce past performance information but where it was otherwise available as required by the RFP; the agency's past performance evaluation was unreasonable because the agency did not consider known relevant adverse performance information; and where the agency unreasonably assigned the awardee an "exceptional" past performance rating of awardee but had not considered certain adverse past performance information that it had received indicating that the awardee had had a number of performance problems.

The Contracting Officer has broad latitude to make performance assessments, which is one of the most highly discretionary tasks for agency evaluators and Source Selection officials. According to the Court of Federal Claims, it is a " 'well-recognized' principle that an agency's evaluation of past performance is entitled to "great deference." For example, the Federal Circuit held the agency's evaluation of the protester's past performance as "less than satisfactory" was not arbitrary and capricious even though the protester's five past performance questionnaires gave the protester overall past performance ratings of "outstanding," "better," and "satisfactory."

Agencies shall monitor their compliance obtaining and storing past performance evaluation requirements information. A recent final rule providing for Government-wide standardized past performance evaluation factors and performance rating categories also requires that past performance information be entered into the Contractor Performance Assessment Reporting System (CPARS), the single Government-wide past performance reporting system. This database accommodates the recent merger of the Past Performance Information Retrieval System (PPIRS), which in turn had been merged in the Architect-Engineer Contract Administration Support System and the Construction Contractor Appraisal Support System modules.

The transition to CPARS creates a single site for "functions such as creating and editing performance and integrity records, changes to administering users, running reports, generating performance records, and viewing/managing performance records." The final rule (1) amends FAR 42.1501(b) to remove a reference to PPIRS and to state that "CPARS is the official source for past performance information," (2) removes from FAR 42.1503(f) a reference to automatic transmission from CPARS to PPIRS, and (3) makes conforming changes throughout the FAR. The transition is part of a consolidation of federal websites, initially, at beta.SAM.gov and, eventually, at SAM.gov.

While related, past performance and experience can be separately evaluated in a solicitation. "Experience" is what the offeror did and past performance pertains to how well the offeror did on the job. In accordance with the solicitation ground rules, a past performance evaluation should—but is not required to—take into account past performance information regarding predecessor companies, key personnel who have relevant experience, or subcontractors that will perform major or critical aspects of the requirement when such information is relevant to the particular procurement.

For bundled and consolidated contracts, Pub. L. No. 114–92, § 867, requires that, when evaluating offers from small business prime contractors that include teaming arrangements, contracting agencies must consider the past performance and capabilities of first-tier subcontractors as constituting part of the capabilities and past performance of the small business prime contractor. Similarly, in evaluating offers from joint ventures, if a joint venture does not demonstrate sufficient capabilities or past performance to be considered for award, contracting agencies must consider the capabilities and past performance of each individual member of the joint venture as the capabilities and past performance of the joint venture as a whole.

Agency discretion extends into the area of selecting the past performance data that is deemed relevant to assessing the risks involved in the contract to be awarded. Agencies are regularly permitted to give greater evaluation credit to work that is highly relevant and to give lesser weight to past performance on work considered not as relevant.

An offeror's mere status as an incumbent contractor, however, does not necessarily warrant special consideration in past performance evaluations. Without more, scant but positive past performance information cannot support a negative rating. While there is no legal requirement that an agency consider all past performance references, GAO has held that some information is simply "too close at hand" to require offerors to shoulder the inequities that spring from an agency's failure to obtain and consider information. Thus, for example, GAO considers relevant past performance questionnaires in an agency's possession on a competing offeror or the awardee to be past performance information—whether adverse or positive—too close at hand to ignore.

Attribution of one entity's past performance to another's is permissible in a source selection, but with limitations. An agency may consider the performance history of one or more of the individual joint venture partners in evaluating the joint venture, provided the RFP is not expressly to the contrary (and the agency meets the recently-enacted rule of Pub. L. No. 114–92, § 867, stated above, regarding evaluation of teaming arrangements). Similarly, an agency may consider an offeror's subcontractor's project execution record when evaluating the offeror's past performance, provided that the solicitation allows for the use of subcontractors and does not prohibit the consideration of a subcontractor's projects during the evaluation.

This area of evaluation very commonly arises with the past performance of subsidiary or affiliated corporations to the proposer submitting the offer. In determining whether such a team member's performance should be attributed to the proposed prime contractor, the agency (apart from Pub. L. No. 114–92, § 867), needs to consider in accordance with the limits of the RFP whether the work force, management, facilities or other resources of one entity may affect contract performance by the other.

Some close distinctions exist in this area. In one GAO decision, an agency unreasonably credited a joint venture with past performance and corporate experience from one partner's separate affiliates, but the problem was the firm would not be relying on those affiliates during contract performance. In another GAO decision, an agency unduly restricted competition when its request for proposals provided that affiliate experience and past performance would not be considered, even if offerors demonstrated that the affiliates would participate meaningfully in performance.

§ 15.9   Price or Cost Evaluation

One key objective of proposal analysis is to ensure that the final agreed-to price is fair and reasonable. The Contracting Officer is responsible for evaluating the reasonableness of the offered prices and the analytical techniques and procedures to be used in the process. The ultimate objective is to ensure that the final price is fair and reasonable; less important is the prices of the individual elements. The complexity and circumstances of each acquisition should determine the level of detail of the analysis required.

A difference exists between price and cost analysis. Price analysis should be used to verify that the overall price offered is fair and reasonable. Price analysis shall be used when cost or pricing data are not required. Cost analysis shall be used to evaluate the reasonableness of individual cost elements when cost or pricing data (see below) are required. Cost analysis may also be used to evaluate information other than cost or pricing data to determine cost reasonableness or cost realism. The Contracting Officer may request the advice and assistance of experts to ensure that an appropriate analysis is performed.

By statute and regulation, price generally must be a substantial point of comparison for award. For this reason, the "build to budget" price evaluation method whereby every offeror proposes the same price is improper for competition purposes because such an approach disregards that price be a meaningful factor in every evaluation and further contradicts an RFP providing for a best value competition. Nevertheless, where estimates are not reasonably available, an agency may establish a notional estimate, consistent with the RFP requirements, to provide a common basis for comparing the relative costs of the proposals.

As indicated above, CICA generally requires that "cost or price must be considered in evaluation of proposals." See 10 U.S.C.A. § 2305(a)(3)(A)(ii) & 41 U.S.C.A. § 3306(c). There are two exceptions. First, 10 U.S.C.A. § 2305 does not require cost or price as a comparative evaluation factor under multiple task or delivery order contracts for the same or similar services where the agency intends to make a contract award to each qualifying offeror. Second, 41 U.S.C.A. § 3306 does not require cost or price as a comparative evaluation factor for certain indefinite delivery, indefinite quantity multiple-award contracts and certain Federal supply schedule contracts for services acquired on an hourly rate, and the executive agency intends to make a contract award to each qualifying offeror.

Where cost/price is a comparative evaluation factor, protesters have argued that under prior Comp. Gen. decisions, an evaluation that considers only whether costs/prices are fair and reasonable reduces cost/price to a nominal evaluation factor and violates CICA. However, in *Sevatec, Inc., et al.*, Comp. Gen. Dec. B-413559.3, et al., 2017 CPD ¶ 3, the GAO held that an agency's use of a "highest technically rated offeror with a fair and reasonable price" evaluation scheme was permissible under the Federal Acquisition Regulation and did not improperly fail to consider price. Statute also permits this approach in limited instances. See § 15.3(b).

A final example of an inappropriate practice would be for the agency to compare proposals to an unreasonable median price that included proposals determined to be unacceptable, ineligible for award, or priced unreasonably high.

(a) Price Analysis

The Government may use various price analysis techniques and procedures to ensure a fair and reasonable price. Examples of such techniques include, but are not limited to, the following:

1.   Comparison of proposed prices received in response to the solicitation. Normally, adequate price competition establishes price reasonableness;

2.   Comparison of previously proposed prices and previous Government and commercial contract prices with current proposed prices for the same or similar items, if both the validity of the comparison and the reasonableness of the previous price(s) can be established; and

3.   Comparison of proposed prices with independent Government cost estimates.

The first two techniques are the preferred techniques. However, if the Contracting Officer determines that information on competitive proposed prices or previous contract prices is not available or is insufficient to determine that the price is fair and reasonable, the Contracting Officer may use any reasonable technique as appropriate to the circumstances applicable to the acquisition. A comparison of an offeror's price to the Independent Government Estimate (IGE) could be irrational where the IGE was based on assumptions that were inapplicable to the offeror given its stated technical approach.

A determination of price reasonableness is a matter of administrative discretion and business judgment that will not be disturbed in a protest unless that determination is clearly unreasonable, fraudulent, or in bad faith.

(b) Cost Analysis

Cost analysis is the review and evaluation of the separate cost elements and profit in an offeror's or contractor's proposal (including cost or pricing data or information other than cost or pricing data), and the application of judgment to determine how well the proposed costs represent what the cost of the contract should be, assuming reasonable economy and efficiency. The Government may use various cost analysis techniques and procedures to ensure a fair and reasonable price, given the circumstances of the acquisition. Various techniques and procedures are available for this purpose.

One such prominent technique is the verification of cost or pricing data and evaluation of cost elements, including the necessity for, and reasonableness of, proposed costs, including allowances for contingencies, projection of the offeror's cost trends, on the basis of current and historical cost or pricing data; the reasonableness of estimates generated by appropriately calibrated and validated parametric models or cost-estimating relationships; and the application of audited or negotiated indirect cost rates, labor rates, and cost of money or other factors. In conducting this evaluation, however, the Contracting Officer shall ensure that the effects of inefficient or uneconomical past practices are not projected into the future.

Another technique is the comparison of costs proposed by the offeror for individual cost elements with actual costs previously incurred by the same offeror; previous cost estimates from the offeror or from other offerors for the same or similar items; other cost estimates received in response to the Government's request; independent Government cost estimates by technical personnel; and forecasts of planned expenditures.

The National Defense Authorization Act for Fiscal Year 2020, Pub. L. No. 116–92, § 803, deals with an offeror's failure to provide Other than Certified Cost or Pricing Data upon Request. This Section amends 10 U.S.C.A. § 2306a(d) to add that: (i) "Contracting officers shall not determine the price of a contract or subcontract to be fair and reasonable based solely on historical prices paid by the Government;" and (ii) if the contracting officer "is unable to determine proposed prices are fair and reasonable by any other means, an offeror who fails to make a good faith effort to comply with a reasonable request to submit [cost or pricing] data . . . is ineligible for award unless the head of the contracting activity . . . determines that it is in the best interest of the Government to make the award to that offeror, based on consideration of pertinent factors," some of which are identified in this Section. See also FAR 15.403–3; DFARS 215.403–3.

(c) Cost Realism and Price Realism Analysis

Cost realism analysis is the process of independently reviewing and evaluating specific elements of each offeror's proposed cost estimate to determine whether the estimated proposed cost elements are realistic for the work to be performed; reflect a clear understanding of the requirements; and are consistent with the unique methods of performance and materials described in the offeror's technical proposal. Thus, an agency would improperly evaluate proposals for cost realism purposes where its evaluation was based on a mechanical application of a Government estimate that did not consider each offeror's unique technical approach.

Cost realism analyses shall be performed on cost-reimbursement contracts to determine the probable cost of performance for each offeror if awarded the contract. The probable cost may differ from the proposed cost and should reflect the Government's best estimate of the actual cost of any contract that is most likely to result from the offeror's proposal. Therefore, even where an agency analyzing cost realism reasonably determined that an offeror did not adequately support its proposed substantial reduction in labor rates, the evaluation can still be faulty where the extent of the agency's resulting upward adjustment was excessive and unreasonable.

This cost shall be used for purposes of evaluation to determine a best value cost. It is determined by adjusting each offeror's proposed cost, and fee when appropriate, to reflect any additions or reductions in cost elements to realistic levels based on the results of the cost realism analysis. An agency will misevaluate proposals for a cost-reimbursement contract when the record does not show a logical connection between the agency's technical evaluation conclusions and its most probable cost evaluation conclusions. In making the source selection decision, the agency would act improperly if it used the offerors' proposed, rather than evaluated, costs.

Many other rules of thumb come into play with cost realism evaluations. For example, ordinarily, normalizing prices involves the measurement of offerors' costs against the same baseline (and will be proper) where there is no logical basis for differences in approach or where there is insufficient information provided with the proposals, leading to the establishment of common estimates by the agency. Where an RFP contemplated the award of a time-and-materials contract with fixed-price, fully burdened labor rates and specifically stated that "time and materials" would be "evaluated on the basis of cost realism," the agency would act improperly by excluding the time and materials labor rates from its realism assessment.

For a fixed price contract, price realism (sometimes inaccurately called cost realism in this context) may also be used on competitive fixed-price incentive contracts or, in exceptional cases, on other competitive fixed-price-type contracts when new requirements may not be fully understood by competing offerors, there are quality concerns, or past experience indicates that contractors proposed costs have resulted in quality or service shortfalls.

Results of the analysis may be used in performance risk assessments and responsibility determinations. An agency has broad discretion on conducting price realism and it can be sufficient when the agency, consistent with the solicitation, compared proposal prices to each other and to the government estimate and further determined whether the prices were commensurate with the proposed technical approaches. However, proposals shall be evaluated using the criteria in the solicitation, and the offered prices for price realism (as contrasted with cost realism) shall not be adjusted as a result of the analysis.

Agencies have continuing challenges in doing defendable price realism assessments. In recent years, GAO has found deficiencies where the agency: did not reasonably consider labor rate realism; improperly considered price realism where RFP did not state this issue would be a factor for award; and where the agency failed to consider a staffing inconsistency between the awardee's price proposal and the technical/management proposal. As with all price evaluation issues, with price realism, the agency must comply with the RFP and not depart from it in a material way without an RFP amendment and the offerors' opportunity for a revised proposal.

(d) Unbalanced Pricing

Unbalanced pricing may increase performance risk and could result in payment of unreasonably high prices. "Unbalanced pricing" exists when, despite an acceptable total evaluated price, the price of one or more contract line items is significantly over or understated as indicated by the application of cost or price analysis techniques.

The greatest risks associated with unbalanced pricing occur when startup work, mobilization, first articles, or first article testing are separate line items; base quantities and option quantities are separate line items; or the evaluated price is the aggregate of estimated quantities to be ordered under separate line items of an indefinite-delivery contract.

All offers with separately priced line items or subline items shall be analyzed to determine if the prices are unbalanced. If cost or price analysis techniques indicate that an offer is unbalanced, the Contracting Officer shall consider the risks to the Government associated with the unbalanced pricing in determining the competitive range and in making the source selection decision. The Contracting Officer also shall consider whether award of the contract will result in paying unreasonably high prices for contract performance. An offer may be rejected if the Contracting Officer determines that the lack of balance poses an unacceptable risk to the Government.

§ 15.10 Profit

FAR policy is that contractors should receive sufficient financial rewards that will stimulate efficient contract performance, attract the best qualified large and small business concerns to government contracts, and maintain a viable industrial base. Thus, it can be seen that the prime function of profit is to motivate the contractor toward efficient and effective contract performance.

Along the same lines, it is not in the government's best interest to negotiate extremely low profits or to calculate profits by using such devices as automatic applications of predetermined percentages to total estimated costs. Indeed, except as required by statute, FAR forbids administrative profit ceilings, either express or de facto.

An example of a recognized statutory profit ceiling is that for experimental, developmental or research work performed under a cost plus fixed fee (CPFF) contract, the fee must not exceed 15% of the contract's estimated cost, excluding the fee itself. Another example would be that for most other cost plus fixed fee contracts, the profit must not exceed 10% of the total estimated cost, not including the profit. This reference to "estimated cost" shows that the profit limitations are based on projected costs, and not the actual costs incurred. On the other hand, a contract negotiated in excess of a statutory profit limitation is unauthorized.

When the price negotiations are not based on cost analysis, contracting officials are not required to analyze an offeror's proposed profit. When the price negotiations are based on cost analysis, then contracting officials ordinarily will use a structured approach under agency procedures to analyze a fair and reasonable approach. This structured approach is a tool for determining the agency's pre-negotiation objective and for ensuring that all relevant factors are considered. Examples of these factors are contractor effort, material acquisition, conversion direct labor, and contract cost risk.

A good example of a structured approach to analyzing profit on contracts where price is to be negotiated is the Department of Defense's (DOD) Weighted Guidelines Method. Used in many DOD contract actions where profit analysis is required, the Weighted Guidelines method is performed through use of DD Form 1547, "Record of Weighted Guidelines Method Application."

Negotiating a profit is *not* the central focus of negotiating prices—the primary objective is the overall price the government will actually pay. Notwithstanding, according to FAR, the Contracting Officer is not to agree on profit or fee without concurrent agreement on cost and type of contract. On the other hand, FAR states that if the contractor demands an unreasonable profit, the Contracting Officer (after having explored all alternative actions) must refer the contract action to higher authority for further review.

§ 15.11 "Best Value" Source Selection

The FAR states that the "objective of source selection is to select the proposal that represents the best value" to the government. "Best value" is defined as "the expected outcome of an acquisition that, in the government's estimation, provides the greatest overall benefit in response to the requirement." FAR describes a "best value continuum" in which the importance of cost or price relative to technical or past performance considerations may vary in different types of acquisitions.

One form of a best value source selection—and probably the most commonly used method—is the "tradeoff process." A tradeoff process is appropriate for use when it may be in the government's best interest to consider award to other than the lowest priced offeror or other than the highest technically rated offeror. This process permits comparisons among cost or price and non-cost factors and allows the government to accept other than the lowest priced proposal.

In best value procurements, the agency may decide to select a lower-technically-rated proposal for a government contract, even if the solicitation emphasizes the importance of technical merit, if the agency decides that the higher price of a higher-technically-rated proposal is not justified. Conversely, an agency properly may select a higher-priced, higher-rated offer where doing so is consistent with the evaluation criteria and the agency reasonably determines that the superiority of the higher-priced offer outweighs the price difference. Both processes exemplify the trade-off method of source selection.

An agency would improperly conduct a tradeoff just between two higher rated, higher priced offers without also considering acceptable, lower priced, lower rated offers. By the same logic, the agency would improperly conduct a tradeoff just between two lower rated, lower priced offers without also considering acceptable, higher priced, higher rated offers.

The FAR suggests that an agency can obtain best value in negotiated acquisitions by using any one or a combination of source selection approaches. For example, in acquisitions where the requirement is clearly definable and risk of unsuccessful contract performance is minimal, cost or price may play a dominant role in source selection. The less definitive the requirements, the more development work required, or the greater the performance risk. However, the more an offeror's technical proposal or performance history may play a dominant role in source selection.

The government's best value source selection decision must be documented and include the rationale for any business judgments or tradeoffs made or relied upon, including benefits associated with additional costs. Generally, the Comptroller General or a court will overturn an agency's best value determination only if it is "not grounded in reason," i.e., it is inconsistent with the RFP's evaluation scheme. Many protests have been sustained where the agency failed to have an adequate record for its analysis. Protests have succeeded where the agency failed to compare all acceptable, but lower priced offers with the higher priced, but higher rated proposal in a tradeoff.

A source selection official may reasonably disagree with the ratings and recommendations of evaluators, but such an official's independent evaluations must also be reasonable, consistent with the stated evaluation factors and adequately documented on why this official disagrees with the evaluators.

§ 15.12 Truth in Negotiations Act

In 1962, Congress passed the Truth in Negotiations Act (TINA). The purpose of the Act is to put the government on an equal footing with contractors in contract negotiations by requiring contractors to provide the government with an extremely broad range of cost or pricing information relevant to the expected costs of contract performance. TINA is now formally termed the Truthful Cost or Pricing Data statute.

TINA, as amended, and the implementing procurement regulations require prime contractors and subcontractors in certain circumstances to submit cost or pricing data to the government and to certify that, to the best of their knowledge and belief, the data submitted are current, accurate, and complete. These rules have had a significant impact on government contractors: where the contractor submits inaccurate, incomplete, or non-current data, the contractor will be subject to contractual, civil, and even possible criminal liability.

(a) Applicability

Although TINA originally applied only to DOD, the National Aeronautics and Space Administration, and the Coast Guard, Congress extended the coverage of the Act to civilian executive agencies in 1985.

The Act now applies to any negotiated contract action expected to exceed $2 million. The dollar threshold for TINA applicability may be adjusted every five years to account for inflation.

When determining the threshold for application of the Act to a contract modification, the price adjustment amount includes increases and decreases totaling more than $2 million in the aggregate. For example, a modification resulting from a reduction of $800,000 and an increase of $1.4 million is a price adjustment exceeding $2 million.

The head of the contracting activity may require cost or pricing data from a contractor when the price of the contract (or modification) is less than the established threshold amount only if the head declares, in writing, that the data must be evaluated by the agency to determine the reasonableness of the contract price. The agency may not require cost or pricing data to be submitted, however, for any contract or contract modification covered by a statutory exemption. When cost or pricing data are not required, the Contracting Officer may nevertheless require the submission of the minimum of data necessary to determine price reasonableness.

(b) "Cost or Pricing Data" Defined

TINA defines the term "cost or pricing data" as follows:

[A]ll facts that, as of the date of agreement on the price of a contract (or the price of a contract modification), or, if applicable consistent with [10 U.S.C.A. § 2306(e)(1)(B)], another date agreed upon between the parties, a prudent buyer or seller would reasonably expect to affect price negotiations significantly. Such term does not include information that is judgmental but does include the factual information from which a judgment was derived.

Under the above definition of cost or pricing data, the contractor must disclose as "facts" the data forming the basis for any judgment, projection, or estimate. The nondisclosure of this data will render the submission incomplete or inaccurate.

The "date of price agreement" means the "handshake" date, even if no contract exists at that time. Data are required to be current as of the time of price agreement. Although some reasonable "lag time" is inherent between the time when data are submitted and the time of price agreement, a contractor's failure to disclose labor rates that were available when prices were negotiated will constitute defective pricing. However, new or changed facts occurring after the "handshake" date need not be disclosed.

"Significant" information necessarily excludes data on which a contractor cannot reasonably have been expected to rely in formulating its price. The concept of a "significant effect" on the price negotiations has been interpreted broadly. For example, in one case it was held that $20,000 out of a target price of $15 million was "significant." In another, an impact of $5,527 on a total price of $2.7 million was considered significant.

(c) Requiring Cost or Pricing Data

Not only does TINA require that contractors submit all cost or pricing data significant to price negotiations at the time of agreement on price, it also requires that they certify that, to the best of their knowledge and belief, the data submitted to the government are accurate, complete, and current. The FAR requires that the contractor do so in a prescribed "Certificate of Current Cost or Pricing Data." The form of the Certificate is set forth in the FAR.

The FAR provides that the Certificate should be submitted "as close as practicable to the date of agreement on price." Thus, a Certificate should not be requested by the government in the solicitation or furnished by the contractor with the proposal. The Certificate covers all cost or pricing data that are "reasonably available" at the "handshake" date.

On May 31, 2019, DOD revised Procedures, Guidance, and Information (PGI) 215.406–2 to conform with the Director, Defense Pricing/Defense Procurement and Acquisition Policy (DP/DPAP) memorandum (Shay Assad Sweep Memo) dated June 7, 2018. The new guidance made clear that the certificate was to be submitted as soon as practicable after the agreement on price (preferably within 5 days), and that contracting officers could no longer consider cost or pricing data submitted after the agreement on price unless they consider the previous agreement on price null and void and reopen negotiations. If the contractor submits cost or pricing data after the agreement on price, the contracting officer must notify the contractor that the data will not be reviewed until after contract award and will be dispositioned in accordance with FAR 15.407–1 and 52.215–10 or 52.215–11, as applicable. In other words, the agency should review the data to determine if it renders defective any of the data received before the agreement.

Note that in defective pricing cases that it is not a defense the prime or subcontractor did not submit a certificate of cost or pricing data when required to do so.

(d) Submission of Data

In October 1997, Standard Forms 1411 and 1448 for submitting and seeking exemptions from submitting cost or pricing data were both eliminated. The FAR still requires submission of essentially identical information but permits it to be submitted in the prime's or subcontractor's own format or in whatever alternate format may be specified in the solicitation.

Some definite rules exist regarding what constitutes a proper submission of cost or pricing data. At a minimum, there must be a reasonable identification of the data. Data vagueness (e.g., using only general terms in revealing lower vendor costs when viewed against the other numerous and detailed price quotations) can lead to a finding that there was no meaningful disclosure. Generally, a contractor cannot escape liability for defective cost or pricing data by proving merely that the government should have been aware that the data were defective. However, a contractor is not obligated to analyze the impact of a raw data update where the government is equally capable of analyzing the data.

Both the DFARS and the NASA FAR Supplement incorporate a proposal adequacy checklist that agencies should use as a tool as part of the price evaluation of certified cost or pricing data.

(e) Submission of Data—When Submitted

TINA requires that data be submitted before the award of a contract or modification expected to exceed the statutory price thresholds, but the FAR requires that data be submitted or identified in writing by the time of agreement on price or another time agreed upon by the parties "as close as practicable to the date of agreement on price." More than one submission of data may be necessary to comply with TINA and the implementing regulations, including a submission with the initial proposal and the updating of the data during negotiations.

(f) Submission of Data—Subcontractor Data

Any contractor or subcontractor that is required to submit cost or pricing data also shall obtain and analyze cost or pricing data before awarding any subcontract, purchase order, or modification expected to exceed the cost or pricing data threshold, unless an exception applies to that action. The contractor shall submit, or cause to be submitted by the subcontractor(s), cost or pricing data to the Government for subcontracts that are the lower of either $13.5 million or more; or both more than the pertinent certified cost or pricing data threshold and more than 10 percent of the prime contractor's proposed price, unless the contracting officer believes such submission is unnecessary.

Under TINA, a subcontractor must certify that required cost or pricing data it submits are accurate, complete, and current. A prime contractor is liable to the extent defective subcontractor (or prospective subcontractor) data cause an increase in price, costs, or fee to the government.

(g) Exceptions and Waivers

TINA provides exceptions from its cost or pricing data submission requirements for prime contracts and contract modifications where the price negotiated is based on (a) adequate price competition, (b) prices set by law or regulation, or (c) the procurement of a commercial item. In addition, in exceptional cases, the head of the contracting activity may waive TINA requirements.

In a recent statute, Pub. L. No. 114–328, § 822: Enhanced Competition Requirement, amends 10 U.S.C.A. § 2306a, Cost or Pricing Data: Truth in Negotiations, to narrow the circumstances in which an offeror for a prime contract entered into pursuant to 10 U.S.C.A. Subtitle A, Part IV, Chapter 137, is required to submit cost or pricing data before contract award. § 15.12(h) below discusses the implementation of the last-mentioned statute.

(h) Price Set by Law or Regulation

A price is "set by law or regulation," making the solicitation exempt from the cost or pricing data submission requirement, if the price is set by "a governmental body." This exception applies chiefly to public utilities and has limited application to other contractors.

(i) Commercial Item Procurements

The FAR provides that any item that meets the definition of a "commercial item" is "exempt from the requirement for cost or pricing data." To qualify for this exemption, the item solicited must satisfy detailed criteria. Specifically, it must be other than real property of a type customarily used for nongovernmental purposes, which has been offered for sale, lease, or license to the general public.

(j) Adequate Price Competition

The first basis for exemption—"adequate price competition"— has resulted in much confusion over the years. The usual method is where two or more acceptable offerors submit reasonable prices. Under the current FAR, price competition can exist even if only one offer is received from a responsible, responsive offeror provided there was a reasonable expectation, based on market research or other assessment, that two or more responsible offerors, competing independently, would submit priced offers in response to the solicitation's expressed requirement. As will be shown below, DOD, NASA and the Coast Guard take a narrower view of this exemption.

Price competition is presumed to be adequate except under circumstances delineated in the FAR. Thus, assuming that a responsible offeror submits a responsive offer, in a competitive environment, the key to finding price competition is whether the contract is to be awarded to the offeror whose proposal represents the best value where price is a substantial factor in the source selection.

Agency regulations may further refine the rules for adequate price competition (or any of the other cost or pricing data exemptions). For example, in the DOD, if there was a "reasonable expectation . . . that two or more offerors, competing independently, would submit priced offers" but only one offer is received, this circumstance does not constitute adequate price competition unless an official at a level above the contracting officer approves the determination that the price is reasonable.

The Federal Acquisition Regulatory Council has issued a final rule to create a separate standard for the Department of Defense, NASA and the Coast Guard for the "adequate price competition" exception to the requirement to submit certified cost or pricing data under the Truth in Negotiations Act. See 84 Fed. Reg. 27494 (June 12, 2019). The final rule provides guidance to DOD, NASA and the Coast Guard consistent with § 822 of Pub. L. No. 114–328.

(k) Waiver

In exceptional cases, the head of an agency may waive cost or pricing data requirements for a particular procurement. The waiver must be in writing, and the authority to grant waivers cannot be delegated.

(l) Liability for Defective Data

The "Price Reduction for Defective Cost or Pricing Data" clause states that if "any price, including profit or fee . . . was increased by any significant amount" because the contractor or subcontractor submitted data "that were not complete, accurate, and current as certified," the contract's "price or cost shall be reduced accordingly."

The contractor's liability is usually measured as the difference between the actual contract price based on the defective data and the price that would have been negotiated had accurate, complete, and current data been disclosed. The FAR also provides that the government is entitled to "recovery of any overpayment plus interest on the overpayments." In addition, if the contractor or subcontractor knowingly or intentionally submitted defective data, it may be liable for a wide variety of civil and criminal penalties, including fines, imprisonment, and suspension and debarment from contracting with the government.

The government has the burden of proof in a defective pricing data case. The elements of the claim are: (1) the information is "cost or pricing data" under TINA; (2) the data were not disclosed, or not meaningfully disclosed, to a proper government representative, and (3) the government relied on the defective data and shows by some reasonable method the amount by which the final negotiated price was overstated. An agency will fail to prove cost overstatement in TINA case where any alleged defective pricing could not have affected the prime contract price. After the government establishes a prima facie case, the contractor will have the burden to rebut the presumption that the natural and probable consequences of the defective data were an overstated contract price.

As stated above, the reliance element is a critical part of any defective pricing case. Frequently, the government's conduct during negotiations will be determinative in concluding whether the requisite reliance was present. For instance, where the government negotiators manifested a lack of confidence in one aspect of the contractor's data and developed their own data based upon the contractor's actual costs, the government failed to establish that the contractor data "would have been of major importance in price negotiations." Furthermore, where negotiations indicated that the government would not have relied on a learning curve, its contention that a learning curve should have been applied to labor cost figures was rejected.

The government's right to a price adjustment will not be affected by any of the following circumstances:

1.   The contractor or subcontractor was a sole source supplier or otherwise was in a superior bargaining position;

2.   The Contracting Officer should have known that the cost or pricing data in issue were defective even though the contractor or subcontractor took no affirmative action to bring the character of the data to the attention of the Contracting Officer;

3.   The contract was based on an agreement about the total cost of the contract and there was no agreement about the cost of each item procured under such contract; or

4.   Cost or pricing data were required, but the contractor or subcontractor did not submit a Certificate of Current Cost or Pricing Data relating to the contract.

Even where the contractor has submitted defective cost or pricing data, the contractor may be entitled to an offset under limited circumstances.

A final rule revises the FAR clauses on price reduction for defective pricing to require that compound interest calculations as required by 26 U.S.C.A. § 6622 (as opposed to simple interest) be applied to Government overpayments as a result of defective cost or pricing data.

C. POST-SELECTION MATTERS

§ 15.13 Notices and Debriefings

The FAR provides for both pre-award and postaward notices to and debriefings of unsuccessful offerors. The rules impose deadlines on the contracting agency to provide notice to unsuccessful offerors, for unsuccessful offerors to request debriefings from the agency, and on the agency to conduct debriefings that are timely requested.

The debriefings are intended to release to disappointed offerors at an early time information they can use to improve future proposals. A debriefing can also allow the offeror to make an informed decision about whether to file a protest challenging the agency's procurement decision. (Protests and debriefings are discussed in Chapter 33.) Notably, even successful offerors are entitled to a post-award debriefing and these sessions often can provide valuable feedback to an awardee.

Statute and the implementing FAR procedures require each solicitation for competitive proposals to include a statement that prescribes minimal information that shall be disclosed in post-award debriefings. The agency's failure to conduct an adequate debriefing, without more, does not create grounds for protest against an award because it is an event post-dating the award decision.

(a) Pre-Award Notices and Debriefings

Under FAR Part 15, the Contracting Officer must notify offerors promptly in writing when their proposals are excluded from the competitive range or otherwise eliminated from the competition, and the notice must state the basis for the determination.

The adequacy of the timing or detail in the rejection notice is a procedural deficiency that has no effect on the validity of an award. The unsuccessful offeror then has three days after receiving the notice of exclusion to submit a written request to the Contracting Officer for a pre-award debriefing. After receiving a timely written request for a pre-award debriefing, the Contracting Officer must "make every effort to debrief the unsuccessful offeror as soon as practicable." However, a debriefing may be delayed for "compelling reasons," and the offeror may also request that the debriefing be delayed until after award.

Pre-award debriefings may be done orally, in writing, or by any other method acceptable to the Contracting Officer. They must include (1) the agency's evaluation of significant elements in the proposal, (2) a summary of the rationale for eliminating the offeror from the competition, and (3) reasonable responses to relevant questions about whether proper source selection procedures were followed by the agency. Pre-award debriefings may not disclose, however, the number of offerors, the identity of other offerors, the content of other offerors' proposals, the ranking of other offerors, the evaluation of other offerors, or any other information that would be prohibited at a post-award debriefing.

(b) Post-Award Notices and Debriefings

After the agency awards the contract, it must notify the unsuccessful offerors in the competitive range within three days that their proposals were not accepted. This written notice must include (1) the number of prospective contractors solicited, (2) the number of proposals received, (3) the name and address of each offeror receiving an award, (4) the items, quantities, and unit prices of each award, unless impracticable, and (5) a general statement of the reasons why the offeror's proposal was not accepted, unless it is otherwise obvious. But, in no event may the agency disclose another offeror's overhead rates, trade secrets, and similar sensitive information during a debriefing.

An unsuccessful offeror has three days after receiving notice of the contract award to submit a written request for a debriefing (although the government may accommodate untimely debriefing requests) but if the request comes after the three day period, minus the extra protester rights associated with timely debriefing requests as explained in Chapter 33. The debriefing should be conducted, to the "maximum extent practicable," within five days after the agency receives the request. The debriefing information should include, at a minimum:

1.   The government's evaluation of the significant weakness or deficiencies in the offeror's proposal;

2.   The cost or price and technical rating of the successful offeror and of the debriefed offeror and past performance information on the debriefed offeror;

3.   The overall rankings of all offerors;

4.   A summary of the rationale for award; and

5.   Reasonable responses to relevant questions about whether the agency followed proper source selection procedures.

The debriefing may not include a point-by-point comparison of the debriefed offeror's proposal with other proposals and may not disclose trade secrets; privileged or confidential manufacturing processes or techniques or commercial and financial information; or the names of individuals who provided past performance information on the offeror.

Pub. L. No. 115–91, § 818, Enhanced Post-Award Debriefing Rights, provides extensive reforms liberalizing the information agencies are required to impart to debriefed offerors. In § 818(a) of the FY 2018 NDAA, Congress directed DOD to revise the Defense Federal Acquisition Regulation Supplement to require, "at a minimum," post-award debriefings for all awards valued at $10 million or more, and to require the disclosure of a redacted source selection determination for all contract awards in excess of $100 million, and, if requested by a nontraditional or small business, for awards in excess of $10 million. These requirements are currently subject to a pending DFARS case and draft proposed rule, which will incorporate the statutory requirements into regulations.

§ 15.14 Corrective Action After Award

Even after they make an award, contracting agencies have broad discretion to take corrective action in a competitive procurement where they determine that such action is necessary to ensure fair and impartial competition. Where the agency's corrective action is otherwise unobjectionable, an agency's request for revised price proposals as part of that process is not improper merely because the awardee's price has been exposed to the competition pursuant to the procedures for notification to unsuccessful offerors (FAR 15.503(b)) or in a post-award debriefing (FAR 15.506(d)).

A limited exception exists to the rules condoning awardee price disclosure where the record establishes that there was no impropriety in the original evaluation and award or that an actual impropriety did not prejudice to offerors. Thus, reopening the competition in this circumstance after prices have been disclosed does not provide any benefit to the procurement system that would justify compromising the offerors' competitive positions, and a protest against the agency's unjustified corrective action may be sustained. Similarly, protest jurisdiction can exist where an initial awardee challenges an agency's corrective action that terminated the initial contract and amended the solicitation.

Rational basis review, rather than a narrowly targeted standard, applies to an agency's corrective action. *Dell Federal Systems, LP v. United States*, 906 F.3d 982 (Fed. Cir. 2018)(disapproving cases to the contrary). An agency's discretion when taking corrective action also extends to a decision on the scope of proposal revisions, and there are circumstances where an agency may reasonably decide to limit the revisions offerors may make to their proposals. Where the corrective action does not also include amending the solicitation, GAO will not question an agency's decision to restrict proposal revisions when taking corrective action so long as it is reasonable in nature and remedies the established or suspected procurement impropriety.

In a rare example of where a tribunal sustained a protest against agency corrective action, the Court of Federal Claims rejected the agency's corrective action to re-open the award previously made to the plaintiff where no defects existed in the proposals and where no solicitation changes were necessary.

For additional discussion of corrective action, see §§ 15.3(a) & (c) above in this chapter.

§ 15.15 Unsolicited Proposals

An "unsolicited proposal" under the FAR is a written offer for a new or innovative idea that a firm submits solely on its own initiative to an agency for the purpose of obtaining a contract. Federal policy is to encourage the submission of unsolicited proposals from private sources because these offers can be a valuable means for obtaining innovative or unique ideas to satisfy agency missions. On the other hand, the agency must satisfy the competition requirements of law and regulation before government acceptance and a contract may result.

FAR contains the policies and procedures for the submission, receipt, evaluation, and acceptance of unsolicited proposals. This subpart does not govern the award of contracts (typically research or development oriented) resulting from the issuance of a solicitation, Broad Agency Announcements, Small Business Innovation Research topics, Small Business Technology Transfer Research topics, Program Research and Development, or any other Government-initiated solicitation or program. Indeed, the above listing shows, as reflected in the FAR, that unsolicited proposals commonly (but not exclusively) pertain to research or development services.

FAR recognizes that unsolicited proposals are a valuable technique for the government to use in relying on private sources to obtain innovative or unique methods to accomplish its missions. At the same time, the regulation narrowly defines just what will qualify as an "unsolicited proposal." The agency may award a contract based on an unsolicited proposal only when the action satisfies the statutory and regulatory policies for full and open competition (and its exceptions).

Chapter 16

TYPES OF CONTRACTS

Analysis

The Federal Acquisition Regulation (FAR) provides that the contract types are grouped into two basic categories for compensation purposes: fixed price contracts and cost reimbursement contracts. Furthermore, within each basic category, the FAR recognizes specific contract types, each also differing in degree of performance risk and profit incentive. This chapter will focus on the most frequently used contract types.

A.   INTRODUCTION

§ 16.1   Restrictions on Types of Contracts

In general, negotiated contracts may be of any type or combination of types as will promote the government's interests. The exceptions to this doctrine are as follows. First, contract types not described in FAR Part 16 are proscribed except as a FAR deviation. Second, various statutes or regulations can restrict the choice of contract type. Thus, federal law and regulation forbids the use of the cost-plus-percentage-of-cost system of contracting as explained in FAR 16.102(c) and § 16.3(a), infra. FAR further states that in sealed bidding, the agency may only use firm fixed price contracts or fixed price contracts with economic price adjustment clauses.

Subject to the statutory and regulatory constraints, contracting officials may exercise sound judgment in choosing the contract type, which decision will stand in a protest absent an abuse of discretion or a violation of the procurement statutes or regulations. The government's goal in selecting the proper contract is to negotiate a contract type and compensation arrangement that will result in reasonable contractor risk and that gives the contractor the greatest possible incentive for efficient performance.

B. CONTRACT TYPES

§ 16.2   Fixed Price Contracts

Fixed price contracts under FAR 16.201 have a preferred status over cost-type contracts because the ultimate cost to the government of the latter type of contract is inherently more uncertain. At the same time, the various fixed price contract types do differ in performance risk allocation and degree of profit incentive.

In keeping with this policy, Pub L. No. 114–328, § 829: DOD Preference for Fixed-Price Contracts, within 180 days of the FY 2017 NDAA's enactment, states the DFARS "shall be revised to establish a preference for fixed-price contracts, including fixed-price incentive fee contracts, in the determination of contract type."

(a) Firm Fixed Price Contracts

Under FAR 16.202, a firm fixed price contract generally is not subject to adjustment based on the contractor's cost experience during performance and thus places the appropriate responsibility, in terms of profits and losses for costs above or below the fixed price, directly upon the awardee.

The major qualification to the above rule is that the contractor is entitled to a price adjustment as allowed by clauses in the contract. The most prominent example is the "Changes" clause. Also, the contractor is entitled to compensation with unusual circumstances, which can include defective specifications, wrongly-withheld superior knowledge and breach of the duty of cooperation and noninterference that would fix liability upon the government and not the contractor for the difficulties encountered, despite the firm fixed-price nature of the contract.

Except when some contract clause allows to the contrary, all the above rules hold true even when the cost increases stem from abnormal increases in the price of supplies or other unusual trade conditions. Accordingly, this contract type provides maximum incentive for the contractor to control costs and to perform efficiently, and also places minimal administrative burdens upon the government and the contractor.

Firm fixed price contracts are well-suited for acquiring commercial products, commercial-type products or other supplies or services on the basis of reasonably definite functional or detailed specifications that will lead to fair and reasonable prices from willing vendors. Firm fixed price contracts are appropriate in these circumstances because the parties should be able to identify any significant performance uncertainties and make reasonable estimates of their cost.

(b) Fixed Price Contracts with Economic Price Adjustment

Under FAR 16.203, a fixed price contract with economic price adjustment (EPA) (formerly called a fixed price contract with escalation) provides for upward or downward revision of the contract price based on the occurrence of described contingencies. The basic purpose of a fixed price contract with an EPA clause is to protect the government in case of a decrease in labor or material and to protect the contractor in the event of an increase. This mechanism has no analogy to a liquidated damages contract clause because the EPA clause does not seek to exact damages in the event of a breach but seeks to minimize contingencies in a fixed price contract.

FAR recognizes three general types of fixed price contracts with EPA: 1. Adjustment based on catalog or market prices established in the contract; 2. Adjustment based on the costs of labor or material that the contractor actually experiences during contract performance; and 3. Adjustment based upon cost indexes of labor or material that are specifically identified in the contract. The overriding goal for all these varieties is that the adjustment will be made on an objective, predetermined basis to the extent possible, as opposed to the offerors' own standards or prices within their control, which would give the contractor an incentive to increase costs unduly during performance.

The use of a fixed price contract with EPA is not appropriate simply because a potential offeror is unable to estimate accurately its labor or material costs. Instead, procurement officials may use this contracting method only when necessary to protect both the government and the contractor from significant fluctuations in labor or material costs or to provide for contract price adjustment in the event of changes in the contractor's established price.

Put another way, serious doubt must exist concerning the stability of market or labor conditions that will exist during an extended contract period such that these contingencies cannot be adequately priced in the offer or identified in the contract. The FAR further provides that price adjustments based on established prices should normally be restricted to industry-wide contingencies, and that price adjustments based on labor and material costs should be limited to contingencies beyond the contractor's control. Similarly, the cases and regulations hold that moving base periods in this type contract is not consistent with its basic nature, because the purpose here is only to protect the contractor against fluctuations from price levels at the time of award.

Because of the variations in circumstances, the FAR does not prescribe a standard clause for an EPA clause with adjustments based on cost indexes of labor or material. Accordingly, the contracting agency must carefully tailor the clause pursuant to agency procedures to meet the specific needs of the acquisition, taking care also to avoid ambiguous escalation provisions.

An EPA clause can be used with any fixed price contract, including firm fixed price contracts or fixed price contracts with incentive or redeterminable provisions. The courts and boards have construed these EPA clauses strictly to include only those cost contingencies assumed by the parties. Absent such a clause (or an equivalent), the risk of labor or material price fluctuations is on the contractor.

§ 16.3   Cost Reimbursement Contracts

Subject to statutory and regulatory limitations, cost reimbursement contracts are suitable for use only when the uncertainties involved in contract performance do not allow the anticipated costs to be estimated with sufficient accuracy to use any type of fixed price contract.

In this regard, the GAO has stated that a procuring activity's lack of experience or success in contracting for certain goods or services may justify the reasonable use of a cost type contract until a contracting history adequate for providing a basis for a fixed price contract is available. Additionally, a cost reimbursement contract may employ more open-ended specifications than a fixed price contract; by its nature, a cost reimbursement contract significantly eliminates undue performance risk since the contractor will be entitled to recoup all allowable costs thereunder.

Pub L. No. 114–328, § 829 adds another layer to the existing limitations on a CO's ability to select a cost-reimbursement contract type set forth in FAR 16.301–2 and 16.301–3. Specifically, FAR 16.301–2 permits the use of cost-reimbursement contracts "only when—(1) [c]ircumstances do not allow the agency to define its requirements sufficiently to allow for a fixed-price type contract . . . ; or (2) [u]ncertainties involved in contract performance do not permit costs to be estimated with sufficient accuracy to use any type of fixed-price contract." Additionally, FAR 16.301–3 requires that (1) "[a] written acquisition plan has been approved and signed at least one level above the contracting officer"; (2) "[t]he contractor's accounting system is adequate for determining costs applicable to the contract or order"; and (3) "[p]rior to award of the contract or order, adequate Government resources are available to award and manage a contract other than firm-fixed-priced (see [FAR] 7.104(e))."

(a) Cost Plus Percentage of Cost Prohibition

The most important limitation regarding employment of cost contracts is the statutory and regulatory prohibition against the "cost plus a percentage of cost system of contracting" (CPPC) (see FAR 16.102(c)). In this method of contracting, the government is obligated to pay the contractor's costs, undetermined at the time the contract is made and to be incurred in the future, plus a profit based on a percentage of these future costs.

The underlying public policy is simply put. Since the contractor's profit in CPPC contracts increases in direct proportion to its incurred costs, the contractor will have every incentive to maximize the government's costs and cause inefficiency and waste in the expenditure of public funds. In effect, the CPPC contractor is penalized for efficient and economical performance and is rewarded for the converse.

The procurement adjudicators have adopted the following test for detecting a potential violation: payment is at a predetermined rate; this rate is applied to actual performance costs; the contractor's entitlement is uncertain at the time of contracting; and profit increases commensurately with increased performance costs. All four conditions must coexist before a violation will be found.

Certain pricing techniques will invariably violate the CPPC proscription. For example, pre-established, nonadjustable overhead rates based on undetermined direct cost elements are improper, as are indirect costs to be paid on a straight percentage basis of overall contract costs. On the other hand, an arrangement for after-the-fact pricing—such as when the contractor receives additional profit with a change order—will not automatically violate the CPPC doctrine under the majority rule. If the parties agree to such an improper arrangement, a CPPC contract will exist even if the parties seek to avoid any difficulty by imposing a ceiling for one or more contract costs. In this situation, the contractor has the same improper profit motivation to increase its costs up to the ceiling level.

(b) Other Limitations

By definition, all cost reimbursement contracts are unfixed at the outset regarding the final costs of performance. Therefore, a cost reimbursement contract will contain one of the standard Limitation of Cost or Limitation of Funds clauses (the former covering fully funded contracts and the latter covering incrementally funded contracts) so that the government does not improperly make expenditures or make obligations in amounts beyond those in existing congressional appropriations.

These clauses provide in part that the government is not obligated to pay the contractor's performance costs incurred above the contract's estimated cost ceiling unless the contractor gives advance written notice of the "overrun" and the government chooses to require continued performance. Several exceptions exist to this rule; for example, where the government is estopped from asserting its rights under the clause, or where the contractor's failure to give timely notice was not within its control.

FAR provides that a commercial contractor will not be entitled to recover its expenses incurred under a cost reimbursement contract unless the cost is "allowable." A cost is allowable when it is reasonable; consistent with the rules of the Cost Accounting Standards Board or with generally accepted accounting principles and practice, as applicable; consistent with the terms of the contract; in compliance with the FAR contract cost principles; and allocable.

The criteria for determining whether a cost is "reasonable" are largely open-ended and subjective. The FAR provides that a "cost is reasonable if, in its nature and amount, it does not exceed that which would be incurred by a prudent person in the conduct of competitive business." In determining whether a cost is reasonable, a number of considerations will be reviewed, including the contractor's "responsibilities to the government, other customers, the owners of the business, employees, and the public at large." A contractor's incurred costs for the FAR covered-contracts are not presumed to be reasonable; rather, "the burden of proof shall be upon the contractor to establish that such cost is reasonable." However, a contractor's decisions regarding its business affairs will be accorded some deference. The government should not superimpose its determinations concerning business matters on those of a contractor.

Generally, a cost is "allocable" when it is assignable or chargeable to one or more contract cost objectives on the basis of relative benefits received or other equitable relationship. Thus, consistent with the general rule, a cost will be allocable when it is incurred specifically for the contract; benefits both the contract and other work (and can be distributed in reasonable proportion amongst these efforts); or the cost is necessary to the overall operation of the contractor's business (although a direct relationship cannot be demonstrated between the cost objective and the cost).

(c) Cost Plus Incentive Fee Contracts

A cost plus incentive fee (CPIF) contract under FAR 16.405–1 is a cost reimbursement contract with an initially negotiated profit that can be adjusted later by a contractual formula based on the relationship of total allowable costs to total target costs.

These contracts are appropriate for use in development and test acquisitions where the contractor can be properly motivated to manage its costs effectively. CPIF contracts will state a target cost, a target fee, minimum and maximum fees, and the fee adjustment formula. After contract performance, the contractor's fee will be determined in accordance with the pre-established formula.

The formula will permit (within limits) increases in fee above the target fee when the total allowable costs are below the target costs and the converse is true when the total allowable costs exceed target costs. When the contractor's total allowable costs are below the range of costs contemplated by the formula, the contractor will receive its allowable costs plus the maximum fee. When the allowable costs are above the formula cost range, the contractor will receive its allowable costs plus the minimum fee.

Thus, a CPIF contract is functionally equivalent to a Cost Plus Fixed Fee Contract (CPFF) when there is an extreme cost underrun or overrun. The Comptroller General has emphasized the need for the parties to conduct meaningful discussions on the proposed targets.

(d) Cost Plus Award Fee Contracts

A cost plus award fee (CPAF) contract under FAR 16.405–2 & FAR 16.305 is a cost reimbursement contract that provides for a base fee fixed at the inception of the contract plus an award fee. The amount of the award fee is based on the government's unilateral evaluation of the contractor's performance at stated intervals. In this respect, the contractor is motivated through the award fee to seek excellence in such areas as quality, timeliness, and cost effective management.

In response to a Federal Circuit decision, *Burnside-Ott Aviation Training Center v. Dalton*, 107 F.3d 854 (Fed. Cir. 1997), FAR provides that CPAF contracts will no longer provide that the amount of the award fee is non-disputable, although FAR retains the rule that the government will set the award fee methodology and award the fee amount. Of course, the parties can negotiate the award fee methodology when included in the solicitation, which is the preferred practice. Under long standing precedent, the contractor may appeal whether the government complied with the established procedures for determining the award fee. Some agency regulations include guidance for evaluating contractor performance for purposes of granting the award fee.

Used principally with service contracts, CPAF contracts are appropriate under the following circumstances. First, the work to be performed is such that it is neither feasible nor effective to devise predetermined objective incentive targets applicable to contract performance requirements. Second, the use of this contract type will enhance the likelihood of meeting acquisition objectives. Third, the agency's additional administrative effort in monitoring performance is expected to be justified by the added benefits. Also, in the Department of Defense, CPAF contracts may not be used as an administrative technique to avoid using a cost plus fixed fee or cost plus incentive fee contract when the criteria for the latter contract types will apply.

(e) Cost Plus Fixed Fee Contracts

A cost plus fixed fee (CPFF) contract under FAR 16.306 is a cost reimbursement contract that provides for payment of a negotiated fee which is fixed at the inception of the contract. The fixed fee will not vary based on actual costs of performance but may be adjusted as a result of changes in the work performed under the contract.

This contract type poses significant cost risk for the agency. It provides the contractor with minimum incentive to control costs precisely because of the predetermined feet arrangement. On the other hand, the fixed fee provision may persuade the contractor to enter into an otherwise risky arrangement from its perspective.

Under FAR, a CPFF contract is suitable in various circumstances. For example, the contract can be proper for performance of research or preliminary exploration or study where the required level of effort is unknown. Such a contract may also be appropriate where the contract is for development and test, and the use of a cost plus incentive fee contract is not practical. On the other hand, a CPFF contract generally is inappropriate for use in the development of "major systems" once the government has established reasonably firm performance objectives and schedules. In the Department of Defense, this contract type can be suitable when the level of effort required is unknown and the standards for use of a cost plus award fee contract are not applicable.

CPFF contracts have two basic forms—completion and term. The "completion" version describes the scope of work by stating a definite goal or target and specifying an end product. Ordinarily, this version requires the contractor to furnish the specified end product—

such as a final report—within the estimated cost, if possible, as a condition for the payment of the entire fixed fee.

When the work cannot be completed within the estimated cost, the Contracting Officer may require more effort at an increased cost, but without a fee increase. The completion version is preferred over the term variety when the work, or specific milestones for the work, can be defined well enough in advance for the development of estimates.

The "term" version describes the scope of work in general terms and requires the contractor to devote a specified level of effort for a particular time period. No end product is envisioned as compared with the completion version. When the Contracting Officer determines that performance is satisfactory, the government will pay the fixed fee upon the expiration of the agreed-upon period, so long as the contractor certifies that it has expended the effort specified in the contract for performing the work.

Renewal is possible, but only as a new acquisition with new costs and fee arrangements. The term version may not be used when the contract obligates the contractor to provide a specific level of effort within a definite time period.

§ 16.4   Indefinite Delivery Contracts

FAR describes three types of indefinite delivery contracts: definite quantity contracts, requirements contracts, and indefinite quantity contracts. These contracts are bilateral instruments wherein the government reserves the right, after the execution of the basic contract, to issue "orders" for specified services or supplies in a particular amount and at a particular time and place as permitted by the basic instrument.

These contract types are "indefinite" in that the exact times or quantities of future deliveries will be unknown at the time of contract award. The principal advantage of indefinite delivery contracts is that they permit government stocks to be maintained at minimum levels and allow direct shipment to the users. Another benefit is that they are based upon a single contract for a specified period of time, which further reduces the government's administrative costs and processing time.

FAR 16.501–2(c) states that indefinite delivery contracts may use any appropriate cost or pricing arrangement. Also, the Comptroller General has held that indefinite delivery contracts may employ orders that use a cost reimbursement compensation approach.

In accordance with the general rule, the agency has reasonable discretion—as guided by the regulatory criteria—in selecting a particular indefinite delivery type contract. One key restriction, implicit in FAR, is that use of indefinite delivery contracts is unauthorized when the agency has available funds and the exact times and quantities of future deliveries are known at the time of contract award. In proper circumstances, agencies may also combine indefinite delivery contract types.

Implementing statute, FAR creates important policies and procedures for indefinite delivery contracts. In one such policy, FAR 16.504(c) establishes a preference to the maximum practicable extent for making multiple awards of delivery order contracts and task order contracts. As stated in FAR, agencies may even make multiple award Architect-Engineer (A-E) contracts subject to A-E selection procedures (see Chapter 36).

A "delivery order contract" means a contract for supplies, and a "task order contract" is a contract for services under the FAR. The terms "issuance" and "award" of a task or delivery order are synonymous.

(a) Definite Quantity Contracts

A definite quantity contract under FAR 16.502 provides for the delivery of a defined quantity of supplies or services for a fixed period, with deliveries scheduled for specified locations upon order. Except as prescribed in the contract, no limitation exists on the number of orders the government may issue. A contract can still be for a definite quantity when it includes options.

FAR permits use of this contract type when the government can determine in advance a definite quantity of supplies or services that will be needed over the entire contract period, and when the supplies or services are regularly available or will be available with a short lead time. These contracts are indefinite only in the sense that the amount or timing of each order is not known at the time of contract award.

In some cases, a contract could arguably be construed as either a requirements contract or a definite quantity contract, such as when the contract calls for "about" or "more or less" a specific number of supply items. The prevailing rule is that the contract will be deemed to be for a definite quantity where the quoted terms were intended to protect against accidental and inconsequential variations in quantity as opposed to when these terms are intended to express a broader scope or to have more extensive significance.

(b) *Requirements Contracts*

A requirements contract is a contract under FAR 16.503 wherein the agency agrees to buy all of its actual purchase requirements for designated supplies or services from a particular supplier, and the supplier agrees, in turn, to fill all the agency's needs during the contract period. Therefore, a contract will not be a requirements contract where it contained no language demonstrating the contractor's exclusive provision of the supplies or services. The government will meet its needs through in-scope orders issued according to the contract schedule (which actions do not have to be synopsized in SAM.gov).

The funds for a requirements contract are typically obligated by each order, not by the contract itself. The agency may include options with a requirements contract, although the agency should not use options when a requirements contract will meet all the agency's needs. The regulation does limit requirements contracts, however, to where the government cannot predetermine the precise quantity of supplies or services that designated government activities will need during a definite time period.

Requirements contracts lack an obligation for the agency to order a specific amount, which raises the issue of whether these agreements are illusory for lack of mutual obligations. A proposed requirements contract will be illusory when it disclaims the government's obligation to order its requirements from the contractor. The procurement adjudicators have held that the agency's obligations are enforceable by its promise to turn to the seller for all such purchase requirements as do develop, even when the contract contains the standard convenience termination contract clause. Thus, a guaranteed minimum—which is sometimes found in these agreements—adds nothing to the enforceability of a requirements contract.

Sometimes, a question may arise on whether a contract is a requirements contract or an indefinite quantity contract (the latter explained in FAR 16.504 & 16.505). Based on the terms of the agreement, as well as the surrounding circumstances, the distinguishing feature is whether the government has committed to satisfying all of its contractual needs from the contractor. Thus, under the majority view, if the contract expressly or impliedly permits the government to assign contractually specified work elsewhere (in-house or to other contractors), the agreement will be deemed an indefinite quantity contract.

If the contract states that the government will purchase those needs from no source other than the contractor, it will be a requirements contract. If a contract is reasonably susceptible of interpretation as either an indefinite quantity contract without minimum agreement or as one for requirements, the procurement adjudicator will uphold it as of the requirements type.

For informational purposes, the Contracting Officer must, as practicable, state in the solicitation and resulting contract a realistic estimated total quantity of the various supplies or services. The estimate is not a contractual guarantee that the government will order the entire quantity or that conditions affecting the contract will be stable and normal. Ensuring the use of the best and most current information available, the Contracting Officer may (with due care) base the agency's anticipated future needs on records of previous requirements and consumption, or on other relevant information.

The agency should not merely parrot current workload figures in the solicitation. When the contractual need arises, the government must issue orders using reasonable discretion and good faith, although the agency's alleged mere improper failure to issue an order is a non-protestable issue of contract administration before the GAO.

FAR has no mandate that a requirements contract place a maximum or minimum limitation upon the estimated requirements. When feasible, however, the regulation requires that a requirements contract shall state the maximum limit of the contractor's obligation to deliver supplies or services, and the government's obligation to order them. The contract also may specify maximum or minimum quantities that the government may purchase under each individual order and the maximum that the government may order during a specified time period, which can be on a multiyear basis. The failure to state a minimum overall quantity will not render the contract invalid, because the agreement to procure all the agency's contractual requirements will constitute sufficient consideration.

The Government can breach a requirements contract by diverting work from the contactor otherwise within the scope of the contract.

(c) Indefinite Quantity Contracts

An indefinite quantity (IQ) contract provides for an indefinite quantity—within stated contract limits—of specific supplies or services to be furnished during a fixed period. According to FAR, IQ contracts may be used when the government cannot predetermine, above the specified minimum, the precise quantities of supplies or services that will be needed during the contract period, and when it is inadvisable for the government to commit itself for more than the stated minimum. Deliveries under an IQ contract are scheduled by placing in-scope orders with the contractor, which orders do not have to be synopsized in the SAM.gov.

Because of the inherent uncertainty of IQ contracts, agencies sometimes have legitimate difficulty in conducting a proper price evaluation for these acquisitions. Citing established principles, the GAO observed in *Lockheed, IMS*, Comp. Gen. Dec. B-248686, 92-2 CPD ¶ 180, that notwithstanding these difficulties, agencies must still give significant consideration to cost during source selection:

> Uncertainty over what ultimately would be needed is not itself a reason to ignore cost, particularly when the cost of the indefinite services is expected to be significant. Uncertainty is inherent in the use of indefinite quantity, indefinite delivery contracts. Nonetheless, in light of the statutory and regulatory requirements that cost be considered in the award of contracts, even when this type of contract is used, cost must be evaluated to the extent possible. To this end, agencies have developed various methods of evaluating proposed costs when level of effort and specific tasks that may ultimately be required during performance are not known. One method is the use of sample tasks or hypothetical plans that are representative of what is anticipated to be acquired during contract performance. Another method is the development of estimates for the various labor categories required.

Nevertheless, agencies still often have difficulty in performing these pricing evaluations. In one solicitation for an ID, IQ contract, the agency did not provide sufficient information to allow a common price evaluation basis because the agency requested unit pricing, but did not provide estimated quantities in the solicitation.

Although it is inherent with an IQ contract that the government is not able to identify all its needs in advance of contracting, an enforceable IQ contract will require the government to order and the contractor to furnish at least a stated minimum of supplies or services that the government is fairly certain to order, which must be more than a nominal amount. A recent Civilian Board of Contract Appeals decision rejected an agency argument that there can be no breach of an ID, IQ contract once the agency has made the minimum guaranteed purchase. The board reasoned that other contract terms implied the contractor would be fairly considered for future work, even after the minimum has been ordered.

It bears emphasis that the necessary flexibility in an RFP for an IQ contract will not excuse the agency from actually identifying its needs in the solicitation. The existence of this stated minimum further helps protect the contractor from the uncertainties of government ordering, provides a means of measuring breach of contract damages, and saves this contract for being illusory for lack of mutual obligations.

An agency will violate the statutory bona fide needs rule under fiscal law where it lacks a legitimate need for the guaranteed-minimum quantities specified in an indefinite-delivery, indefinite-quantity contract in the fiscal year of the award. As indicated above, FAR states that an IQ contract must announce a stated minimum quantity that can be ordered under the contract (but which need not necessarily be designated on a contract schedule line item basis).

Where the contract had no guaranteed minimum it is an invalid ID/IQ contract, entitling contractor only to payment for work actually performed. Conversely, FAR requires the contract to announce a stated maximum estimate. In obtaining the basis for this maximum quantity, the Contracting Officer may rely on the records of past requirements and consumption or on other reasonable data, but the maximum quantity should be realistic and based on the most current information available.

Furthermore, the contract may specify maximum or minimum quantities that the government can order under each task or delivery order and the maximum that it may order during a particular time period. The government may be liable under an ID, IQ contract for damages if the contractor can show by a preponderance of evidence that the government: (1) failed to prepare an estimate in good faith, (2) prepared an estimate negligently, or (3) failed to use reasonable care).

Lockheed Martin Integrated Sys., Inc., ASBCA 59508 et al., 17-1 BCA ¶ 36597, addressed FAR 42.202, which states generally that prime contractors are responsible for managing their subcontractors. The ASBCA held that unless FAR 42.202 appears in the prime contract, the Government will lack a cause of action against the prime contractor for its failure to manage its subcontractor's inefficient incurrence of costs.

It bears emphasis that the seller under a standard IQ contract simply agrees to provide whatever quantity of goods or services that the buyer chooses to purchase from the seller, as limited by the contract. With a standard IQ contract, even if the buyer has requirements above the stated minimum, it is not obligated to purchase them from the seller but may resort to other sources. Accordingly, contracting on an indefinite quantity basis poses certain risks that potential contractors can address in their proposed prices.

FAR 16.504(c) states a strong preference for multiple awards of indefinite-quantity contracts under a single solicitation for the same or similar supplies or services to two or more sources. However, all awardees must be given a fair opportunity to compete for each task or delivery order placed under multiple award contracts, with some exceptions.

One such exception to the multiple award preference is where only one contractor is qualified to meet the agency's needs for unique or highly specialized supplies or services. The key issues that the Contracting Officer must consider in determining the number of contracts to be awarded are (a) the scope and complexity of the contract, (b) the expected duration and frequency of task or delivery orders, (c) the mix of resources a contractor must have to perform satisfactorily, and (d) the ability to maintain competition among the awardees throughout the contract's period of performance.

It is critical to understand that a different set of protest rules exists for the award of task or delivery orders under IQ contracts as opposed to protests against the award of the basic IQ contracts themselves.

Implementing 10 U.S.C.A. § 2304c(d) (for military agencies) and 41 U.S.C.A. § 4106(f) (for civilian agencies) (FASA), FAR 16.505 provides that no protest under FAR subpart 33.1 is authorized in connection with the issuance or proposed issuance of an order under a task-order contract or delivery-order contract, except—

(A) A protest on the grounds that the order increases the scope, period, or maximum value of the contract; or

(B)(1) For agencies other than DOD, NASA, and the Coast Guard, a protest of an order valued in excess of $10 million (41 U.S.C.A. § 4106(f)); or

(2) For DOD, NASA, or the Coast Guard, a protest of an order valued in excess of $25 million (10 U.S.C.A § 2304c(e)).

GAO has exclusive jurisdiction for protests of orders in excess of the thresholds stated in para. (B)(1, 2). above. There are no similar dollar threshold rules for prime contracts as compared with orders thereunder.

The COFC has held that the FASA bar on protests in connection with the issuance and proposed issuance of task and delivery orders precludes protests of agency's planning process for a sole source task order. By contrast, COFC has said that the task order protest bar of 41 U.S.C.A. § 4106(f) does not apply to a protest involving a task order under a blanket purchase agreement.

The GAO, however, has accepted one other qualification to the "no protest" general rule. Thus, the GAO will accept protest jurisdiction with a "down selection," i.e., where the RFP for a task order under a multiple award ID, IQ contract contemplated only a single competitive source selection for specific items based on the proposals submitted in response to that RFP, and did not involve an assignment of work based on further competition among the awardees. Similarly, GAO will consider a protest that the agency had failed to consider a small business set aside under the statutory and regulatory criteria before the agency places such a task or delivery order. GAO also will accept protests against Blanket Purchase Agreements, which are not considered task or delivery order contracts.

Some divisions of authority exist on the contractual nature of task orders. A split exists between the GAO and the ASBCA on whether delivery or task orders represent the government's exercise of existing contract rights, as held by the ASBCA, or whether they are separate stand-alone acquisitions, as held by GAO. An authority split also exists between the Court of Federal Claims and the GAO on whether the protest bar exists to task order modifications. Yet another division of authority exists between the Court of Federal Claims and the ASBCA, where the judges have disagreed on whether the tribunals retain Contract Disputes Act jurisdiction for a breach of a fair opportunity to compete. See Edwards, Postscript: Breadth of Loss of the Fair Opportunity to Compete, 20 Nash & Cibinic Rep. ¶ 59 (Dec. 2006).

Pub. L. No. 110–417, § 863, implemented by FAR subpart 16.5, requires—in general—competitive procedures for purchases over the simplified acquisition threshold under multiple-award contracts (MACs). These competition procedures include those that provide notice (including a description of the work and the bases for evaluation) to all contractors under the MAC and afford those contractors a "fair opportunity" to be considered for award. DOD contracts already were subject to substantially similar requirements under Defense FAR Supplement, which was imposed by § 803 of the FY 2002 National Defense Authorization Act (Pub. L. No. 107–107).

For actions over the applicable threshold, the scope of GAO's exclusive protest jurisdiction over MATOC orders is determined by the value of the task order as awarded, rather than the amount stated in the protester's proposal. GAO's jurisdiction over a task order protest includes the value of task order option to extend services under FAR 52.217–8 when it was part of the total evaluated price. Splitting procurements to avoid the threshold is improper.

The National Defense Authorization Act for FY 2020, Pub. L. No. 116–92, § 874, addresses post-award explanations for unsuccessful offerors for certain contracts. It states that by June 17, 2020, the FAR "shall be revised to require that" for "an offer for a task order or delivery order . . . greater than the simplified acquisition threshold [currently, $250,000] and less than or equal to $5,500,000 issued under an [IDIQ] contract, the contracting officer shall, upon written request from an unsuccessful offeror, provide a brief explanation as to why such offeror was unsuccessful." This explanation shall include "a summary of the rationale for the award and an evaluation of the significant weak or deficient factors in the offeror's offer." This is not the equivalent of a debriefing, which offerors are entitled to after an award of an order exceeding $5.5 million. See FAR 16.505(b)(1)(iv)(E), (b)(6).

§ 16.5   Time-and-Materials and Labor Hour Contracts

(a) Time-and-Materials Contracts

With a time-and-materials (T & M) contract, the contractor will provide services for a specified time period at fixed hourly rates for various labor categories described in the schedule. These rates will include employee wages, as well as a burden for general and administrative expenses, overhead and profit. Additionally, the contractor will be reimbursed for certain other costs of performance, such as applicable travel, materials, and material handling charges. Because the contractor is compensated on an hourly basis for a specific time for its "best efforts" rather than for a particular end product such as a completed supply item or service, T & M contracts are level-of-effort contracts.

T & M contracts are disfavored and may be used only in limited cases. As recognized in FAR, the contractor under this arrangement has every incentive to maximize its labor hours and cause inefficiencies, because its overall profit and overhead compensation will increase accordingly. Therefore, the agency may use a T & M contract only when it is not possible at the time of contract placement to estimate accurately the extent or duration of the work or to anticipate costs with any reasonable degree of confidence.

Also, the government must monitor contractor performance to ensure that the contractor uses efficient methods and effective cost controls. If a T & M contractor does not support its labor costs with data, it may be required to return payments, because it has a contractual duty to keep accurate records. Some examples of where T & M contracts can be appropriate are for acquisition of engineering and design services; dies and special tooling; repair, maintenance, and overhaul work; and of work to be performed in emergency situations. FAR imposes additional limitations on use of T & M contracts. First, the Contracting Officer may use this instrument only after executing a Determination and Finding (D & F) that no other contract type is suitable. (In some agencies, a higher level official must approve this determination.). Second, the contract must contain a ceiling price that the contractor may exceed at its own risk, except with Contracting Officer approval.

A standard contract clause used in T & M contracts, indicates that this ceiling actually functions like a limitation-of-cost provision characteristic of cost reimbursement contracts. The inclusion of overhead and profit in the fixed rates for labor saves the contract from being a cost plus a percentage of cost system of contracting (CPPC). The Government under a time and materials contract (or a labor hour contract)(described in § 16.5(b) below) is obligated under FAR 52.232–7 to pay a contractor in full for hours its employees worked, regardless of whether the contractor paid the salaried employees for those hours.

A final FAR rule establishes procedures for the raising of ceiling prices or otherwise changing the scope of work for time-and-material or labor-hour contracts and orders. Under the new procedures, agencies must document an analysis of pricing and other relevant factors before determining that the revision of the ceiling price is in the best interest of the Government.

(b) Labor Hour Contracts

A labor hour contract is a variation of the time-and-materials contract and differs only in that the contractor provides no "materials" to the agency. Thus, a labor hour contract basically provides for the procurement of services at specified fixed hourly rates that include direct and indirect labor, overhead, and profit. The same FAR rules on application and limitations for use of time-and-materials (T & M) contracts apply for labor hour contracts.

One confusing element of labor hour contracts, noted above, is that under the definition, the contractor provides no "materials" to the agency. The problem with this definition is that "materials " under the FAR on T&M contracts includes such items as "other direct costs," e.g., incidental services for which there is not a labor category specified in the contract, travel, computer usage charges, and applicable indirect costs. Thus, literally interpreted, a contractor under a labor hour contract cannot provide travel or charge overhead but the opposite undoubtedly occurs every day.

§ 16.6   Letter Contracts

A letter contract is a written preliminary contractual instrument (or part of an instrument) that authorizes the contractor to commence performance immediately. In effect, this contract instructs the awardee, "Move out, and we'll settle the remaining details later."

Given their preliminary nature, letter contracts—which can be either the fixed price or cost reimbursement type—are usually in the form of an actual letter (with attachments) to be countersigned by the contractor. The procurement adjudicators have held that these agreements are enforceable only when they contain the basic elements of a contract. Therefore, if the agency conditions its acceptance of the letter contract on the execution of the superseding definitive agreement, there will be no enforceable agreement.

The letter contract should be as complete and definite as possible under the circumstances. Thus, this instrument must contain a negotiation "definitization"—finalization—schedule, including a date for submission of the contractor's price proposal and a target date for definitization within 180 days after the date of the letter contract or before completion of 40% of the work, whichever occurs first. The parties may authorize an additional period in extreme cases in compliance with agency procedures.

When the parties reach agreement, the definitized agreement will supersede the letter agreement. If the parties cannot negotiate a definite contract—and both parties are under a duty of good faith negotiation—the contractor is nevertheless required to proceed with the work. The Contracting Officer may then determine, in accordance with agency procedures, a reasonable price or fee subject to appeal as provided in the Disputes Clause of the contract.

Undefinitized actions such as letter contracts are disfavored precisely because their largely open-ended nature encourages the contractor to incur maximum costs and thereby pose high risk for the agency. Indeed, the Government Accountability Office (GAO) has noted that these agreements could violate the rules against cost plus a percentage of cost system of contracting contracts (see FAR 16.102(c)) when the contractor completes the work before definitization. Thus, the regulations impose additional controls on use of this contract type. The most important of these restrictions are described below.

First, FAR requires the Contracting Officer to obtain the prior written determination of the head of the agency's contracting activity (or a designee) that no other contract type is suitable. In addition, FAR mandates that the agency include a standard contract clause,

Limitation of Government Liability, to state the government's maximum liability for the costs of performance prior to definitization.

Generally, this ceiling will not exceed 50% of the estimated cost of the definitive contract. The reason for this clause is to ensure that the contractor does not incur costs in excess of amounts available in appropriations or apportionments available for that contract. Finally, FAR requires the inclusion of the standard contract clauses required by regulation for the type of definitive contract contemplated as well as any other appropriate clauses. It further bears emphasis that even though letter contracts frequently are based on urgency, they can be competitive or noncompetitive. Thus, the agency must comply with the FAR competition requirements when the agency uses other than full and open competition in making the award.

Implementing § 812 of the National Defense Authorization Act for Fiscal Year 2010, a DFARS rule makes requirements for DOD management and oversight of certain unpriced change orders consistent with those that apply to other undefinitized contract actions.

Other controls are in place. Under the revised 10 U.S.C.A. § 2326, "[n]o undefinitized contractual action [UCA] may extend beyond 90 days without a written determination by the Secretary of the military department concerned, the head of the Defense Agency concerned, the commander of the combatant command concerned, or the Under Secretary of Defense for Acquisition, Technology, and Logistics (as applicable) that it is in the best interests of the military department, the Defense Agency, the combatant command, or the [DOD], respectively, to continue the action."

§ 16.7   Agreements to Enter into Contractual Commitments

(a) Basic Agreements

FAR establishes the policies and procedures for what may be called agreements to enter into contractual commitments. In one variety, a basic agreement (BA) is a written instrument of understanding between the parties, but it is not a contract. Instead, this arrangement contemplates separate future contracts to be awarded thereunder.

These separate contracts will incorporate by reference or attachment the required and applicable contract clauses described in the basic agreement. Therefore, neither party assumes any obligation simply by executing the agreement. A BA should be used when the government contemplates a substantial number of separate contracts to be awarded during a particular period and where the agency has experienced significant recurring negotiating problems with the contractor. BAs may be used with negotiated fixed price or cost reimbursement contracts.

Each BA will grant either party the unrestrained right to discontinue the future applicability of the arrangement by giving 30 days advance written notice to the other side. The agency must review the agreement at least annually to ensure that it conforms to the FAR requirements. FAR sets three limits upon basic agreements. First, they may not cite appropriations or obligate funds. Second, they may not state or imply any agreement by the government to place future contracts or orders with the vendor. Third, they may not be used to restrict competition.

(b) Basic Ordering Agreements

A basic ordering agreement (BOA) resembles a Basic Agreement, with two principal qualifications. First, a BOA will contain a description, as specific as practicable, of the supplies or services to be ordered. Second, it will contain methods for pricing, issuing, and delivering future orders.

It bears emphasis that a true BOA is not a contract, but that the orders issued thereunder will be individual contracts. Similarly, the BOA by itself does not create a binding obligation on the government's part to order any goods or services from the BOA vendor. A BOA does not resemble a requirements contract—a BOA is only an understanding, not an obligation, that the agency may enter into future contracts should the need for certain supplies or services arise. On the other hand, the contractor will be obligated to perform orders issued under the BOA's standards.

A BOA is appropriate for use when it is needed to expedite contracting for substantial requirements that are uncertain at the time of agreement. The proper use of this arrangement can create economies by reducing administrative lead time, inventory investment, and inventory obsolescence because of design changes.

According to FAR, BOAs will state the following terms:

1. A description of the methods for determining prices;

2. The delivery terms (or the method for determining them);

3. The government purchasing activities authorized to issue orders;

4. The point at which each order will become a binding contract;

5.   A statement that the failure to reach agreement on price for any order issued before the price is established will constitute a dispute under the Disputes Clause of the BOA; and

6.   Special data pertaining to "fast pay" procedures, as applicable.

The agency must review BOAs annually and revise them as necessary to ensure that they conform to the FAR requirements. The agency may revise BOAs only by modifying the basic agreement and not by revising the individual orders. A BOA modification may not retroactively affect orders previously issued.

The Contracting Officer must maximize competition before issuing an order under a BOA. Thus, the FAR synopsis requirements will control, as will the FAR competition requirements. The use of a BOA may not be prejudicial to other offerors. In sum, the Contracting Officer must treat each order under a BOA as if the contract were awarded independently of the BOA. Ordinarily, the Contracting Officer may neither make a final commitment nor authorize the contractor to begin work on an order unless the prices have been established. Limited exceptions exist to this rule, such as where the order has a ceiling price and there is a compelling and unusual urgency (but no order may be priced retroactively in its entirety).

Chapter 17

OPTIONS

Analysis

§ 17.1   Basic Concepts

The Federal Acquisition Regulation (FAR) prescribes the policies and procedures for the use of options, which are quite common in federal acquisitions. Except as provided by agency regulations, these FAR rules are inapplicable to the following classes of contracts: services involving the construction, alteration, or repair of real property; architect engineer services; and research and development services. In practice, however, most agencies follow the standard option policies even for these excepted categories.

An "option" under the FAR refers to the government's unilateral right in the contract whereby, for a specified time, the government may choose to (1) purchase additional supplies or services called for by the contract, or (2) extend the term of the contract. Put another way, an option under the procurement regulations is an unaccepted, irrevocable offer from the contractor to sell upon agreed terms, which binds the contractor after being unilaterally accepted by the government in its discretion. Therefore, the contractor derives no benefit from the mere existence of the option, and the government is not bound in any sense until it acts upon the standing offer.

An option should be clear and definite and should not require further negotiations to work out important and essential terms. This doctrine stems largely from the view that an option can be a contract on its own terms and therefore must contain all the prerequisites for an enforceable agreement. Therefore, the essential terms of an option and the corresponding commitment on the part of the contractor ordinarily have to be established at the time the underlying contract is awarded, although there is some authority to the contrary as will be explained below. If they are not fully established, the prevailing view is that there is no option for exercise by the government.

To bind the optionor (the contractor), the government's acceptance of the option must be "unqualified, absolute, unconditional, unequivocal, unambiguous, positive, without reservation, and according to the terms and conditions of the option." Otherwise, the government will terminate its power of option acceptance and make a counter offer, which may be accepted by the contractor as permitted by the contract and the procurement laws and regulations.

A key exception to this rule is that where the contractor-caused delay prevents the agency from timely exercising the option, the option exercise will still be valid if the agency exercises the option as soon as practicable thereafter. Another exception is that if the government's "acceptance" revises the option beyond the scope of the contract, the action must satisfy, as applicable, the FAR competition requirements.

§ 17.2   Use of Options

The Contracting Officer may include an option in a solicitation and resulting contract when this determination is in the government's best interests and does not unduly restrict competition. In view of the agency's primary responsibility to determine its minimum needs, the Comptroller General has said that a mere difference of opinion between the agency and a protester concerning the agency's needs for an option is not sufficient to upset an agency's determination. Instead, for a challenge to succeed, the record must contain clear evidence that the decision to include an option is arbitrary or unreasonable.

Notwithstanding the potential benefits of options, the FAR also recognizes their possible anti-competitive effect. Each inclusion of an option is a single source transaction. Accordingly, FAR imposes various restrictions on use of options. For example, the Contracting Officer ordinarily may not use options when the solicitation's foreseeable requirements involve quantities of supplies or services large enough to permit the recovery of startup costs and the production of the required items at a reasonable price, and there are delivery requirements far enough into the future to permit competitive acquisition, production and delivery.

Furthermore, the Contracting Officer may not use options when the market prices for the supplies or services involved are likely to change substantially over the life of the contract. The rationale here is to preclude offerors from including undue contingencies in their pricing. In contrast to its earlier cases, the GAO no longer imposes any per se restrictions on the permissible quantity of option items in relation to the basic contract quantity. Agencies may impose such restrictions, however, by regulation.

§ 17.3   Exercise of Options

It bears emphasis that those who propose on government contracts bear the risk that the agency may not exercise the option. When the government does exercise an option, the Contracting Officer ordinarily must provide any required advance written notice thereof (which could include an e-mail message) to the contractor in compliance with the means for communicating the exercise and the time period as stated in the contract.

Ordinarily, the contract will contain standard FAR clause, "Option to Extend the Term of the Contract," when firm performance extensions are contemplated. When no period for the exercise is stated, the Contracting Officer must exercise the option during the period of performance then in effect. Ordinarily, the option exercise will be effective on the date received by the contractor, unless otherwise agreed to by the parties.

In *AllWorld Language Consultants, Inc.*, B-411481.3, 2016 CPD ¶ 12, GAO held in construing FAR Part 8 that an agency could not exercise options included in an Federal Supply Schedule (FSS) order after the underlying FSS contract's ordering period had expired, even if the FSS order containing the option was issued *during* the FSS contract's ordering period. It remains undecided whether the same general doctrine governs outside of FAR part 8. See generally Jay Devecchio, Government Contractor ¶ 265, FEATURE COMMENT: Keeping Your Options Open—Why Not To Worry About GAO's *AllWorld* Decision On Task Order Options, 58 No. 29 Govt Contractor ¶ 265 (August 3, 2016).

(a) Form and Timing of Notice

The contractor cannot be held bound when the government fails to give the requisite timely notice to exercise the option. On the other hand, the notice requirement included in the contract exists for the protection of the contractor, and so it may waive this right expressly or by conduct.

Therefore, under one line of authority when the incumbent contractor accepts a late option exercise, the boards of contract appeal have indicated that a valid obligation can result even as the out of time exercise could entitle the contractor to an equitable adjustment on a constructive change theory. See *TECOM*, IBCA No. 2970 A-1, 95-2 BCA ¶ 27607. Other cases say when the agency attempts exercise an option after its expiration, the action is a nullity as an option exercise because the option is no longer part of the contract (absent a savings clause). The only way for the agency to obtain the supplies or services is through a sole source under CICA and FAR 6.302–1. See *Seven Resorts, Inc. v. United States*, 112 Fed. Cl. 745 (2013); *Washington National Arena Limited Partnership*, B-219136, 85-2 CPD ¶ 435.

In almost all instances, contractors rarely will object to the mode or timing of the option exercise, and the contractor may waive the departure from option terms. Contractors rarely regret the original bargain or look for a means to exit the contract. In one CBCA case, the government's failure to exercise the option after initially providing notice to the contractor of the agency's intent to exercise that option was not a breach of the covenant of good faith and fair dealing.

A contractor's willingness to accept a late option does not excuse the agency from obeying the competition rules. As indicated above, the question of timely notice for option exercise must be distinguished from whether the option is still viable. The GAO observed in the *Washington National Area* case, cited above, if the option performance term has expired, the agency no longer has an option to exercise, regardless of whether the contractor is willing to accept the delinquent notification. In this situation, the contract action can only be justified as an urgency acquisition or a sole source procurement. This doctrine, however, has not been reconciled with the views of the board of contract appeals mentioned above.

(b) Best Interests Requirement

Because the proper exercise of an option permits an agency to satisfy current needs for goods or services without going through formal competitive procedures, the FAR provides for transactions encompassed by FAR Part 17 that before an option can be exercised the agency must ensure that the option exercise is in its best interests.

FAR 17.207 requires that the Contracting Officer may exercise an option only after executing a written determination that funds are available; that the requirement covered by the option satisfies an existing government need; that the exercise of the option is the most advantageous method of filling the government's needs; that price and all other relevant factors have been considered; the performances of the contractor has been acceptable, and that the option had been synopsized in accordance with FAR (except where an exemption applies).

The Contracting Officer must further document for the contract file that the option exercise complies with the terms of the option and the requirements of the FAR, including the competition requirements. The exercise of unpriced options is improper absent independent compliance with the requirements for noncompetitive actions. Supplementary agency regulations may impose additional agency obligations.

(c) Competition Rules

In general, an option exercise under FAR 17.207(f) will meet the competition requirements of FAR where the option was evaluated as part of the initial competition, and where the option is exercisable at an amount contained in or reasonably determinable from the contract. This rule is particularly important with FAR 52.217–8, which is a contract option clause when exercised allows a six month performance extension. This clause is primarily intended to serve as a bridge contract for the agency to cover its mission where a disappointed offeror files a protest against a successor contract award to the contract recently performed.

Subject to certain restraints, such as the statutory requirement that funds be available, contracting officials have broad discretion on whether to exercise an option or to proceed with a separate, new procurement. In deciding whether an option or a new procurement is most advantageous to the government, and considering price and other factors, the Contracting Officer must base his decision on one of the following considerations:

1. The agency issues a new solicitation which fails to produce a better offer than the option. The Contracting Officer should not use this method of testing the market when the agency anticipates that the option represents the most advantageous offer;

2. The Contracting Officer's informal analysis of prices or examination of the market indicates that the option is more advantageous; or

3. The time between the option exercise and the award of the basic contract is so short that the option price appears to be the most advantageous to the government. When relying on this theory, the Contracting Officer must consider factors such as market stability and the need for continuity in government operations.

If the agency issues an RFP to solicit new offers for items covered by a contractor's options, the agency must advise offerors that their offers will be compared with the options. This comparison is decisive regarding the award. Furthermore, this disclosure stems from the agency's general obligation to provide offerors with sufficient detail about the evaluation criteria so as to ensure equal treatment of the competitors.

(d) Protests and Disputes

Often, the agency's decision to forego exercising an option will cause a financial loss for the contractor, who might have invested heavily in equipment or incurred other startup costs in the expectation that the annual renewal options would be exercised. In reviewing protests from incumbent contractors on this basis, the Comptroller General has said that offerors take the risk when proposing on a government contract that the agency might not exercise a unilateral option. The agency may even make this determination without making a cost comparison between a new acquisition and an option exercise.

Absent a prejudicial violation of applicable statutes or regulations, the GAO has held repeatedly that the issuance of a new solicitation rather than an option exercise, or the failure to exercise an option at all, is a matter of contract administration outside the GAO's bid protest function, even when the contractor alleges agency bad faith in the decision. The sole exception is that the GAO will consider such a protest when the agency failed to exercise the option after conducting a competition to determine whether the option would be exercised.

Similarly, the Court of Federal Claims has recently held that the government's alleged improper bad faith failure to exercise an option is a contract dispute under the Contract Disputes Act and not a protest under the revised Tucker Act. Again, the chance for success is small.

By contrast, the GAO has considered numerous protests from aggrieved prospective offerors that a new acquisition is required because the agency allegedly improperly exercised an incumbent contractor's option. Frequently, the protesting firm was a competitor on the original acquisition who now alleges that it can guarantee a lower price than the awardee for the option items. On what basis may such a protest succeed?

In responding to such allegations, the GAO generally will not question the exercise of an option unless the protester shows that applicable regulations were not followed or that the agency's determination to exercise the option, rather than conduct a new procurement, was unreasonable. The intent of the regulations is not to afford a firm that offered higher prices under an original solicitation an opportunity to remedy this business judgment by undercutting the option price of the successful offeror.

While it may be appropriate in certain circumstances for a Contracting Officer to contact all available sources to determine whether an option price is most advantageous, such a procedure is not mandated by regulation. The FAR grants the Contracting Officer wide discretion in determining what constitutes a reasonable check on prices available in the market; therefore, no requirement exists for resoliciting before exercising an option simply because a competitor guarantees a lower price after the option exercise.

On the other hand, an option exercise will be questionable when the agency's requirements have changed significantly since the original contract award and where the agency makes no real effort to determine whether the option exercise will be the most advantageous method of meeting its requirements. Similarly, an option exercise is improper when it fails to meet the FAR 17.207 competition standards.

If the agency wishes to revise the option terms, and if price competition is unavailable, the safest course of action is for the agency to exercise the option "as is" (with no express or implied conditions) and then to make any revisions to the terms in compliance with the standard Changes Clause. Otherwise, an option that requires additional negotiations on price or on other material terms can be challenged as an improper sole source award.

Part IV

SOCIOECONOMIC
PROGRAMS

Chapter 19

SOCIOECONOMIC
REQUIREMENTS

Analysis

Although the government's primary interest in procuring goods and services is to obtain them on a competitive, best value basis, the government has also implemented various socioeconomic objectives throughout the procurement process. Thus, programs have been created (and implemented through FAR Part 19) that provide certain contracting preferences to small and small disadvantaged businesses, women-and disabled veteran-owned small businesses, and small businesses located in historically underutilized business zones (HUBZones). This chapter will focus primarily on the FAR based programs.

With an exception for certificates of competency (discussed below), according to FAR 19.000(b), FAR Part 19 currently applies only in the United States or its outlying areas (although a proposed FAR change as of the date of this writing aims to change this rule to apply outside these areas).

It bears noting that the Small Business Administration regulations, 13 C.F.R. § 125.2(c)(1), state that agencies are required to foster the participation of small business concerns as prime contractors and subcontractors in the contracting opportunities of the Government regardless of the place of performance of the contract. This regulation goes beyond the bounds of the current FAR 19.000(d) and its limitation to the United States and its outlying areas, therefore placing agencies in a bind on whether the FAR or the SBA regulations is controlling.

No cases address this FAR/SBA discrepancy. Because this Hornbook primarily analyzes the FAR, it will go with the FAR policies, even though a FAR change is likely and the usual rule is that the SBA regulations control over the FAR in a conflict. Readers are advised to check the continuing validity of FAR 19.000(d) when researching a small business issue.

In addition to meeting small business objectives, contracting officers must comply with other socio-economic policies arising under various laws, such as the federal environmental laws and labor standards statutes. This chapter discusses many of these preferences and requirements. Note that some of the laws addressed in this chapter do not apply to contracts for the acquisition of commercial items, such as the Drug-Free Workplace Act and the Walsh-Healey Act.

§ 19.1   Small Business Preferences

(a) Small Business Concerns

To qualify for preferential procurement treatment as a "small business concern," a business concern must be independently owned and operated and not dominant in its field of operation and must qualify as a small business under the size standard applicable to the procurement. Size standards, which are stated in terms of either maximum number of employees or maximum annual receipts, are established by the Small Business Administration (SBA) on an industry-by-industry basis using the North American Industrial Classification System (NAICS).

On December 17, 2018, President Trump signed into law the Small Business Runway Extension Act of 2018, Pub. L. No. 115–324. The Act changes the formula for determining whether a firm meets revenue-based small business size standards by lengthening the period for calculating average annual receipts from three years to five years. The Act does not change any revenue limits or impact size standards for manufacturing contracts, which are based on employee count. The purpose of the change is to prevent firms from prematurely becoming ineligible for small business programs because of spikes in revenue. The Small Business Act has issued its final rule implementing the Runway Act. See 84 Fed. Reg. 66561 (Dec. 5, 2019); 84 Fed. Reg. 29399 (June 24, 2019).

The SBA publishes a table listing the small business size standards for each industry classification. The GAO has no protest jurisdiction regarding small business size standards and standard industrial classifications. Challenges of established size standards or the size status of particular firms, and challenges of the agency's selected standard industrial classification, may be reviewed by the SBA.

By comparison, the GAO has held that where the awardee was found by the SBA to be other than small based on a timely size protest filed after award on a small business set-aside, and this determination was not appealed, the agency, in the absence of legitimate countervailing reasons, should have terminated the contract and obtained these services from a small business. Furthermore, the Court of Federal Claims has jurisdiction to decide matters otherwise within the SBA's jurisdiction insofar as the court can grant relief without remanding the case to the SBA's Office of Hearings and Appeals.

Section 1341 of Pub. L. No. 111–240 states that an application or proposal submitted to a government procurement officer, or even registration in a government data base, to be considered for a small business set aside indicating that the applicant is a small business, will be considered an affirmative, willful and intentional certification that the business meets the qualifications to be designated as a small business concern.

DOD has issued a final rule amending the DFARS to clarify that entering into a contract may cause a small business to eventually exceed the applicable small business size standard. 80 Fed. Reg. 30116 (May 26, 2015).

The Small Business Administration has issued its long-awaited final rule providing for a new mentor-protégé program for all small businesses. Prior to the creation of this new program, the SBA maintained a mentor-protégé program that was limited to only 8(a) small businesses. See 81 Fed. Reg. 48558 (July 25, 2016).

(b) Contract Set-Asides

The most common method by which the government gives preference in its procurements to small business concerns is by "setting aside" i.e., restricting, all or part of a proposed procurement for exclusive participation by small business concerns.

A set-aside will be present when the solicitation contains language expressly identifying the procurement as a set-aside. "Tiered" or "cascading" set-asides—i.e., an RFP procedure that divides a competition into tiers based on socio-economic classifications—also are permissible under SBA regulations and the FAR.

Some recent statutes and regulations address set asides. In accordance with § 1347 of the Small Business Jobs Act, Pub. L. No. 111–240, no order of precedence exists among the 8(a) Program (subpart 19.8), HUBZone Program (subpart 19.13), or Service-Disabled Veteran-Owned Small Business (SDVOSB) Procurement Program (subpart 19.14), according to FAR 19.203(a), as amended. For acquisitions above the "simplified acquisition threshold (see Chapter 13), however, Contracting Officers must consider an 8(a), HUBZone or SDVOSB set-aside or sole-source award before using a general small business set-aside. SBA's Women Owned Small Business program provides for parity with the 8(a), HUBZone and SDVOSB programs.

To avoid the problem of front organizations purporting to be small business concerns, FAR 52.219–14 prescribes a minimum percentage of the cost of contract performance incurred for employees of the small business concern, depending on whether the contract is for services, supplies, or general construction.

Some socio-economic programs exist outside the FAR framework. For example, the Veterans Entrepreneurship and Small Business Development Act of 1999, 38 U.S.C.A § 8127, expands existing programs and establishes new assistance programs for veterans, especially those with service-related disabilities, who own at least 51% of and control a small business concern. See *Kingdomware Technologies, Inc. v. United States*, 136 S. Ct. 1969, 195 L.Ed.2d 334 (2016)(analyzing program). The Small Business Administration (SBA) has implemented a final rule that shifts to the SBA the responsibility for the Department of Veterans Affairs' verification of veteran-owned small businesses (VOSBs) and service-disabled VOSBs (SDVOSBs). See 83 Fed. Reg. 48908 (Sept. 28, 2018).

(c) Total Set-Asides

Each contract for supplies or services that has an anticipated dollar value exceeding $3,500 ($20,000 for acquisitions as described in FAR 13.201(g)(1)), but not over the usual simplified acquisition threshold of $150,000 ($750,000 for acquisitions described in paragraph (1)(i) of the simplified acquisition threshold definition at FAR 2.101) will be exclusively for small business participation unless the Contracting Officer determines that there is not a reasonable expectation of obtaining offers from two or more responsible small business concerns that are competitive in terms of market price, quality, and delivery. Contracts more than the simplified acquisition threshold (see Chapter 13) must be set-aside for exclusive small business participation if there is a reasonable expectation that (1) offers will be received from at least two responsible small business concerns offering the products of different small business concerns, and (2) award will be made at fair market prices. An unrestricted solicitation will be improper when the Contracting Officer failed to conduct adequate market research or to consider the responses to the agency's pre-solicitation notice of a possible set-aside.

(d) Partial Set-Asides

Under the FAR, if the criteria for a total small business set-aside are not met, a portion of an individual procurement—not including construction—generally must be set-aside for exclusive small business participation when (a) the requirement is severable into two or more economic production runs or reasonable lots, (b) one or more small business concerns are expected to be able to furnish the set-aside work at a fair market price, and (c) the procurement exceeds the simplified acquisition threshold.

When the government decides to use a partial set-aside under FAR 19.502–3, the procurement is divided into a nonset-aside portion and a set-aside portion. Offers are first obtained on the nonset-aside portion from all interested firms, whether or not they are small business concerns. After the award prices for the nonset-aside portion have been determined, negotiations are conducted— exclusively with small business concerns—for the set-aside portion. However, to be eligible to participate in those negotiations, a small business concern must have submitted a responsive offer on the nonset-aside portion. As a general rule, awards of the set-aside portion are made at the highest unit price for each item awarded on the nonset-aside portion, adjusted to reflect transportation and other cost factors considered in evaluating offers on the nonset-aside portion.

The Small Business Act and the FAR address multiple award contracts and small business set asides. In 2013, the SBA regulations implementing the revised Small Business Act changed the definition of a partial small business set aside (which version the FAR has not yet adopted as of the publication of this Hornbook). A "partial set-aside" under the SBA regulations occurs with a multiple award contract. When market research indicates that a total set-aside is not appropriate, agencies may use this partial set-aside technique where the procurement can be broken up into smaller discrete portions or categories, such as contract line items, special item number, functional area, or any other means for identifying various parts of a requirement as identified by the contracting officer. The key prerequisite is that two or more small business concerns are reasonably expected to submit an offer on the set-aside part or parts of the requirement at a fair market price.

This discrepancy between the FAR and SBA regulations on partial small business set asides is unfortunate. The agencies and offerors should be able to rely on the FAR without consulting the SBA regulations on such a basic point. The usual rule is that where the FAR and SBA regulations are inconsistent, the SBA procedures will govern in an area of SBA jurisdiction (as they should in the above circumstance).

Under FAR 15.503, in procurements that have been set-aside for small businesses, either on a total or partial basis, the contracting agency must inform each unsuccessful offeror, in writing, of the identity of the apparent successful offeror prior to making award. Where an agency fails to provide pre-award notification of the identity of the prospective awardee on a small business set-aside, and the awardee is ultimately found by the SBA to be other than small based upon a timely size protest filed after award, the agency should terminate the contract and obtain the services from a small business offeror.

(e) Certificates of Competency

Under certain circumstances, the SBA has statutory authority to certify the responsibility of any small business concern. A Certificate of Competency (COC) is a written certification by the SBA that a particular small business has the capability to perform a specific government contract.

Contracting Officers must accept a COC as establishing conclusively all elements of a prospective contractor's responsibility, including capability, competency, capacity, credit, integrity, perseverance, tenacity, and limitations on subcontracting. The COC program is thus a procedural method by which small business concerns are given special treatment in government procurements.

If a Contracting Officer determines that a small business otherwise in line for the contract lacks certain elements of responsibility, the Contracting Officer must withhold award and refer the matter to the SBA. The SBA then offers the small business an opportunity to apply for a COC. If a Contracting Officer has substantial doubt as to the concern's ability to perform, the Contracting Officer and the SBA must make every effort to reach a resolution before the SBA takes final action on a COC. An appeal process exists within the SBA hierarchy if the agency disagrees with the local SBA officials. However, the ultimate determination of the SBA whether to issue a COC is conclusive and must be accepted by the Contracting Officer.

The SBA can refuse to issue a COC for a reason not questioned by the Contracting Officer. As a result, it is possible that a Contracting Officer could be legally required to award a contract to a small business concern even though the Contracting Officer believes the firm is not qualified to perform the contract. Note that the SBA's denial of a COC to a small business concern does not necessarily prohibit the Contracting Officer from making an award to the concern—although that outcome would be a rarity. The SBA's denial, however, would not preclude that concern from competing for other contracts.

In limited circumstances, the GAO will review protests concerning referrals made under the COC program, or the issuance of, or refusal to issue, a COC. GAO will review such protests when they show possible bad faith on the part of governmental officials, or when they present allegations that the SBA failed to follow its own published regulations or failed to consider vital information bearing on the firm's responsibility because of the manner in which the information was presented to or withheld from the SBA by the procuring agency. The COFC has protest jurisdiction to review the SBA's denial of an offeror's application for a COC.

(f) Small Disadvantaged Businesses

A firm that qualifies as a "small business concern owned and controlled by socially and economically disadvantaged individuals"— commonly known as a small disadvantaged business (SDB)—is accorded greater preference in procurement than an ordinary small business concern. To qualify as an SDB, a firm must (1) meet the Small Business Act's definition of "small business concern,"(2) be at least 51% owned or controlled by socially and economically disadvantaged individuals, and (3) be under the control of such individuals for its management and daily business operations.

SDBs may qualify for the SBA's "8(a) program" (discussed below). The SBA's regulations have changed the requirements for firms that certify their status as small disadvantaged businesses for purposes of federal prime contracts and subcontracts. Currently, only those firms that have applied to and been certified as small disadvantaged businesses by SBA may certify themselves to be small disadvantaged businesses for federal prime and subcontracts. The rule allows firms to self-represent their status for subcontracting purposes without first receiving SBA certification.

A rare decision by the Supreme Court in the procurement field injected some uncertainty into the validity of some small business FAR regulations. In *Adarand Constructors, Inc. v. Pena*, 515 U.S. 200, 115 S. Ct. 2097, 132 L.Ed.2d 15 (1995), the Court held that race-based affirmative action programs must meet a strict scrutiny test to withstand constitutional challenges. This decision resulted in a major governmental review and reform of affirmative action programs as federal and state agencies devised programs that were not as race-conscious and that complied with the Supreme Court's strict scrutiny test.

In response to *Adarand*, among other things, the SBA's regulations governing the SDB programs were revised to reflect new categories of individuals considered to be socially and economically disadvantaged. Also, courts have held that the statute underlying the Small Business Administration's (SBA) 8(a) business development program, 15 U.S.C.A. § 637, uses facially race-neutral terms of eligibility to identify individual victims of discrimination, prejudice or bias, without presuming that members of certain racial, ethnic or cultural groups qualify for the program See *Rothe Dev., Inc. v. U.S. Dep't of Def.*, 836 F.3d 57 (D.C. Cir. 2016).

(g) The "8(a)" Program

One of the most important advantages available to an SDB contractor is the right to participate in the SBA's "8(a) program" (derived from § 8(a) of the Small Business Act). Under this program, the SBA obtains contract awards from other agencies and subcontracts the work—in whole or in part—to eligible SDB contractors.

Based on the 1998 amendments to the SBA's 8(a) program regulations, the SBA may also delegate its contracting authority to agencies, thus allowing them to enter into 8(a) contracts directly with program participants. These delegations of authority remove the SBA from its traditional contract "middleman" or oversight role but do not affect the SBA's authority to determine the eligibility of firms to participate in the 8(a) program. They also do not change the fact that the SBA remains the prime contractor (at least in theory). Indeed, the regulations continue to provide that the SBA enters into the contract and the 8(a) firm is a subcontractor.

In addition to the entry requirement that the individual on whom the firm's SDB status is based have a net worth of less than $250,000, to be eligible to participate in the 8(a) program, a small business must have been in business for two full years and have demonstrated a "potential for success." An SDB's eligibility to receive awards under the 8(a) program is limited to nine years, after which the firm is considered to have "graduated" from the program. The nine year program term may be shortened only by termination, early graduation or voluntary graduation. Unfortunately, experience has shown that many 8(a) business concerns do not become viable businesses after graduation.

Procurements appropriate for inclusion in the 8(a) program may be identified by the SBA, a program participant, or the procuring agency. Contracts with an 8(a) concern may be awarded under the program on either a sole-source or a competitive basis. Awards are made on the basis of competition restricted to eligible 8(a) program participants if (1) there is a reasonable expectation that at least two eligible participants will submit offers and the award can be made at a fair market price, and (2) the anticipated contract price will exceed $7 million for manufacturing and $4 million for all other contract opportunities.

The SBA may appeal to the agency head a Contracting Officer's decision (a) not to make a particular acquisition available for award under the 8(a) program, (b) to reject a specific 8(a) firm for award of an 8(a) contract, or (c) on the terms and conditions of a proposed 8(a) contract, including the estimated fair market price.

An agency would improperly reject as ineligible an 8(a) joint venture's proposal merely because the SBA had not approved the 8(a) joint venture agreement prior to proposal submission.

(h) Subcontracting

Another method for furthering the government's preference for small businesses in procurements is encouraging the use of such businesses as subcontractors. Except for contracts performed totally outside the United States and contracts for personal services, all contracts exceeding the simplified acquisition threshold must include a clause requiring the contractor to award subcontracts to small business concerns and SDBs, as well as to women owned small business concerns, veteran-owned small business concerns, service disabled veteran-owned small business concerns, and HUBZone small business concerns, (discussed below), "to the fullest extent consistent with efficient contract performance."

Under this clause, the prime contractor retains the right to determine if a small business concern has the capability to perform a subcontract. Generally, the government will not question the prime contractor's decision in this regard because the prime contractor is responsible for the performance of its subcontractors.

Solicitations with subcontracting possibilities for supply and service contracts expected to exceed $7,000,000 and for construction contracts expected to exceed $1.5 million must contain a clause requiring the prospective contractor to submit a subcontracting plan outlining—in detail—the efforts the contractor will make to ensure that small business concerns, SDBs, women-and veteran-owned small businesses, and HUBZone small businesses will have an equitable opportunity to compete for subcontracts. Separate versions of the clause are prescribed for negotiated and sealed-bid contracts. The plan must be approved by the Contracting Officer, and the approved plan will be included in the resulting contract. If the prime contractor fails to make a "good faith effort" to comply with its small business subcontracting plan, it could be assessed liquidated damages.

The Small Business Act and SBA regulations require that, on supply contracts set aside for small businesses, a small business must perform at least 50 percent of the cost of manufacturing the supplies (not including the cost of materials). This "Non-Manufacturer Rule (NMR)" is an exception to this performance requirement, and provides that a firm that is not a manufacturer may qualify as a small business on supply contracts set aside for small businesses if, among other items, it supplies the product of a small business located in the United States. Pub. L. No. 114–92, § 864, amends the Small Business Act to provide that the NMR "shall not apply to a contract that has as its principal purpose the acquisition of services or construction."

(i) Women-Owned Small Businesses

By statute, there is a government-wide goal to award at least 5% of all federal prime contracts and subcontracts each fiscal year to women-owned small businesses. To implement this policy, an Executive Order requires the SBA to establish an Assistant Administrator for Women's Procurement and, among other things, to create a web site to provide timely information about contract opportunities for women-owned small businesses.

The ownership and control standard for women-owned small businesses is similar to that for other small businesses. To be considered women-owned, the firm must be 51% owned by one or more women or, if the firm is publicly owned, one or more women must own 51% of the firm's stock. The daily operation and management of the firm must also be controlled by one or more women.

The SBA's regulations, 13 C.F.R. Part 127, originally effective October 1, 2008, as modified, authorize Contracting Officers to restrict competition to eligible Women Owned Small Businesses. The FAR also has implementing guidance.

The Small Business Administration has issued a final rule authorizing contracting officers to award sole-source contracts to women-owned small businesses and economically disadvantaged WOSBs (EDWOSBs) in certain circumstances. See 80 Fed. Reg. 55019 (Sept. 14, 2015).

(j) Veteran-Owned Small Businesses

The purpose of the Veterans Entrepreneurship and Small Business Development Act of 1999 is to expand existing programs and to establish new assistance programs for veterans, especially those with service-related disabilities, who own at least 51% of and control a small business concern. The Act aims to accomplish its purposes by (1) expanding the eligibility for certain small business assistance programs to include veterans, (2) directing certain federal agencies to enhance small business assistance to veterans, and (3) establishing new institutions to provide small business assistance to veterans or to support the institutions that provide such assistance. Among other things, the Act amends the Small Business Act to establish a government-wide participation goal for small businesses owned and controlled by service-disabled veterans of 3% of the total value of prime contract and subcontract awards for each fiscal year.

FAR implements the Veterans Benefit Act of 2003, Pub. L. No. 108–183, § 36(a), 117 Stat. at 2662 (codified at 15 U.S.C.A. § 657f(a)), which creates a procurement program for small business concerns owned and controlled by service-disabled veterans. Under the FAR, subpart 19.14, set-asides and sole source awards are possible for such concerns.

Mandatory statutory provisions in 38 U.S.C.A. § 8127 require the Department of Veterans Affairs to apply the Rule of Two, a set-aside for veteran-owned businesses, to all contracting determinations. Section 8127 does not allow the VA to evade the Rule of Two on the ground that the VA has met its contracting goals or on the ground that the VA has placed an order through the Federal Supply Schedule, the U.S. Supreme Court has held in reversing the Court of Appeals for the Federal Circuit. See *Kingdomware Techs., Inc. v. United States*, 136 S. Ct. 1969, 195 L.Ed.2d 334 (2016).

The U.S. Court of Appeals for the Federal Circuit has held that the Veterans Benefits, Health Care, and Information Technology Act of 2006 (VBA), Pub. L. No. 109–461, requires the Department of Veterans Affairs to undertake a "rule of two" analysis to determine the propriety of awarding a contract based on competition restricted to veteran-owned small business before procuring from any other source, including a nonprofit agency for the blind or significantly disabled under the Javits-Wagner-O'Day Act (JWOD). *PDS Consultants, Inc. v. United States*, 907 F.3d 1345 (Fed. Cir. 2018).

(k) HUBZone Small Businesses

The "HUBZone Empowerment Contracting Program," established by Congress in the Small Business Reauthorization Act of 1997, is intended to provide contracting assistance to qualified small businesses located in "historically underutilized business zones" (HUBZones) in an effort to increase employment opportunities, investment, and economic development in those areas.

To qualify for certification by the SBA as a HUBZone small business concern, a small business must be 100% owned and controlled by United States citizens, have its principal place of business located in a HUBZone, and have at least 35% of its employees residing within the HUBZone.

A HUBZone small business concern under a HUBZone set aside must be a HUBZone concern both at the time of its initial offer and at the time of contract award. For general construction or general construction by special trade contractors, the HUBZone small business concern generally must spend at least 50 percent of the cost of contract performance incurred for personnel on its own employees or subcontract employees of other HUBZone small business concerns. An SBA rule regarding the HUBZone program allows a declined or decertified HUBZone small business to reapply 90 calendar days after the decline or decertification decision is rendered, rather than to wait one year to reapply for admission.

Under the program, Contracting Officers may set-aside contracts for competition restricted to qualified HUBZone small business contractors where there is a reasonable expectation that at least two responsible HUBZone contractors will submit offers and award can be made at a fair market price. If only one HUBZone small business contractor can satisfy a requirement and the anticipated contract price will not exceed $6.5 million for manufacturing or $4 million for all other contract opportunities, the contract may be awarded to the HUBZone small business on a sole-source basis.

In procurements conducted using full and open competition, a HUBZone small business concern is eligible for a 10% price evaluation preference. GAO has held that even where the HUBZone offeror's proposal was already lower in price than the large business's proposal, the agency is still required to apply the 10 percent HUBZone price preference. The HUBZone regulations on set-asides properly implement the revised Small Business Act. HUBZone firms can have more than one office, and its principal office, i.e., where most of its employees work and the linchpin for HUBZone eligibility, can differ from its headquarters.

The prior version of the enabling statute for the HUBZone program gave this program priority over the 8(a) and service disabled veteran owned business programs. After conflicting advice among the courts, the GAO and the Department of Justice, the Small Business Jobs Act 0f 2010, Pub. L. No. 111–240, implemented by FAR 19.203, stated that these programs have equal stature in the procuring agency's discretion.

(l) Other Procurement Preferences

Other examples of a procurement preference are for (a) historically black colleges and universities and minority institutions, to include set-asides for acquisition of research, studies or services from these institutions, (b) local and small business concerns located in the vicinity of a military installation that is being closed or realigned, (c) businesses that reside or primarily do business in geographic areas affected by major disasters or emergencies, (d) certain Native Hawaiian organizations, (e) state licensing agencies for the blind, (f) nonprofit agencies employing persons who are blind or severely disabled, (g) Federal Prison Industries, and (h) Native Americans.

(m) Contract Bundling

Contract "bundling"—the combination of two or more smaller contracts into one large contract—may preclude small businesses from participating effectively in government contracts as prime contractors. The Small Business Reauthorization Act of 1997 amended the Small Business Act to require agencies to conduct market research and to coordinate with small business advisors before proceeding with an acquisition strategy that could lead to bundling and to justify the use of bundling by identifying anticipated benefits. This form of bundling differs from the consolidation of agency requirements that can unduly restrict competition in contravention of the Competition in Contracting Act.

More recently, as will be explained below, the FAR imposes further controls on contract bundling. An agency's failure to perform the analysis required by the Act and the related regulations can be grounds for protest.

(n) Small Business Jobs Act of 2010

Subtitle C of The Small Business Jobs Act of 2010, Pub. L. No. 111–240, 124 Stat. 2504, September 27, 2010, makes numerous changes to small business contracting policies. Part I addresses contract bundling and consolidation, Part II states new requirements for subcontracting integrity, Part III considers the acquisition process, and Part IV analyzes small business size and status integrity. Some important policies in Part III relate to reservation of contract awards for small businesses, agency accountability, payment of subcontractors, and repeal of the Small Business Competitiveness Demonstration Program.

Some highlights from Part IV concern policy and presumptions, updated size standards, and small business contracting parity.

The Department of Defense, General Services Administration and NASA issued a final rule to amend the Federal Acquisition Regulation to implement §§ 1312 and 1313 of the Small Business Jobs Act of 2010, Pub. L. No. 111–240, on Government-wide contract consolidation and bundling, and § 1671 of the National Defense Authorization Act for Fiscal Year 2013, Pub. L. No. 112–239. See 81 Fed. Reg. 67763 (Sept. 30, 2016). The final rule incorporates regulatory changes made by the Small Business Administration on contract consolidation and bundling. See 78 Fed. Reg. 61113 (Oct. 2, 2013).

§ 19.2   Equal Access to Justice Act

The Equal Access to Justice Act (EAJA) is another example of the preferences accorded to small businesses. Under the Act, eligible small business concerns may recover attorney fees and expenses from the government if it prevails in an administrative proceeding or a civil action brought by or against the government and if the government's position in the litigation was not "substantially justified." A court or board cannot hear a party's claim for attorney fees under EAJA unless it has jurisdiction over the action and until the party makes a formal application. The filing deadline is 30 days from the first business day after the government's deadline for filing an appeal has expired.

(a) Eligibility

Recovery of fees and expenses under the EAJA is limited to prevailing parties that qualify under the Act's net worth and size limitations. For individuals, the Act limits recovery to persons whose net worth did not exceed $2 million at the time the court action or board appeal was initiated. Eligible businesses must have a net worth of no more than $7 million and no more than 500 employees at the time the court action or board appeal was initiated.

Note that when a subcontractor's claim is brought in the name of the prime contractor, it is the net worth of the prime contractor that will be considered in determining the party's small business status. The government cannot be a prevailing party under the EAJA.

(b) "Prevailing Party"

In determining what constitutes a "prevailing party" in litigation against the government, the courts and boards of contract appeals have held that the small business (a) need not prevail on every claim, (b) must prevail on a claim that is more than "de minimis," (c) cannot be a "prevailing party" if the matter is not litigated (even if it is negotiated to a successful conclusion). In sum, to demonstrate that it is a "prevailing party," an applicant for award of attorney fees under EAJA must show that it obtained an enforceable judgment on the merits or a court-ordered consent decree that materially altered the legal relationship between the parties, or the equivalent of either of those outcomes.

The award of attorney fees and costs under EAJA requires only that the plaintiff achieve substantial relief against the government, not that there must be an identity between the relief sought and the relief granted.

A recent United States Supreme Court case, *Astrue v. Ratliff*, 560 U.S. 586, 130 S. Ct. 2521, 177 L.Ed.2d 91 (2010), has held that the award of EAJA fees is to the prevailing party, not its attorney, and therefore may be offset against the contractor's pre-existing debt owed to the government.

(c) Government Position Not "Substantially Justified"

The EAJA provides that a court or board may not award attorney fees or expenses to an eligible, prevailing party if the government's position in the litigation was "substantially justified." Whether the position of the government was substantially justified is determined on the basis of "the administrative record, as a whole, which is made in the adversary adjudication for which fees and other expenses are sought" or "the record (including the record with respect to the action or the failure to act by the agency upon which the civil action is based) which is made in the civil action for which fees and other expenses are sought."

Where an agency violates a regulation, it will be difficult for a tribunal to find the agency's position substantially justified unless there is conflicting precedent regarding the controlling law or significant constitutional questions.

A timely EAJA attorney fee application can be amended after the 30-day filing period has run to cure an initial failure to allege that the government's position in the underlying litigation lacked substantial justification.

To be considered "substantially justified," the government's position must have had a reasonable basis in law and fact and be "justified to a degree that would satisfy a reasonable person." The government has the burden of proving that its position was substantially justified.

Although the issue is case-specific, the government's position in one piece of litigation was substantially justified where the case was a close one of first impression and where the contractor recovered only 18% of its claim. In another case, the government's position was not substantially justified where the government failed to (1) recognize industry customs and practice, and (2) produce an important witness, and where the government's interpretation of the contract either ignored or rendered meaningless a significant portion of the contract's specifications. Thus, the logic and factual information supporting the actual merits of the government's position is the central issue for deciding whether its position was "substantially justified."

(d) Amount of Recovery

The EAJA permits prevailing parties to recover the reasonable expenses of expert witnesses, the reasonable cost of any study, analysis, engineering report, test, or project necessary for the preparation of the party's case, and reasonable attorney fees. Attorney fees are subject to a $125-per-hour limit, but this limit may be increased as allowed by statute if justified for cost-of-living increases or for a special factor, such as limited availability of qualified attorneys for a particular legal subject matter.

Most of the boards of contract appeals have held that in the absence of an agency regulation authorizing a fee higher than the statutory cap, the boards cannot exceed the cap even when it could have been justified by a special factor. Nevertheless, knowledge in government contract law is not a special factor that would warrant justifying an increased standard hourly rate.

Decisions addressing the amount of fees and expenses recoverable under the EAJA have held that the applicant will be compensated only for hours billed to the contractor. Furthermore, the extent of a contractor's success is a crucial factor in determining the proper amount of an award. Where the plaintiff achieved only limited success, the forum should award only that amount of fees that is reasonable in relation to the results obtained.

Other decisions have (a) held that a contractor appearing "pro se" cannot recover attorney fees for his or her own services, (b) ruled that embraces the fees of paralegals, which may be recovered at market rates, (c) allowed the recovery of expert witness fees, deposition costs, and fax and courier expenses, and (d) concluded that attorney fees incurred by a subcontractor in an appeal sponsored by the prime contractor were not recoverable.

The court or board may reduce or deny an EAJA award if the prevailing party engaged in conduct that unduly and unreasonably protracted the litigation. One court reduced an award of expenses where the prevailing party's attorney's efforts were unsatisfactory in a material respect—failing to cite key cases that the court later found and ultimately relied upon.

§ 19.3   Nondiscrimination Requirements

(a) "Equal Opportunity" Clause

The primary clause for implementing the policy of equal employment opportunity under the FAR is the "Equal Opportunity" clause, 52.222–26, (promulgated under Executive Order 11246 as amended). This clause—with some exceptions—must be incorporated into all prime contracts and subcontracts more than $10,000. However, if the contract is less than $10,000 but the contractor has been awarded contracts or subcontracts aggregating more than $10,000 in any previous 12-month period, the clause must be included in the current contract.

Under the "Equal Opportunity" clause, contractors are (1) prohibited from discriminating against any employee or applicant for employment on the basis of race, color, religion, sex, or national origin and (2) required to take affirmative action to ensure nondiscriminatory employment practices.

Such affirmative action applies not only to hiring practices but to practices related to hiring—such as promotion, demotion or transfer, recruitment or recruitment advertising, layoff or termination, rates of pay or other forms of compensation, and selection for training or apprenticeship. For contracts and subcontracts of $10 million or more, excluding construction, contracting officials generally must obtain pre-award clearances to ensure the firms' compliance with equal employment opportunity requirements.

In addition to complying with the "Equal Opportunity" clause, non-construction prime contractors and subcontractors with (a) 50 or more employees and (b) either (1) nonexempt contracts or subcontracts of $50,000 or more or (2) government bills of lading expected to exceed $50,000 in any 12-month period, must develop— within 120 days from the time performance of a contract begins—a written affirmative action program for each of their establishments, complete with detailed goals and timetables. Construction contractors with nonexempt construction contracts must comply with contract terms and conditions specifying affirmative action requirements applicable to covered geographical areas or projects and applicable rules and regulations promulgated by the Secretary of Labor.

(b) Miscellaneous Requirements

Title VII of the Civil Rights Act of 1964, Executive Order 11141, the Federal Rehabilitation Act of 1973, the Americans with Disabilities Act of 1990, and the Vietnam Era Veterans

Readjustment Assistance Act of 1972 also impose some nondiscrimination requirements on federal contractors. Title VII makes it unlawful for employers with 15 or more employees to discriminate on the basis of race, color, religion, sex, or national origin, while Executive Order 11141 establishes a federal policy against discrimination on the basis of age. Although contract clauses prohibiting age discrimination are not required, the FAR requires agencies to bring this policy to the attention of contractors and to request compliance if a person makes a valid complaint.

In implementing the Rehabilitation Act, another social engineering policy, the FAR directs that all government contracts or subcontracts over $10,000 must contain an affirmative action clause stating that the contractor "shall not discriminate against any employee or applicant because of physical or mental disability." This clause need not be used, however, if the contract work is performed outside the United States by employees recruited outside the United States or if the clause terms have been waived by the contracting agency.

The Americans With Disabilities Act mandates strict personnel rules so that the disabled can be assured of fair employment practices (as well as changes in the physical makeup of some contractor facilities to provide reasonable work accommodations).

To carry out the Vietnam Era Veterans Readjustment Assistance Act, the FAR directs that, in the absence of a waiver by the contracting agency, all contracts or subcontracts exceeding $10,000 contain a clause requiring affirmative action to employ (and advance) qualified disabled veterans and veterans of the Vietnam era.

(c) Administration and Enforcement

The Office of Federal Contract Compliance Programs (OFCCP), operating under authority delegated by the Secretary of Labor, is responsible for the administration and enforcement of the government's equal employment policies. Complaints received by the Contracting Officer alleging violations of the Executive Order establishing these policies and contractors' inquiries regarding their compliance status or their right to appeal enforcement sanctions are to be referred to the OFCCP for resolution. If the OFCCP determines that a contractor has violated the policies of the Executive Order, regulations of the Secretary of Labor, or applicable contract clauses, it may impose the following sanctions:

1.   Publication of the name of the contractor or its union;

2.   Cancellation, termination, or suspension of all (or part) of the contractor's contracts;

3.   Debarment of the contractor from future government contracts (or extensions or modifications of existing contracts) until the contractor has established and carried out personnel and employment policies in compliance with Executive Order 11246 and the regulations of the Secretary of Labor; and

4.   Referral to the Department of Justice or the Equal Employment Opportunity Commission for appropriate civil or criminal proceedings.

Title VII of the Civil Rights Act is enforced by the Equal Employment Opportunity Commission. The Commission is authorized to investigate charges of discrimination, to secure voluntary compliance with the Act, and to initiate suit against the violating contractor if voluntary compliance fails. Under Title VII, an aggrieved person may also sue the contractor in United States District Court seeking an injunction or damages.

§ 19.4   Labor Standards Requirements

Along with meeting the requirements of executive orders, Government contractors must comply with the labor standards imposed under various federal statutes, notably the Walsh-Healey Act, the Service Contract Labor Standards Act (SCLSA), the Wage Rate Requirements (Construction), and the Contract Work Hours and Safety Standards Act. These statutes were enacted to prevent substandard wage rates and working conditions in the performance of government contracts.

(a) Walsh-Healey Act

The Walsh-Healey Act establishes labor standards for government contracts in excess of $10,000 to manufacture or furnish materials, supplies, articles, and equipment. The Act applies to prime contractors. However, if a subcontractor is performing the work of a prime contractor, it may be considered a substitute manufacturer or supplier and will then be subject to the Act. The Act covers only those employees actually engaged in (or connected with) the manufacturing and supply process and not to office or custodial workers, executive-level personnel, or outside sales personnel.

Contracts subject to the Walsh-Healey Act must contain the following stipulations:

1.   Employees manufacturing or furnishing the contract items will be paid no less than the prevailing minimum wage for persons performing similar work (or in the particular industry) in the locality

where the contract is to be performed (as determined by the Secretary of Labor); and

2.   These employees (a) will be compensated at applicable overtime rates for work in excess of 40 hours in one week, (b) will not be required to perform under working conditions that are hazardous, unsanitary, or dangerous to health and safety, (c) are over 16 years of age, and (d) are not convict laborers.

Both statutory and regulatory exemptions are available under the Walsh-Healey Act. Statutorily exempted from the Act's requirements are supply contracts for specifically authorized "open market" purchases (commercial items), perishables, agricultural products, and contracts made by the Secretary of Agriculture in purchasing agricultural products. Regulatory exemptions are granted at the discretion of the Secretary of Labor where such exemptions would further justice and the public interest.

Examples of regulatory exemptions include contracts for public utility services and contracts for supplies manufactured outside the United States, Puerto Rico, and the Virgin Islands. Exemptions for specific contracts or classes of contracts may be granted by the Secretary of Labor provided that requests include a finding by the agency head stating the reasons why the conduct of government business will be seriously impaired unless the exemption is granted.

The Secretary of Labor is charged with the administration and enforcement of the Walsh-Healey Act. Penalties for violating the Act include (1) terminating the contract for default and charging the contractor for the excess costs of reprocurement, (2) debarring the contractor from contracting with the government for up to three years, and (3) assessing damages in the amount of unpaid wages plus liquidated damages of $10 per day for each underage worker or convict improperly employed. Penalties are collected by the government on behalf of the employees by withholding payments on the contract or, if necessary, through court action.

(b) Service Contract Labor Standards Act

The Service Contract Labor Standards Act (SCLSA) establishes labor standards for contracts that are primarily for services. Under the Act, government contracts and subcontracts over $2,500 whose principal purpose is to furnish services in the United States through the use of service employees must contain provisions regarding minimum wages, fringe benefits, safe working conditions, notification to employees of minimum allowable compensation, and equivalent federal employee classifications and wage rates. A new website, https://wdolhome.sam.gov, allows a single location for a person to obtain SCLSA wage determinations for official contract actions.

The Act does not apply to service contracts that are performed (a) exclusively by executive-level, administrative, or professional personnel or (b) primarily by bona fide executive, administrative, or professional employees when service employees are only a minor factor in the performance of the contract. In addition, the Act's coverage specifically excludes (1) contracts for construction, alteration, or repair of public buildings, (2) supply contracts covered by the Walsh-Healey Act, (3) transportation contracts, (4) communications contracts, (5) contracts for public utility services or for operating postal contract stations, and (6) contracts for individual personal services.

The Secretary of Labor is authorized to administer the SCLSA and enforce its requirements. Contractors that do not comply with certain minimum wage levels and working conditions face sanctions, such as the withholding of payments or debarment from government contracting. While traditionally the Department of Labor is charged with ensuring SCLSA compliance, an agency may need to question an offeror's compliance with the SCLSA in two instances. First, an agency must consider SCLSA compliance when it is conducting a cost realism analysis in a competition for a cost-type contract. Second, an agency must consider SCLSA compliance if there is an indication on the face of an offer that the offeror does not intend to pay SCLSA mandated wage rates. This doctrine requires a clear intent not to comply with the SCLSA on the face of the offer, and not merely incorrect classifications or wage rates within an offer.

In a recent GAO case, the contracting officer properly concluded that offeror's labor rates were reasonable when they were all significantly higher than the applicable SCLSA rates even though they were significantly lower than the incumbent's rates and the Government estimate. An agency cannot properly find a protester's wage rates unrealistic when they were higher than those required by the SCLSA. A contractor will not be entitled to receive contract reformation and is still subject to the SCLSA where its misreading of the contract was based on its erroneous business decision to ignore the SCLSA wage requirement clauses in the solicitation.

An employee on an SCLSA covered contract has standing to bring a False Claims Act (FCA) action premised on false certifications of company compliance with the SCLSA because the FCA violation arises from the claim for payment, not from the underlying SCLSA violation.

(c) Davis Bacon Act

The most important requirement of the Davis Bacon Act (renamed Construction Wage Rate Requirements statute but still called the Davis Bacon Act even on the Department of Labor's (DOL) website) is that contractors (and subcontractors) must pay mechanics and laborers employed directly on the work site no less than minimum wages, including basic hourly rates and fringe benefits payments, as determined by the DOL and as set forth in the DOL wage determination included in the contract.

Courts have divided on whether the Davis Bacon Act pre-empts or otherwise precludes a state law cause of action, be it statutory or common law, seeking payment of wages required by the Act. A new website. https://wdolhome.sam.gov allows a single location to obtain DBA wage determinations for official contract actions.

Mechanics and laborers (including apprentices and trainees) are those who work primarily with the strength and skills of their hands and bodies. Clerks, bookkeepers, superintendents, guards and watchmen, technical workers, and engineers are generally not considered mechanics and laborers. The Act is intended to protect employees from substandard earnings by fixing a floor on their wages on government contracts; it is not designed to protect contractors. The Act also permits the President to suspend the Act in a national emergency; thus, President Bush in 2005 temporarily suspended the Act in a limited geographical area after Hurricane Katrina.

The Act applies to contracts in excess of $2,000 for the construction, alteration, or repair (including painting and decorating) of public buildings or public works within the United States. Thus, the Act applies to domestic construction-type work—as distinguished from the (a) manufacturing or furnishing of supplies, materials, and equipment and (b) rendering of services. Generally, the Act applies only if the contract as a whole is for construction, alteration, or repair; it does not apply to contracts only incidentally involving construction work (even if such work exceeds $2,000). However, the Act has been held to cover the construction of a building to be leased to the government.

Some contracts are hybrids of construction with service or supply elements. DBA will apply to the construction work under such contracts when (a) the construction work is to be performed on a public building or work, (b) the contract contains specific requirements for a substantial amount of construction exceeding the DBA threshold, and (c) the construction work is physically or functionally separate and segregable from the other work required by the contract.

"Incidental" construction work or construction that is so merged with non-construction work or fragmentary in location or time will not invoke the DBA. Accordingly, in challenging before the GAO the agency's estimate of work in the solicitation subject to the Davis Bacon Act, the protester must show that the government did not use the appropriate statutory and regulatory criteria, or that the estimates are not based on the best information available, or otherwise misrepresent the agency's needs, or result from fraud or bad faith.

The minimum wages to be paid various classes of laborers and mechanics are based on the wages the Secretary of Labor determines to be the "prevailing" wages being paid to corresponding classes of laborers and mechanics employed on similar projects in the political subdivision (city, town, village, county, etc.) where the work is performed. The Secretary of Labor determines the prevailing wage rates based on data voluntarily submitted, field surveys, or formal hearings.

Often, wage rates bargained for by building trade unions are accepted as "prevailing." Where little or no similar work has been performed in the immediate area, the nearest employment center from which workers might be drawn—even though outside the county in which the work is to be performed—may be used. Determinations of prevailing wages by the Secretary of Labor generally are not reviewable.

Wage determinations set forth minimum rates to be paid by craft (painter, laborer, carpenter, etc.). Apprentices registered in government programs may be paid lower rates. A Contracting Officer's order to pay a higher wage rate to correct an erroneous wage determination rate can be a compensable contract change. Note that wage determinations may not prescribe how the work will be performed (for example, painting with a brush rather than with a spray). Such instructions are the province of the contract specifications.

The most critical problem in the administration and enforcement of these wage determinations is the classification of workers by craft. An employer may attempt to pay workers in a low-wage classification (e.g., as helpers) rather than pay the higher wages specified for craftsmen. As a result, the DOL has promulgated rules allowing use of helpers only where their duties are clearly defined and distinct from journeymen and laborer classifications in the area. The standard for classification of workers is the "area practice." Any generally accepted practice in the construction area will usually be acceptable. A contracting agency does not, however, owe a legal duty to clarify DOL employee classifications.

The GAO in a protest will not review the propriety or correctness of a DBA wage determination, because this decision is the responsibility of (and may be appealed through) the DOL. On the other hand, the GAO will consider on the merits a protest that the agency improperly included the DBA clauses in a solicitation; here, the protester must show either that the agency did not apply the appropriate statutory and regulatory criteria or that the agency acted fraudulently or in bad faith.

The implementing FAR clause requires that all on-site workers be paid in accordance with the wage determination included in the contract. DOL issues the wage determination (including labor classifications for the project and the minimum hourly wages and fringe benefits that must be paid for each classification) before the contract bidding or negotiation commences. Thus, all prospective contractors are supposed to have an opportunity to include these wages in their bids and offers.

The solicitation must indicate which "wage schedule" is to apply to which work. For example, it may specify a "building" wage schedule for certain work and a "heavy and highway construction" wage schedule for other work. Where the wage determination is invalid (and even rescinded), a contractor that has paid the employees according to the DOL wage determination will be entitled to an equitable adjustment.

If the wage determination does not include a labor classification for an employee actually working on the project, the contractor must request a "conformance" from the Contracting Officer. A conformance is a new labor classification with a wage rate based on wage rates for similar work in the project area. If the contractor and the Contracting Officer are in agreement, the new classification is reported to DOL, which may approve, modify, or reject it.

Wage conformances are judicially reviewable under the Administrative Procedure Act. In one case, the GAO has held the agency was not required to incorporate the predecessor contract's wage conformance in a solicitation for equipment calibration and maintenance services, because (a) wage conformances are not binding, unlike wage determinations, (b) the DOL must approve new wage conformances for each successor contract, and (c) the wage conformances under the predecessor contract was available under the Freedom of Information Act.

The minimum wage schedule is not a representation that such wages will be sufficient to attract workers to the particular job. However, where the government mistakenly incorporates wage rate schedules that are lower than the actual minimums, it may be required to correct the schedules and grant the contractor an adjustment in the contract price. Conversely, the government cannot obtain credit on reduction of an erroneous wage determination. The contractor is required to post the scale of wages in a prominent and easily accessible place at the work site.

The Davis Bacon Act mandates that wages must be paid not less often than once a week. Rebates and kickbacks cannot be taken after wages are paid, and only certain listed deductions from wage payments are permitted. The payment of the prescribed wage rates may not be avoided by special arrangements with workers—such as "subcontracting" with a partnership made up of workers—or obtaining their agreement to lower wages. The contractor must submit to the Contracting Officer payrolls and a certificate affirming payment and must maintain payroll records for three years. False payroll information may result in civil and criminal penalties.

The DOL wage determination also will include "fringe benefits," which are contributions made, or obligations incurred, for medical or hospital care, pensions, compensation for injuries or illness resulting from occupational activity, unemployment benefits, life insurance, disability and sickness insurance, accident insurance, vacation and holiday pay, apprenticeship, or any other fringe benefit specifically enumerated in the wage determination or expressly approved by the Secretary of Labor. Fringe benefits may be conferred by (1) paying amounts in cash to the laborer or mechanic, (2) irrevocable contributions to a fund, (3) incurring obligations to provide benefits, or (4) any combination of these methods.

Failure by the contractor to pay required wages can result in several sanctions, including termination of the contract for default and assessment of excess reprocurement costs (see Chapter 49) and debarment of the contractor for three years from contracting with the government.

The government may also withhold payment due the contractor to the extent necessary to cover any wage underpayment and may pay these funds directly to the contractor's work force. These withholdings are generally accomplished under the contract's "Withholding of Funds" clause, 52.222–7, which permits the Contracting Officer to withhold monies for labor violations from payments otherwise due the contractor.

If, after receiving written notice, the contractor does not pay the required monies to its employees, payments to the contractor will be withheld to cover the underpaid wages. The clause also authorizes suspension of future payments until the violations cease. In addition, to provide funds for the payment of violations that occurred on previously completed contracts, DOL may order progress payments withheld on a current contract even though the contractor is in full compliance with all labor standards provisions—this practice is referred to as "cross-compliance" withholding. If the withheld funds are insufficient to cover the underpayments, the workers may sue the contractor and its surety for the difference.

Administration and enforcement responsibilities under the Davis Bacon Act are divided primarily between two government agencies:

The first agency is the procuring agency's Contracting Officers, who are responsible for administration (inserting wage determinations in contracts, reviewing payrolls for compliance, and conducting investigations to determine compliance with labor standards provisions) and enforcement (for example, withholding contract funds for wage underpayments and initiating debarments).

Contracting agencies are required to keep payroll records for three years and periodically audit the contractor's compliance, either on the agency's own initiative or on receiving a complaint about a possible violation. A significant part of the monitoring process includes a determination of the proper classification of workers—that is, determining if the employee's wage classification fits with the employee's actual work performed.

The other agency is the Department of Labor (DOL) which makes wage determinations and is responsible for assuring coordination of administration by all federal agencies. DOL also conducts compliance audits. DOL's audits include a review of payroll records filed, a review of apprenticeship and training program documentation, fringe benefit program documentation, and confidential interviews with employees regarding their wage rates, labor classifications, and descriptions of their actual work.

Generally, DOL wage determinations may be disputed only through the DOL's administrative processes. But when that administrative process is complete, the contractor may seek a price adjustment for the effects of the DOL's wage determination under the contract's "Price Adjustment" or "Changes" clauses. A contractor that has failed to pay workers in accordance with the Davis Bacon Act and that falsely certified payments at prevailing wages can be subject to a qui tam action for a False Claims Act violation (see Chapter 3).

Congress has passed legislation to move responsibility for Davis-Bacon Act wage claim processing from the Government Accountability Office to the Department of Labor. The law will replace references to the United States Comptroller General in 40

U.S.C.A. §§ 3144, 3703(b)(3) with references to the Secretary of Labor.

Issues will arise on whether a proposal met the RFP's term on Davis Bacon Act compliance. Thus, in one case, GAO has denied a protest that awardee's unrealistically low price would not permit the contractor to meet required DBA labor rates where no indication exists that the awardee took exception to any RFP clauses, including the DBA clauses. In a second case, the GAO found that the, agency's evaluation of an awardee's proposal as responsive to the terms of the solicitation was unreasonable because the awardee did not expressly commit to pay Davis Bacon Act-required wage rates, but rather committed to pay those rates for a subset of the anticipated work, In another decision, however, GAO said that the Contracting Officer unreasonably evaluated the awardee's proposal as responsive to the terms of the solicitation, where the record showed that the agency inquired about whether the awardee's price included a commitment to pay solicitation-required wage rates for reconstruction of the existing building, and the awardee's response did not expressly commit to pay those rates. These decisions are not reconcilable.

(d) Contract Work Hours and Safety Standards Act

The Contract Work Hours and Safety Standards Act supplements the Davis Bacon Act by providing that government contractors and subcontractors must calculate the wages of every laborer and mechanic employed on a public works contract on the basis of a standard workweek of 40 hours. Work in excess of this amount is permitted, but the contractor must pay overtime wages of not less than one-and-one-half times the basic rate of pay. These requirements are similar to the overtime provisions imposed on supply contractors by the Walsh-Healey Act. The Work Hours Act also forbids working conditions that are unsanitary, hazardous, or dangerous to employee health or safety.

By its terms, the Work Hours Act applies to (1) any contract involving the employment of laborers or mechanics on a public work of the United States, a United States territory, or the District of Columbia and (2) any other contracts involving employment of laborers and mechanics (a) to which the United States, the District of Columbia, or any territory is a party, (b) that are made on their behalf, or (c) that are financed by loans or grants from, or insured or guaranteed by, the United States and are subject to wage standards. Mere government insurance or guarantee of the financing of work does not bring a contract under the coverage of the Act.

The Act excludes from coverage (1) contracts for transportation or communications, (2) contracts for the purchase of materials available in the open market, (3) contracts subject to the Walsh-Healey Act, and (4) contracts below $150,000. Also, under a provision of the Work Hours Act giving the Secretary of Labor the authority to provide exemptions to the Act, exemptions have been made, for example, for construction contracts involving work in foreign countries.

(e) Disputes

The general rule is that boards of contract appeals and courts lack jurisdiction over labor standards matters that are reserved exclusively for resolution by the DOL (which would include matters under the Act).

A qualification to this rule is the Court of Federal Claims and boards of contract appeals may still entertain a dispute that centers on the mutual contract rights and obligations of the parties even though matters reserved to and decided exclusively by the DOL are part of the "factual predicate." Thus, the former GSBCA held that it had jurisdiction to hear an appeal that an agency's assessment of liquidated damages under the Act was improper because the agency itself had breached the contract by failing to incorporate the proper collective bargaining agreement into the contract.

§ 19.5   Domestic and Foreign Product Preferences

The Buy American Act (BAA), the Trade Agreements Act (TAA), and other statutes and implementing regulations create preferences in government procurement for the acquisition of United States domestic goods and services and for goods and services of certain United States trading partners. The statutes and regulations in this are extremely complex, and so the discussion below is necessarily general.

To ensure compliance with the BAA, TAA, and other domestic and foreign product preference requirements, contractors must file documentation certifying the country of origin of the products they plan to supply to the government. A false certification—in addition to making the contractor vulnerable to suspension and debarment from government contracting and to potential civil and criminal action—also exposes a contract award to a potential protest.

(a) Buy American Act

The BAA and its implementing regulations provide an advantage to "domestic end products" and "domestic construction materials" over foreign products and materials when the government acquires supplies and construction materials. This advantage is achieved through the application to foreign products of an evaluation factor that increases the cost of foreign products and materials solely for purposes of evaluating offers. The BAA is not applicable at the subcontract level.

Specifically, the BAA and its implementing regulations restrict the government's purchase of supplies for use in the United States to "domestic end products." A "domestic end product" is an "unmanufactured end product mined or produced in the United States" or an "end product manufactured in the United States, if the cost of its components mined, produced, or manufactured in the United States exceeds 50% of the cost of all of its components." DOD has issued a rule amending the DFARS to implement a policy that the Buy American Act "component test" does not apply to commercial off the shelf (COTS) item acquisitions. The waiver allows a COTS item to be treated as a domestic end product if it is manufactured in the United States, without tracing the origin of the item's components.

A CO may acquire a foreign end product if (a) the agency head grants a waiver, (b) the end product is not mined, produced, or manufactured in the United States in sufficient and reasonably available commercial quantities of satisfactory quality, or (c) the cost of the domestic end product is "unreasonable."

The cost of a domestic end product is "unreasonable" if, after the addition of an evaluation factor to a foreign offer, the domestic offer is still more expensive. In a civilian agency procurement, if there is a domestic offer competing with a foreign offer, and if the foreign offer has the low price before application of the BAA, the Contracting Officer must increase the price of the foreign end product by 6% if the domestic offer is from a large business or by 12% if the domestic offer is from a small business. In DOD procurements, the CO must apply a 50% evaluation factor.

In construction contracts to be performed in the United States, the BAA and its implementing regulations require the government to use only "domestic construction materials." A "domestic construction material" is an "unmanufactured construction material mined or produced in the United States" or a "construction material manufactured in the United States, if the cost of its components mined, produced, or manufactured in the United States exceeds 50% of the cost of all of its components."

A Contracting Officer may acquire foreign construction materials if (1) the agency head determines that applying the BAA restrictions to a particular construction material would be impracticable or inconsistent with the public interest, (2) the particular construction material is not mined, produced, or manufactured in the United States in sufficient and reasonably available commercial quantities of satisfactory quality, or (3) the cost of domestic construction material is "unreasonable."

The cost of a domestic construction material is "unreasonable" if, after the addition of an evaluation factor to the offered price of the foreign construction material, an offer containing only domestic materials continues to have the higher price. Specifically, the CO evaluates an offer proposing to use foreign construction materials by adding 6% of the cost of the foreign construction materials to the offered price unless the head of the agency specifies a higher percentage. This evaluation factor applies to construction contracts with the DOD as well.

(b) Balance of Payments Program

The Balance of Payments Program restricts the Department of Defense's (a) purchase of supplies that are not domestic end products for use outside the United States and (b) use of construction materials that are not domestic for performance of construction contracts outside the United States. The Program's restrictions, which apply outside the United States, are similar to those of the BAA, which apply within the United States. It uses the same definitions and evaluation procedures as the BAA, except that a 50% evaluation factor generally is used to determine unreasonable cost.

(c) Trade Agreements Act

Congress enacted Title III of the TAA in 1979 to implement the Tokyo Round and, in a 1994 amendment, the Uruguay Round of the General Agreement on Tariffs and Trade Government Procurement Agreement. The TAA promotes nondiscrimination in government procurement by allowing the President to waive discriminatory laws, such as the BAA, for certain categories of goods coming from certain "designated countries." In contrast to the BAA, which imposes an evaluative penalty on foreign offers but allows them to be considered as so evaluated, the TAA bars the government from purchasing noncompliant goods. The TAA is not applicable at the subcontract level.

Specifically, the TAA and its implementing regulations (1) waive application of the Buy American Act and the Balance of Payments Program to the end products and construction materials of designated countries and (2) restrict purchases in acquisitions subject to the TAA to United States-made end products or eligible products (designated, Caribbean Basin, or North American Free Trade Agreement country end products) unless offers for such end products either are not received or are insufficient to fulfill the requirements.

The DOD has compiled a comprehensive list of products subject to the TAA; if a product is not included on the list, the TAA does not apply. With some exceptions, the TAA applies to acquisitions whose estimated value exceeds the dollar threshold set periodically by the United States Trade Representative, with a much lower threshold typically used for supplies or services as compared with construction. When the restrictions of the Buy America Act or the Balance of Payments Program are waived for eligible products, offers of such products receive equal consideration with domestic offers.

A final rule has amended the FAR to implement a revision by the United States. Trade Representative to the list of least-developed countries that are designated countries under the Trade Agreements Act of 1979. This final rule amends the FAR to revise (a) the definitions of "designated country" and "least developed country" and (b) the definition of "designated country."

A decision of the Court of International Trade (CIT) marks the first time that the Court has applied the "substantial transformation" test for an end product's country of origin under the Trade Agreements Act of 1979 (TAA), Pub. L. No. 96–39, codified at 19 U.S.C.A. §§ 2511–2518. *Energizer Battery, Inc. v. United States*, 190 F. Supp. 3d 1308 (Ct. Int'l Trade 2016).

(d) Berry Amendment

The Berry Amendment provides that the DOD may not use appropriated funds to acquire certain items, unless they have been grown, reprocessed, reused or produced in the United States. Some examples are identified food, clothing, and canvas products. Where the solicitation incorporates the Berry Amendment's domestic source requirements, a firm may not receive the contract when pre-award information indicates that the firm would not comply with the domestic preference.

§ 19.6   Environmental Protection Requirements

The FAR includes provisions prescribing acquisition policies and procedures supporting the government's program for protecting and improving the quality of the environment through pollution control, energy conservation, identification of hazardous material, and use of recovered materials.

For example, Contracting Officers must consider energy conservation and efficiency data along with estimated cost and other relevant factors in the preparation of plans, drawings, specifications, and other product descriptions. Whenever hazardous materials will be introduced into the workplace, all apparent successful offerors (before award) and all contractors (at the time of delivery) must provide the Contracting Officer with a "Material Safety Data Sheet" identifying (a) all hazards to which workers may be exposed, (b) relative symptoms and appropriate emergency treatment, and (c) proper conditions for safe use and exposure.

The Resource Conservation and Recovery Act of 1976, as amended, and an Executive Order require agencies, among other things, to implement affirmative procurement programs favoring the purchase of products made with recovered materials. When agencies purchase these Environmental Protection Agency-designated products above certain thresholds, contractors must submit estimates or, in some cases, certifications of the percentage of recovered materials used in contract performance. Other environmental requirements apply when contractors use of radioactive materials and ozone-depleting substances, impose various compliance obligations on contractors operating at federal facilities, and mandate toxic chemical release reporting.

§ 19.7   Drug-Free Workplace Act

In response to the increasing problem of illicit drug use, the government has taken steps to counteract drug use among government employees and in the government contractor workplace. The Drug-Free Workplace Act of 1988 requires that for contracts in excess of the simplified acquisition threshold (except for contracts for commercial items), contractors must establish and maintain a drug-free workplace as a condition of maintaining their current contracts and eligibility for future contracts.

As specified in the FAR "Drug-Free Workplace" contract clause, contractors must agree that they will provide a drug-free workplace by taking the following steps:

1.   Publishing a statement (a) notifying employees that the unlawful manufacture, distribution, dispensing, possession, or use of a controlled substance is prohibited in the contractor's workplace and (b) specifying the actions that will be taken against employees who violate that prohibition;

2.   Providing all employees engaged in the performance of the contract with a copy of this statement and notifying employees in writing that they must abide by the statement's terms;

3.   Establishing an ongoing drug-free awareness program to inform employees about (a) the dangers of drug abuse in the workplace, (b) the contractor's drug-free workplace policy, (c) any available drug

counseling, rehabilitation, and employee assistance programs, and (d) the possible penalties for drug abuse violations occurring in the workplace;

4.   Requiring that employees directly involved in performing a government contract notify the contractor within five days of any criminal drug conviction for a violation occurring in the workplace; and

5.   Notifying the Contracting Officer in writing about any such conviction within 10 days after receiving notice of the conviction and, within 30 days of receiving notice, either taking "appropriate personnel action" against the employee (up to and including termination) or requiring the employee to participate in an approved drug abuse assistance or rehabilitation program.

A contractor's failure to comply with the requirements of the "Drug-Free Workplace" clause or to make good faith efforts to provide a drug-free workplace may result in suspension of contract payments, termination of the contract for default, or the contractor's suspension or debarment from government contracting. However, the head of the contracting agency may waive these actions if necessary to prevent a severe, detrimental disruption of the agency's operations.

Before enactment of the Drug-Free Workplace Act, DOD had issued a "Drug-Free Work Force" clause as part of its own procurement regulations. The DOD clause requires defense contractors to institute and maintain a program to achieve a drug-free work force. To identify potential drug users, the clause includes a requirement for drug testing by the contractor of employees who hold "sensitive positions," a requirement that goes beyond the provisions of the Drug-Free Workplace Act and the FAR. The clause must be included in all DOD contracts (except for contracts for commercial items, to be performed outside the United States, or below the simplified acquisition threshold) (a) that involve access to classified information or (b) when the Contracting Officer determines it necessary for reasons of national security or for the purpose of protecting the health and safety of those using or affected by the contract's performance or end-product.

§ 19.8   Immigration Policies

Under a February 1996 Executive Order, as amended, contractors that knowingly hire illegal immigrants may be debarred from federal contracting. The Order gives the Attorney General the responsibility to investigate whether contractors have hired illegal immigrants, to hold hearings, and to transmit determinations to the contracting agency, which will then consider the contractor for debarment.

Executive Order 13465, "Economy and Efficiency in Government Procurement Through Compliance with Certain Immigration and Nationality Act Provisions and Use of an Electronic Employment Eligibility Verification System," directs executive departments and agencies to require, as a condition of their contracts, that contractors agree to use an electronic eligibility verification requirement system, designated by the Homeland Security Department, to verify whether the contractor has hired only those persons lawfully within the United States. The requirement applies to all persons hired during the term of the contract to perform duties within the United States and assigned by the contractor to work in this country. A final FAR rule implements the Executive Order.

§ 19.9   Defense Base Act

The Defense Base Act ("DBA"), 42 U.S.C.A. §§ 1651–54, is a workers' compensation-like statute that limits damages available to some contractor employees working on Government contracts outside of the United States. The DBA provides contractors with a tool to limit liability for injuries to such overseas employees. When applicable, the DBA, like workers' compensation statutes, limits an employer's liability for on-the-job injuries.

Part V

GENERAL CONTRACTING REQUIREMENTS

Chapter 27

INTELLECTUAL PROPERTY

Analysis

---

§ 27.1   In General

The federal government and contractor community have been engaged for some time in a dialogue on the policies governing contractors' intellectual property. This exchange of views has centered primarily on the treatment to be accorded patents, technical data, and computer software and software documentation. The issues pertain to the rights of the government, the contractor, and third parties; these matters are likely the most difficult and complex of any subject in this Hornbook. Indeed, as will be seen in this chapter, contractors may be held to have waived or forfeited rights in their valuable intellectual property, even though the subjective intent might have been otherwise.

This chapter reviews the government's intellectual property policies as incorporated into statute and regulation. The focus will be on (1) patents, especially the problems of infringement and indemnification, (2) contractors' rights with respect to their technical data and computer software and software documentation, and (3) copyright policy under government contracts. The discussion considers the Federal Acquisition Streamlining Act of 1994 (FASA) and its extensive policy revisions in this area as well as the evolving policy of the Department of Defense (DOD) as expressed in statute and regulation regarding rights in commercial technical data and commercial computer software and software documentation.

§ 27.2   Patents

(a) Title vs. License

A recurring issue deals with which party—the government or the contractor—retains title to patents resulting from work performed under government research and development (R & D) contracts.

The two schools of thought in this area are divided between (a) those who favor a title policy under which the government would retain title to any patent resulting from an invention first conceived or reduced to practice under an R & D contract (the phrase "reduced to practice" is meant to include the construction of at least a functioning model of the invention), and (b) those who favor a license policy under which the contractor/inventor retains full title to the patent for commercial purposes, while conveying a nonexclusive, nontransferable, paid-up (royalty-free) license to the government to use the invention for government purposes.

The basic rationales in support of these divergent positions should be clear. On the one hand, it is logical to require a contractor to grant to the government title to inventions that directly result from publicly funded work. On the other hand, it is true that innovation is greatly enhanced by providing contractors with the economic incentive of a monopoly position. All things being equal, contractors are more likely to develop innovative technology when title to any resulting patents will remain in their possession.

(b) Current Government Policy

The government's current position with regard to R & D contracts is basically the license policy. For many years, the allocation of patent rights varied throughout federal agencies, depending on the needs of each agency.

In 1980, Congress passed a law that added provisions covering patent rights in inventions made with federal assistance to Title 35 of the United States Code. The law granted small businesses, universities, and other nonprofit scientific or educational organizations the right to retain title to inventions derived under federally funded R & D contracts and grants. The government acquires a nonexclusive, irrevocable, paid-up license to use the subject invention for its own purposes. Furthermore, under the statute, the government may modify the rights of the contractor or grantee only where (a) national security is threatened, (b) the contractor is operating a government-owned research or production facility, or (c) other exceptional circumstances exist. Although this law created a uniform government policy and new opportunities for small businesses and nonprofit organizations, it did not change government policy for other contractors.

However, in February 1983, President Reagan issued a memorandum directing the heads of all departments and agencies to extend the benefits of the 1980 law to all R & D contractors, including large businesses and for-profit organizations. The major premises underlying the 1983 presidential memorandum are as follows: (1) patented processes or products developed under federal programs have significant commercial value, (2) properly used, they can improve industrial productivity and the overall national economy, and (3) allowing the contractor to retain title is the best incentive for developing an invention's commercial potential.

Under the memorandum, the government continues to retain at least a royalty-free license in all subject inventions. An exception can be made to waive all government rights when (a) it is necessary to obtain an agreement with a uniquely qualified contractor, or (b) the contract involves cosponsored, cost-sharing, or joint venture R & D, and the contractor is making a substantial contribution of funds, facilities, or equipment to the work performed.

In an age when much new technology is being developed with private funds, this patent policy provides federal agencies with the necessary flexibility to contract for R & D work on terms that contractors will accept and that will promote participation of technologically sophisticated contractors in government programs. For example, the government supports basic research in computer technology with the active cooperation of firms that have developed their own technological base. These firms would be reluctant to apply their expertise if the government could acquire a royalty-free license to all inventions made under the R & D program.

Note, however, that because patent policy for large businesses and for-profit institutions is established by presidential decree and not by statute, it is subject to change by later administrations or preemption by existing or future statutes/regulations.

(c) FAR Coverage

The government policy set forth in the presidential memorandum discussed above—promoting the commercialization of patentable results of federally funded research by granting to all contractors, regardless of size, the title to patents made in whole or in part with federal funds in exchange for royalty-free use by or on behalf of the government—is reflected in the Federal Acquisition Regulation (FAR) and the various FAR "Patent Rights" clauses. The Department of Defense (DOD) is not governed by the FAR on patent rights but adheres to separate DOD FAR Supplement (DFARS) instructions and solicitation/contract terms.

In an important decision, the Federal Circuit in *Campbell Plastics Engineering & Mfg., Inc. v. Brownlee*, 389 F.3d 1243 (Fed. Cir. 2004), has held that absent the contractor's proper disclosure to the government about the contractor's unique manufacturing process, the contractor's failure to timely identify the process as an "invention" under the applicable FAR patent rights clause enabled the agency to acquire title to the invention. The court reached this result even though (a) the law generally disfavors forfeiture of rights, and (b) the contractor's failure to comply with the reporting requirement caused no prejudice to the agency.

(d) Contractor Title Rights

FAR 52.227–11, "Patents Rights—Ownership by the Contractor" clause requires the contractor to disclose to the government in writing any "subject invention"—that is, "any invention of the Contractor made in the performance of work under this contract."

Recently, the FAR clause on patent rights and ownership by the contractor modified the definition of "subject invention," by making the concept a two-step process involving both the terms "subject invention" and how it was "made." The revised FAR clause also clarified that the rights accruing under the patent clause are intended to flow through the tiers to the government and not to the higher tier contractor.

(e) Government License Rights

When the contractor elects to retain title, the government under FAR 27.302(c) retains a "nonexclusive, nontransferable, irrevocable, paid-up license to practice or have practiced for or on behalf of the United States the subject invention throughout the world." That license gives the government the right to allow other contractors, including competitors of the licensor, to produce the item for sale to the government. When the government is the only or the major consumer of the invention, the license the government retains under the "Patent Rights" clause could deprive the contractor of much of the benefit of its title in the invention.

(f) Patent Infringement

One of the basic rights of a patent holder is the right to prevent or enjoin others from the unauthorized use, sale, or production of the patent holder's invention. Where the patent infringer is a government contractor (or the government), however, the right of a patent holder to seek an injunction against the infringer has been significantly altered.

Government contractors are protected by statute from suits by other contractors for patent infringement. Under 28 U.S.C.A. § 1498, a suit in the United States Court of Federal Claims against the government is the exclusive remedy for a patent owner who claims its patented invention has been infringed either by the government or by someone acting for the government. Therefore, the patent holder must proceed against the government (not the infringing contractor), and it may sue to enforce its rights only in the Court of Federal Claims.

A company's allegations that a product of its patented process was used in, or imported into, the United States by or for the United States stated a claim against the Government for infringement under 28 U.S.C.A. § 1498(a), which is not limited by the limits on patent infringement set out in 35 U.S.C.A. § 271(a).

Statute also provides that the government may be liable for "reasonable and entire compensation" (i.e., money damages) for the "unauthorized use" of a patent but will not be liable for the tort of "patent infringement." This language means the patent holder may not seek the remedy of injunctive relief against the government but is limited to monetary compensation (usually equivalent to a fair licensing fee).

Along similar lines, if a solicitation for bids or proposals incorporates technical descriptions of supplies or equipment that authorize or effectively permit patent (or license) infringement, a protest on this issue will not be considered on the merits. More importantly, the government (or its contractor) may continue to use the patented invention once "reasonable compensation" has been paid. Therefore, under this statutory scheme, the contract work may proceed uninterrupted even when an infringement has occurred, while the patent holder may seek its limited remedy of monetary compensation for the infringement.

To implement the statutory policy in this area, an "Authorization and Consent" clause, FAR 52.227–1, is to be included in most government contracts. These clauses are normally broad and generally provide that the government gives its authorization and consent to a contractor to use any invention covered by a United States patent in the performance of its contract. This authorization also extends to subcontracts performed under a prime contract.

If a court finds that the "Authorization and Consent" clause applies, the court will normally dismiss a claim of patent infringement brought against the contractor-infringer. On occasion, however, a lack of authorization and consent has been found, as in one case where the court concluded that a refuse collection contractor used patented equipment when it was not required to do so either by the specifications or by the Contracting Officer. The Federal Circuit in *Zoltek Corp. v. United States*, 442 F.3d 1345 (Fed. Cir. 2006), held that an unauthorized patent use lawsuit cannot be maintained against the government if some steps described in the underlying method patent are practiced outside the United States. The court further held ruled that there is no separate Fifth Amendment claim based on the government's taking of the rights provided by the patent.

(g) Contractor Indemnification of Government

The government may be liable for damages caused by an infringement of a patent by a government contractor, or the government may pass the liability on to the infringing contractor by means of a "Patent Indemnity" clause, FAR 52.227–3. Under such a clause, the contractor agrees to indemnify the government for any damages suffered by the government as a result of the contractor's infringement of a patent. "Patent Indemnity" clauses are usually not considered to be appropriate for inclusion in R & D contracts, however, because they tend to restrain the creativity of contractors performing such work.

In construction, service, and supply contracts of a commercial type, however, government policy requires that the ultimate liability for patent infringement be placed on the contractor. These contracts routinely include both an "Authorization and Consent" clause and a "Patent Indemnity" clause. However, a "Patent Indemnity" clause is not mandatory in negotiated contracts (except those involving construction) but may be used in certain circumstances.

(h) Contractor Notice and Assistance

The "Notice and Assistance Regarding Patent and Copyright Infringement" clause, FAR 52.227–2, requires contractors to report to the Contracting Officer "promptly and in reasonable written detail" all notices or claims of patent (or copyright) infringement that are made against them as a result of their contract work. Under the clause, contractors must also—if a claim or suit is ultimately brought against the government—assist the government in its defense and furnish it with all available documentation pertaining to the claim. Prime contractors must flow this clause down to supply and service subcontracts at all tiers.

§ 27.3   Technical Data and Computer Software

Technical data and computer software are even more controversial subjects than patents. Some persons (mostly in the federal agencies) strongly believe that the government should have unlimited rights to data and software that came into existence in connection with the performance of a publicly funded contract. Others (mostly in industry) argue, however, that requiring a contractor to relinquish valuable proprietary rights stifles innovation and discourages companies from doing business with the government. Both the FAR and the DOD FAR Supplement (DFARS) approaches to the government's rights in technical data and computer software are discussed below.

(a) Regulations

Government contractors must be aware of two different sets of rules for data and software rights—those found in the FAR governing civilian agency procurements and in the DFARS for DOD procurements.

The FAR seeks to balance the interests of agencies predominantly involved in the procurement of commercial products and the interests of government suppliers. The general approach of the FAR is to require delivery of only the minimum data essential to use and maintain the contract product. Similarly, the DFARS seeks a fair balance between the interests of the procuring agencies and their suppliers. Because defense procurements typically involve the acquisition of large, complex systems, the DFARS is considerably more detailed than the FAR and provides rules for a greater variety of licenses and situations. Similarly, although both the FAR and the DFARS set forth specific procedures for contractors to follow to protect data and software delivered to the government, the DFARS requirements (discussed briefly below) are more complex.

Even in DOD, however, the increased emphasis on commercial buying—brought about in large measure by FASA—has resulted in changes to the DFARS regarding the government's rights in technical data and computer software. Thus, although significant differences exist between the two sets of rules, with respect to commercial item acquisitions, both the FAR and DFARS generally limit the government's rights in technical data and computer software to those rights that the contractor customarily provides to the public.

(b) Types of Government Rights

The extent of the government's rights in contractors' technical data and computer software usually depends on whether government funds were used to develop the data or item, component, process, or computer software. Thus, the government typically acquires more limited rights to data or software developed at private expense than it does when public funds are used.

Several types of standard government licenses in technical data and computer software have evolved.

First, the government may obtain unlimited rights to technical data or software, thus gaining the right to use, reproduce, modify, or disclose the data or software as it wishes. Use of this technique, however, runs the risk of deterring knowledgeable prospective contractors from competing because they would naturally be reluctant to disclose technical information that may contain their trade secrets.

Second, the government may obtain no rights by permitting the contractor to withhold data—for example, when the government does not need the data to use the item.

Third, the government may require delivery of technical data, but permit the use of restrictive legends on the data and agree to hold such information in confidence—without, most importantly, using the data to enable another contractor to compete with the developer. This third technique provides the government with limited rights to use and release the data in certain circumstances, but not for commercial purposes or in competitive procurements. The government ordinarily obtains restricted rights (similar to limited rights) in computer software.

Another type of data rights, government purpose license rights, is mentioned only in the DFARS and provides an intermediate level of negotiated government rights between limited rights and unlimited rights. A license of this variety permits the government to use the data for its own purposes, such as authorizing a third party to use the data for the purpose of becoming a competitor for future government purchases (but not for commercial purposes) or becoming a competitor with the developer for a business opportunity created by a commercial organization. In addition, Contracting Officers may tailor data rights to the specific procurement by negotiation, and agencies may develop differing rights in their FAR supplements.

(c) FAR Coverage

As indicated above, the basic government policy on rights in data as stated in the FAR is that the rules of all procurement agencies and their implementation by government personnel should "strike a balance between the government's need and the contractor's legitimate proprietary interest" in the data.

This policy encourages the development and availability of innovative technology for government use by preserving private proprietary rights, while recognizing that it is often necessary for government agencies "to carry out their missions and programs, to acquire or obtain access to many kinds of data produced during or used in the performance of their contracts."

The FAR contains separate terms on the government's rights in technical data and computer software. Where the contract prescribes the transfer of ownership of contractor-prepared computer programs, however, there will be no conflict with the FAR rights in data clause.

(d) Technical Data Under the FAR

The FAR instructs that, except as provided by agency-specific statutes, the government will seek to "acquire only the technical data and the rights in that data customarily provided to the public with a commercial item or process." The Contracting Officer is directed to assume that data delivered under a contract for commercial items was developed exclusively at private expense and is therefore subject to limited rights. If a contract for commercial items requires the delivery of technical data, appropriate clauses delineating the rights in such data will be included in the solicitation and contract.

(e) Computer Software and Software Documentation Under the FAR

The FAR directs that commercial computer software and software documentation shall be "acquired under licenses customarily provided to the public to the extent such licenses are consistent with Federal law and otherwise satisfy the government's needs."

The government's rights generally will only be those specified in a license, which is normally contained in an addendum to the contract. Thus, contractors will not be required to (1) "[f]urnish technical information related to commercial computer software or commercial computer software documentation that is not customarily provided to the public," or (2) "[r]elinquish to, or otherwise provide, the government rights to use, modify, reproduce, release, perform, display, or disclose commercial computer software or commercial computer software documentation," except as the parties agree.

Recently, the FAR was revised to clarify the definition of computer software, most importantly, to exclude computer databases and computer software documentation from the concept. This change means that databases and documentation will be treated, and will need to be marked, as technical data. The FAR definition of computer software is now identical to the DOD formulation.

In another revision, the FAR defines "commercial computer software," which means "any computer software that is a commercial item." Similar to the DOD practice, the FAR provides that commercial computer software is to be acquired under licenses customarily provided to the public to the extent the license is consistent with federal law and otherwise satisfies government needs.

(f) DFARS Coverage

In June, 1995, DOD made significant changes to its technical data policies. These changes included (a) deleting the concept that the government obtain unlimited rights in technical data and the like that were developed at private expense if development "was required for performance of the contract."

Now an item is deemed to be unlimited rights material if the costs of its development were allocated to a government prime or subcontract; (b) clarifying that all development accomplished with costs charged to contractor indirect cost pools is considered development at private expense; (c) requiring that, with some exceptions, DOD receive only "the technical data customarily provided to the public with a commercial item or process;" and (4) providing separate policy treatment and contract clauses for technical data and for computer software and computer software documentation.

More recent DOD policy guidance underscores the importance of engaging in certain practices permitted by the DFARS, including (1) emphasizing the use of specially negotiated license rights; (2) exercising flexibility when negotiating patent rights; (3) using performance-based acquisition strategies that may obviate the need for data and/or rights and (4) acquiring only data and/or rights to data that are truly needed for a given acquisition. Statute requires the DOD to issue policy guidance on the negotiation and acquisition of technical data rights for agreements not covered by the FAR.

The DOD rules are constantly changing and both agencies and industry must struggle to keep current. For example, Pub. L. No. 114–328, Amendments Relating to Technical Data Rights, § 809(b)(5), amends 10 U.S.C.A. § 2320 to provide that the United States "shall have government purpose rights in technical data pertaining to an interface between an item or process and other items or processes that was developed in part with Federal funds and in part at private expense." However, DOD may negotiate rights that extend beyond Government-purpose rights "in any case in which the Secretary of Defense determines, on the basis of criteria established in the regulations, that negotiation of different rights in such technical data would be in the best interest of the United States."

In a final example, Pub. L. No. 115–391, Continuation of Technical Data Rights During Challenges, § 866, modifies 10 U.S.C.A. § 2321 to permit the DOD to exercise certain rights in technical data while a dispute over the scope and nature of DOD's data rights is pending before the United States Court of Federal Claims or a board of contract appeals, provided that the secretary of defense or of a military department, signs a written determination that "compelling mission readiness requirements" will not permit waiting for the COFC's or board's decision.

(g) Technical Data Under the DFARS

The DFARS contains separate terms for acquiring rights in contractor technical data depending on whether commercial or noncommercial items are involved.

Commercial Items—As noted above, DOD acquires only the technical data customarily provided to the public with a commercial item or process, except technical data that "(1) [a]re form, fit, or function data, (2) [a]re required for repair or maintenance of commercial items or processes, or for the proper installation, operating, or handling of a commercial item, either as a stand-alone unit or as a part of a military system, when such data are not customarily provided to commercial users or the data provided to commercial users is not sufficient for military purposes; or (3) [d]escribe the modifications made at government expense to a commercial item or process in order to meet the requirements of a government solicitation."

Noncommercial Items—The DFARS provides that for noncommercial items, DOD acquires only the technical data and rights in that data sufficient to satisfy its needs. Thus, solicitations and contracts must specify, by separate line items where possible, the technical data to be delivered, and must establish or reference procedures for determining the technical data's acceptability.

(h) Computer Software and Software Documentation Under the DFARS

The DFARS treatment of rights in computer software and software documentation also varies depending on whether commercial or noncommercial items are involved.

Commercial Items—The DFARS provides that DOD will have only the rights specified in the license agreement under which the commercial computer software or software documentation was obtained. If rights not conveyed by the license are necessary, the government must negotiate with the contractor to determine if there are acceptable terms for conveying such rights.

Noncommercial Items—The DFARS provides that DOD will acquire only the computer software or software documentation necessary to satisfy its needs. Solicitations and contracts must (1) specify the computer software or software documentation to be delivered, (2) establish (where practicable) separate line items for the computer software and related documentation as well as procedures for determining their acceptability, and (3) require that computer software and related documentation that are to be furnished with restrictions be identified prior to delivery.

Offerors are not required to sell or otherwise relinquish to the government any rights in computer software and related documentation beyond the standard grant of license, except for (1) corrections or changes furnished to the government, (2) software or documentation that is otherwise available to the public or has been released or disclosed by the contractor without any restrictions or is otherwise obtained by the government with unlimited rights, and (3) software and documentation that were initially furnished with restrictions that have expired.

(i) DFARS Procedures

The DFARS sets forth procedures to be followed by contractors to secure data rights protection. If a contractor intends to deliver technical data to the government with restrictions on its use, it must identify those items or processes, to the maximum extent practicable, prior to delivery.

This prior notice requirement serves as the basis for identifying all technical data restrictions applicable to the government unless the Contracting Officer challenges the validity of the contractor's assertions. As discussed above, the standard rights that a contractor grants to the government are unlimited rights, government purpose rights, or limited rights.

To preserve "limited rights" in data, the contractor must (1) identify those restricted documents in an attachment to the contract, and (2) mark them with a restrictive legend. The following information should appear in the legend: (a) the contract number and contractor name, (b) the date the data will be subject to unlimited rights (if applicable), and (c) an indication (by circling, underscoring, etc.) of the specific data to which the legend applies.

The legend must appear on each piece of data submitted to the government for which "Limited Rights" are claimed, and the government must include the legend on all reproductions of the data. A similar marking requirement applies to data submitted subject to "government purpose" license rights."

If a contractor—through inadvertence or otherwise—submits data without a restrictive legend, the data will be considered to have been submitted with unlimited rights. Thus, in a United States Court Federal Claims case, *Ervin & Associates, Inc. v. United States,* 59 Fed. Cl. 267 (2004), because the contractor failed to affix the FAR-required notices to the data, the government's rights were unrestricted despite separate contractor correspondence with the agency stating that the material was proprietary and could not be reproduced to third parties.

However, the contractor may identify other data not originally marked if it does so within six months of the data's delivery, provided (1) the failure to mark is based on new information or inadvertent omission, and (2) the proposed marking is justified.

Note, however, that marking the item with a restrictive legend will not protect information not otherwise entitled to protection. Therefore, the government is free to use an idea generally known in the trade, even though the idea was submitted to the government as a trade secret. On the other hand, merely because design and development are part of the contractor's obligation under a contract does not necessarily mean that a particular item was developed at government expense. The contractor may still show that it previously developed the item.

The DFARS contains "validation" procedures that the government may use to review or challenge restrictive markings on data. The Contracting Officer accomplishes a pre-challenge review by asking the contractor to furnish a written justification for any restriction asserted, which the Contracting Officer then reviews. After determining that a challenge to a restrictive marking is warranted, the Contracting Officer must send written notice to the contractor setting forth the grounds for the challenge and giving the contractor an opportunity to justify the current validity of the restrictive marking.

Where the contractor fails or refuses to do so, and the government intends to pursue the matter, the Contracting Officer will then issue a final decision on the validity of the restrictive marking. This decision can be appealed in the disputes process (see Chapter 33).

(j) Enforcing Data Rights

Misuse of proprietary contractor data related to a government contract can occur either inside or outside the procurement process. There are essentially three remedies available to a contractor for data misuse by the government: (a) an injunction (and declaratory relief) to stop a threatened disclosure; (b) a "bid protest" remedy—to counter a threat to disclose as an error in the course of a contract competition; or (c) money damages—in cases where the government has already made a disclosure to the public.

Regarding the above protest remedy, where a firm believes that a government solicitation improperly incorporates the vendor's proprietary data, the protester must show that its material was marked as proprietary or confidential or that it was disclosed in confidence; and the material involved significant time and expense in preparation and contained material or concepts that could not be independently obtained from publicly available information or common knowledge. *Ingersoll Rand Co.*, B-236391, 89-2 CPD ¶ 517. Even where the protester has established proprietary rights in the material, a recommendation for a sole-source award or a requirement for each offeror to purchase a license from the protester would be an extraordinary GAO remedy.

An injunction to stop the data disclosure can be obtained only from a court. No grounds for such relief will exist where the agency properly releases proprietary data, such as where it is in the public domain. The boards of contract appeal have jurisdiction over a claim that the Government breached the contract by disclosing a contractor's proprietary data.

Where the government violates the contractor's rights under the FAR rights in data clause the government will be liable to the contractor for its lost profits, as contrasted with the speculative relief for the contractor's diminished net worth or lost contract claims. Finally, if the misuse has occurred or cannot be prevented, monetary compensation—based on a theory of breach of contract or unconstitutional taking of property, for example—may be available from the government. A tort remedy of wrongful disclosure of a trade secret is another possible remedy.

The United States Court of Appeals for the Federal Circuit has established a very stringent rule for firms that submit unsolicited proposals containing proprietary information to the Government. In *Xerxe Group, Inc. v. United States*, 278 F.3d 1357 (Fed. Cir. 2002), the court affirmed a decision of the Court of Federal Claims holding that the submitter's failure to place a notice on each page of an unsolicited proposal relinquished any rights pertaining to information on the unmarked pages even though the submitter placed the required legend on the cover page of the proposal.

Pub. L. No. 111–383, § 801 authorizes the DOD to disclose technical data to a litigation support contractor, although that contractor (which may include an expert or technical consultant) must assure the Defense Department, by agreement, that the technical data will be protected and will not be used to compete for future contracts. A final rule amends the DFARS to implement a section of National Defense Authorization Act of 2010 that provides authority for certain types of Government support contractors through an agreement to have access to proprietary technical data or computer software belonging to prime contractors and other third parties.

Pub. L. No. 111–383, § 824, calls for the secretary of defense to issue guidance ensuring the Government's access to technical data produced at the Government's expense, to promote competition and ensure that the United States is not required to pay more than once for the same technical data.

§ 27.4   Copyright

Copyright protection extends to any original work of authorship in any tangible medium of expression. Generally, the owner of a copyright has the exclusive rights, among others, to (1) reproduce the copyrighted work and (2) prepare derivative works. Thus, copyrighted material is not available to the general public for reproduction without the permission of the copyright owner through a license or other conveyance. Computer software, for example, which may be delivered by a contractor in connection with a government contract, is often published and copyrighted.

The general government policy is to preserve contractors' rights under the copyright laws while ensuring that its own use of copyrighted material will not be considered an infringement of the copyright. Under the FAR, contractors are normally authorized, without the permission of the government, to establish a claim to copyright in technical or scientific articles based on or containing data first produced in the performance of a government contract containing the "Rights in Data-General" clause and published in academic, technical, or professional journals and similar works.

Otherwise, the permission of the Contracting Officer is required to establish a claim to copyright subsisting in data first produced in the performance of a contract, unless a special FAR clause is used. The FAR states that assent will normally be given but lists several broad grounds on which the Contracting Officer may deny the request.

The DFARS uses "for guidance" the same policies with respect to copyrights as it does for technical data and computer software and software documentation. DOD generally takes the position that— unless a work is designated a "special work"—a contractor may copyright any work of authorship first generated under a contract as long as the contractor grants to the government a royalty-free license to use the work for government purposes. Where the primary purpose of the contract is the creation of a "special work" (such as an audiovisual work or departmental history), however, the government retains ownership and control of the work.

The exclusive remedy for copyright infringement against the government is to sue for reasonable compensation in the United States Court of Federal Claims. The court has no jurisdiction under the Digital Millennium Copyright Act of 1998, 17 U.S.C.A. §§ 1201 et seq., for copyright infringement.

Chapter 29

TAXES

Analysis

§ 29.1   In General

This chapter explains the policies and procedures for (a) using tax clauses in contracts (including foreign contracts), (b) asserting immunity or exemption from taxes, and (c) obtaining tax refunds. It explains Federal, State, and local taxes on certain supplies and services acquired by executive agencies and the applicability of such taxes to the Federal Government. It is for general information and does not present the full scope of the tax laws and regulations.

Contract tax problems vary widely. Agencies must resolve specific tax questions by reference to the applicable contract terms and to the pertinent tax laws and regulations. To achieve consistent treatment within an agency, Contracting Officers or other authorized personnel shall consult the agency-designated counsel before negotiating with any taxing authority for either determining whether a tax is valid or applicable or obtaining exemption from, or refund of, a tax.

Similarly, before purchasing goods or services from a foreign source, the Contracting Officer should consult the agency-designated counsel for information on foreign tax treaties and agreements in force and on the implementation of any foreign-tax-relief programs and to resolve any other tax questions affecting the prospective contract.

§ 29.2   State and Local Taxes

The Federal Government generally is immune from direct State and local taxation. An example would be where state taxing authorities attempted to tax a federal entity's phone bill. Whether any specific purchase or lease is immune, however, is a legal question requiring advice and assistance of the agency-designated counsel. When economically feasible, executive agencies shall take maximum advantage of all exemptions from State and local taxation that may be available. If appropriate, the Contracting Officer shall provide a Standard Form 1094, United States Tax Exemption Form or other evidence listed in the regulation to establish that the Government is making the direct purchase.

Agencies should not normally designate prime contractors and subcontractors as agents of the Government for the purpose of claiming immunity from State or local sales or use taxes. Before any activity contends that a contractor is an agent of the Government, it must refer the matter to the agency head for review.

When the prime contractor or subcontractor under a prime contract makes the purchase, as opposed to the Government, the right to an exemption of the transaction from a sales or use tax may not rest on the Government's immunity from direct taxation by States and localities. It may rest instead on provisions of the particular State or local law involved, or, in some cases, the transaction may not in fact be expressly exempt from the tax. The Government's interest shall be protected by using the Federal Acquisition Regulation (FAR) procedures.

Frequently, property (including property acquired under the progress payments clause of fixed-price contracts or the Government property clause of cost-reimbursement contracts) owned by the Government is in the possession of a contractor or subcontractor. Situations may arise in which States or localities assert the right to tax Government property directly or to tax the contractor's or subcontractor's possession of, interest in, or use of that property. In such cases, the Contracting Officer shall seek review and advice from the agency-designated counsel on the appropriate course of action.

§ 29.3   Contract Coverage

Most cost reimbursement type contracts will apply the FAR cost principle making federal, state and local taxes allowable except as proscribed by regulation. Most of the discussion in this chapter will concern fixed price contracts, the most common pricing arrangement. See generally, Steven W. Feldman, *Contractor Liability for Taxes under FAR 52.229–3: When Are Equitable Adjustments Permissible?*, 44 Procurement Lawyer 1 (Summer 2009).

For most fixed price contracts to be performed wholly or partly in the United States, the solicitation must contain mandatory clauses requiring the contract price to contain (with limited exceptions) all applicable federal, state, and local taxes and duties. Upward equitable adjustments after award are available in a limited way, for example, the contract price shall be increased by the amount of any after-imposed Federal tax, provided the Contractor warrants in writing that no amount for such newly imposed Federal excise tax or duty or rate increase was included in the contract price, as a contingency reserve or otherwise. Downward equitable adjustments also can occur, for example, the contract price shall be decreased by the amount of any after-relieved Federal tax.

No legal requirement exists for a solicitation to advise offerors that a particular jurisdiction does or does not impose a particular tax for a particular product. A standard contract clause (one of several) requires that the contract price include all applicable taxes constitutes notice to all offerors that proposals will be evaluated on a tax-included basis, instructs that the offerors must ascertain whether any taxes apply and mandates inclusion of these taxes in the price. The most widely-used clause is FAR 52.229–3, Federal, State and Local Taxes.

Thus, the primary purpose of soliciting offers on a tax-included basis is to limit the government's payment obligation to the price offered—the contractor will be precluded from successfully claiming at a later date that the government should reimburse the firm for any taxes that the firm ultimately has to pay which allegedly were not contemplated when the firm submitted its proposal. Also, competition on a mutual tax-included basis ensures commonality of evaluation, although the GAO has not objected to an offer "on a 'tax-excluded' basis" permitted by the solicitation when the cost and amount of the tax is specified elsewhere in the offer and commonality remains among the offerors.

Offerors have the burden of determining taxes because they are generally more familiar with the application of state and local taxes than is the contracting agency. Nearly all states and many localities impose taxes or duties, and the rules vary greatly from one jurisdiction to another. Additionally, contracting agencies ordinarily are not sufficiently familiar with the offerors' operations to make these taxability determinations. Furthermore, it would be inappropriate for agencies to shoulder the administrative burden of examining the tax situation (and to make assessments of the various state and local tax laws) for each offeror who may submit a proposal. An offer taking exception to a solicitation requirement that price be on a tax-included basis can be found unacceptable for award.

The cases have strictly enforced the above "Federal, State and Local Taxes" clause. Because the standard FAR clause contains no provision for post-contractual relief from after-imposed state or local taxes, the contractor bears the risk of such increases, even if it omitted the tax through no fault of its own. Where offeror submits an offer on a tax exempt basis, it still bears the ultimate responsibility for any tax liability that may arise from the contract.

Two clauses used in cost reimbursement contracts, FAR 52.232–20, Limitation of Cost, and 52.232–22, Limitation of Funds, does not necessarily bar recovery of state general excise taxes that the contractor and its partners were required to pay, even though the taxes exceeded the amount of funds allotted to the contract.

Chapter 30

COST ACCOUNTING STANDARDS

Analysis

---

§ 30.1   In General

In 1970, Congress passed a statute directing the establishment of the Cost Accounting Standards Board (CAS Board). The statute directed the Board to promulgate cost accounting standards that would achieve uniformity and consistency in the cost accounting practices followed by prime contractors and subcontractors in estimating, accumulating, and reporting costs under negotiated defense prime contracts and subcontracts.

In general, it was agreed that the Standards should (1) not require the application of precisely prescribed methods of computing each different type of cost; (2) not be limited to cost-reimbursement contracts, but rather, should apply to all types of negotiated prime and subcontracts; (3) evolve from sound commercial cost accounting practices and should be compatible with generally accepted accounting principles; and (4) require contractors to maintain contract performance records in conformity with the standards and with the approved practices set forth in disclosure statements.

In addition, the CAS Board was directed to prepare regulations requiring contractors, as a condition of contracting with the government, to (1) disclose in writing their cost accounting practices and (2) agree to a contract price adjustment in the event of noncompliance with applicable CAS or failure to follow disclosed or established cost accounting practices.

The CAS Board carried out its mission with vigor, promulgating regulations that established a number of individual standards (which are collectively referred to as the Cost Accounting Standards (CAS)) as well as requirements for contractor disclosure statements and contract price adjustments. The Board also promulgated regulations covering its own operations. However, the first Board ceased to exist on September 30, 1980, after Congress failed to appropriate funds for the Board's FY 1981 operations.

In 1988, a new, independent CAS Board was created. This legislation provided that all standards, interpretations, modifications, rules, regulations, waivers, and exemptions promulgated by the first CAS Board would "remain in effect unless and until amended, superseded or rescinded by the new Board," and gave the Board exclusive authority to promulgate, amend, interpret, and rescind the CAS.

The Board is composed of the Administrator of the Office of Federal Procurement Policy, one representative each from the Department of Defense (DOD) and the General Services Administration, and two private sector members. Its makeup and functions undergo constant scrutiny from the procuring agencies and the private sector.

In 1992, the CAS Board promulgated a recodified set of administrative rules and Standards, and the Federal Acquisition Regulation (FAR) was amended to reflect the recodifications. This amendment removed the CAS rules and regulations from FAR Subpart 30.3 and placed them in an appendix to FAR Part 30. In addition, the FAR was amended to conform to CAS Board changes regarding the criteria, thresholds, and procedures for applying the CAS to negotiated contracts. Where the CAS and FAR cost allowability provisions conflict, the CAS will govern.

Pub. L. No. 114–328, § 820(a) amends 41 U.S.C.A. § 1501 to establish certain duties for the Cost Accounting Standards Board, for example, to ensure that the cost accounting standards used by Federal contractors rely, to the maximum extent practicable, on commercial standards and accounting practices and systems. The Defense CAS Board, a separate entity, is defunct. Pub. L. No. 116–92, Div. A, Title VIII, § 810(a), Dec. 20, 2019, 133 Stat. 1487.

§ 30.2   Applicability

The CAS and the Board's regulations are inapplicable to certain defense and nondefense negotiated prime and subcontracts as explained in 48 CFR 9903.201–1. Implementation of the CAS and contractor disclosure requirements is accomplished by including a notice in solicitations and a "Cost Accounting Standards" clause in contracts. Thus, the solicitation will advise prospective offerors whether the proposed contract is subject to the CAS Board's requirements.

The CAS principles are the most relevant for contract administration, although they occasionally pertain to contract formation issues. The GAO has held that the CAS requirements and contract accounting principles establish rules for the consistent accumulation and reporting of cost data and do not require that an offeror base its fixed prices upon any particular allocation of costs.

The COFC has noted that the CAS statute primarily protects the Government from unwarranted contract performance costs and prohibits windfalls to the Government. *The Boeing Co. v. United States*, 143 Fed. Cl. 298 (2019).

§ 30.3   Exemptions and Waiver

Under 48 C.F.R. § 9903.201–1(b), the following categories of contracts and subcontracts are exempt from all CAS requirements:

(1)   Sealed bid contracts.

(2)   Negotiated contracts and subcontracts not in excess of the Truth in Negotiations Act (TINA) (now Truthful Cost or Pricing Data statute) threshold, as adjusted for inflation (41 U.S.C.A. § 1908 and 41 U.S.C.A. § 1502(b)(1)(B)). For purposes of this paragraph (b)(2), an order issued by one segment to another segment shall be treated as a subcontract.

(3)   Contracts and subcontracts with small businesses.

(4)   Contracts and subcontracts with foreign governments or their agents or instrumentalities or, insofar as the requirements of CAS other than 9904.401 and 9904.402 are concerned, any contract or subcontract awarded to a foreign concern.

(5)   Contracts and subcontracts in which the price is set by law or regulation.

(6)   Contracts and subcontracts authorized in 48 C.F.R. § 12.207 for the acquisition of commercial items.

(7)   Contracts or subcontracts of less than $7.5 million, provided that, at the time of award, the business unit of the contractor or subcontractor is not currently performing any CAS-covered contracts or subcontracts valued at $7.5 million or greater.

(8) to (12) [Reserved]

(13) Subcontractors under the NATO PHM Ship program to be performed outside the United States by a foreign concern.

(14) [Reserved by 76 FR 49368]

(15) Firm-fixed-price contracts or subcontracts awarded on the basis of adequate price competition without submission of certified cost or pricing data.

As indicated above, implementing § 823(a) of the Duncan Hunter National Defense Authorization Act for Fiscal Year 2009, the Cost Accounting Standards Board has issued a final rule eliminating the former CAS exemption at 48 C.F.R. § 9903.201–1(b)(14) for contracts and subcontracts executed and performed entirely outside the United States.

In some instances, all or part of the CAS Board's Standards and requirements may be waived for a particular prime contract or subcontract. The head of an agency is authorized to waive CAS requirements for contracts or subcontracts under $15 million if the official determines, in writing, that the performing business unit (a) is engaged primarily in the sale of commercial items, and (b) would not otherwise be subject to the CAS requirements. CAS requirements may also be waived for contracts exceeding $15 million in "exceptional circumstances" (i.e., when a waiver is necessary to meet the needs of the agency).

§ 30.4   Types of CAS Coverage

There are two types of CAS coverage—"full" and "modified." Full coverage applies to a business unit of any contractor that (a) receives a single CAS-covered contract or subcontract of $50 million or more or (b) received $50 million or more in net CAS-covered awards during its preceding cost accounting period. A contractor subject to full coverage must follow all of the Standards.

A business unit that receives a covered contract of less than $50 million may elect modified CAS coverage if the covered contracts that it was awarded in the immediately preceding cost accounting period totaled less than $50 million. Modified coverage requires that the business unit comply with CAS 401, CAS 402, CAS 405, and CAS 406 (all discussed below).

A recent clause, FAR 52.230–4, sets forth the rules for disclosure and consistency of the cost accounting practices applicable to foreign concerns. The clause makes clear that CAS does not apply to contracts with foreign concerns otherwise exempt from CAS coverage and that "foreign business concerns" do not include foreign governments or their agents or instrumentalities.

§ 30.5   Contractor Obligations

The "Cost Accounting Standards" FAR clause, along with its companion clauses, must be inserted in contracts and subcontracts subject to full coverage under the Cost Accounting Standards. The basic clause requires contractors and subcontractors to do the following:

1.   Disclose in writing their cost accounting practices by completing a "Disclosure Statement;"

2.   Follow their disclosed practices consistently in estimating, accumulating, and reporting costs;

3.   Comply with all of the individual CAS in effect on the contract award date; and

4.   Agree to an adjustment of the contract price when the contractor or subcontractor fails to comply with existing Standards or its own disclosed practices.

Besides implementing the substance of the CAS Board's enabling statute, the "Cost Accounting Standards" clause also establishes the contract price adjustment procedure to be followed whenever a contractor makes a cost accounting practice change. (Hereinafter, the term "contractor" in Chapter 30 includes "subcontractor" except as stated otherwise.)

The clause identifies several types of adjustments in various provisions. One element permits an upward adjustment in contract price only when a new Standard is issued that has the effect of increasing the cost of a previously-awarded covered contract. Another element requires downward adjustment, if appropriate, pursuant to a "voluntary" cost accounting change by the contractor but does not permit upward adjustment. A third element entitles the contractor to an adjustment for a "voluntary" cost accounting change, without regard to increased costs to the government, if the Contracting Officer finds the change to be "desirable" and "not detrimental to the interests of the government." Finally, a fourth element deals with the consequences of a failure, whether unintentional or inadvert, to comply with the Standards or the contractor's disclosed accounting practices. This liability is equal to the amount of the increased costs paid by the government as a result of noncompliance.

For more than 50 years, both the former United States Court of Claims (now Federal Circuit) and, until recently, the ASBCA have held that the Government may not retroactively disallow costs, or retroactively disapprove a contractor's cost accounting practices, when a contractor has detrimentally relied on the Government's acquiescence or approval of those costs or cost accounting practices. Because the rule is based on the questionable doctrine of equitable estoppel against the government, the ASBCA rejected this principle in *Tech. Sys., Inc.*, ASBCA 59577, 17-1 BCA ¶ 36,631.

In the case of CAS noncompliance, compound interest runs from the date on which the CAS noncompliance occurs through the date that the Government receives full compensation, i.e., interest continues to accrue until the Government receives full payment of principal and interest.

Beginning in April 1993, the CAS Board embarked on a lengthy rulemaking proceeding intended to modify the definition and administration of cost accounting practice changes. The rule, as finalized some seven years later, deals primarily with the cost impact of changes in a contractor's cost accounting practices—including those associated with external restructuring activities.

First, the rule—to encourage greater reliance on the "desirable" change provisions in the CAS—provides that changes in a contractor's cost accounting practices may be deemed "desirable" even if such a determination has the effect of raising the prices to the government on existing CAS-covered contracts or subcontracts. Secondly, the rule discusses three additional types of cost accounting practice changes: (a) required changes (those that a contractor must make in order to comply with the CAS due to award of an additional CAS-covered contract) for which the government pays the increased costs, (b) unilateral changes (changes from one compliant practice to another that do not satisfy the "desirable" change criteria) for which offsets of increases and decreases are permitted so long as there is no net upward price adjustment, and (c) noncompliant practices for which the government is required to adjust the prices of CAS-covered contracts to avoid paying any increased costs in the aggregate.

Finally, in DOD contracts, the rule contains a term exempting from the CAS cost impact process those cost accounting practice changes causally related to external restructuring activities associated with contractor business combinations. This exemption is conditioned on a written determination by the Secretary of Defense that the projected savings from the change will (a) be at least twice the amount of the costs allowed, or (b) exceed the amount of costs allowed—where the new business combination preserves a critical capability that might otherwise be lost.

§ 30.6   Disclosure Statements

Unless exempted from filing requirements, a contractor covered by the CAS is obligated to file a "Disclosure Statement"—a written description of the contractor's cost accounting practices and procedures. A standard solicitation provision used in CAS-covered contracts requires certain offerors to submit information regarding its disclosure statement and the cost accounting standards.

No requirement exists under the FAR for a contractor submitting cost or pricing data (see Chapter 15) to disclose whether it is, or may be, in noncompliance with their Disclosure Statement or Cost Accounting Standards that the cognizant federal agency official has determined to have an immaterial cost impact. As indicated above, the "Cost Accounting Standards" clause for full-coverage contracts imposes this requirement. Specifically, the contractor shall:

> By submission of a Disclosure Statement, disclose in writing the Contractor's cost accounting practices ... including methods of distinguishing direct costs from indirect costs and the basis used for allocating indirect costs. The practices disclosed for this contract shall be the same as the practices currently disclosed and applied on all other contracts and subcontracts being performed by the Contractor and which contain a Cost Accounting Standards (CAS) clause. If the Contractor has notified the Contracting Officer that the Disclosure Statement contains trade secrets and commercial or financial information which is privileged and confidential, the Disclosure Statement shall be protected and shall not be released outside of the government.

The government has certain responsibilities regarding Disclosure Statements. For example, after including an appropriate notice in the solicitation for a proposed contract to indicate that the contract is subject to CAS Board requirements, the Contracting Officer must ensure that offerors submit required Disclosure Statements. The appropriate government auditor is designated to conduct an initial review of Disclosure Statements. Thereafter, the cognizant Administrative Contracting Officer determines whether a Disclosure Statement is adequate and notifies the contractor in case of any deficiencies.

In a recent GAO decision, the agency reasonably determined that an incorporated joint venture awardee satisfied the requirement for Cost Accounting Standards disclosure statement where the proposal included disclosure statements originally submitted by, and concerning cost accounting systems of, the joint venture members/subcontractors.

(a) Time of Submission

Currently, any contractor that was awarded a single CAS-covered contract of $50 million or more, or, together with its segments, received $50 million or more in net CAS-covered awards during its preceding cost accounting period, must submit a completed Disclosure Statement before award of its first covered contract in the immediately following cost accounting period. However, if the first CAS-covered contract is received within 90 days of the start of the cost accounting period, the contractor is not required to file until the end of 90 days.

If a Disclosure Statement is required, a separate Disclosure Statement must also be submitted for each segment of a company whose costs included in the total price of any CAS-covered contract or subcontract exceed the Truth in Negotiations Act (TINA) (now Truthful Cost or Pricing statute) threshold current at the time, unless the contract or subcontract is exempt from CAS requirements or the division's CAS-covered awards were both less than 30% of total segment sales and less than $10 million in the most recently completed cost accounting period.

(b) Form of Submission

The standard Disclosure Statement is submitted on Form CASB-DS-1, a lengthy document, which can be obtained from the cognizant Administrative Contracting Officer. Offerors must file their CASB-DS-1s with both the Administrative Contracting Officer (the original and one copy) and the cognizant auditor (one copy).

The DS-1 form in its latest (1996) version consists of eight parts that address, among other things, the cost of money, postretirement benefits, and employee stock option plans. Most emphasis is given to Part VII, "Deferred Compensation and Insurance Costs." This DS-1 form reduces some of the detailed reporting previously required and also clarifies the requirements for annual updating. The DS-1 form emphasizes the concept of full disclosure, which can prevent a deficient filing as well as subsequent compliance problems.

§ 30.7   Individual Standards

The individual CAS helps ensure a more uniform treatment of costs incurred by government contractors. The Government bears the burden of proving that a contractor's accounting practices do not comply with the CAS.

A close relationship exists between the CAS and the cost principles. For example, one of the factors for determining cost allowability set forth in the FAR Subpart 31.2 cost principles is consideration of applicable CAS Board "Standards." Nonetheless, the CAS are not based on cost principles. Collectively, they represent the government's view of acceptable cost accounting techniques. Even though the Standards do not determine categories or individual items of cost that are allowable, it is more likely that the costs expended will be deemed allowable if the CAS are followed.

The 19 individual CAS are discussed briefly below. Each Standard is designated as "CAS" followed by a three-digit number corresponding to the sections in Title 48 of the Code of Federal Regulations where each Standard has been codified. The FAR Appendix contains the CAS and the related rules and regulations of the CAS Board.

CAS 401—Consistency in Estimating, Accumulating, and Reporting Costs. CAS 401 establishes the fundamental requirement that a contractor's practices used in estimating costs for proposals must be consistent with the cost accounting practices the contractor uses in accumulating and reporting those costs.

CAS 402—Consistency in Allocating Costs Incurred for the Same Purpose. CAS 402 requires that each type of cost be allocated to a contract only once, and only on one basis (i.e., only as a direct cost or as an indirect cost). However, CAS 402 does not require direct cost treatment for bid and proposal costs incurred to enhance chances of winning a follow-on contract.

CAS 403—Allocation of Home Office Expenses to Segments. CAS 403 establishes criteria for allocation of home office expenses to segments reporting directly to one home office, based on beneficial or causal relationships.

CAS 404—Capitalization of Tangible Assets. CAS 404 requires contractors to establish and adhere to capitalization policies that satisfy criteria set forth in the Standard.

CAS 405—Accounting for Unallowable Costs. CAS 405 sets forth guidelines for early identification and treatment of unallowable costs.

CAS 406—Cost Accounting Period. CAS 406 includes criteria for the selection of time periods to be used as cost accounting periods for cost estimating, accumulating, and reporting.

CAS 407—Use of Standard Costs for Direct Material and Direct Labor. CAS 407 provides for the use of standard costs for estimating, accumulating, and reporting costs.

CAS 408—Accounting for Costs of Compensated Personal Absence. CAS 408 is intended to assure that personal absence costs are assigned to the accounting period in which the related labor is performed and the related wage and salary costs are recognized.

CAS 409—Depreciation of Tangible Capital Assets. CAS 409 establishes criteria for assigning depreciation costs to the proper cost accounting period and for consistent allocation to cost objectives.

CAS 410—Allocation of Business Unit General and Administrative Expenses to Final Cost Objectives. This Standard sets forth criteria for allocating the cost of management and administration—i.e., general and administrative expense—of a business unit based on beneficial or causal relationships.

CAS 411—Accounting for Acquisition Costs of Material. CAS 411 provides methods for using material inventory records to determine acquisition costs.

CAS 412—Composition and Measurement of Pension Cost. CAS 412 establishes the components of pension cost, the basis for measuring such costs, and the criteria for assigning these costs to cost accounting periods.

CAS 413—Adjustment and Allocation of Pension Costs. CAS 413 gives guidance for adjusting pension costs by measuring actuarial gains and losses and assigning them to accounting periods. If a pension plan is terminated, the government has been held to be entitled to share in the proceeds reverting to a contractor from the termination.

CAS 414—Cost of Money as an Element of the Cost of Facilities Capital. CAS 414 provides for explicit recognition of the cost of money for facilities capital as an element of contract cost.

CAS 415—Accounting for the Cost of Deferred Compensation. This Standard applies to the cost of all deferred compensation except for compensated personal absence and pension plan costs covered, respectively, by CAS 408 and CAS 412.

CAS 416—Accounting for Insurance Costs. CAS 416 provides criteria for measurement of insurance costs, assignment to accounting periods, and allocation to cost objectives.

CAS 417—Cost of Money as an Element of the Cost of Capital Assets Under Construction. CAS 417 provides for the determination of an imputed cost of money to be included in the capitalized cost of acquisition of assets constructed for a contractor's own use.

CAS 418—Allocation of Direct and Indirect Costs. CAS 418 provides for consistent determination of direct and indirect costs. It does not apply to the allocation of indirect cost pools covered by other Standards.

CAS 420—Accounting for Independent Research and Development and Bid and Proposal Costs. This Standard sets forth criteria for the accumulation of independent research and development and bid and proposal costs and their allocation to cost objectives.

In addition to the Standards, the CAS Board periodically has issued "Interpretations" as appendices to certain Standards.

Interpretations were added to CAS 401 and CAS 402 in 1976, and one was added to CAS 403 in 1980. The Board also has published "Comments" concerning some of the factors that it has considered in issuing particular Standards and Interpretations.

Chapter 32

PAYMENT AND FINANCING

Analysis

§ 32.1 In General

Payment and financing are related subjects in government contracting; both concern how much money a contractor can expect to receive from the government under various types of contracts. Contract payments typically are made in exchange for actual work performed, while various forms of government financing may be available before a contract product or service is delivered and accepted. Agency regulations commonly supplement the Federal Acquisition Regulation (FAR) in these areas and should be consulted.

Contractors do not always submit timely invoices for their work, which can create administrative problems for government agencies in resolving unliquidated obligations. If the contractor fails to submit a completion invoice or voucher in a timely manner, the Contracting Officer may determine the amounts due to the contractor under the contract and record this determination in a unilateral modification to the contract. This determination must be issued as a final decision under the Contract Disputes Act. In a number of agencies, this problem has been alleviated to an extent by the general requirement for electronic invoices.

Perhaps more importantly for small business concerns, The National Defense Authorization Act for FY 2020, Pub. L. No. 116–92, § 873, and the National Defense Authorization Act for 2019, Pub. L. No. 115–232, § 852, address accelerated payments applicable to contracts with certain small business concerns under the Prompt

Payment Act. See also 84 Fed. Reg. 25225 (May 31, 2019)(DOD proposal to implement 2019 Act).

As a matter of policy, Contracting Officers provide financing only to the extent needed for prompt and efficient performance, considering the availability of private financing and the impact of predelivery expenditures and product lead times on working capital. There are a variety of available methods: (1) progress payments, (2) advance payments, (3) performance-based payments, (4) commercial item purchase financing, and (5) other methods, such as private financing and government loan guarantees.

To minimize risk to the government, the regulations also provide that when a contractor requests financing, the Contracting Officer should consider the financing methods in the following order of preference—(a) private financing without government guarantees, (b) "customary" contract financing, (c) loan guarantees, (d) "unusual" contract financing, and (e) advance payments.

§ 32.2   Contract Payments

Obviously, contractors are critically interested in when they will receive payment from the government and how much they will be paid. Performance-based payments are the government's preferred means of contract financing under most negotiated, fixed-price contracts, and their use (if both parties agree) is required unless deemed impracticable. Under this system, payments are tied to specific, predetermined goals rather than guaranteed to be made on certain dates.

Payment may also be available from the government in some situations to assist the contractor in financing completion of the contract work. If the government believes that the contractor has not performed its contractual obligations, however, the government may interrupt or withhold payments it otherwise owes the contractor. Similarly, if the government believes that the contractor owes it money, it may "offset" those amounts against other funds due the contractor. This section reviews these and other payment issues.

(a) Standard Contract Clauses

The FAR provides different "payments" clauses depending on the nature of the contract. Two of the most often-used clauses are the (1) "payments" clause for fixed-price supply contracts (this clause is also authorized for use in fixed-price service contracts and contracts for nonregulated communication services) and (2) the "Payments Under Fixed-Price Construction Contracts" clause.

Both clauses provide for payment of the contract price for accepted supplies or services upon the contractor's submission of proper invoices. Under some payment clauses, the Contracting Officer is entitled to a retainage and to withhold final payment until the contractor executes a release of claims.

The "payments" clause for fixed-price supply contracts, provides that the government shall pay the contractor "upon the submission of the proper invoices or vouchers," the stipulated prices "for supplies delivered and accepted or services rendered and accepted." If this clause is the only payment term in the contract, the supply contractor must finance all of its work and expenses until its first substantial delivery is made and accepted.

This circumstance means that the supply contractor must use its working capital to pay material suppliers, vendors, employees, and other creditors. Special facilities and equipment might have to be purchased with the contractor's own funds—all before receiving any payment from the government. Often, there will be a substantial interval between the incurrence of such costs and the receipt of payment.

The standard "Payments under Fixed-Price Construction Contracts" clause requires the government to pay the contractor the contract price after "(1) Completion and acceptance of all work; (2) Presentation of a properly executed voucher; and (3) Presentation of release of all claims against the Government." This clause contains special elements regarding the retention of a percentage of progress payment amounts and the ownership of material and work covered by progress payments.

(b) Partial Payments

The government is authorized to make partial payments "for accepted supplies and services that are only a part of the contract requirements." The "payments" clause also authorizes payment for "partial deliveries accepted by the Government" where warranted or where the contractor requests it and the amount due is at least $1,000 or 50% of the total contract price. Partial contract payments are not technically a method of contract "financing" because they depend on delivery and acceptance of contract items. They can, however, reduce a contractor's need for financing by providing interim payments during contract performance.

(c) Electronic Funds Transfer

Federal law requires that Electronic Funds Transfer (EFT) be used to make all contract payments, subject to certain exceptions (e.g., payments to be received outside the United States or in other than United States currency; payments under certain classified contracts; and payments from a government office that loses the ability to release payment by EFT). EFT—which includes Automated Clearing House transfers, Fedwire transfers, and transfers made at ATM machines—is defined as any transfer of funds, other than a transaction originated by cash, check, or similar paper instrument, that is initiated through an electronic terminal, telephone, computer or magnetic tape, for the purpose of ordering a financial institution to debit or credit an account.

The FAR EFT procedures include payments by government wide commercial purchase cards. For these types of transactions, the contractor is instructed to initiate charges to a government account with a third party. The third party then makes the payments and the agency is instructed that to the extent that the requested payment would otherwise be approved, the charge against the purchase card should not be disputed when the third party reports it to the government.

Prospective contractors must be registered in the System for Award Management (SAM) database prior to the award of a contract, with limited exceptions, such as for classified contracts. All solicitations and contracts that utilize the SAM database as their source of EFT information are required to include the "Payment by Electronic Funds Transfer—System for Award Management" clause. Other contract-related clauses, to be used as appropriate, are also included in the FAR.

§ 32.3   Prompt Payment Act

The government's "slow pay" proclivities in the past affected some contractors' financial stability, occasionally obligated borrowing to finance continued performance, and likely convinced some contractors not to work with the government anymore.

To avoid this result, Congress passed the Prompt Payment Act in 1982. The Act provided, among other things, that the government pay interest penalties for late payments. In 1999, regulations implementing the Act were codified, providing further rules and guidance. These regulations (a) address the increased use of electronic commerce financial systems, (b) promote the use of government wide commercial purchase cards and accelerated payment methods, and (c) reflect the EFT requirements of the Debt Collection Improvement Act of 1996.

(a) Applicability of the Act

The Prompt Payment Act generally applies—at least according to one board of contract appeals judge—where the government simply "cannot get its act together" to pay the contractor on time.

The Act applies to government delay in paying undisputed invoices. It does not apply where the contractor's entitlement is in dispute or where questions exist regarding the contractor's compliance with the contract's requirements. The Act also does not apply to government delays in acting on change orders or requests for equitable adjustment, or to delays in payments made solely for financing purposes (such as advance payments or progress payments based on cost or percentage or stage of completion).

It does apply, however, to partial or periodic deliveries of supplies or performance of services and to progress payments and retainage due under construction contracts. However, construction contractors must include with each progress payment request a certification and substantiation of the amount requested.

(b) Interest Penalties

Under the standard FAR clauses, payment is generally due from the government on the submission of invoices or vouchers or the completion of work.

Under the Prompt Payment Act, the government's due date for making a payment (if the contract does not specify a particular date) is 30 days after the government receives a proper invoice for the amount due. The 30 days is computed from the later of the dates when (1) the person or place designated by the agency in the contract to first receive an invoice actually receives a proper invoice from the contractor or (2) the seventh day after delivery of the contract property or performance of the contract services, unless actual acceptance by the government is earlier or the contract specifies a longer period.

Interest is calculated from the day after the payment due date through the payment date at the interest rate in effect on the day after the payment due date. For up to one year, interest penalties remaining unpaid at the end of any 30-day period will be added to the principal and subsequent interest penalties will accrue on that amount until paid. However, interest penalties will not continue to accrue (a) after the filing of a claim for such penalties under the Contract Disputes Act, or (b) for more than one year.

Note also that late payment penalties must be paid without regard to whether the contractor has requested payment of such penalty. A notice stating the amount of the interest penalty, the number of days late and the rate used should accompany such payments.

(c) "Proper" Invoices

Interest does not begin to accrue until the contractor submits a "proper" invoice to the government. The FAR provides a checklist of information a proper invoice must contain. If the invoice is defective, the government has seven days after receipt of the invoice to alert the contractor and explain the deficiencies.

(d) Government Remedies

The government is entitled to withhold payment to a contractor in certain circumstances generally having to do with the contractor's failure to perform. As noted above, the government may suspend progress payments, for example, for contractor nonperformance. Similarly, "Payments Under Fixed-Price Construction Contracts" clause authorizes the Contracting Officer to retain 10% of payments due the contractor to protect the government unless the Contracting Officer finds that "satisfactory progress was achieved." The government is also entitled to withhold payment to contractors that fail to meet certain obligations under various labor statutes.

(e) Common-Law Offset

The government can interrupt or reduce payments to a contractor when the government seeks to use funds otherwise due the contractor under the contract to offset (also called "setoff") debts of the contractor allegedly arising either under the affected contract or independently. Indeed, the government has the inherent authority to recover sums illegally or erroneously paid, and it cannot be estopped from doing so by the mistakes of its officers or agents.

A board is not authorized to grant a stay of the government collection by offset against contract payments An agency official's poor judgment in making a payment, i.e., where the official acts within his authority but makes a conscious decision with known risks, does not entitle the government to recoup such an erroneous payment.

(f) Debt Collection Act

Although the government has a "long-standing common law right to administratively offset contract debts against contract payments," under the Debt Collection Act of 1982, the government may not collect debts unless it follows certain procedures—such as notice to the debtor, providing the debtor an opportunity to inspect agency records and decisions relating to the claim, and permitting the debtor an opportunity to negotiate a repayment agreement with the agency.

For many years, there was controversy in the courts and boards of contract appeals over whether the government had to comply with Debt Collection Act procedures before collecting contract debts through offset. The controversy was largely resolved in 1993 by the United States Court of Appeals for the Federal Circuit, which held in *Cecile Industries, Inc. v. Cheney*, 995 F.2d 1052 (Fed. Cir. 1993), that the Act does not apply to the use of contract funds to satisfy claims relating either to the same contract or to a different contract. The decision did not address, however, whether the Debt Collection Act procedures apply to the government's use of contract funds to offset non-contract debts.

The FAR contains procedures governing the government's ascertainment and collection of contract debts. Under the regulations, the government cannot issue a demand for payment until the Contracting Officer issues a final decision on the debt under the contract's "Disputes" clause. The demand for payment must include notice to the contractor that it may request a deferment of collection if immediate payment is not practicable or the amount is disputed.

Debt deferral is more likely if the contractor has appealed the Contracting Officer's debt decision under the Contract Disputes Act or the contractor is a small business or financially weak. If, within 30 days, payment is not completed and deferment is not requested, the government may begin withholding contractor funds to offset the debt.

Absent a contract clause requiring the contractor to pay interest on a government claim, the Debt Collection Act requires contractors to pay prejudgment interest on government claims based on the contract.

§ 32.4   Progress Payments

One of the most important and frequently used ways in which the government assists contractors in financing their contracts is to make periodic progress payments as contract performance proceeds. Progress payments may be based on either the costs incurred in performance or on a percentage or stage of completion.

Under the FAR, progress payments based on a percentage or stage of completion are typically used only in construction contracts and are not governed by the FAR's financing provisions. Similarly, progress payments typically are not made under cost-reimbursement contracts. Progress payments are payments under fixed-price contracts that are based on the contractor's incurred costs and are limited by the contract price.

An important point about progress payments is that the government generally will not make such payments if they were not provided for in the contract as awarded, unless the contractor agrees to furnish additional consideration, for example, a promise to do more work.

(a) Progress Payment Amounts

The regulations set forth "customary" limits on the percentage of incurred costs for which progress payments may be made. Under the FAR, the customary rate is 80% of the "total costs of performing the contract" for large businesses and 85% for small businesses. Progress payments at a higher rate may not be included without advance agency approval.

Under the standard "Progress Payments" clause, the contractor may bill the government only for amounts that have been paid by cash, check, or other forms of payment. Following the elimination of the so-called "paid cost" rule in March 2000, all contractors—both large and small—may also bill for monies that will be paid to subcontractors (a) in accordance with the terms of a subcontract or invoice, and (b) ordinarily prior to submission of the contractor's next payment request to the government.

Under the same clause, contractors must exclude from their progress payment billings costs that are not "reasonable, allocable to this contract, and consistent with sound and generally accepted accounting principles and practices," costs that are ordinarily capitalized and subject to depreciation or amortization, and costs incurred by subcontractors and suppliers. In addition, to encourage the contractor to provide progress payments to subcontractors, the government will reimburse contractors for the total amount of "customary" progress payments made to subcontractors.

Pub. L. No. 111–240, § 1334, protects small business subcontractors by creating a reporting requirement for prime contractors with a small business subcontractor where the subcontractor is paid less than the contracted price for work after it is completed. Also, if payment to a subcontractor is more than 90 days overdue on a government contract where the government has already paid the prime contractor, the prime must report this fact.

A final FAR rule implements temporary guidance set forth in Office of Management and Budget Memoranda M–12–16, dated July 11, 2012, and M–13–15, dated July 11, 2013, regarding accelerated payments to small-business subcontractors. The rule also creates a new clause (FAR 52.232–40) to this effect.

(b) Progress Payments and Title to Property

To assure some security for the progress payments made, the standard "Progress Payments" clause provides that the government has title to all property "allocable or properly chargeable" to the contract. This includes, for example, materials, inventories, work-in-process, special tooling and test equipment, and other nondurable items necessary to perform the contract. The contractor may dispose of such property only with the consent of the Contracting Officer. The "title" provisions of the clause have caused difficulty regarding the scope of the government's interest in contractor state property in tax cases and in bankruptcy proceedings.

(c) Suspension or Reduction of Progress Payments

The standard "Progress Payments" clause gives the Contracting Officer express authority to reduce or suspend progress payments in six specified circumstances. For example, if the Contracting Officer finds there is "substantial evidence" the contractor has failed to comply with a material contract requirement, failed to make adequate progress, or is delinquent in paying subcontractors or suppliers, the Contracting Officer can suspend or reduce progress payments. Suspension of progress payments is also justified if the contractor's financial condition is such that it is unlikely the contract can be completed. Not surprisingly, progress payments may also be suspended or reduced where there is substantial evidence that the contractor's progress payment request is based on fraud.

If the parties enter the contract with the understanding that it will be financed solely by progress payments on a cost basis, the government's unjustified failure to make prompt progress payments excuses any duty of further performance of the work by the contractor. Of course, in that case, the contractor must establish that the government's failure to make progress payments was the primary cause of the contractor's inability to continue performance. If—despite the government's unjustified suspension of progress payments—the contractor is able to continue performance, the government will be liable for additional costs incurred as a result of that suspension.

§ 32.5 Advance Payments

Where no other financing is available, the government may agree to make advance payments to a contractor, i.e., payments made before the contractor acquires any materials for or does any work under a contract. Although authorized by statute, advance payments entail substantial risk for the government and so are made only "sparingly" and where the head of the agency determines in writing that advance payments are in the public interest.

As a practical matter, few contractors will be eligible to receive advance payments. The FAR identifies several types of contracts that may be targeted for advance payments, including experimental research and development contracts with nonprofit institutions or contracts with financially weak contractors whose technical ability is considered essential or highly classified contracts.

If advance payments are authorized, the contract must contain the "Advance Payments" clause. Under this clause, advance payments are made only at such times as the contractor's financial necessity dictates, and must be approved by a special "administering office" of the government. The contract clause also requires that advance payments be deposited in a special bank account and that withdrawals from that account be countersigned by a government official. The use of the funds is restricted to paying allowable costs incurred under the contract. Finally, the clause requires the contractor to pay interest on the advance payments made.

§ 32.6 Performance-Based Payments

Performance-based payments are the preferred government financing method when the Contracting Officer finds them practical and the contractor agrees to their use. FAR subpart 32.10 on performance based payments does not apply to (a) noncommercial item contracts that are not cost-reimbursement contracts, (b) contracts for architect/engineer services or construction or for shipbuilding or ship conversion, alteration or repair, where the contracts provide for progress payments based upon a percentage or stage of completion, or (c) contracts awarded through sealed bid procedures.

Pursuant to the "Performance-Based Payments" clause, these payments may be made on the basis of (1) performance based upon quantifiable, objective methods, (2) the accomplishment of defined events, or (3) other quantifiable measures of results. They may be used where (a) the parties agree on the performance-based payment terms, (b) the contract is a definitized, fixed-price type contract, and (c) the contract does not provide for any other method of contract financing (except for certain advance payments or guaranteed loans).

The FAR provides that the bases for performance-based payments may be either specifically described events (i.e., milestones) or some measurable criterion of performance. Each event or performance criterion must be an integral and necessary part of contract performance and must be identified in the contract, along with a description of what constitutes successful performance of the event or attainment of the performance criterion. An event need not be a critical one, but its successful performance must be readily verifiable. Events or criteria may be either severable or cumulative. But payment for a cumulative event or criterion may not be made until the dependent event or criterion has been successfully completed.

§ 32.7   Commercial Item Purchase Financing

The FAR, as directed by the Federal Acquisition Streamlining Act of 1994 (FASA), makes a fundamental distinction between government financing of purchases of noncommercial and commercial items.

The FAR contains distinct policies for financing commercial item contracts. It notes first, that since it is the contractor's responsibility to provide all the resources needed for performance of commercial item contracts, financing of such contracts is normally also the contractor's responsibility. However, in some markets the provision of financing by the buyer is a commercial practice. In these markets, appropriate financing terms may be included when this is in the government's best interests.

(a) Permissible Categories

Government financing for commercial purchases is allowed under the following circumstances:

1.   The contract item being financed is a commercial supply or service whose price exceeds the simplified acquisition threshold;

2.   It is appropriate or customary in the commercial marketplace to make financing payments for the item;

3.   Financing is in the best interests of the government under standards established by the individual agencies;

4.   Adequate security (as specified in the solicitation) is obtained;

5.   Prior to the performance of the contract work, the aggregate of commercial advance payments does not exceed 15% of the contract price;

6.   The contract is awarded under competitive procedures, or if only one offer is solicited, adequate consideration is obtained if the financing is expected to be substantially more advantageous to the offeror than its normal method of customer financing; and

7.   The Contracting Officer obtains concurrence from the payment office concerning liquidation provisions when required.

(b) Types of Payments

The FAR states that financing of commercial purchases is expected to be different from that used for noncommercial purchases, although the Contracting Officer is permitted to adapt techniques and procedures from the traditional noncommercial methods. Three types of payments are discussed in the FAR:

1.   Commercial advance payments—These are payments made before any performance of work under the contract. The aggregate of these payments may not exceed 15% of the contract price;

2.   Commercial interim payments—these are any payments that are not commercial advance payments or delivery payments. An interim payment is given to a contractor after some work has been done; or

3.   Delivery payments—these are payments for accepted supplies or services, including payments for accepted partial deliveries.

§ 32.8   Loan Guarantees

Guaranteed loans are available only to "borrowers performing contracts related to national defense." Loan guarantees are made by Federal Reserve Banks on behalf of designated "guaranteeing agencies" to enable contractors to obtain financing from private sources under contracts for the acquisition of supplies or services for the national defense. Notably, many agencies in recent years, such as the DOD, have not requested congressional authorization for these guarantees.

§ 32.9   Private Financing

Contractors may finance a government contract in much the same way as they would finance a commercial contract—by obtaining financing through a commercial bank or financial institution. As might be expected, commercial financing is the government's preferred financing method. Because private financing institutions typically require a contractor to assign to it the proceeds of the contract to be financed as security for any funds advanced, the government imposes restrictions on these transactions. If contract proceeds are to be assigned in exchange for a loan, the contractor must comply with the Assignment of Claims Act and the Anti-Assignment Act and their implementing regulations.

The Act prohibits the assignment of federal government contracts (and the assignment of claims against the federal government). The policy is to prevent fraud and multiple claims, which further protects the government's right to determine its contracting partner. An unauthorized attempt to transfer an interest in a government contract, such as the contract proceeds, may result in an agency or judicial declaration that the transfer is null and void.

However, to encourage private financing of government contracts, a transfer of contract proceeds is exempt from the Act's prohibitions where the proceeds exceed $1,000 and "are assigned to a bank, trust company, or other financing institution" for the purpose of facilitating performance of the contract. To effect a valid assignment under the Act, however, the contractor must strictly comply with the regulatory procedures set forth in the FAR. Thus, the plaintiff has the burden to show that there is a bona fide financial institution.

One major exception to the Act is any transfer that is incidental to a corporate merger, consolidation, reorganization or by operation of law in which there is no probability that the United States could suffer injury in respect to outstanding claims. Additionally, the government may forego the protection of the statutory prohibitions against the assignment of contractual rights if the Contracting Officer gives clear assent to the assignment. The transfer of government contracts should be upheld if the government recognizes the transaction explicitly, such as through a novation, or implicitly, through ratification or waiver.

Chapter 33

PROTESTS, DISPUTES
AND APPEALS

Analysis

The chapter first reviews the forums and remedies available to disappointed would-be contractors that protest their exclusion from a competition or from the award of a contract or that challenge an alleged solicitation irregularity. Protests may be lodged against a government agency in opposition to a contract solicitation, award (anticipated or actual), or other action in which the protester has a direct economic interest. Most protesters are actual or prospective bidders or offerors. Protesters have a choice of three forums in which to argue their case: the procuring agency, the Government Accountability Office (GAO), and the United States Court of Federal Claims (COFC).

The second focus of the chapter is the contract disputes process. In 1978, Congress restructured the disputes process in the Contract Disputes Act of 1978 (CDA), setting forth a standard procedure to be used by all executive agencies. Among other things, the CDA (1) increased the authority of the Contracting Officer to settle disagreements and of the agency boards of contract appeals to determine the merits of disputes, (2) broadened the types of claims that are subject to the disputes process and made government claims against contractors subject to the process, (3) set time limitations on the issuance of Contracting Officer decisions on contractor claims, (4) created accelerated and expedited schedules for the resolution of small claims, (5) provided contractors with a choice of forum for challenging an adverse Contracting Officer decision (appeal to the appropriate agency board of contract appeals or filing suit in the COFC), and (6) gave both the government and contractors the right to appeal adverse board or COFC decisions.

The disputes process is frequently evolving through amendments to the CDA and reorganization of the judicial system. For example, the Federal Courts Improvement Act of 1982 replaced the trial division of the Court of Claims with the United States Claims Court (later changed again to the United States Court of Federal Claims) gave the Court "exclusive" jurisdiction to grant declaratory and injunctive relief regarding federal contract disputes, and established the Court of Appeals for the Federal Circuit— successor to the appellate division of the Court of Federal Claims, among other tribunals—to hear appeals from both the boards of contract appeals and the United States Court of Federal Claims.

The Federal Courts Administration Act of 1992 changed the name of the Claims Court to the Court of Federal Claims, gave the court jurisdiction to decide non-monetary government contract disputes (thus making court and board jurisdiction under the CDA virtually identical), and provided that a defect in the certification of a contractor's claim did not deprive the boards or the COFC of jurisdiction over that claim. Several years later, the Federal Acquisition Streamlining Act of 1994 (FASA) altered, among other things, the dollar threshold in the CDA for claim certification.

A. PROTESTS

§ 33.1   Protests to the Agency

Under FAR subpart 33.1, the least formal, least expensive, and quickest of these choices of forums for pursuing a protest is the procuring agency itself. An agency protest may only be filed by an "interested party"—an actual or prospective offeror whose direct economic interest would be affected by the award of a contract or the failure to award a contract." As defined in the FAR, a "protest" means a written objection by an interested party to a solicitation or cancellation of a solicitation, an award or proposed award of a contract, or the termination or cancellation of a contract award if the written objection alleges that the termination or cancellation is based on improprieties in the award of the contract.

(a) Procedures

Implementing a 1995 Executive Order, the FAR instructs agencies to provide for the inexpensive, informal, procedurally simple, and expeditious resolution of protests, including, where appropriate, the use of alternative dispute resolution techniques, third-party neutrals, and another agency's personnel. The FAR directs all parties to use their best efforts to resolve protest matters initially at the Contracting Officer level through "open and frank discussions."

The filing and timeliness requirements for agency protests closely parallel the procedures at the GAO. Thus, for example, the protester must be an "interested party" and the protest must include a detailed statement of the legal and factual grounds for complaint. The same type of suspension of award or performance process applicable at the GAO also applies to agency protests. The protester is entitled to request an independent review of the merits of its agency protest at a level above the Contracting Officer. Agencies must advise firms whether this independent review is available as an alternative to consideration of the matter by the Contracting Officer or as an appeal of the Contracting Officer's protest decision.

Note that a higher-level agency review of the Contracting Officer's protest decision will not extend the deadlines for filing a timely protest at the GAO. Thus, any subsequent protest to the GAO—whether or not an agency appellate review is conducted—must be filed within 10 days after the protester obtains actual or constructive knowledge of the initial adverse agency action.

(b) Remedies

The remedy before award is simple: corrective action should be taken if the protester establishes a legal deficiency with the solicitation, or that the contract should be awarded to another party—unless the agency decides it no longer needs the product (in which case the procurement should be canceled). After award, the Contracting Officer may void the improperly awarded contract (an unusual option) or terminate the contract for the government's convenience (see Chapter 49). If the protest decision directs a re-evaluation, the protester could be entitled to the contract after the completion of this process. In addition, if the agency concludes that a protest is meritorious because of the agency's noncompliance with a statute or regulation, it may pay the protester the cost (excluding profit) of pursuing the protest, including reasonable (capped) attorney, consultant, and expert witness fees together with bid or proposal preparation costs.

In sum, if, in connection with an agency protest, the head of an agency determines that a solicitation, proposed award, or award does not comply with the requirements of law or regulation, the head of the agency may—

(1) Take any action that could have been recommended by the Comptroller General had the protest been filed with the Government Accountability Office;

(2) Pay appropriate costs as stated in FAR 33.104(h).

§ 33.2   Protests to the GAO

CICA governs the GAO's process for handling protests, which is further implemented by GAO's bid protest regulations. GAO has a helpful publication, "Bid Protests at GAO: A Descriptive Guide (10th ed. 2018)," available at its website, http://www.gao.gov. The GAO's protest decisions are available on GAO's website for a relatively short period. They are also available on WESTLAW ("CG" database) and in full-text form in COMPTROLLER GENERAL'S PROCUREMENT DECISIONS published by Thomson Reuters.

A GAO Final Rule has implemented the Electronic Protest Docketing System (EPDS). See https://www.gao.gov/assets/690/687917.pdf. In 2018, the Government Accountability Office amended its bid protest regulations to establish an electronic filing and document dissemination system, as required by § 1501 of the Consolidated Appropriations Act for Fiscal Year 2014, Pub. L. No. 113–76. See 83 Fed. Reg. 13817 (Apr. 2, 2018). The amendments also include administrative changes to reflect current practice, to streamline the bid protest process, and to make clerical corrections.

According to GAO, the EPDS will be the sole means for filing documents in connection with a protest, with two exceptions: (1) Documents containing classified material, and (2) documents that, for reasons of size or format, are not suitable for filing through EPDS. GAO has posted guidance on EPDS at https://www.gao.gov/products/D17931.

Section 1501 amended 31 U.S.C.A. § 3555(c) to direct the Comptroller General to "establish and operate an electronic filing and document dissemination system" and to authorize the collection of filing fees to fund the new system. Thus, protests are filed and required documents and information generally are disseminated electronically.

(a) Definitions

A GAO "protest" means a written objection by an interested party to a solicitation or cancellation of a solicitation, an award or proposed award of a contract, or the termination or cancellation of a contract award if the written objection alleges that the termination or cancellation is based on improprieties in the award of the contract.

GAO's bid protest jurisdiction is based on a finding that the protest concerns a procurement of property or services by a federal agency. Accordingly, GAO's bid protest regulations disclaim jurisdiction over various other types of complaints. Examples of such exclusions are: matters of contract administration, small business size standards and standard industrial classifications, and challenges to the suspension or debarment of contractors. The Comptroller General's jurisdiction also does not turn on whether appropriated funds are involved or on whether the competition requirements of CICA apply. By comparison, GAO has jurisdiction to hear objections to agency action that will result in the "award" of instruments (such as Blanket Purchase Agreements) that are not themselves contracts, but which will give rise to binding contracts when orders are in place. An agency's award of an intergovernmental support agreement (IGSA) is a procurement contract within the Government Accountability Office's protest authority.

GAO's jurisdiction generally does not extend to awards made by others "for" the government; accordingly, absent a request by the federal agency concerned, GAO will not take jurisdiction over such procurements. GAO continues to take jurisdiction, however, where it finds that a subcontract essentially was awarded "by" the government such that the prime contractor's role in the procurement was essentially ministerial as it was merely acting as a conduit for the government.

Protestors must be an interested party. An "interested party" is generally defined as "an actual or prospective bidder or offeror whose direct economic interest would be affected by the award of a contract or by the failure to award a contract." Determining whether a party is "interested" involves consideration of various factors, including the nature of the issues raised, the benefit or relief sought by the protester, and the party's status in relation to the procurement.

Thus, for example, where there are intermediate parties between the awardee and the protester that have a greater interest in the procurement than the protester, the GAO generally considers the protester's interest to be too remote to confer interested party status. Some per se rules exist in this area, for example, a suspended or debarred firm is not an interested party to challenge a solicitation or an award. Somewhat surprisingly, however, a firm can be an interested party to compete on an amended solicitation when the firm did not submit an offer on the original solicitation, provided that the changes to the RFP were so significant that they justify an RFP cancellation rather than an amendment.

Corporate transactions can complicate whether a firm is an interested party A parent corporation is not an interested party to protest its wholly owned subsidiary's elimination from competition if the subsidiary is a separate and distinct legal entity with which the Government would contract. By contrast, a corporate restructuring that occurred between the time the offeror submitted its proposal and the award decision, under which the protesting entity was transformed from an unincorporated division of a corporate parent into a new, stand-alone incorporated entity, does not necessarily affect the protester's status as an interested party.

One exception to the general definition of an interested party is that GAO considers the official submitting the Federal agency tender in many public-private competitions conducted under OMB Circular A-76 to be an interested party. See Chapter 7 (explaining A-76 program). By comparison, GAO in the A-76 arena has denied an employee agent interested party status where the protester represents a group of employees whose positions are not at risk as a consequence of the contemplated contracting decision in a private public competition.

This doctrine concerning A-76 and government outsourcing is only of academic interest at this time. Public Law 111–118, § 117 has suspended public/private competitions under OMB Circular A-76 until the Department of Defense complies with § 325 of the Fiscal Year 2010 National Defense Authorization Act, Pub. L. No. 111–84, which requires the Department to conduct a comprehensive review of A-76 policies. Hence, until the moratorium is lifted on these competitions, the rules on representation of government employees in government outsourcing cases lacks practical application.

The regulations define many other important terms, such as "adverse agency action," "days," "federal agency," and when a document is "filed" with GAO.

(b) Content of Protest

As with an agency protest, a protest filed with the GAO need not be in any particular format but must be in writing, concise, and logically arranged. The protest must be signed by the protester or its representative and addressed to the GAO's general counsel.

Perhaps the most important pleading requirement from the GAO's regulations is for a detailed statement of the factual and legal grounds for complaint. GAO has interpreted this requirement to mean that the protester must provide, at a minimum, either allegations or evidence sufficient, if uncontested, to establish the likelihood of the protester's claim of improper agency, including some specific explanation of the bases for the protester's concerns.

Accordingly, a protest founded upon mere speculation or rumor provides no basis for questioning the propriety of a procurement. Prejudice is an essential element of any viable protest, and even where the record establishes a procurement deficiency, GAO will sustain a protest on this basis only with a substantial possibility of competitive prejudice to the displaced protester.

In the context of a protest challenging the terms of a solicitation, competitive prejudice occurs where the challenged terms place the protester at a competitive disadvantage or otherwise affect the protester's ability to compete. Regarding an award decision, GAO will not sustain a protest unless the protester demonstrates a reasonable possibility that it was prejudiced by the agency's actions, that is, unless the protester demonstrates that, but for the agency's actions, it would have had a substantial chance of receiving the award.

(c) *Filing Deadlines*

The GAO's bid protest regulations establish three basic filing deadlines, as explained below. These "strict" rules serve the dual requirements of giving the parties a fair opportunity to present their cases and of resolving protests expeditiously without unduly disrupting or delaying the acquisition process. The GAO will give the protester the benefit of the doubt, however, when a legitimate question exists on whether the protest is timely.

First, under the GAO's bid protest regulations, 4 C.F.R. Part 21, any protest based upon alleged solicitation improprieties that are apparent before bid opening or the time and date set for receipt of initial proposals must be filed with the GAO before these times. GAO is open only during working days Thus, if the solicitation's closing time is 3:00 p.m., EST on a Tuesday, but an aggrieved party files a solicitation protest with the GAO at 6:00 p.m. EST that same day, the protest will be late. This rule holds true because GAO's business hours are 8:30 a.m. to 5:30 pm EST. Therefore under the GAO's rules, the protest will be deemed to be filed the next business day at 8:30 a.m. Improprieties that did not exist in the initial solicitation but that are subsequently incorporated must be protested no later than the next closing time for receipt of proposals following their incorporation.

The GAO has clarified that protest filings due by 5:30 p.m. (EST) pursuant to 4 C.F.R. § 21.0(f) are timely filed if received by GAO any time before "the clock reaches 5:31 p.m." In *Government Acquisitions, Inc.*, B-408426, B-408426.2, 2013 CPD ¶ 277 (Comp. Gen. 2013), the

GAO accepted as timely filed the protester's comments and supplemental protest, even though they were filed at 5:30 p.m. and 35 seconds on the due date.

Second, any other protest must be filed no later than 10 days after the basis of the protest is known or should have been known (whichever is earlier). GAO has ruled that a protest of award will be untimely when filed more than 10 calendar days after receipt during business hours of the agency's email notification of award (and explanation for the award decision and proposal rejection of the recipient). The firm's receipt of an agency email with such an explanation of the protest decision during regular business hours constitutes notice of basis for protest.

In a procurement based upon competitive proposals, an agency must provide such a debriefing (i.e., a "required" debriefing) when an offeror submits a written request that is received by the agency within three days after the date on which the offeror received notice of its exclusion from the competition or of the contract award (see Chapter 15). Where an offeror has requested a required debriefing, with respect to any basis for a protest that is known or should have been known either before or as a result of the debriefing, the offeror has until 10 days after the date the debriefing is held to file a protest with the GAO. The offeror, however, may not file the protest before the date offered for the required debriefing.

Third, if the protester previously filed a timely agency protest, but the agency denies or dismisses the protest, the GAO will consider any subsequent protest on the same grounds to the GAO filed within 10 days of the protester's obtaining actual or constructive knowledge of initial adverse agency action as long as the initial protest was filed with the agency within the GAO's time limits or within the agency's time limits if they are more restrictive.

If the agency protest concerned an alleged solicitation impropriety, the GAO will consider a subsequent protest if it is filed within 10 days of the protester's obtaining actual or constructive knowledge of initial adverse agency action, even if the GAO protest is filed after bid opening or the closing time set for receipt of proposals. Where the protester received the agency's protest decision by mail on a non-business day, but where the protester did not review or even open the envelope at that time, the filing period will begin on the next business day.

Fourth, in a rarely permitted exception, GAO may consider, upon good cause shown, or where GAO determines that a protest raises issues significant to the procurement system, a protest that is untimely. "Good cause" under this exception means circumstances that arose from some compelling reason beyond the protester's control that prevented it from filing a timely protest. A "significant issue" refers to an issue that is of widespread interest to the procurement community that GAO has not considered previously. In one case, GAO invoked the significant issue exception and sustained the protest but because the protester did not raise the issue in a timely manner, GAO did not recommend reimbursement of protest costs.

(d) Automatic Suspension of Contract Award or Performance

If a protest is filed with the GAO before award, the agency is automatically prohibited from awarding a contract for the particular services or supplies covered by that agreement after the agency has received notice of the protest, unless the head of the contracting activity makes a written finding that (a) "urgent and compelling circumstances" will not permit waiting for the Comptroller General's decision, and (b) award is likely to occur within 30 days of release of the written finding. Thus, the agency can override the automatic stay of the award as outlined in FAR 3.104(b).

If the award has occurred, and a protester files its challenge after award, CICA provides for an automatic statutory stay of performance as outlined in FAR 33.104(c). If a protest is filed after award and the agency receives notice of the protest from the GAO within 10 calendar days after award or within five days after a required debriefing date offered to the protester, whichever is later, the Contracting Officer must suspend contract performance immediately or terminate the awarded contract. Notice to the agency must come from the GAO. Notice from the protester will not suffice.

CICA permits the agency to override the stay of performance. In accordance with agency procedures, the head of the contracting activity may, on a nondelegable basis, authorize contract performance, notwithstanding the protest, upon a written finding that—

(i)   Contract performance will be in the best interests of the United States; or

(ii) Urgent and compelling circumstances that significantly affect the interests of the United States will not permit waiting for the GAO's decision.

The stays will continue unless the agency effects an override of the stay in accordance with FAR 33.104 or if GAO disposes of the protest. The automatic CICA stay also will apply to a protest of a re-affirmed award following a corrective action.

The "agency" in this sense, noted above, does not necessarily mean the procuring activity; thus, in the United States Army Corps of Engineers, where the GAO properly notifies the Corps' headquarters in Washington, D.C., that notification will govern a protest concerning a procurement conducted by a Corps procuring activity in Huntsville, Alabama.

For purposes of the automatic stay rule, in asserting that urgent and compelling circumstances require immediate performance, the agency must consider (1) the adverse consequences that will occur without the stay, (2) reasonable alternatives to the override, (3) the potential cost of proceeding with performance, including the costs associated with a potential sustained protest, as compared with the benefit of the approach being considered for addressing the agency's need, and (4) the impact of the override on competition and the integrity of the procurement system.

Although GAO will not review the agency's rationale to override the statutory stay, COFC has jurisdiction over such complaints from "interested parties" as defined by the revised Tucker Act. The agency has to explain in a convincing way why the override is the only reasonable method for meeting an important agency mission. Thus, for example, the court has determined that the agency improperly allowed an override when it simply relied on the reasons it used to award the new contract. In another example, the COFC found the agency's override decision to be arbitrary and capricious because the agency did not consider alternatives to the override decision and made no serious attempt to analyze the override's effect on the integrity of the procurement system.

Generally, experience has shown the COFC generally will subject the government's explanation to intense scrutiny (notwithstanding the more lenient Administrative Procedure Act review, which is whether the decision was arbitrary, capricious, an abuse of discretion, or otherwise not in accordance with law). The agency's best course of action is to place the work under an existing contract or a new bridge contract, neither of which are circumventions of the automatic CICA stay so long as the agency preserves all the contract work under protest.

(e) Agency Report and Comments

After receiving a protest, the GAO will contact the procuring agency involved (normally by telephone, followed by a confirming letter) within one day to request a detailed report and copies of all pertinent documents. Immediately after receipt of the GAO's written notification, the agency will give notice of the protest to the contractor (if award has been made) or (if no award has been made) to all parties that appear to have a reasonable chance of receiving award if the protest is denied.

The agency report must be submitted to the GAO within 30 days after the GAO notified the agency by telephone that a protest had been filed or within 20 days after receipt of a determination (rarely invoked) to use the express option procedures. The agency report should contain copies of all documents relevant to the protest as well as the Contracting Officer's signed statement of facts, including a best estimate of the contract's value, a memorandum of law, findings, actions, and recommendations, and any additional information or evidence not provided in the protest file.

If the agency defends the protest before the GAO, the Comptroller General will give little, if any, weight to a source selection official's statement made in the agency report in a response to the protest that irrespective of any agency evaluation error, he or she would have made the same source selection decision. GAO gives little weight to such post-protest judgments (and others like them), which are prepared in the heat of the adversarial process, because they may not represent the fair and considered judgment of the agency, which is a prerequisite of a rational evaluation and source selection process.

Post hoc arguments are entitled to "lesser weight" because "judgments made in the heat of an adversarial process may not represent the fair and considered judgment of the agency, which is a prerequisite of a rational evaluation and source selection process," the Comp. Gen. said in *Boeing Sikorsky Aircraft Support*, Comp. Gen. Dec. B-277263.2, et al. 97-2 CPD ¶ 91. If the truth be told, GAO (probably legitimately) suspects that it is the agency counsel behind all these suddenly refined and supposedly persuasive agency reasons for the earlier decision.

On the other hand, in reviewing an agency's evaluation of offerors' proposals, GAO does not limit its consideration to contemporaneously documented evidence, but instead considers all the information provided, including the parties' arguments, explanations, and any hearing testimony. Thus, post-protest explanations that provide a detailed rationale for contemporaneous conclusions, and simply fill in previously unrecorded details, will generally be considered in GAO's review of the rationality of selection decisions—so long as those explanations are credible and consistent with the contemporaneous record, *Carahsoft Technology Corporation*, B-401169, B-401169.2, 2009 CPD ¶ 134.

When the agency submits its report to the GAO, it must furnish copies to the protester and to any firms that have achieved admission to the case as intervenors. These parties ordinarily are the awardee or, if no award has been made, bidders or offerors with a substantial prospect of receiving the award if the protest is denied. In distributing copies of the protest, the agency commonly redacts information the protester marks as proprietary. If another party intervenes and seeks GAO permission to participate in the protest, such as an awardee that desires to defend the award, GAO will typically require that the party's counsel or other representative review the unredacted protest under a protective order.

Documents covered by a protective order will be released only in accordance with the terms of that order. The GAO may issue a protective order controlling access to proprietary, confidential, or source-selection-sensitive material at the request of a party or on its own initiative. In considering the propriety of granting or denying an applicant admission to a protective order, GAO will review each application in order to determine whether the applicant is involved in competitive decision-making and whether there is otherwise an unacceptable risk of inadvertent disclosure of protected information should the applicant be granted access to protected material. The GAO has the inherent authority to dismiss a protest when a protester abuses the bid protest process, which can include violations of a protective order.

After receiving the agency report, the protester may file a request with the GAO for additional documents from the agency no later than two days after the existence of the documents or their relevance is known or should have been known, whichever is later. The agency must provide the documents and a list to the GAO and other parties within two days of the request.

Ordinarily, the protester and any intervenors must file their comments on the agency report with the GAO within 10 days (or five days if the express option is used) after receiving the report. Copies should be sent to the Contracting Officer and to other participating parties. If a hearing is held these comments are due within five days after the hearing. GAO recently has modified its protective order procedures to streamline use of protected information in bid protests filed with the United States Court of Federal Claims.

(f) Hearings

The GAO has the discretion to hold a hearing at the request of the agency, the protester, or other party or on its own initiative. Hearing are a relatively rare occurrence, and GAO ordinarily will allow one when there is a factual dispute between that parties that cannot be resolved without an oral examination and which requires GAO to assess witness credibility, or where an issue is so complex that proceeding with written supplemental pleadings will clearly be a less efficient and more burdensome method than holding a hearing. All parties must file comments within five days of the close of the hearing.

(g) Time for Decision

The GAO will issue decision on a protest within 100 days from the date of its filing with the GAO or within 65 days under the express option procedures.

(h) Flexible Alternative Procedures

In addition to the procedures outlined above, the GAO's bid protest regulations provide that the GAO "may use flexible alternative procedures to promptly and fairly resolve a protest." The GAO commonly uses two alternative techniques to resolve protests— outcome prediction and negotiation assistance.

Outcome prediction is used when the GAO attorney at the working level who will draft the protest for eventual GAO management level review strongly believes that one side will win if the protest continues. The GAO attorney calls the two sides together and explains the predicted outcome of the protest and the reasons for that prediction. If the predicted loser then takes steps to settle the protest so that a written decision will be unnecessary (i.e., the protester withdraws the protest or the agency takes corrective action), the GAO closes the case.

If outcome prediction does not prompt affirmative action by the parties, the GAO will issue a written decision on the merits. Where negotiation assistance is used, the GAO attorney acts as a facilitator to assist the parties in reaching a settlement. If the parties are unable to reach a settlement, the protest is decided under the GAO's standard protest procedures.

GAO also may employ other means to facilitate protests, including summary decisions and the use of status calls and other conferences.

(i) Reconsideration

The protester, an intervenor, or the agency may request the GAO to reconsider a protest decision. A request for reconsideration must be filed with the GAO (with copies provided to all parties) no later than 10 days after the basis for reconsideration is known or should have been known, whichever is earlier. The filing of a request for reconsideration does not require the agency to withhold contract award or suspend contract performance. GAO will deny a request for reconsideration based solely on repetition of arguments made during the original protest and statements of mere disagreement with the decision. Moreover, the GAO will not grant reconsideration on the basis of evidence that could have been offered during the original protest proceedings.

(j) Remedies

In conducting corrective action in consequence of a valid protest, the process can be extensive. Among other responses, an agency can reasonably reopen discussions, solicit new final proposals, reevaluate offers and make a new source selection decision to resolve evaluation errors. The GAO may, if it determines that the protested solicitation, proposed award, or award does not comply with a statute or regulation, recommend that the agency (a) refrain from exercising options under the contract, (b) immediately recompete the contract, (c) issue a new solicitation, (d) terminate the contract, (e) award a contract that complies with statutes or regulations, (f) take any combination of the above actions, or (g) implement other recommendations the GAO determines necessary to promote compliance. Where the agency has determined that an award or performance of the contract is in the government's best interest, and overrides the automatic stay notwithstanding a pending protest, the GAO's recommendation must ignore any cost or disruption from terminating, recompeting, or re-awarding the contract.

In addition, if the GAO concludes that a protest is meritorious because of the agency's noncompliance with a statute or regulation, it may recommend that the agency pay the protester the cost (excluding profit) of pursuing the protest, including reasonable (capped) attorney, consultant, and expert witness fees together with bid or proposal preparation costs. The protester must file a claim for such costs within 60 days of the GAO's recommendation that the agency pay these costs. If the parties are unable to agree on the amount of costs, the GAO will, on the protester's request, recommend to the agency the amount of costs that it should pay.

Where a procuring agency takes corrective action in response to a protest, GAO may further recommend that the agency reimburse the protester its protest costs where, based on the circumstances of the case, GAO determines that the agency unduly delayed taking corrective action in the face of a clearly meritorious protest, thereby causing the protester to expend unnecessary time and resources to make further use of the protest process to obtain relief. A protest is "clearly meritorious" when a reasonable agency inquiry into the protest allegations would have shown facts disclosing the absence of a defensible legal position.

Generally, GAO will consider a successful protester entitled to costs incurred with respect to all issues pursued, not merely those upon which it prevails. On the other hand, GAO will deny a claim for costs where protester failed to adequately document the claim and inappropriately aggregated allowable and non-allowable costs such that they could be not be sufficiently distinguished. Protest costs need not be allocated between clearly meritorious protest issues and other protest issues if all issues were intertwined parts of the same basic objection.

GAO will limit a successful protester's recovery of protest costs where a part of its costs is allocable to a losing protest issue that is so clearly severable as to essentially constitute a separate protest. Issues are intertwined where they share a common core of facts, are based upon related legal theories, and are otherwise not readily severable.

A protester seeking to recover its protest costs must submit sufficient evidence to support its monetary claim; GAO will base its decision for a cost claim upon the facts and circumstances of that claim. The amount claimed may be recovered to the extent that the claim is adequately documented and is shown to be reasonable. For protesters other than small businesses, attorney fees are capped at $150 per hour except for special circumstances.

A GAO decision is not binding as with a court or board decision; the decision is technically a recommendation. If the agency does not fully implement the GAO's recommendations within 60 days of receiving them, the head of the contracting activity must report the failure to the GAO within five days after expiration of the 60-day period. The report must explain why the GAO's recommendations, exclusive of costs, have not been followed by the agency. This report also goes to Congress. Thus, it may be said that the GAO's decision is de facto binding. On the other hand, the details of implementing GAO's recommendations for corrective action are within the sound discretion and judgment of the contracting agency.

§ 33.3   Protests to the United States Court of Federal Claims

As a result of the Administrative Dispute Resolution Act of 1996 (ADRA), which in turn amended the Tucker Act, COFC is now the sole federal judicial trial forum in which disappointed bidders or offerors may pursue a protest.

(a) Jurisdiction

By statute, the COFC has jurisdiction to consider (1) objections to a solicitation or to a proposed or actual award of a contract and (2) alleged violations of a statute or regulation in connection with a procurement or a proposed procurement. Some cases have gone quite far in the interpretation of this authority, well beyond the GAO's protest jurisdiction. Resolving a split within COFC, the Federal Circuit has held that the ADRA provides the basis for protest jurisdiction within COFC over procurement contracts. The Federal Circuit no longer follows the prior common law implied contract of fair consideration of bids or proposals as that authority. *Resource Conservation Group, LLC v. United States*, 597 F.3d 1238 (Fed. Cir. 2010).

Because the COFC in deciding protests must use the Administrative Procedure Act (APA) standard of review, a protester may allege that the agency either (a) violated an applicable procurement statute or regulation or (b) acted in an arbitrary and capricious way or abused its discretion. The COFC has declined to assume protest jurisdiction over matters relating to an agency's administration of a contract, requests to enjoin agencies from reporting derogatory contractor past performance information, or whether a GAO protest process should be enjoined.

Even though COFC is an Article I court under the federal Constitution, and not an Article III court, COFC bid protests are subject to the traditional doctrines governing all federal judicial actions, including the justiciability doctrines of ripeness and mootness

(b) Standing

To bring a protest at the COFC, the protester must be an "interested party," although the jurisdictional statute does not define the term. The Federal Circuit held in *Rex Service Corp. v. United States*, 448 F.3d 1305 (Fed. Cir. 2006), that the quoted term in the ADRA is construed in accordance with the definition of the same term in the Competition in Contracting Act, which governs GAO bid protests. Thus, the parties encompassed by that term are actual or prospective bidders or offerors whose direct economic interest would be affected by the award of the contract or the failure to award the contract.

Standing to protest differs from proving the entitlement to relief on the merits. The COFC will consider the plaintiff's plausible allegations and merely ask whether, if they turn out to be correct, whether the plaintiff has a substantial chance of receiving the award. Prejudice or injury in this sense is a necessary element of standing, although COFC will examine prejudice similar to what typically occurs at the GAO to determine whether the plaintiff shall be afforded relief.

The standing question can arise in numerous settings. For example, a protester will not be an interested party at the COFC to challenge a sole source award where the party has failed to establish it was a qualified, responsible bidder A successor-in-interest to an actual offeror is an interested party with standing to protest under the Administrative Dispute Resolution Act, 28 U.S.C.A. § 1491(b). For a firm to have standing to protest a sole-source procurement for which the agency required potential contractors to submit a capability statement, a protester must have submitted the statement within the time set in the agency's notice of intent to award a sole-source contract.

For COFC protests, the aggrieved firm that has not actually submitted an offer must be expecting to submit an offer prior to the closing date for receipt of the offers. Accordingly, where a firm makes a business decision not to submit an offer on the procurement and has failed to file a timely protest against the solicitation, such a firm is no longer a "prospective bidder" to establish its status as an interested party under the revised Tucker Act.

The COFC expounded on the "substantial chance" test for standing in *Preferred Systems Solutions, Inc. v. United States*, 110 Fed. Cl. 48 (2013), where the COFC agreed that the protester had demonstrated a sufficiently direct economic interest to establish standing. Ruling that a protester need not be "next in line" for award to invoke the court's jurisdiction, but rather within the zone of active consideration for the award, the court found the protester had standing despite its ranking fourth out of five offerors.

The COFC permits intervenors in both pre-award and post-award protests. The applicable rules of intervention can be found in Court of Federal Claims Rule 24. A party may participate as an *amicus curiae* in a COFC case within the discretion of the court.

(c) Source of Procedures

In addition to the COFC's basic rules and the Federal Rules of Evidence, the Appendix C of the COFC's Rules of Procedure governs the court's protest procedures. The Federal Circuit in *Blue & Gold Fleet, L.P. v. United States*, 492 F.3d 1308 (Fed. Cir. 2007), has ruled, by analogy, that the timeliness rules of the Government Accountability Office regarding challenges to solicitations apply in Tucker Act protests.

(d) Filing of the Complaint

One of the innovations brought about by Appendix C of the COFC's Rules of Procedure is a requirement that, absent exceptional circumstances, protesters must give the Department of Justice, the

Clerk of the Court, the involved agency, and the apparent awardee 24 hours' advance notice of an anticipated protest.

A protest action begins with the filing of a complaint stating the nature of relief sought, along with a civil cover sheet. Because there is no automatic stay of award or of performance in COFC protests, a protester should move for a temporary restraining order or a preliminary injunction as soon as possible after the filing of its complaint. The protester should also file a motion for a protective order that will outline the procedures to be followed for access to such information. Appendix C of the COFC's Rules of Procedure has sample forms for (a) a protective order, (b) an application for access by outside or inside counsel, and (c) an application for access by experts or consultants.

(e) Summary Judgment

Most protest actions at the COFC are resolved before a trial or final hearing on the merits through a motion for summary judgment or a distinct process for relief based on the administrative record. This last method amounts to a "paper trial," where the court bases its judgment solely on the documents in the record. Discovery is rare, but can take place in proper circumstances, such as with well-grounded allegations of agency bias. COFC may request expert affidavits, rebuttal affidavits, and written closing arguments to reach a decision.

The administrative record may be supplemented only if the omission of extra-record evidence would preclude effective or meaningful judicial review, which differs from mere post-hoc rationalizations. Thus, for example, the record may be supplemented with relevant information that by its very nature would not be found in an agency record, for example, evidence of bias, prejudice, or bad faith

(f) Alternative Dispute Resolution

Alternative Dispute Resolution (ADR) procedures are available for use in protest actions at the COFC. The use of ADR at the court is governed by its General Order No. 44.

(g) Standard of Review

A protest proceeds in two steps. First, COFC determines whether the government acted without rational basis or contrary to law when evaluating the offers and awarding the contract. Second, if the COFC finds that the government's conduct fails the APA review under 5 U.S.C.A. § 706(2)(A), then it proceeds to determine, as a factual matter, if the bid protester was prejudiced by that conduct. *Bannum, Inc. v. United States,* 404 F.3d 1346 (Fed. Cir. 2005).

As noted earlier, the APA standard of review applies to protests at the COFC. Thus, in most protests, the COFC will determine whether the agency' actions were arbitrary, capricious, an abuse of discretion, or not otherwise in accordance with law. To prevail on this basis, a protester must prove (1) that there was subjective bad faith on the part of the government, (2) there was no reasonable basis for the agency's decision, (3) the procuring officials abused their discretion, or (4) pertinent statutes or regulations were violated. A statutory or regulatory violation is not necessarily grounds for a valid protest.

(h) Burden of Proof

The protester bears the burden of proving its protest allegations. To prevail in a protest at the COFC, the protester must demonstrate that (a) there was a significant error in the procurement process, and (b) the error "competitively prejudiced" the protester (i.e., but for the error, there was a substantial chance that the protester would have received the award.) Competitive prejudice for a solicitation protest means a non-trivial competitive injury that can be redressed by judicial relief. In a post-award protest based on a procurement defect occurring during the evaluation and award process, a protester demonstrates prejudice if it shows that "absent the error, it would have a chance of receiving the contract award that is more than merely speculative."

An agency's notice of intent to make a sole-source award was a final action and ripe for review, the United States Court of Federal Claims has held. But the protester lacked standing because it did not satisfy a requirement for award and therefore did not show that it had a substantial chance of receiving the award. *Ideogenics, LLC v. United States,* 145 Fed. Cl. 666 (2019).

In *Orion Technology, Inc. v. United States,* 704 F.3d 1344 (Fed. Cir. 2013), the Federal Circuit held that the "substantial chance" test (rather than the more lenient "non-trivial competitive injury" test) should be used in post-proposal, pre-evaluation protests to determine the standing requirement of having "a direct economic interest" in the procurement.

Even after the enactment of the revised Tucker Act by way of the Administrative Dispute Resolution Act (ADRA), the court's review of procurement decisions is "extremely limited in scope." The agency is accorded wide discretion in its evaluation of bids and proposals and in its application of procurement regulations. This deference is particularly great when a negotiated procurement is involved and is greater still in a "best value" procurement, i.e., where the agency balances an RFP's announced price and non-price evaluation factors. Where the decision-making process involves a review of technical matters, the court will accord the agency the highest degree of deference.

Where the record before the agency does not support the agency action, or if the reviewing court simply cannot evaluate the challenged agency action on the basis of the record before it, the proper course, except in rare circumstances, is for COFC to remand to the agency for additional investigation or explanation.

(i) Reconsideration and Appeal

An unsuccessful protester at the COFC has two options for obtaining further judicial consideration of its protest. First, the protester may file a motion for reconsideration with the COFC within 10 days after the entry of judgment. Generally, the motion must be based on a manifest error of law or a mistake of fact. Second, the protester may appeal the COFC's decision to the United States Court of Appeals for the Federal Circuit by filing a notice of appeal with the COFC clerk within 60 days after the judgment or order. The Federal Circuit will review the COFC's legal conclusions *de novo*, but it will disturb the court's factual findings only if they are clearly erroneous.

B. DISPUTES

§ 33.4   Contract Disputes—Overview

Most government contracts are performed and paid for in satisfactory fashion. When disputes go unresolved, however, the contract contains a mechanism known as the "Disputes" clause that allows the contract work to continue while an orderly settlement of the dispute is sought.

If a mutually acceptable settlement cannot be attained, the Contracting Officer has the power to decide the issue unilaterally. A contractor that disagrees with the Contracting Officer's decision may elect to file an action with the appropriate agency board of contract appeals or the Court of Federal Claims. The government also has rights under the "Disputes" clause, although not identical to the contractors. Thereafter, the U.S. Court of Appeals for the Federal Circuit can hear an appeal. Most of the discussion in this chapter will focus on contractor claims, except as indicated.

One of the more important changes made by the CDA was the extension of the disputes process to all claims of either party "relating to" a contract. Before the CDA was enacted, only claims "arising under" the terms of a government contract were subject to the jurisdiction of the agency boards of contract appeals. Therefore, boards did not have the authority to hear breach of contract claims against the government because breach claims were considered to arise "outside" the contract's terms. The contractor had to sue the government in court for breach of contract. The CDA established that all claims "relating to" a contract are subject to the disputes procedure regardless of whether relief is available under the contract's terms.

The COFC's jurisdictional statutes are broad. In *Slattery v. United States*, 635 F.3d 1298 (Fed. Cir. 2011), the Federal Circuit overruled cases precluding Tucker Act (and likely Contract Disputes Act) jurisdiction over claims against non-appropriated fund instrumentalities. Although the jurisdictional separation of claims between "breach of contract" and claims "arising under" the contract was resolved by the CDA, the term "arising under the contract" still has some legal significance. For example, the contractor's duty under FAR 52.233–1 to proceed with performance pending resolution of the dispute, the amount of the contractor's recovery, or the contractor's notice obligations may be affected by whether the remedy sought by the contractor is based on a contract clause. Federal district courts lack jurisdiction over cases within the CDA's exclusive dispute-resolution process.

The CDA broadened the coverage of the disputes process, but it did not extend it to all government contracts or procurement actions. For example, grants, cooperative agreements, and subsidy arrangements do not typically qualify as CDA "procurement" contracts, nor are cases challenging debarments or suspensions of contractors from government contracting subject to CDA jurisdiction.

The CDA applies to "any express or implied contract" entered into by "an executive agency" of the United States for "(1) the procurement of property, other than real property in being; (2) the procurement of services; (3) the procurement of construction, alteration, repair or maintenance of real property; or (4) the disposal of personal property." Contracts with foreign governments or agencies are normally excluded. However, the statutory exclusions have been narrowly construed.

Not all controversies that may arise during the performance of a government contract are subject to CDA procedures. In implementing the CDA, the FAR gives the Contracting Officer authority "to decide or resolve all claims arising under or relating to a contract subject to the Act," but this authority "does not extend to— (a) a claim or dispute for penalties or forfeitures prescribed by statute or regulation that another federal agency is specifically authorized to administer, settle, or determine; or (b) the settlement, compromise, payment, or adjustment of any claim involving fraud." Claims for relief that have been held to be outside the Contracting Officer's jurisdiction because they involve "penalties or forfeitures" within the purview of "another federal agency" include, for example, labor-related disputes.

Agency boards are frequently requested to stay their CDA proceedings so as not to interfere with pending or ongoing criminal or civil proceedings. In considering whether to stay the proceedings, the boards have balanced the competing interests of the contractor's statutory right to an expeditious resolution of its contract claim against the government's interest in avoiding duplicative litigation and prejudice to its investigation.

§ 33.5   The Disputes Path

The "Disputes" clause prescribed by the FAR implements the CDA. This clause defines the term "claim," describes how claims are submitted ("in writing . . . within 6 years after accrual of the claim") and which claims (those exceeding $100,000) must be certified by the contractor. It imposes an obligation on the Contracting Officer to decide the claim within certain time limits and states that such decision "shall be final unless the contractor appeals or files a suit as provided" in the CDA.

The Act also permits the parties to agree to use alternative dispute resolution (ADR) techniques to resolve their dispute, provides for the payment to the contractor of interest on any amounts found due the contractor, and requires the contractor to "proceed diligently" with contract performance pending final resolution of the dispute.

(a)   Contracting Officer

The FAR disputes process begins with the presentation of a claim by the contractor to the Contracting Officer or by the transmission of a government claim to the contractor. The Contracting Officer has two primary roles in the disputes process: to settle disagreements and to render decisions on contractor and government claims.

In addition, it is the government's policy "to try to resolve all contractual issues in controversy by mutual agreement at the contracting officer's level." The standard "Disputes" clause expressly permits the parties to consent to alternative dispute resolution (ADR) techniques to resolve a claim. Parties must provide a written explanation if they reject an offer of ADR.

If negotiation fails, however, the Contracting Officer's second duty is to issue a final decision on a contractor's claim, usually within 60 days. If the decision is adverse to the contractor, the contractor may appeal the Contracting Officer's decision either to the appropriate board of contract appeals (within 90 days) or the Court of Federal Claims (within twelve months) (except that a claim filed a year and a day qualifies as "twelve months" under COFC rules). The contractor similarly may appeal a government claim, most commonly, a termination for default or a withholding of monies.

Once an action is brought following a contracting officer's decision, the review is de novo, which means that the parties start in court or before the board with a clean slate and not being necessarily bound by the contracting officer's fact findings or legal conclusions.

(b) Boards of Contract Appeals

Boards of contract appeals serve as the administrative forums for deciding the merits of claims that the parties have been unable to resolve at the Contracting Officer level. The CDA broadened the authority of the boards by specifically giving each agency board jurisdiction "to decide any appeal from a decision of a contracting officer . . . relative to a contract made by its agency."

In exercising this jurisdiction, an agency board is authorized "to grant any relief that would be available to a litigant asserting a contract claim in the United States Court of Federal Claims." Accordingly, the boards, in addition to carrying out their traditional role of deciding disputes arising under the contract, are able to (1) order the agency to modify, reform, or rescind contracts in the case of bid mistakes, and (2) decide the merits of cases involving breach of contract theories.

Boards have no authority under the CDA to grant relief for claims based on the United States Constitution or to order specific performance or injunctive relief. *Kansas City Power & Light Co. v. United States*, 131 Fed. Cl. 161 (2017). Similarly, alleged fiscal law violations did not support a contractor action for rescission of the contract and quantum meruit recovery, the Armed Services Board of Contract Appeals has held in dismissing the appeal. *Parsons Gov't Servs., Inc.*, ASBCA 60663, 17-1 BCA ¶ 36743.

Where the Government's offset defense sought to reduce plaintiff's damage claims against the Government by the amount of plaintiff's insurance recoveries, the offset defense was not a Contract Disputes Act claim. Therefore, the CDA did not require that the defense be first submitted to and addressed by the contracting officer, the United States Court of Federal Claims (COFC) has held.

As of January 8, 2007, all boards of contract appeals for civilian agencies, except the boards of the U.S. Postal Service and the Tennessee Valley Authority, were consolidated into the Civilian Board of Contract Appeals (CBCA). The Chairman of the former General Services Administration Board of Contract Appeals became the chairman of the CBCA, whose website is https://www.cbca.gov/. The Armed Services Board of Contract Appeals remains the main tribunal for the military departments whose website is http://www.asbca.mil/index.html.

A final rule revises, reorders and clarifies the ASBCA's rules, updates contact information, accounts for changing technology, and inserts two addenda: Equal Access to Justice Act procedures and alternative methods of dispute resolution, previously were not formally contained in the rules.

(c) Court of Federal Claims

The CDA allows the contractor the option to elect between appealing an adverse Contracting Officer's decision to a board or filing suit directly in the COFC. Because the Federal Courts Administration Act of 1992 expanded the jurisdiction of the COFC to include nonmonetary government contract disputes, the jurisdictions of the boards and the court with respect to government contracts have been virtually identical. The pretrial, trial, and decision procedures used by the two forums are also substantially similar.

(d) Court of Appeals for the Federal Circuit

The Court of Appeals for the Federal Circuit acts as the reviewing authority in cases that are appealed (by either party) after receipt of an adverse decision from a board or the COFC. Both parties—the contractor and the government—have 60 days after the date the judgment or order is entered to file an appeal of a COFC decision and 120 days to file an appeal of a board decision. The Federal Circuit has ruled that it has no jurisdiction over appeals from board decisions filed after the expiration of the prescribed 120-day period and no authority to waive the statutory period. The Supreme Court reviews government contract cases decided by the Federal Circuit only when they, at least potentially, would have far-reaching precedential effect.

§ 33.6   The Claim and the Contracting Officer's Decision

This portion of the chapter reviews the first steps in the disputes process—the submission of a claim to the Contracting Officer and the Contracting Officer's decision on that claim. Not every request by a contractor to the government qualifies as a "claim," nor does every communication from the Contracting Officer to the contractor on a subject in disagreement constitute a "decision" under the Contract Disputes Act (CDA) and the contract's "Disputes" clause.

The succeeding sections in this chapter examine (a) the two types of claims that may begin the disputes process: contractor claims or government claims, (b) how a claim is asserted, (c) the rules relating to the issuance of a final decision by the Contracting Officer on the claim, and (d) where the Contracting Officer's decision on the claim is adverse to the contractor, the factors and consequences of the contractor's decision to litigate the dispute in a board of contract appeals or COFC.

(a) Contractor Claims vs. Government Claims

The claim that begins the disputes process is usually a contractor claim. This demand may be a claim "arising under" some remedy-granting clause of the contract, such as the "Changes" or "Suspension of Work" clauses, for more money or more time (or both) to complete the contract.

Alternatively, the contractor may allege a claim "relating to the contract," such as a breach of the contract by the government or for equitable relief, such as reformation, based on a bid mistake. Although a subcontractor may not file a claim directly with the Contracting Officer, a prime contractor may sponsor a claim—commonly called a "pass through claim"—on a behalf of a subcontractor. A surety is not a "contractor" under the CDA, absent privity with the government.

The government may assert a claim against the contractor. For example, it may seek reimbursement of excess costs caused by defective performance, recovery of overpayments made to the contractor, a reduction in the contract price caused by defective pricing or failure to comply with the Cost Accounting Standards, imposition of a termination for default or an assessment of liquidated damages.

Note that regardless of which party is asserting the claim, it must, under the CDA, be submitted within six years of its accrual, except for government claims based on fraud. In implementing the CDA, the FAR defines "accrual of a claim" as occurring "when all events, which fix the alleged liability of either the government or the contractor and permit assertion of the claim, were known or should have been known."

Sometimes it is difficult to distinguish between "contractor claims" and "government claims." For example, a question involving cost allowability is often resolved in the context of a claim asserted by the government in the form of a formal notice to the contractor of cost disallowance. The contractor may also file a "claim" with the Contracting Officer seeking an interpretation, in the form of a Contracting Officer's final decision, of cost allowability issues.

Before an appeal is proper, both contractor and government claims must be the subject of a Contracting Officer's final decision or, in the case of a contractor claim, be "deemed" denied by the Contracting Officer. This final decision is a jurisdictional prerequisite with a dispute before a board or the COFC.

In a recent development, the Federal Circuit *M. Maropakis Carpentry, Inc. v. United States*, 609 F.3d 1323 (Fed. Cir. 2010), held that contractor which seeks an adjustment of contract terms must meet the jurisdictional requirements and procedural prerequisites of the Contract Disputes Act for a "claim" asserted as an affirmative defense or as a defense to a Government claim. The *Maropakis* case, however, has its limits. COFC has rejected the government's *Maropakis* argument that a contractor's assertion of Government delay as a defense was required to be the subject of a CO final decision; the reason for the court's holding was the defense was already within the scope of the contractor's Contract Disputes Act claim for an equitable adjustment.

Relying on *Maropakis*, supra, and *Laguna Constr. Co. v. Carter*, 828 F.3d 1364 (Fed. Cir. 2016); 58 GC ¶ 264, the Federal Circuit in *Securiforce Int'l Am., LLC v. United States*, 879 F.3d 1354 (Fed. Cir. 2018), has explained that a contactor defense that merely contests an agency action, without more, is not a claim for money and affirmative defenses must be submitted to the CO for decision only if the defense seeks a change in the terms of the contract—for example, an extension of time or an equitable adjustment.

(b) Claim Submission

The submission of a claim to the Contracting Officer initiates the disputes process. As mentioned above, the contractor's claim triggers the Contracting Officer's obligation to make a timely decision on the claim and begins the running of interest on the claim amount. Thus, whether and when a contractor "claim" has arisen is of basic importance.

Government claims usually commence with a demand letter notifying the contractor of the potential claim and giving the contractor an opportunity to respond. Interest on a government claim begins to run when the contractor has received the government's initial written demand for payment.

(c) Definition of "Claim"

The CDA contains no definition of "claim." But it does specify two of a claim's key requirements: (1) all claims by a party "shall be in writing and submitted to the contracting officer for a decision," and (2) all contractor claims over $100,000 must be certified. The "Disputes" contract clause, however, defines a claim as "a written demand or written assertion by one of the contracting parties seeking, as a matter of right, the payment of money in a sum certain, the adjustment or interpretation of contract terms, or other relief arising under or relating to this contract." Thus, the CDA procedures will apply to where a contractor or the government seeks relief through a claim.

Along with meeting the certification requirement, the claim must (a) be in writing, (b) request monetary relief in a sum certain or the interpretation of the contract's terms or some other kind of relief under or relating to the contract, and (c) demand a final decision. The claim may implicitly or explicitly request the final decision, although the Contracting Officer may not issue a valid final decision if the contractor explicitly states it does not desire such a decision.

Although no particular form or wording is required to state a claim, a contractor must submit "a clear and unequivocal statement that gives the contracting officer adequate notice of the basis and amount of the claim." A claim need not be submitted as a single document and, in fact, several communications taken together may constitute a claim. But to qualify as a claim, there must be a manifestation of a "present, positive intention to seek an equitable, monetary or other adjustment of the contract terms, as a matter of right." The sufficiency of a claim is based on the totality of the circumstances, including the claim document, the correspondence, and the parties' continuing discussions.

A contractor's use of the Defense Federal Acquisition Regulation Supplement certification for a request for equitable adjustment (REA) was sufficiently close to the CDA certification language, and the contractor was entitled to correct its certification, the Armed Services Board of Contract Appeals has held in denying the Government's motion to dismiss for lack of jurisdiction. *Air Servs., Inc.*, ASBCA 59843, 15-1 BCA ¶ 36146.

The CDA requires that a claim by either party be submitted to the Contracting Officer for a decision. The CDA "submission" element for a contractor claim requires the contractor to commit the claim to the Contracting Officer and to yield to his authority to make a final decision. Furthermore, where the contractor asserts related, but distinct, claims, each must satisfy the CDA requirements.

However, the boards and courts have allowed some flexibility in interpreting this submission requirement. For instance, the Armed Services Board of Contract Appeals (ASBCA) has stated that a claim need only be submitted "in a manner reasonably calculated to be received by the Contracting Officer authorized to decide the claim," concluding that submission of a claim to the legal officer rather than to the contractually designated area engineer fulfilled this requirement.

The "Disputes" clause also states that a "voucher, invoice, or other routine request for payment that is not in dispute when submitted is not a claim under the [CDA]." Much litigation has resulted from this relatively simple language, primarily over whether both "routine" and "non-routine" requests were required to be "in dispute" to qualify as CDA claims.

In 1995, the United States Court of Appeals for the Federal Circuit in *Reflectone, Inc. v. Dalton,* 60 F.3d 1572 (Fed. Cir. 1995), seemingly put the matter to rest, holding that (1) non-routine demands for payment—such as a request for an equitable adjustment—need not be in dispute as to either amount or liability when first submitted to the Contracting Officer to qualify as a CDA claim, and (2) if a routine request for payment is filed, the parties must first reach an impasse before the request can attain claim status. In one recent case, the ASBCA determined the contractor stated a "non-routine" payment request that was a routine monthly progress payment request when the invoice was originally submitted to the contracting officer for payment.

It bears emphasis, however, in accordance with the above Federal Circuit decision, that a request for an equitable adjustment can be a monetary claim only when it also constitutes a written demand seeking as a matter of right the payment of money in a sum certain, and is certified by the contractor if it exceeds $100,000.

A subsequent decision by the Federal Circuit, *James M. Ellett Const. Co. Inc. v. United States*, 93 F.3d 1537 (Fed. Cir. 1996), introduced a degree of uncertainty in this area when it concluded that although a termination for convenience settlement proposal is a non-routine submission, negotiations must reach an impasse before the settlement proposal can be considered a CDA claim. As a result, it is now possible that a contractor's request for "prompt action and decision" could be interpreted as an invitation for further settlement negotiations and thus does not trigger the start of the claims process.

The Federal Circuit in *Systems Development Corp. v. McHugh*, 658 F.3d 1341 (Fed. Cir. 2011), has since clarified this point, holding that requirement for an "impasse" to create a claim goes only to termination for convenience settlement proposals and does not apply to claims for equitable adjustment on contracts, even if there is a termination for convenience.

Another decision ruled that the prime contractor's submissions to the Government did not constitute a Contract Disputes Act claim because they asserted a routine request for payment of overhead costs. These fine distinctions in the cases summarized above, resulting in different outcomes, are the key to deciding whether under the particular facts, the contractor has filed a compensable claim.

(d) Sum Certain

The requirement is that a monetary claim be for a "sum certain." Generally, a "good faith estimate" of the amount allegedly due will meet this requirement. Even a reservation of the right to seek additional "acquisition savings" has been held not to render an otherwise acceptable claim uncertain. But care must be taken. In one case, *McElroy Mach. & Mfg. Co., Inc.,* ASBCA No. 39416, 92-3 B.C.A. (CCH) ¶ 25107, a board of contract appeals found that a claim for a sum certain that reserved the right to include additional line items and to otherwise "modify the presentation" was, in fact, simply a "predicate for negotiations" and not a proper CDA claim.

A board or court has authority to award compensation in excess of the amount stated in a certified claim. The rationale is the amount specified may be revised or refined without recertification as long as it is based on the original claim.

(e) Claim Certification

The CDA and the implementing "Disputes" clause state that "a written demand or written assertion by the contractor seeking the payment of money exceeding $100,000 is not a claim under the Act until certified." The CDA provides as follows:

> For claims of more than $100,000, the contractor shall certify that the claim is made in good faith, that the supporting data are accurate and complete to the best of his knowledge and belief, that the amount requested accurately reflects the contract adjustment for which the contractor believes the government is liable, and that the individual executing the certification is duly authorized to certify the claim on behalf of the contractor.

The intent behind the certification requirement is deter fraud and to discourage contractors from submitting unwarranted or inflated claims. This policy does not require unqualified certainty that the amount claimed is correct, so long as the contractor reasonably believes that it has a right to recover the amount requested. No certification is required for a government claim.

Various rules exist for determining the claim amount. For example, the aggregate effect of the increased and decreased costs will determine the threshold for claim certification, but not the amount of any government claims. Next, claims based on a common or related set of operative facts will be one claim. In a third example, separate claims that total less than $100,000 each require no certification, even if their combined total exceeds $100,000. Invoices, detailed cost breakdowns and other supporting financial documentation need not accompany a CDA claim as a jurisdictional requirement.

If a claim in excess of $100,000 is not properly certified, the CDA provides that the Contracting Officer has no obligation to render a final decision if, within 60 days after receipt of the claim, the Contracting Officer notifies the contractor, in writing, of the reasons the attempted certification is defective.

The FAR defines a defective certification as one that alters or otherwise deviates from the FAR certifying language or that is not executed by a person duly authorized to bind the contractor. However, a defective certification does not necessarily deprive a court or board of jurisdiction over the claim as long as the defect is corrected before the entry of final judgment by the court or a board's final decision. Interest on the claim accrues from the date that the Contracting Officer initially received the claim.

Note that a certification is correctable only if the defect is "technical in nature." Certifications made with intentional, reckless, or negligent disregard of the applicable statutory requirements are not correctable. Nor does the statutory authority to correct deficiencies extend to supplying a certification where none was submitted initially. Where a certification was missing a signature, it was not a defective certification that deprived a board of contract appeals or the COFC of jurisdiction.

Although the rules regarding who may sign a claim certification were previously complex and strictly construed, the CDA and the "Disputes" clause now provide that the certification "may be executed by any person duly authorized to bind the contractor with respect to the claim." Thus, for example, a contractor's senior project manager can be a proper certifying official.

The FAR specifies mandatory language for the claim certification. The certification contains four assertions: (1) the claim is made in good faith, (2) the supporting data are accurate and complete to the best of the contractor's knowledge and belief, (3) the amount requested accurately reflects the contract adjustment for which the contractor believes the government is liable, and (4) the certifier is duly authorized to certify the claim on behalf of the contractor. Exact recitation of the certification language is not required, provided the certification substantially complies with the statutory requirements. Also, a CDA certification would not be defective merely because the term "request" was twice substituted for "claim."

§ 33.7   Contracting Officer's Decision

If the Contracting Officer and the contractor are unable to resolve their dispute through a negotiated settlement agreement, the Contracting Officer must issue a decision (called a "final decision") under the "Disputes" clause on the contractor's claim. The Contracting Officer's final decision is the final rejection of the contractor's claim by the government and the predicate for the litigation process.

Contracting Officers may reconsider, withdraw, or rescind a final decision before the expiration of the appeals period. A Contracting Officer also could vacate the "final" decision inadvertently by reopening consideration of the claim, such as by agreeing to meet with the contractor to discuss the matters in dispute. The Contracting Officer will restart the appeal period after reconsideration of a final decision only by issuing a new final decision.

(a) Role in Disputes Process

The Contracting Officer's decision—whether express or a "deemed" denial—is a jurisdictional prerequisite to the contractor's filing an appeal to a board of contract appeals or a suit on the claim in the Court of Federal Claims. Because in one case the subject matter was a new claim versus the claim that was before the Contracting Officer, the Civilian Board of Contract Appeals refused jurisdiction by way of a *Hamilton* stipulation that the Contracting Officer had informally considered the claim and if asked for a final decision would have denied the claim, per *United States v. Hamilton Enterprises*, 711 F.2d 1038 (Fed. Cir. 1983).

As stated in the previous section, the contractor may appeal either the denial of its own claim or the contracting officer's acceptance of a government claim. Once the appeal period has lapsed, the contractor cannot challenge the merits of the decision judicially. Also, if the claim is pending in litigation, a Contracting Officer has no authority to issue a final decision on the claim because the exclusive governmental authority in this situation rests with the

Department of Justice. Under 28 U.S.C.A. § 516, the Department of Justice gains exclusive authority to act in the pending litigation, and that exclusive authority divests the CO of his authority to act on and issue a final decision on the claim.

Boards lack jurisdiction over claims relating to the acceptability of bids or proposals for awards or to de facto suspensions and debarments. The boards and courts are similarly without jurisdiction to consider a government claim or counterclaim absent a valid Contracting Officer's final decision on the claim or counterclaim and an appeal of that decision by the contractor. One exception to this rule is that the government need not obtain a final decision when it wishes to exercise its common law right of setoff. Another qualification is that when a claim is suspected to be fraudulent, the contracting officer shall refer the matter to the agency official responsible for investigating fraud but that step does not necessarily justify staying the proceedings until the board takes such an unusual action.

The Contracting Officer must make a personal and independent decision. An agency may not reverse the Contracting Officer's final decision through the appointment of a successor Contracting Officer who would make another determination. On the other hand, the Contracting Officer may rely upon the advice of other officials in arriving at the final decision, such as technical and legal personnel. No requirement exists for the Contracting Officer to conduct a personal investigation of the facts of the claim before rendering the final decision.

(b) Content

The FAR contains detailed guidance on the Contracting Officer's duties with respect to deciding claims. It provides that when a claim—by or against a contractor—cannot be settled by agreement, the Contracting Officer must (1) review the pertinent facts, (2) secure assistance from legal and other advisors, (3) coordinate with other government offices to the extent necessary, and (4) prepare a written decision.

The final decision must be in writing and shall include (a) a description of the claim or dispute, (b) reference to pertinent contract provisions, (c) a statement of the factual areas of agreement or disagreement, (d) a statement of the Contracting Officer's decision with supporting rationale, and (e) a demand for payment when the decision finds that the contractor is indebted to the government. By presenting the decision in some detail, the Contracting Officer will aid in eliminating undisputed matters from litigation. On the other hand, the CDA states that specific findings of fact are not required and will not be binding in subsequent litigation.

The Contracting Officer's decision must include a paragraph containing language such as the following, notifying the contractor of its appeal rights:

> This is the final decision of the Contracting Officer. You may appeal this decision to the agency board of contract appeals. If you decide to appeal, you must, within 90 days from the date you receive this decision, mail or otherwise furnish written notice to the agency board of contract appeals and provide a copy to the Contracting Officer from whose decision the appeal is taken. The notice shall indicate that an appeal is intended, reference this decision, and identify the contract by number. With regard to appeals to the agency board of contract appeals, you may, solely at your election, proceed under the board's—
>
> (1) Small claim procedure for claims of $50,000 or less or, in the case of a small business concern (as defined in the Small Business Act and regulations under that Act), $150,000 or less; or
>
> (2) Accelerated procedure for claims of $100,000 or less.
>
> Instead of appealing to the agency board of contract appeals, you may bring an action directly in the United States Court of Federal Claims . . . within 12 months of the date you receive this decision.

This paragraph notifies the contractor (1) that the document is a final decision of the Contracting Officer and (2) of its right of appeal. Without this paragraph or equivalent language, a contractor could argue that the Contracting Officer's communication did not start the time period for filing an appeal or suit or be forced to treat all significant communications from the Contracting Officer as final decisions to protect its appeal rights.

The Court of Federal Claims in several cases has construed the above referenced one year CDA appeal period. These decisions hold that an appeal filed within a year and a day from the claimant's receipt of the Contracting Officer's decision would be timely The rationale is that the Rules of the Court of Federal Claims exclude the day the claimant receives the decision in calculating the 12 month period.

The standard "boilerplate" paragraph eliminates uncertainty and provides a clear date for determining when the contractor must file a notice of appeal or complaint. However, where the "boilerplate" language is included but contains incorrect information, the contractor must demonstrate that it detrimentally relied on the incorrect advice to justify an untimely filing. For this reason, whether a final decision contains a defective notice of appeal rights is not, by itself, sufficient to suspend the 90-day period for filing a notice of appeal; the controlling question is whether the defective notice prejudiced the contractor.

(c) Timing

Before enactment of the CDA, the timing of the issuance of the final decision was within the discretion of the Contracting Officer, subject only to the limits of "reasonableness." As a result, contractors sometimes complained of lengthy and unnecessary delays in the issuance of Contracting Officers' decisions on their claims. The CDA established specific time limits for the issuance of decisions and provides contractors with appropriate remedies in case the limitations are not met.

If the contractor's claim does not exceed $100,000, the CDA requires that the decision be issued within 60 days after the Contracting Officer receives a written request from the contractor that a decision be rendered or within a reasonable time after receipt of the claim if the contractor does not make such a request. If the claim exceeds $100,000, the Contracting Officer must either (a) issue a decision within 60 days after receiving a certified claim or (b) notify the contractor within that period of the time within which a decision will be issued.

The FAR provides that the Contracting Officer's final decision on submitted claims must be issued "within a reasonable time" taking into account the size and complexity of the claim, the adequacy of the contractor's supporting data, and any other relevant factors.

In the event of undue delay on the Contracting Officer's part, the CDA allows a contractor to request "the tribunal concerned" (the board or court) to direct the Contracting Officer to issue a decision within a specified time period. The contractor has no right, however, to obtain a more detailed final decision than the Contracting Officer already has issued. If the Contracting Officer fails to act within the period of time ordered, the failure may be a "deemed denial" that authorizes the contractor to commence an appeal to the board or a suit in the Court of Federal Claims without a Contracting Officer's final decision. In one case, the CBCA granted the contractor a deemed denial and rejected the government's attempt to justify its failure to issue a decision based on the workload of its attorneys.

(d) Delivery

The Contracting Officer must mail, or otherwise furnish, a copy of the final decision to the contractor. Delivery to a contractor employee can be proper notice. The government should maintain all evidence of the date of contractor receipt of the decision, so that a board or court can determine the commencement of the appeal period. Usually, the agency will use certified mail, return receipt requested. Where the agency uses a facsimile transmission, which can be permissible, the Contracting Officer should confirm receipt and create a memorandum of the confirmation.

(e) Contractor's Duty to Proceed

A unique feature of government contracting is the requirement that even while the parties are contesting some aspect of contract performance, the contractor generally must continue with its performance under the contract as directed by the Contracting Officer. The "Disputes" clause provides that the contractor "shall proceed diligently with performance of this contract, pending final resolution of any request for relief, claim, appeal, or action arising under the contract, and comply with any decision of the Contracting Officer."

Requiring the contractor to proceed with work pending an appeal protects the government by preventing interruption of the work. A Contracting Officer's direction to proceed with the work is a matter of contract administration that is not appealable separately from the underlying claim. Thus, if the contractor refuses or fails to proceed in accord with the Contracting Officer's decision, the contract may be terminated for default.

The phrase "arising under the contract" limits this obligation to proceed to disputes not involving breach of contract claims. Therefore, the FAR provides an alternate clause for use in contracts where "continued performance is necessary pending resolution of any claim arising under or relating to the contract." The alternate language requires the contractor to proceed with performance regardless of the nature of the claim in dispute.

C. APPEALS

§ 33.8   Contractor's Decision to Appeal

The CDA gives only contractors, not the government, the right to challenge Contracting Officer decisions. It also gives them a choice of forum in which to do so. Under the Act, contractors may either appeal the Contracting Officer's decision to a board of contract appeals or bypass the boards and bring an action against the government directly in the COFC. The contractor chooses a forum by filing a Notice of Appeal at the board (within 90 days) or by filing a complaint (within one year) in the COFC. According to the ASBCA, the contractor can establish the timeliness of an appeal with testimonial evidence despite an untimely postmark.

Initiating an action at a board or the COFC is an election of remedies that will bar a later action in the other tribunal if the first tribunal had jurisdiction. A contractor may also appeal different claims under a single contract to different forums, although the Court of Federal Claims may order consolidation of the cases or transfer the suit to the agency board involved.

§ 33.9   Appeal to the Board of Contract Appeals

The succeeding sections will review the procedures of an administrative appeal—that is, the appeal by the contractor of the Contracting Officer's decision on the claim to the agency board of contract appeals. The procedures of the Armed Services Board of Contract Appeals (ASBCA)—the most prominent board—are typical of the rules of the various other boards.

(a) Taking the Appeal—Jurisdiction

Before a contractor brings an appeal to a board of contract appeals, it should determine whether the board is empowered to hear the appeal under the Contract Disputes Act (CDA). The CDA applies to all disputes arising under government contracts, unless a more specific statute provides another remedy. However, a board may only hear an appeal from a properly filed claim. The ASBCA has jurisdiction to decide appeals regarding contracts made by the Department of Defense or an agency that has designated the ASBCA to decide the appeal.

(b) Standing

Both sides should consider whether the contractor has standing to bring its case before the board. In this regard, the CDA grants the boards of contract appeals jurisdiction over appeals by and against a "contractor," defined as "a party to a government contract other than the government." Thus, a surety generally is not a contractor under the statute. The qualification is a surety may file a claim when it has privity of contract with the government.

(c) Notice of Appeal

The mechanism that initiates an appeal to a board of contract appeals is the filing of a Notice of Appeal by the contractor of the Contracting Officer's final decision. Under the ASBCA's procedures, which is essentially the same as the CBCA's and will be used for illustrative purposes in this Hornbook, this notice is filed directly with the board, and a copy is given to the Contracting Officer. Under the CDA, this notice must be filed no later than 90 days after the contractor receives the Contracting Officer's decision. The 90-day CDA appeal period is jurisdictional and not subject to waiver or tolling. In calculating the 90-day period, the date of receipt of the Contracting Officer's decision is excluded and the date of filing the Notice of Appeal is included.

If the Government proves by objective evidence that a contracting officer's decision was received at the location designated by the contractor for receipt of correspondence, the 90-day appeal period effectively commences.

Another qualification exists to the 90 day rule. In an ASBCA case, the board rejected the government's motion to dismiss a contractor's appeal as untimely, even though the appeal was filed at the Board 128 days after the Contracting Officer's Final Decision (COFD). Here, the contractor filed its notice of appeal with the Contracting Officer five days after the Contracting Officer issued a COFD, but the COFD did not include the address of the ASBCA and the Contracting Officer never forwarded the contractor's notice of appeal to the Board.

(d) Rule 4 File

ASBCA Rule 4 requires the Contracting Officer, within 30 days after receiving the docketing notice, to assemble and transmit to the board "an appeal file consisting of all documents pertinent to the appeal." These documents (known popularly as the "Rule 4 file") include (a) the Contracting Officer's decision, (b) the contract and all pertinent specifications, amendments, plans, and drawings, (c) all relevant correspondence, (d) any relevant transcripts, affidavits, or statements, and (e) any additional information considered relevant to the appeal. In part, the government's Rule 4 submission is a form of initial discovery. The appellant, within 30 days after receiving the Rule 4 file, may transmit to the board (with two copies to the government) any documents not contained in the file that the appellant considers relevant to the appeal.

Either party may object to the inclusion of a particular document or documents in the Rule 4 file. If an objection is made, the document will be removed from the Rule 4 file and the party that introduced the document will have the opportunity to offer it into evidence as would be done with any other non-Rule 4 file documents.

Rule 4 states that, if neither party objects, the documents contained in the file automatically become part of the record upon which the board will render its decision. In such cases, the documents in the file are treated as authentic and genuine, although the presiding ASBCA judge has discretion to accord them whatever weight is deemed appropriate in the course of deciding the appeal.

Regarding discovery, the boards frown on hardball tactics and, especially, upon a party's disregard for the rules of the board. In one case, a board granted the appellant's motion to impose sanctions against the VA for abuse of the discovery process, finding that the VA's response to the appellant's discovery requests was "discourteous," "egregious, "violated repeated promises" to the appellant, and "disregarded Board orders."

(e) Abbreviated   Proceedings—Submission   Without Hearing

The ASBCA permits either party to waive a hearing and submit its case on the record before the board. This simplified procedure is best suited for cases involving relatively small, uncomplicated claims where the time and expense of trying the case likely would exceed the dollar amount in controversy. Under this procedure, affidavits, depositions, answers to interrogatories, and the like may be used to supplement the documentary evidence in the Rule 4 file. In addition, the board may allow the parties to engage in oral argument and to submit briefs in support of their positions.

The ASBCA Rules give an important admonition regarding a case submitted on the record: "Submission of a case without a hearing does not relieve the parties from the necessity of proving the facts supporting their allegations or defenses."

(f) Expedited Appeals

An appellant with a claim of $50,000 or less, or in the case of a small business concern, $150,000 or less, may elect to use the expedited procedure. Under this procedure, the board should, wherever possible, decide the case within 120 days of the appellant's election.

Within 15 days after receiving the appellant's election notice, the judge must contact both parties (frequently through a telephone conference call) and (1) identify the issues, (2) establish a simplified procedure appropriate to the particular appeal involved, (3) determine whether either party wants a hearing and, if so, fix a time and place for it, (4) require the government to furnish all the additional documents relevant to the appeal, and (5) establish an expedited schedule for resolution of the appeal. Pleadings and discovery will be allowed only to the extent that they are consistent with the requirement to issue a decision within the four-month period.

Written decisions in expedited appeals are rendered by a single judge and are short, containing only summary findings of fact and conclusions of law. Moreover, if there has been a hearing, the presiding judge has the discretion to render an oral decision in the appeal at the conclusion of the hearing. Decisions in expedited appeals are not published, are of no precedential value, and may not (in the absence of fraud) be appealed.

(g) Accelerated Appeals

If the amount of the claim is less than $150,000, an appellant may elect to have a decision rendered by the board within 180 days, wherever possible, after the election is made. One board has held that where, during litigation, the amount of the appellant's claim is increased to over the applicable dollar threshold (because of a change in the method of calculating hourly rates of pay), the appeal was no longer entitled to accelerated treatment. A board may not waive the statutory monetary limitation even if both parties agree. However, an appellant will be permitted to waive any recovery in excess of the statutory limit in order to qualify for the accelerated procedure.

Accelerated proceedings follow a pattern similar to expedited proceedings. The parties will be encouraged (to the extent possible consistent with adequate presentation of their factual and legal positions) to waive pleadings, discovery, and briefs. Moreover, the board is given discretion to shorten time periods prescribed or allowed elsewhere in the ASBCA Rules.

The presiding judge renders written decisions in accelerated proceedings with the concurrence of a vice chairman of the board. Such decisions are published, may be appealed in the normal manner, and are valid precedent.

§ 33.10 ADR and the ASBCA

Alternative dispute resolution (ADR) techniques—broadly defined as any voluntary method of dispute resolution short of formal litigation—are available to the parties before and after the issuance of a Contracting Officer's final decision regardless of the amount in dispute. All of the agency boards of contract appeals invite the parties to use ADR.

(a) Evaluating Whether ADR Is Appropriate

The ASBCA encourages parties to consider the option of using ADR procedures when deciding how they will process their appeals. Since mid-1989, the ASBCA has included with every docketing notice a separate "Notice Regarding Alternative Methods of Dispute Resolution." This notice explains the available ADR processes under the Board's auspices, discusses the procedures to be used if the parties agree to use one of those techniques, and explains the alternatives available if ADR is not successful.

Although ADR is potentially available for any dispute under the CDA, not every appeal lends itself to resolution through ADR procedures. The Administrative Dispute Resolution Act mandates that a government agency "shall consider not using" ADR procedures if (1) the agency needs a precedential decision, (2) the dispute involves a significant issue of government contract policy requiring development of the law, (3) the agency has a special need to maintain established policy or avoid variations in decisions, (4) the dispute involves parties that would not be parties to the ADR proceeding, (5) there is a need to develop a full public record, or (6) the agency has a significant need to retain jurisdiction over the matter.

Additional factors that disfavor use of ADR include the likelihood that the case will settle without assistance from a board as well as the existence of issues that can be decided on motions for summary judgment or on the record under ASBCA Rule 11 (submission without a hearing).

(b) Initiating the ADR Process

The decision to use ADR procedures must be by voluntary agreement of the parties. Nevertheless, the CDA, as amended by Administrative Disputes Resolution Act (ADRA), requires that a party rejecting a request for ADR provide the other party with the specific reasons for rejecting the request. In the case of the Contracting Officer, the CDA requires that the explanation cite, if applicable, the conditions identified by ADRA that militate against the use of ADR procedures, while in the case of the contractor, the requirement is imposed through the standard "Disputes" clause. A number of agencies have promulgated additional ADR policies.

Typically, parties interested in ADR procedures sign a joint letter to the board requesting their use. It is also acceptable for one party to write on behalf of both, as long as the request reflects that the other party concurs. A request by one party will not be accepted, although the board may refer the request to the other party for evaluation. If the parties have decided upon the ADR method they wish to pursue, they should include a copy of their proposed draft agreement with their request.

(c) Basic ADR Techniques

There are two basic kinds of ADR—binding and nonbinding— although there are also many variations of both. The ASBCA's "Notice Regarding Alternative Methods of Dispute Resolution" identifies three ADR techniques regularly and successfully used at the ASBCA: (a) summary trial with binding decision, (b) settlement judge, and (c) mini-trial. The first is a binding ADR method, while the other two are nonbinding approaches to dispute resolution. Nonbinding ADR proceedings are substantially more flexible than binding ADR and permit the parties to retain more control over the process. Not surprisingly, nonbinding ADR tends to be more popular with the parties than binding ADR and accounts for approximately 55% of the ADR proceedings at the ASBCA.

§ 33.11 Appeal to the Court of Federal Claims

Two federal courts play key roles in the government contract disputes process—the United States Court of Federal Claims (COFC) and the United States Court of Appeals for the Federal Circuit. Under the Contract Disputes Act (CDA), contractors have the right of direct access to either the agency board of contract appeals or the COFC to challenge an unfavorable Contracting Officer decision. The Federal Circuit serves as the appellate forum for the review of decisions of both the boards and the COFC, regardless of which party is seeking review.

(a) Jurisdiction

Congress has defined the COFC's jurisdiction in the Tucker Act. Under this statute, the COFC has jurisdiction over claims against the United States involving an "express or implied [-in-fact] contract." It does not have jurisdiction over claims against the government based on promissory estoppel or an implied-in-law contract. For claims brought under the CDA, the COFC, like the boards of contract appeals, lacks jurisdiction over any claims not raised in the Contracting Officer's final decision and those made against a federal agency that operates with non-appropriated funds.

The court has declined to assume jurisdiction over matters simply relating to an agency's administration of a contract. For the court to have jurisdiction over a contract dispute, all that is required is that a valid contract be pleaded. Therefore, where a contractor asserts that a government contract exists, the court has jurisdiction to determine whether a valid contract ever came into being.

In part, the COFC's claims jurisdiction under the Tucker Act is limited to claims "founded either upon the Constitution, or any Act of Congress, or any regulation of an executive department" where that constitutional provision, act of Congress, or regulation mandates the payment of money. A provision of law is "money-mandating" if the statute or regulation is reasonably amenable to a reading that it mandates a right to recovery of damages. While such a reading is not to be lightly inferred, a fair inference that money damages are allowable under the statute or regulation in question will suffice. The COFC may award attorney's fees under the Equal Access to Justice Act.

The Federal Courts Administration Act of 1992 eliminated a source of controversy regarding the COFC's CDA jurisdiction over non-monetary claims by amending the Tucker to expressly give the court jurisdiction over disputes "concerning termination of a contract, rights in tangible or intangible property, compliance with cost accounting standards, and other nonmonetary disputes." Following the Federal Circuit's decision in *Securiforce Int'l Am., LLC v. United States*, 879 F.3d 1354 (Fed. Cir. 2018), the boards and courts have scrutinized nonmonetary claims to assess whether a claim is in substance a monetary one and whether it must follow the procedures for such claims.

However, the COFC does not have authority under the CDA to grant specific performance or to consider contractor attempts to obtain a declaratory judgment in advance of either a dispute or a Contracting Officer's final decision. The Tucker Act, not the CDA, provides jurisdiction over third party beneficiary claims against the government.

(b) Alternative Dispute Resolution

The court's use of ADR procedures is governed by its General Order No. 44, which permits the use of settlement judges, mini-trials, third-party neutrals, or any other ADR technique that the parties find appropriate.

The use of ADR is both flexible and voluntary and should be employed early in the litigation process in order to minimize discovery. The court views the use of ADR as being most appropriate where the parties anticipate lengthy discovery followed be a protracted trial—these requirements typically are met where the amount in controversy exceeds $100,000 and it is anticipated that a trial will extend for more than one week.

When mini-trials are used, for example, the general approach would be that (a) the entire mini-trial process, including discovery and trial, should conclude within one to three months, (b) the parties' senior management with full settlement authority and with first-hand knowledge of the underlying dispute should participate, and (c) discovery should be expedited, limited in scope where feasible, and concluded at least two weeks before the mini-trial, (d) at the close of discovery a prehearing conference will be held, (e) the hearing will be informal and will generally not exceed one day, and (f) at the conclusion of the mini-trial, all concerned will meet to discuss resolution of the dispute.

The judge will be available to play an active role in these discussions or to render an advisory opinion regarding the merits of the claim. Discovery taken for the purpose of the mini-trial may be used in any further judicial proceedings if settlement is not achieved.

§ 33.12 Court of Appeals for the Federal Circuit

The Federal Circuit has jurisdiction over appeals from decisions of the COFC and of the boards of contract appeals under the CDA. Note that only "final" decisions from the boards of contract appeal are appealable. This requirement "deters litigants from harassing opponents and clogging the courts with expensive and time-consuming appeals." For example, under this standard, the Federal Circuit refused to review a board decision that decided liability but did not determine the amount of recovery. By contract, interlocutory appeals are permissible from the COFC where the trial judge so certifies the appeal.

The party wishing review of a board decision must file a Petition for Review with the Clerk of the Federal Circuit within 120 days of receipt of the board's decision. The court has no authority to waive the prescribed statutory appeal period. A party appealing an unfavorable decision of the COFC must file a Notice of Appeal with the Clerk of the Court of Federal Claims within 60 days of entry of the court's judgment or order.

For the government to appeal an adverse board decision, it must obtain the prior approval of both the agency head and the Attorney General. Before enactment of the CDA, only the contractor was permitted to appeal an adverse board decision; the government could not appeal. Now both parties may challenge the decision on an equal basis. A government appeal of a COFC decision requires the prior approval of the Attorney General.

(a) Review of Board Decisions

The standards to which the Federal Circuit must adhere when it is reviewing a board decision are set forth in the following language from the CDA:

> [T]he decision of the agency board on any question of law shall not be final or conclusive, but the decision on any question of fact shall be final and conclusive and shall not

be set aside unless the decision is fraudulent, or arbitrary, or capricious, or so grossly erroneous as to necessarily imply bad faith, or if such decision is not supported by substantial evidence.

Boards have no authority to certify interlocutory appeals to the Federal Circuit.

(b) Review of COFC Decisions

The Federal Circuit reviews COFC decisions for errors of law but will not set aside findings of fact unless they are "clearly erroneous." As a practical matter, the "clearly erroneous" standard is similar to the "substantial evidence" standard applied to board decisions, although the Federal Circuit has indicated that board findings may be accorded greater deference under the "substantial evidence" test than COFC findings under the "clearly erroneous" test.

Part VI

SPECIAL CATEGORIES OF CONTRACTING

Chapter 35

RESEARCH AND DEVELOPMENT CONTRACTING

Analysis

§ 35.1   In General

Federal Acquisition Regulation (FAR) Part 35 (along with its implementing regulations) prescribes the special policies and procedures pertaining to research and development (R & D) contracting. The primary purpose of R & D contracting is to advance scientific and technical knowledge to achieve agency and national goals As noted in the Department of Defense FAR Supplement, there are several categories of R & D contracting: research, exploratory development, advanced development, engineering development, and operational systems development.

R & D contracts differ from most other forms of contracting for supplies and services in that the contractual objectives cannot be precisely described in advance. As stated in the FAR, the reason for this uncertainty is that "It is difficult to judge the probabilities of success or required effort for technical approaches, some of which offer little or no early assurance of full success." To encourage these scientific advances, agencies must provide an environment in which the work can be pursued with reasonable flexibility and minimum administrative burdens.

R & D efforts can be accomplished either by contract or grant, or by a cooperative agreement. R & D contracts are permissible only when the principal purpose of the acquisition is for the direct benefit or use of the federal government. The agency may use grants or cooperative agreements when the principal purpose of the transaction is to stimulate or support research and development for another public purpose.

The Federal Technology Transfer Act encourages technology transfer from federal government operated laboratories to private industry. To effectuate this purpose, the act authorizes federal agencies to permit the director of any government operated laboratory to enter into a "CRADA"—a cooperative research and development agreement—with a private entity.

This agreement is a type of contractual relationship between a federal laboratory and a nonfederal party for research and development purposes. Congress did not intend, however, that a CRADA be used as a substitute for procurement contracts or cooperative agreements where otherwise required by law. Thus, the award of cooperative agreements is not protestable under the Competition in Contracting Act (CICA) unless some threshold showing exists that a cooperative agreement was used inappropriately where a procurement contract is required. A firm has standing to challenge the award of a CRADA only where it presents a substantial question on whether the CRADA is being used as a means to circumvent the federal procurement laws.

An increasingly important aspect of R & D contracting is the use of federally funded research and development centers (FFRDCs) to perform R & D work. The government has a special relationship with FFRDCs. An FFRDC is a privately operated, but publicly funded under a long-term contract or sponsoring agreement with a federal sponsoring agency and are established to meet some special research or development need which cannot (at the time) be met as effectively by existing in-house or contractor resources. An example of a FFRDC would be the Lawrence Livermore National Laboratory, which is a Department of Energy-sponsored research institution concentrating on nuclear sciences.

Although FFRDCs do not compete for the work they conduct for their sponsors, regulation and case law prohibit these centers (but not their parent organizations or the parent's affiliates) from competing under a federal agency RFP for other than the operation of an FFRDC with any non-FFRDC concern as either a prime contractor or a subcontractor. On the other hand, a sole source award to an FFRDC could be permissible under the CICA and FAR requirements.

Furthermore, CICA and FAR specifically recognize that the agency may exclude one or more sources from competing for an award if that would be in the interest of national defense in establishing or maintaining a FFRDC. Before an agency may establish a FFRDC, or change its basic purpose and mission, FAR requires the agency to publish three notices over a 90-day period in the SAM.gov and the Federal Register, except the notice is not needed when the action is required by law.

In addition to the rules governing FFRDCs, several statutes govern the agencies' authority to conduct certain R & D contracting actions. For example, under 10 U.S.C.A. § 2358, the Secretary of Defense (subject to presidential approval) may engage in basic and applied research projects necessary to DOD basic and applied research responsibilities. This statutory authority extends to contracting for research and development projects with such entities as educational or research institutions or private businesses, or by providing such entities with grants.

The above law further provides that projects funded with DOD monies must have a potential connection to military functions or operations. In addition, the "Bayh Amendment" prohibits the use of appropriated funds for entering into contracts with foreign entities for the performance of R & D contracts for weapons systems or other military equipment for the DOD when there is a United States entity equally competent to carry out the R & D and willing to do so at a lower cost. Except as required by law or regulation, the usual FAR rules of negotiated procurement will apply to R & D contracting.

§ 35.2   Work Statements

The solicitation's scope of work must be a clear and complete statement of the area of exploration (for basic research) or the end objectives (for development and applied research).

"Basic research" means research directed toward increasing knowledge in science and is theoretical rather than practical in nature. In basic research, the emphasis is on achieving specified objectives and knowledge rather than predetermined end results. "Development" means the systematic use of scientific and technical knowledge in the design, development, testing, or evaluation of a potential new product or service (or of an improvement to an existing product or service) to meet specific performance requirements or objectives. "Applied research" is effort that ordinarily follows basic research, it attempts to determine and exploit the potential of scientific discoveries or technological improvements, and seeks to advance the state of the art.

The government's requirements in R & D contracting can be either for the furnishing of technical effort with a report on the results or the development of a tangible end item designed to achieve specific performance characteristics. Therefore, the work statement should be structured so that it does not inappropriately mix level-of-effort language with task completion language, although it would seem possible to have both approaches in the same statement of work if they are identified as discrete tasks. Moreover, if the agency is only seeking the furnishing of technical effort with a report on the results, it should not include language that requires the development of a tangible end item.

Another common pitfall in work statements for R & D contracting is that the wording should match the contract type. For example, the work statement for a cost reimbursement contract promising the contractor's best efforts for a fixed term would be phrased differently than a work statement for a cost reimbursement completion contract promising the contractor's best efforts for a defined task. Under the same logic, work statements for a cost reimbursement contract as opposed to a fixed price contract should be tailored accordingly. Similarly, extensive modifications to an R & D contract are to be expected, because of the experimental nature of the work, although impermissible out-of-scope changes are possible with this type contract.

Because the focus of R & D contracting is to advance scientific and technical knowledge, the specifications in an R & D solicitation will usually be performance oriented as opposed to having many design requirements. In such acquisitions, the GAO has said that the agency is soliciting innovative and independent approaches to the work, and that offerors will be rated on that basis.

§ 35.3   Contract Methods

R & D contracting is characteristically accomplished by negotiation because the precise specifications necessary for sealed bidding are generally not available. Despite the difficulty of drafting such specifications, agencies are not excused from satisfying the FAR's full and open competition requirements in conducting these procurements.

Consistent with the usual rule, the Contracting Officer has discretion (except as limited by law or regulation) to select the appropriate contract type for an R & D acquisition. Because technical considerations are so important for R & D contracts, the Contracting Officer should make this decision only after obtaining the recommendations of agency technical personnel.

Fixed price contracts are technically permissible for R & D contracts but are a good idea only in the rare circumstance when the goals, objectives, specifications, and cost estimates are suited for a fixed price, as opposed to a cost reimbursement, arrangement. Indeed, FAR states that government must typically assume greater risks in R & D contracting and the DOD FAR Supplement provides that fixed price contracts will not ordinarily be used in development program for R & D efforts. When the use of cost and performance incentives is desirable and practicable, the agency may consider fixed price incentive and cost plus incentive fee contracts in that order of preference. In all situations, the contract type must be tailored to the work required.

Follow-on production contracts are common in R & D contracting. Characteristically, such contracts are fixed price because the designs are more firmly established, risks are reduced, and the production tooling, equipment, and processes are established. FAR cautions, however, that a final commitment to undertaking specific product development and testing should be avoided until:

1.   Preliminary exploration and studies have indicated a high degree of probability that development is feasible; and

2.   The government has determined both its minimum requirements and desired objectives for product performance and schedule completion.

Increasingly, agencies in research and development contracting are bypassing the FAR and are using their "Other Transactions" (OT) authority as allowed by statute. The Department of Defense is the chief purveyor of this method and so this Hornbook will emphasize the practices and procedures in the DOD. The Undersecretary of Defense for Acquisition and Sustainment (USD, A&S) has issued a new Guide on Other Transactions. See https://www.dau.edu/guidebooks/Shared%20Documents/Other%20Transactions%20(OT)%20Guide.pdf.

Under certain circumstances, DOD can enter into an "Other Transaction" agreement instead of a traditional procurement contract. OT agreements are generally exempt from federal procurement laws and regulations.

Generally, DOD can use its other transaction authorities for three purposes:

1.   conduct research,

2.   develop prototypes, or

3.   contract for follow-on production of a successful prototype project.

Congress has been active in this area. Section 867, Pub. L. No. 115–91, Preference for Use of Other Transactions and Experimental Authority, provides "[i]n the execution of science and technology and prototyping programs," the secretary of defense should "establish a preference ... for using" (a) "transactions other than contracts, cooperative agreements, and grants entered into pursuant to" 10 U.S.C.A. §§ 2371, 2371b, and (b) "authority for procurement for experimental purposes pursuant to" 10 U.S.C.A. § 2373.

DOD's other transaction authorities are found in two sections of law:

10 U.S.C.A. § 2371 grants DOD the authority to use other transactions to carry out basic, applied, and advanced research projects. DOD regulations treat these projects as financial assistance instruments, not as contracts.

10 U.S.C.A. § 2371b permits the use of other transactions to conduct prototype projects and follow-on production.

OTs can only be used for prototypes if one of the following applies:

☐ at least one nontraditional defense contractor significantly participating in the project;

☐ all significant participants are small businesses or nontraditional defense contractors;

☐ at least one-third of the total cost of the prototype project is provided by nongovernment participants; or

☐ the senior procurement acquisition official provides in writing an explanation of the exceptional circumstances justifying an OT.

Follow-on production can only be conducted when

☐ the underlying prototype OT was competitively awarded, and

☐ the prototype project was successfully completed.

The key definitions of some of these terms are:

Basic research is conducted to gain more comprehensive knowledge or understanding of the subject under study without specific applications in mind.

Applied research is conducted to gain knowledge or understanding to meet a specific, recognized need.

Advanced research includes efforts that have moved into the development and integration of hardware for field experiments and tests.

Prototype—the term prototype is not defined in the statute. DOD generally describes a prototype as a physical, virtual, or theoretical model used to evaluate the technical or manufacturing feasibility, or effectiveness, of what is intended to come later. It need not be a physical model; prototypes can involve designs, novel applications of commercial technologies.

GAO has noted that the "other transaction" authority provided to the Department of Defense is generally limited to basic, applied, and advanced research projects. See *MorphoTrust USA, LLC*, 2016 CPD ¶ 133 at 8 n.14. Other Transactions do not have the hallmarks of a typical procurement contract. See *Rick's Mushroom Serv., Inc. v. United States*, 76 Fed. Cl. 250, 258 (2007) (agreement will be a procurement contract where it contemplates the transfer of goods or services directly to the government; there is evidence of a buyer-seller relationship; and a direct benefit accrued to the government.)

GAO also has said that agreements issued by an agency under its "other transaction" authority "are not procurement contracts, and therefore we generally do not review protests of the award, or solicitations for the award, of these agreements under our bid protest jurisdiction." *Rocketplane Kistler*, B-310741, 2008 CPD ¶ 22 at 3. GAO has also observed that it will review, however, a timely protest that an agency is improperly using its "other transaction" authority. *See Rocketplane Kistler, supra.*

In its most recent decision, the Government Accountability Office reaffirmed it has no discretion to expand its bid protest jurisdiction to address a protest asserting that an agency improperly evaluated a proposal for an Other Transaction Agreement (OTA), the U.S. Comptroller General said in dismissing a protest for lack of jurisdiction. *MD Helicopters, Inc.*, B-417379, 2019 CPD ¶ 120.

§ 35.4   Solicitations

Although the requirements for full and open competition apply to R & D contracting, FAR policy is that the government need not seek an "inordinate number" of R & D proposals. Indeed, FAR states that, if it is not practicable for the agency to solicit all apparently qualified sources, the agency need only solicit a "reasonable number" of offers. The reason is that the evaluation of proposals from sources lacking the appropriate qualifications is costly and time-consuming for both government and industry. Therefore, contracting officials should initially distribute solicitations only to technically qualified firms. Cognizant agency personnel should make appropriate recommendations to the Contracting Officer as to which firms should be qualified.

The primary focus of the evaluation factors in R & D solicitations is to determine the most technically qualified firm. FAR contains a list of recommended evaluation factors, such as (but not limited to) the offeror's understanding of the scope of work; the availability and competence of the firm's engineering, scientific, or technical personnel; and the offeror's experience. Because precise specifications are not ordinarily available in R & D contracting, the agency should ensure that the specifications and the evaluation factors are consistent.

In addition to including evaluation factors regarding technical competence, the Contracting Officer must consider management evaluation factors such as (but not limited to) cost management techniques and subcontracting practices. Although cost or price is not normally the deciding factor in R & D source selections, cost or price is still a factor for consideration and should not be disregarded in arriving at a selection that best satisfies the government's needs at a fair and reasonable cost. Indeed, price can become the discriminator for award between technically equal proposals in R & D procurements.

The agency should ensure that each prospective offeror understands the details of the work and the government's interpretation of the work statement. Thus, in the Department of Defense, the Contracting Officer may include in the RFP the government's estimate of the man-year effort under a research contract. For complex efforts, the Contracting Officer should afford prospective offerors the opportunity to comment on the RFP. A pre-proposal conference can be appropriate in this regard.

§ 35.5   Evaluation and Award

Generally, the agency should award a contract to the offeror which proposes the best ideas or concepts and which has the highest competence in the specific field of science or technology involved, consistent with those qualifications needed for successful performance of the work. The agency should not award a contract to obtain capabilities that exceed those needed for successful performance of the work. Of course, the award must be consistent with the announced request for proposal evaluation factors.

As stated in section § 35.4, above, cost or price considerations normally are secondary in R & D contracting, but it is still important for the agency to evaluate the proposed contractor's price or cost estimate. The reasons for this review are to ensure that the price or cost is reasonable and to determine whether the contractor has the requisite understanding of the project, its risks, and the need to organize and perform the work. Traditional cost or price analysis under FAR Part 15 can be useful here.

Another important consideration during the negotiation of most R & D contracts is information concerning the contractor's plan for subcontracting any portion of the experimental, research or development effort. This area is important because R & D contractors are substantially selected based on their scientific competence and so it is necessary for the agency to know whether the subcontractors have the requisite qualifications. To avoid any difficulties, contracts for either fixed price or cost reimbursement contracts will require the Contracting Officer's advance approval for the placement of a subcontract that has as one purpose experimental, developmental, or research work.

According to statute and regulation, Department of Defense contracts for R & D services may not be performed over a period exceeding 10 years from the date of initial award, unless the department or agency notifies Congress. This notice is required within 30 days after the initial award date or date of modification, as applicable, or, if no prior notice was given, not later than 30 days after the date on which performance exceeds 10 years. Otherwise, there is no bar in the FAR to extending an R & D contract beyond five years.

If the agency rejects a small business for an R & D award because it is not considered responsible, the usual policies from FAR for referring the matter to the Small Business Administration for a Certificate of Competency (see Chapter 19) will apply. Similarly, the usual rules from FAR on debriefing offerors should be applicable.

§ 35.6   Broad Agency Announcements

Frequently, the agency will use the standard FAR Part 15 negotiation (see Chapter 15) procedures (as modified by other FAR requirements) in R & D contracting. At the same time, the regulations recognize an alternative methodology of source selection for R & D contracts based on broad agency announcements (BAA) (with peer or scientific review).

This BAA will be general in nature, identify areas of research interest, and function somewhat like the usual solicitation. The BAA is a contracting method for acquiring basic and applied research ordinarily directed toward advancing the state of the art or increasing knowledge or understanding rather than focusing on a specific system or hardware solution. The BAA must include the criteria for selecting proposals, the method of evaluation, and the instructions for submitting proposals. However, the BAA does not contain a specific statement of work, and no formal solicitation is issued.

According to the FAR, the primary bases for selecting proposals under a BAA are technical qualifications, importance to agency programs, and funding availability. The firms' cost realism and reasonableness also must be considered to the extent appropriate. If a firm objects to the use of BAA procedures for an acquisition, it must protest to the GAO, if that is the forum selected, before the time set for receipt of proposals. COFC follows the same principle.

BAA contracting is allowed only when the agency reasonably anticipates receiving meaningful proposals with varying technical/scientific approaches. As stated above, the BAA procedure is for the acquisition of basic and applied research and for that part of development not related to specific system or hardware procurement.

The BAA will seek the participation of all offerors capable of satisfying the government's needs (although there is no common due date for proposals), and its availability will be published in the SAM.gov and possibly in noted scientific, technical, or engineering journals. No requirement exists, however, for the agency to make the usual synopsis of a proposed contract action as would be required under FAR subpart 5.2; the publication of the availability of the BAA in the SAM.gov and the noted scientific journals, if used, will usually suffice.

The agency must evaluate proposals submitted in response to the BAA in accordance with the announced evaluation criteria through a peer or scientific review process. It is this combination of adherence to the BAA procedures and the use of peer or scientific review that will qualify the acquisition as a competitive procedure under the CICA and FAR. The principles from FAR on advisory and assistance services with respect to the use of outside evaluators are applicable, and the rules from FAR concerning organizational conflict of interest will also be mandatory. The composition of BAA evaluation boards is within agency discretion and is not subject to challenge absent proof of bias or conflict of interest.

In rating offers, the agency must prepare written evaluation reports on individual proposals, but no requirement exists for rating proposals against each other. The proposals are not submitted against a common work statement but only against a broad statement of the agency's areas of research interest. The proposers are not competing against each other but are attempting to show that their proposed research meets the government's needs. The agency is not under any obligation to award a contract, because the agency has discretion to fund only those efforts which it believes are suitable.

The GAO has indicated that the usual requirements for competitive fairness apply to BAA acquisitions. Thus, agencies using the BAA procedures are required to identify the major evaluation factors but are not required to disclose other evaluation considerations reasonably related to or encompassed by the stated criteria. Similarly, the GAO will not disturb an agency's evaluation of proposals, provided that it was reasonable and in accordance with the stated criteria. Another familiar principle is that the offeror has the burden to submit an adequately written proposal that will establish compliance with the agency's requirements.

One unresolved question under BAA procedures is whether federally funded research and development centers (FFRDCs) may compete with other private entities for the award. Under one view, FFRDCs may pursue such awards, because the noncompetition prohibition in FAR extends only to competition in response to RFPs; a BAA is not an RFP. On the other hand, the spirit of the regulations would seem to prohibit such competition, and so a revision to the regulations to address this issue appears advisable. Another unresolved BAA question is the extent to which the agency may hold discussions with the firms about their proposals before award.

The Department of Defense has issued a final rule (a) adding solicitation of science and technology proposals, including by broad agency announcement (BAA), to the definition of "other competitive procedures" that meet competition requirements, and (b) increasing the maximum duration and value of a related contract authority for advanced prototype development. See 84 Fed. Reg. 4364 (Feb. 15, 2019).

The final rule adds DFARS 235.016(a) to define science and technology proposals, for purposes of BAA awards, as including the above-mentioned proposals. DOD noted that a BAA is one method for soliciting science and technology proposals. The final rule adds DFARS 235.006–71(a) to specify that a BAA with peer or scientific review for the award of science and technology proposals in accordance with 235.016(a) fulfills the requirement for full and open competition.

§ 35.7   Small Business Innovation Research Program

The Small Business Innovation Development Act of 1982, as amended, requires that agencies with extramural R & D budgets exceeding $100 million yearly for Fiscal year 1992 or any Fiscal year thereafter, set aside specified percentages of their budgets for award of contracts, grants, or cooperative agreements to small business concerns participating in Small Business Administration (SBA) approved small business innovation research (SBIR) programs. The underlying policy of this set-aside program is to strengthen the competitive free enterprise system and to allow the orderly development of the national economy by giving small business concerns special assistance in the R & D area. An agency's SBIR set-aside program should only be applied to those agency programs funded through an R & D appropriation and presented to the

Congress as part of its detailed budget breakdown constituting R & D as defined by the Act.

The selection of research proposals under the Act is a competitive procedure under the CICA, although the law does not require an award to any particular proposer. The statute is implemented not through the FAR system but by a Small Business Administration Policy Directive published in the Federal Register. Unsolicited proposals are ineligible for SBIR awards, as are any other proposals not submitted in response to the SBIR solicitation.

When the agency determines its needs for the SBIR program, it will furnish the information to the SBA. The SBA will then issue a quarterly presolicitation announcement covering all participating agencies. Concurrently, the procuring agency will publish a SAM.gov notice announcing the current research categories at least 15 days before issuance of the request for proposal. Agency SBIR solicitations will be issued in accordance with the SBA's master schedule and using a uniform SBA format with proposals due by a common cutoff date. Because these acquisitions are not conducted under FAR Part 15, some agencies prohibit formal discussions or submission of final proposal revisions to avoid unfairness to one or more proposers.

The SBIR program has three possible phases. Under Phase I, small businesses are invited to submit proposals under an RFP to submit research on one or more topics specified in the participating agency's annual SBIR program solicitation. Typical evaluation criteria for these Phase I awards would be scientific or technical quality of the proposal; the qualifications of the offeror's principal investigator; key staff and consultant qualifications; adequacy of the available facilities; anticipated benefits to the agency's research and development effort; adequacy of the proposed effort to show progress toward demonstrating the feasibility of the concept; and cost to the government. Under Phase II, firms that received Phase I awards may, on their own initiative, submit proposals for further development work on the topic. Phase III contemplates that, unlike Phases I and II, non-SBIR funds will be used to pursue commercial applications of the research or development.

When a competing firm protests an SBIR acquisition, the GAO's review is limited to determining whether the agency violated any applicable regulations or solicitation provisions or whether the agency acted fraudulently or in bad faith. The protester's mere disagreement with the agency's judgment will not suffice. The GAO follows this standard of review because the agency has significant discretion to decide which proposals, if any, it will accept.

The usual rules governing interpretations of solicitations, allegations of agency bad faith, cancellation of an RFP, and referral of small business concerns to the SBA for certificates of competency, before the GAO will also apply to these procurements. Also, in accordance with the usual rule, a protester before the GAO must challenge an apparent solicitation deficiency before the closing date for receipt of proposals. COFC follows the same principle.

Chapter 36

CONSTRUCTION AND ARCHITECT-ENGINEER CONTRACTS

Analysis

A. CONSTRUCTION CONTRACTS

§ 36.1   Construction Contracts—Overview

The initial part of this chapter provides an overview of the basics of construction contracting and some of the similarities and differences between construction and other contract types. The chapter also discusses a frequent subject for contractor claims, differing site conditions.

"Construction" has an elaborate Federal Acquisition Regulation (FAR) definition. It means the construction, alteration or repair (including dredging, excavation and painting) of buildings, structures, or other real property. Examples of items in these categories are bridges, dams, highways, and power lines. "Construction" does not include the manufacture, production, or furnishing of personal property.

A major government construction project is usually preceded by a contract between the government and an architectural-engineer (A-E) firm to submit a design for the structures to be built or renovated and to draft the drawings and specifications that will be followed by the construction contractor. The "design-bid-build" delivery method is the traditional construction delivery method. Design and construction are sequential and contracted for separately, usually with two contracts and two contractors.

Sometimes the government elects to use the "design-build" method, which means combining design and construction in a single contract with one contractor. A variation is known as the "two-phase design-build" selection procedure. Here, a limited number of offerors (normally five or fewer) are selected during Phase One to submit detailed proposals for Phase Two. The "two-phase" procedure is intended for use where design work must be performed by offerors before developing price or cost proposals, and offerors will incur substantial expenses in preparing offers.

The "Specifications and Drawings for Construction" clause, required to be included in most fixed-price construction contracts that exceed the simplified acquisition threshold (see FAR Parts 13 & 2.101), states that "[a]nything mentioned in the specifications and not shown on the drawings, or shown on the drawings and not mentioned in the specifications, shall be of like effect as if shown or mentioned in both."

The clause further provides that "[i]n case of a difference between the specifications and drawings, the specifications shall govern." However, "[i]n case of a discrepancy in the figures in the drawings or in the specifications, the matter shall be promptly submitted to the Contracting Officer, who shall promptly make a determination in writing."

Ordinarily, contractors are required to make pre-bid/offer inquiries about patent ambiguities in the proposed contract documents or risk any additional costs that are incurred if their interpretation is incorrect. The purpose of requiring the pre-bid/proposal inquiry is to prevent contractors from taking advantage of ambiguities in government contracts by adopting narrow interpretations in preparing their bids/proposals and then, after the award, seeking equitable adjustments to perform additional work the government actually wanted. However, if an ambiguity can be satisfactorily resolved (e.g., by the "Order of Precedence" clause), the contractor may proceed without first seeking clarification.

Contractors generally are not required, however, to "ferret out" hidden ambiguities and errors in the construction documents even if those documents oblige the contractor to "verify" the design. Because the doctrine has the effect of relieving the government from consequences of its own poorly drafted contracts, it has been applied only to contract ambiguities that are judged so "patent and glaring" that it is unreasonable for a contractor not to discover and inquire about them.

Usually, the work will be divided into individual items with separate unit prices in a bidding or pay schedule. Even though not included in any specific pay item, work that is clearly required by the contract must be performed without additional compensation. Except for the "two-phase" process discussed above and A-E services, which are acquired through negotiations, sealed-bidding procedures are frequently used for routine construction contracts to be performed in the United States, and the contract award will be for a lump sum, except when a cost reimbursement contract is appropriate. Alternatively, for the more complex projects, the government may seek competitive proposals for construction projects, such as where discussions about the offers are necessary, and non-competitive construction projects are also possible.

Some contracts contain elements of both construction and supply or service contracts. A contract with such mixed elements shall include clauses applicable to the predominant part of the work. If the contract is divided into parts, the clauses applicable to each portion shall be included. A DFARS regulation (222.402–70) provides helpful guidance for contracts containing mixed construction/services required for installation support contracts.

§ 36.2 Construction Contracts vs. Supply Contracts—Similarities and Differences

The basic principles of government contracting are the same whether a contract is for supplies or construction, although supply contracts involve more varied procedures and contract types than construction contracts. Thus, the policy favoring full and open competition, the preferences for small businesses and other groups, the rules limiting the authority of government agents, the government's duty of fairness and noninterference with contractors, policies regarding patents and data, and the other fundamental policies and procedures reviewed in earlier chapters in this Hornbook with regard to supply contracts apply with equal force to construction contracts.

The main distinctions between supply and construction contracts are the different physical environments in which they are performed and to the differences in the nature of the contract work. Some of the most significant differences between supply and construction contracting are discussed below.

(a) Government Control

Whereas supply contracts are typically performed in a production facility owned or leased by the contractor and generally under its control, a construction contract is more commonly performed on government property. The construction contractor, even when it is responsible for quality control, is subject to a great deal more surveillance and control by government inspectors and other government representatives than is the supply contractor.

A burdensome feature of construction contracts is the number of reports the contractor frequently must file with the government. Daily reports of work accomplished are often required, as well as reports involving (a) quality control activities, (b) safety procedures, (c) labor disputes, (d) construction or completion schedules, and (e) descriptions—even samples—of materials the contractor proposes to use.

(b) Work Site

Whether the contract is performed on a government-owned site or in a government-controlled facility also poses problems of access to the work site by the contractor's employees, subcontractors, and material suppliers. Other difficulties faced by the construction contractor are interference from possible concurrent government activities conducted while work is being performed and from the activities of other government contractors, as well as the possible damage or loss of equipment and materials after work hours.

The contractor is also responsible for maintaining a safe and clean work site. Moreover, even though the work is commonly done on federal property, the construction contractor can be responsible for properly disposing of hazardous substances.

(c) Contract Clauses

Construction contractors must also comply with the standard clauses used only in construction contracts. For example, the standard "Permits and Responsibilities" clause makes the contractor "responsible for all damages to persons or property that occurs as a result of [its] fault or negligence." That clause also makes the contractor responsible for all materials delivered and work performed "until completion and acceptance of the entire work, except for any completed unit of work, which may have been accepted under the contract." The "Permits and Responsibilities" clause also requires the contractor to obtain "any necessary licenses and permits" and comply with federal, state, and local safety standards.

In a second example, the "Payments under Fixed-Price Construction Contracts" clause provides that at the time of each progress payment, the contractor work shall become the sole property of the government even as the contractor remains liable for the repair of any damaged work. Thus, a contractor could be required to bear the cost of work and material damaged, stolen or otherwise removed from the contract site when partial acceptance has yet to occur.

In a third example, the "Performance of Work by the Contractor" clause is intended to assure adequate interest in and supervision of all work involved in larger projects—those exceeding $1.5 million (with some qualifications, such as under small business set asides)—by requiring the general contractor to perform a significant part of the contract work (set forth in the contract in terms of a percentage that reflects the minimum amount of work that must be so performed) with its own forces. Ordinarily, specialty construction effort in heating, plumbing, and electrical work is subcontracted and should not be considered in establishing the amount of work to be performed by the prime contractor.

(d) Bonds

Construction contractors must also comply with statutory bonding requirements designed to protect both the government and subcontractors. Such bonding is permissible on a regulatory basis, but only rarely so, for non-construction contracts. The Miller Act requires construction contractors, for projects exceeding $150,000 that are to be performed in the United States, to furnish payment and performance bonds. Statute may provide for limited exceptions.

For contracts between $35,000 and $150,000, the Contracting Officer selects two or more payment protections from a selection of five alternatives, giving "particular consideration" to inclusion of an irrevocable letter of credit as one of the selected alternatives. If a payment bond is required or selected it must be for the total amount payable under the contract unless the Contracting Officer finds such amount is impractical (but in no case can the amount be less than the performance bond).

A "performance bond" secures the contractor's performance of its work under the contract. If the contractor defaults on the contract by failing to complete its work or by performing defective work, the contractor and the surety are both liable to the obligee (i.e., the government) in the amount needed to correct the default, up to the penal sum of the bond. The performance bond is generally co-extensive with the contractor's obligations under the contract and imposes on the surety all obligations imposed upon the contractor by its contract or by law with respect to performance under the contract.

Unless the Contracting Officer determines that a lesser amount will adequately protect the government, performance bonds must be for 100% of the original contract price—with an opportunity for increasing if the contract price increases. It bears emphasis that if the government departs from or alters the terms of the bonded contract, the surety will be discharged from its obligations if it can show injury, loss, or prejudice.

A "payment bond" assures payments as required by law to all persons supplying labor or material in the prosecution of the work for in the contract. With a dispute, subcontractors regularly seek to enforce their right to payment from prime contractors under Miller Act payment bonds, commencing suit in the United States District Court where the work was performed. Upon the request of a subcontractor/supplier, actual or prospective, the Contracting Officer must provide it certain information about the payment bonds, such as the name and address of the surety, and the penal amount of the bond.

A subcontractor faced with an insolvent prime contractor may not, however, sue the government directly to recover its losses or for the government's failure to require the prime to post a Miller Act payment bond. The failure of the prime contractor to furnish these bonds when required or the furnishing of forged bonds may form the basis for terminating the prime contract for default. A performance bond reinsurance agreement may not replace the required payment bond.

Statutory and regulatory requirements for payment and performance bonds for construction contracts reflect significant or deeply ingrained public procurement policy and, if the clauses were omitted from a construction contract, they are incorporated by operation of law under the *Christian* doctrine (see Chapter 1).

(e) Labor Standards

Construction contractors are subject to stringent statutory and regulatory requirements regarding the treatment and payment of laborers. Construction contract labor standards laws and rules are reviewed in Chapter 19.

(f) Changes and Delays

One of the most notable features of many construction projects is the number of contract modifications that may be necessary in performing the contract. Construction contracts are often routinely changed during performance about some aspect of the work. These modifications should take the form of ordered changes under the "Changes" clause or as constructive changes (see Chapter 43).

Such changes to the contract work frequently disrupt the project's schedule, however, and can increase its costs. Suspensions of work under a construction contract's "Suspension of Work" clause also frequently form the basis for contractor claims under construction contracts. The subject of work suspensions is discussed in greater detail in Chapter 42.

(g) Default Termination

As mentioned in Chapter 49, terminations for default are less frequent in construction projects than in supply contracts. In construction contracts, the imposition of liquidated damages for delayed completion of work is also more common. The government may collect liquidated damages until the time reasonably required to complete the work. Forgoing its right to terminate a contract for default does not waive the government's right to assess liquidated damages for late completion of the contract (see Chapter 11).

The "Default" clause for construction contracts varies from the supply contract "Default" clause in some respects. For example, the construction contract "Default" clause renders the surety liable for any damage to the government based on the contractor's failure to complete the work within the specified time. The clause also does not require the government to issue a cure notice to the contractor before terminating a contract for default. In addition, the clause requires the contractor to notify the government in writing of the causes of any excusable delay, such as fires, floods, or strikes.

A major advantage for construction contractors is that they are entitled to payment for the value of work they have performed at the time of a termination for default, whereas supply contractors may get nothing for the work they have completed but not delivered. Because the surety company that has guaranteed performance by issuing a performance bond usually completes defaulted construction contracts, disputes concerning repurchase actions and excess costs of completion are relatively rare after clear evidence exists that the agency has issued a termination of a construction contract for default.

(h) Fiscal Constraints

The government operates under numerous statutory and regulatory restrictions on use of appropriated funds for construction.

In one case, the contractor cited 10 U.S.C.A. § 2801 et seq. as requiring major construction to be funded by Military Construction funds and 10 U.S.C.A. §§ 2801, 2802 and 2805 as requiring notice to Congress and approval for all military construction projects in excess of $3 million. In opposition, the government in this case primarily relied on *United Pacific Insurance Company v. United States*, 464 F.3d 1325 (Fed. Cir. 2006). *United Pacific* held that § 2805 did not contemplate a private cause of action, and Parsons cited no "language in the other two statutes . . . that might dictate a different result," the ASBCA said in dismissing Parsons' appeal for failure to state a claim on which relief can be granted. *Parsons Gov't Servs., Inc.,* ASBCA 60663, 17-1 BCA ¶ 36743.

§ 36.3   Construction Contracts vs. Service Contracts

It can sometimes be difficult to distinguish construction and service contracts. The hallmark of a service contract is it does not involve alteration, repair or construction of real property.

"Service contract" means a contract that directly engages the time and effort of a contractor whose primary purpose is to perform an identifiable task rather than to furnish an end item of supply or to perform construction. A service contract may be either a nonpersonal or personal contract. It can also cover services performed by either professional or nonprofessional personnel whether on an individual or organizational basis. Some of the areas in which service contracts are found include the following:

1.   Maintenance, overhaul, repair, servicing, rehabilitation, salvage, modernization, or modification of supplies, systems, or equipment;

2.   Routine recurring maintenance of real property;

3.   Housekeeping and base services;

4.   Advisory and assistance services;

5.   Operation of government-owned equipment, real property, and systems;

6.   Communications services;

7.   Architect-Engineering;

8.   Transportation and related services; and

9.   Research and development.

§ 36.4   Differing Site Conditions

(a) Overview

When a construction contractor encounters a subsurface or otherwise physically concealed site condition that differs from what was indicated in the contract or from what would normally be expected, the situation encountered is referred to as a "differing site condition." In the absence of a contract clause allocating the risk of unknown subsurface conditions between the parties, a construction contractor generally assumes the risk of increased costs that may result from unforeseen site conditions.

To discourage contractors from including undue contingency increments in their prices—and thus needlessly increasing the cost of government construction—the government has developed a contract clause called "Differing Site Conditions" (along with a companion clause, "Site Investigation and Conditions Affecting The Work") that substantially shifts the risk of subsurface or unknown site conditions to the government. As indicated above, the differing site conditions clause exists to take at least some of the gamble on subsurface conditions out of bidding. Instead of necessitating high prices for the contractor to protect against risks inherent in limited pre-offer knowledge, the clause allows the parties to deal with actual subsurface conditions after work begins when more accurate information can be uncovered.

This chapter next examines the workings of that clause, the different types of differing site conditions (usually designated as "Type I" or "Type II" condition), the contractor's duty to investigate the site, and the effect of government efforts to disclaim liability for differing site conditions.

(b) The FAR Clause

The FAR's standard "Differing Site Conditions" clause requires the contractor to "promptly, and before the conditions are disturbed" provide written notice to the Contracting Officer of any (1) subsurface or latent physical conditions at the site that differ materially from those indicated in the contract, or (2) unknown physical conditions at the site of an unusual nature that differ materially from those ordinarily encountered.

If such conditions increase or decrease the contractor's cost of, or time required for, performance, the clause requires that an equitable adjustment in the contract's price and schedule be made. "Differing site conditions" may include not only natural conditions, involving such things as rock and water, but also man-made physical conditions.

(c) The Notice Requirement

The notice requirement of the "Differing Site Conditions" clause affords the government the opportunity to inspect the condition and modify the contract requirements if necessary, or even abandon the contract work if it is no longer feasible. Usually, the government modifies the contract, but failure to follow the notice requirements may result in the rejection of a contractor's otherwise valid differing site conditions claim.

The notice provision of the "Differing Site Conditions" clause probably would not be enforced, however, if the government had either actual or "constructive" (i.e., as a matter of law, but not necessarily of fact) knowledge of the physical conditions that the contractor encountered. In addition, if the Contracting Officer decides a claim for a differing site condition on its merits, the government may be held to have waived the notice requirement. Similarly, where the contractor's failure to give notice does not prejudice the government's interest, the contractor's claim usually will not be barred.

Just as the contractor is obliged to proceed with contract performance in the case of a contract change (see Chapter 33), the contractor is obliged to proceed with the contract work if so directed after notifying the government of a differing site condition. A contractor is not entitled to stop work while waiting for a government decision on its equitable adjustment proposal.

(d) Types of Conditions

Differing site conditions are usually classified as "Type I" or "Type II" conditions. The major difference between the two is that in Type I conditions, the contractor compares conditions actually encountered with the conditions represented in the contract, while in a Type II condition, the contractor compares the conditions actually encountered with the conditions that would usually be encountered, given the nature and location of the work. A contractor may also argue in the alternative both types of conditions in its proposal and any follow-up claim.

(e) Type I Conditions

The great majority of differing site condition claimants seek recovery for conditions that are different than those that are indicated in the contract. Because the clause refers to "subsurface or latent" in the disjunctive, the condition need not be underground. Indeed, even the term "subsurface" has been held not limited to underground conditions.

To prove a Type I differing site condition, the contractor must show that (1) the contract documents positively indicated the site conditions that form the basis of the claim, (2) the contractor reasonably interpreted the contract, (3) the contractor reasonably relied upon its interpretation of the contract documents, (4) the conditions actually encountered differed materially from those indicated in the contract, (5) the conditions encountered were unforeseeable based on all the information available at the time of bidding, and (6) the contractor was damaged as a result of the material variation between the expected and the encountered conditions.

Examples of Type I conditions include the following: (a) rock in an excavation or dredging area where the rock was not indicated by soil boring information made available by the government to bidders and included in the contract, (b) larger or denser boulders than indicated by government test borings, and (c) a substantially greater quantity of rock in an excavation area than indicated in test borings. In one case, the ASBCA denied a Type I differing site condition claim because the soil profile, the soil characteristics, and the moisture content encountered by the contractor should have been anticipated.

(f) Type II Conditions

The second type of differing site condition is an "unknown physical condition" of an "unusual nature" differing "materially from those ordinarily encountered and generally recognized as inhering in work of the character provided for in the contract"

The Type II condition is less frequently alleged and more difficult to prove than the Type I condition. It requires proof of the recognized and usual physical conditions at the contract site, the actual physical conditions, the difference in the conditions from the known and the usual, and the fact that the different conditions caused an increase in contract performance.

To recover for a Type II claim, a contractor must demonstrate that (1) the condition was not known to the contractor, (2) it could not have been anticipated from either an inspection or from general experience, and (3) it varied from the norm in similar contracting work.

Type II claims have succeeded, for example, where the contractor encountered (a) highly corrosive ground water; (b) the presence of cattle bones beneath an inlet structure; and (c) gravel composed of more dense, hard concrete than was usually found in the area.

(g) Excluded Conditions

Certain types of conditions—such as those resulting solely from unusually severe weather, acts of God, or acts of the government in its sovereign capacity—are not considered to fall within the protection of the "Differing Site Conditions" clause. Examples of such conditions include the following: hurricanes, excessive rainfall, frozen ground, excessive snowfall, drought, and flooding due to natural causes.

(h) Standard "Site Investigation" Clause

When a solicitation calls on prospective contractors to do a site investigation before submitting their bids or offers, they have a duty to do so. This duty is underscored by the admonition contained in the "Site Visit (Construction)" provision, which states that "offerors or quoters are urged and expected to inspect the site where the work will be performed."

The same concept is expressed in the FAR's "Site Investigation and Conditions Affecting the Work" clause. If the contractor does not conduct a site investigation, or does so in a careless manner, it likely will not be compensated for differing site conditions that a reasonable investigation would have revealed.

(i)   Limitations on Duty

The site investigation requirement relates to the foreseeability of the differing site condition. If the condition could have been discovered by a "reasonably prudent contractor" during a reasonable site inspection, a claim based on the condition will be denied. A reasonable site investigation does not require the employment of geologists or other experts; the test is what a reasonably experienced and intelligent contractor-layperson could discover in an economical and practicable way. However, the contractor will be held responsible for discovering "patent indications, plainly, to a layman, contradicting the contract documents."

If the contract documents are silent as to what conditions may be encountered, the contractor may have an obligation to inquire whether the government has borings or other pertinent data, or to seek clarification of inconsistent drawings. This would be particularly true where the specifications as a whole indicate that such information is available and would be of use in determining the overall contract conditions. Contractors are generally not required to inspect documents that are not a part of the contract.

(j)   Government's Duty to Cooperate

A contractor is not required to inspect a work site if it is denied access by the government, or if sufficient time to inspect has not been allocated by the government. Similarly, if the government possesses important information regarding site conditions, which it knows or should know the contractor does not possess, it has a duty to disclose this information.

(k)   Liability Disclaimers

Efforts by the government in the contract to disclaim liability in contract specifications or other contract documents for differing site conditions do not normally preclude the contractor's recovery, provided the contract contains the standard "Differing Site

Conditions" clause and the contractor is otherwise able to prove it is entitled to recovery under the clause.

B. ARCHITECT-ENGINEER SERVICES

§ 36.5   Architect-Engineer Services

(a) The Brooks Act

The Brooks Act, 40 U.S.C.A § 1101 et seq., and FAR subparts 36.1 & 36.6 prescribe special policies and procedures for the acquisition of A-E services. In essence, the Brooks Act procedures, and the restrictions to contracting only with A-E firms, apply to the procurement of those services which uniquely or to a substantial or dominant extent logically require performance by a professionally licensed and qualified A-E firm.

The chief difference between Brooks Act procurements and standard selection procedures under the FAR is that price competition is not part of the source selection process. The goal of these special selection procedures is to ensure as extensive an evaluation of alternative technical approaches and design concepts as is possible without the agency's requiring actual design work to be performed by prospective contractors. The sole qualification to this last statement is that the agency may require design work from the competing firms when a design competition is authorized.

The succeeding sections will examine in more depth the definition of these services, review the competition and source selection policies, and consider other applicable contracting procedures.

(b) Definitions

Under the Brooks Act and the FAR, "A-E services" means:

(1) Professional services of an architectural or engineering nature, as defined by state law, if applicable, which are required to be performed or approved by a person licensed, registered, or certified to provide such services;

(2) Professional services of an architectural or engineering nature performed by contract that are associated with research, planning, development, design, construction, alteration, or repair of real property; or

(3) Such other professional services of an architectural or engineering nature, or incidental services, which members of the architectural and engineering professions (and individuals in their employ) may logically or justifiably perform. Such services can include studies, investigations, surveying and mapping, tests,

evaluations, consultations, comprehensive planning, program management, conceptual designs, plans and specifications, value engineering, construction phase services, soils engineering, drawing reviews, preparation of operating and maintenance manuals, and other related services.

Except for "incidental services" as defined in FAR, if the services do not require performance by a registered or licensed architect or engineer, then FAR advises that the agency should procure those services under either simplified purchase, sealed bidding or negotiated procedures, even though an A-E could conceivably perform the work. The determination of whether a proposed procurement is subject to Brooks Act procedures is made by the Contracting Officer on a case by case basis, and this decision is within the sound discretion of procuring officials subject to the above definitional limitations.

Sometimes, the anticipated contractual statement of work includes both A-E services and other services. In these instances, the Contracting Officer must deem the services overall to be A-E services for purposes of following the FAR selection procedures if the statement of work substantially or to a dominant extent specifies performance or approval by a registered or licensed architect or engineer. If the statement of work does not specify such performance or approval, then the Contracting Officer must follow the usual simplified purchase, sealed bidding or negotiation procedures, as applicable.

(c) SAM.gov Notice

The first public step in most A-E acquisitions is an announcement of the agency's requirement in the SAM.gov, which announcement is designed to enhance competition among A-E firms. The predecessors to the SAM.gov, FedBizOpps and the *Commerce Business Daily,* were the prior sources for this notice. The GAO has said that the announcement is tantamount to a solicitation of interested firms.

This public announcement under the FAR will state the agency' intent to follow the Brooks Act and to contract for these services based on demonstrated competence and qualifications of prospective contractors to perform the effort. The notice must include brief details with respect to location, scope of services required, cost range and limitations, type of contract, estimated starting and completion dates, and any significant evaluation factors. The agency will make the source selection based on current performance data on hand and the firms' qualifications statements provided to the government except when a design competition is authorized.

(d) Selection Criteria

As required by agency regulations, the selection criteria must be stated in their relative order of importance, should be project-specific, and in all cases may not relate either directly or indirectly to possible contractor fees. Except as limited by statute or regulation, agencies have broad discretion in determining the relative importance of these criteria.

Under the FAR, the SAM.gov notice must inform interested firms that the agency will evaluate each prospective contractor with regard to the following factors:

1. Professional qualifications necessary for satisfactory performance of required services;

2. Specialized experience and technical competence in the type of work required, including where appropriate experience in energy conservation, pollution prevention, waste reduction, and the use of recovered material;

3. Capacity to accomplish the work in the required time;

4. Past performance on contracts with government agencies and private industry in terms of cost control, quality of work, and compliance with performance schedules;

5. Location in the general geographical area of the project and knowledge of the locality of the project; *provided,* that application of this criterion leaves an appropriate number of qualified firms, given the nature and size of the project; and

6. Acceptability under other appropriate evaluation criteria.

In the Department of Defense (DOD), an example of mandatory "other appropriate evaluation criteria" is consideration of the volume of work awarded by the DOD in the previous 12 months. DFARS further provides that secondary factors such as equitable distribution of the work may not control in the source selection, and that the agency should not reject the most qualified firm in the interests of equitable distribution of contracts.

(e) Evaluation Boards

When the agency acquires A-E services, it must provide for one or more permanent or ad hoc A-E evaluation boards (which can include preselection boards, as permitted by agency regulations) to be composed of members who, collectively, have experience in architecture, engineering, construction, and government and related acquisition matters. The preselection board where applicable essentially frees the selection board from considering firms with no real chance for award, although the selection board may disagree and add firms from the pool of available A-E firms for consideration.

Under the general direction of the agency head (or a delegee), the evaluation board will:

1.   Review the current data files on eligible firms as well as the firms' responses to the SAM.gov notice regarding the specific project;

2.   Evaluate the firms in accordance with the established selection criteria outlined in the FAR;

3.   Hold discussions (which can be face-to-face) with at least three of the firms deemed most highly qualified (known as the "short list") regarding concepts and the relative utility of alternative methods of furnishing the required services (but no discussion is permitted regarding possible contractor fees); and

4.   Prepare a selection report for the agency head or other designated selection authority recommending in order of preference at least three firms deemed to be the most highly qualified to perform the required services; this report also must describe the discussions and evaluations conducted by the board to allow the selection authority an intelligent basis for decision.

Although price is a critical factor in the ultimate award of the contract, it bears repeating that price issues are irrelevant to the final rankings. The reason why price considerations must be absent from the A-E rankings is that Congress was convinced that any consideration of proposed fees would result in undue pressure on the firms to lower their proposed fees, which in turn would adversely affect the quality of the design by favoring the selection of less skilled firms and those concerns willing to provide a lower level of effort.

Congress also determined that price is unimportant at this point in the acquisition because such cost generally represents a small part of the total cost of construction and are kept under control by the six percent statutory fee limitation as compared with the value of the project as constructed.

(f) Documentation of Qualifications

To be considered for an A-E contract, a firm must file with the appropriate office or board the standard form (SF) 330, Architect Qualifications, Part II (which is submitted annually), which is used to obtain information about the firm's general professional qualifications, and when applicable, SF 330, Part I, which is used to obtain specific information about the firm's qualifications. The agency will also examine performance data on file regarding the competing firms.

(g) Selection Authority

In reviewing the evaluation board's recommendations, the agency head or other designated selection authority must make the final selection decision with the advice of appropriate technical and staff representatives. The final selection will be a listing, in order of preference, of the firms considered the most highly qualified to perform the work.

Although the selection authority may not add firms to the selection report, this official may disagree with the evaluation board's rankings. In such an instance, this official must document the file on why another firm is deemed best or better qualified. If the selection authority considers the firms offered to be unqualified, or if he believes the report is inadequate for any other reason, this official must record the reasons and return the report through channels for corrective action. All firms on the final selection list are considered "selected firms" for purposes of negotiation under the FAR and the board must promptly be informed of the final selection.

(h) Simplified Purchase Selections

As authorized by the agency, the procuring activity may use an abbreviated process to select firms for A-E contracts expected to be within the simplified acquisition threshold.

(i) Negotiations and Award

Unless otherwise specified by the selection authority, the final selection authorizes the Contracting Officer to commence negotiations with the firms deemed the most qualified, beginning with the most preferred firm in the final selection. At this point, the agency must employ the usual FAR negotiation procedures (as supplemented by agency regulations), which means that the agency must issue a Request for Proposals (RFP) (with the usual terms and conditions).

In the next step, the agency will receive a proposal from the firm (usually consisting of a price proposal, the standard representations and certifications, and acceptance of the solicitation's material terms and conditions). The RFP should not inadvertently preclude the firm from proposing modern design methods. In determining whether the proposed price is fair and reasonable, the agency is to take into account the estimated value of the service, and the scope, complexity, and professional nature thereof.

Under the FAR, the agency may reasonably terminate negotiations where the agency and the offeror cannot come to a mutually acceptable agreement (a rarity). When the agency cannot negotiate a mutually satisfactory contract with the firm, the FAR states that the Contracting Officer must obtain a written Final Proposal Revision (FPR) from the firm, notify it that negotiations have been terminated, and then initiate negotiations with the next rated firm on the final selection list. (It might be questioned why this pointless FPR must be requested if a satisfactory agreement is not possible.).

The usual organizational conflict of interest rules (see Chapter 9) apply to selection of A-E firms, and the same is true for the rule against personal services contracts (see FAR 7.104), although FAR does exclude A-E services from the definition of advisory or assistance services (see FAR subpart 37.2).

One additional FAR prohibition peculiar to A-E purchases is the agency may not award the follow-construction contract to the firm that designed the project (or to its subsidiaries or affiliates), except when the agency head or designee determines otherwise through a waiver. The prohibition is intended to eliminate the conflict of interest and apparent unfair competitive advantage an A-E firm (or its affiliates) would have in seeking a construction contract after having prepared the specifications for the same project.

The standard principles of contract interpretation will apply to A-E contracts. For instance, the ASBCA has held that the contractor with a firm fixed price contract has no entitlement for additional compensation for design changes resulting from government review when the contract already contemplated those reviews and changes.

Part VII

CONTRACT MANAGEMENT

Chapter 42

DELAYS AND SUSPENSIONS OF WORK

Analysis

The effect of a delay in contract performance on the contractor and the government depends on the cause of the delay and the contract clause involved. Generally, the government agrees in the contract, through the "Government Delay of Work" clause and "Stop-Work Order" clause (for supply and service contracts) or the "Suspension of Work" clause (for construction contracts), to compensate the contractor in both time and money for the delays the government causes. On the other hand, the contractor is responsible for both the time and cost of delays that it causes or that are within its control. Normally, if the delay was caused by events beyond the contractor's control, the contractor will be excused for the delay in performance (under the contract's "Default" clause) but is responsible for the additional costs caused by the delay.

This chapter discusses two types of delays in the context of supply, service and construction contracts. First, it examines suspensions of work that are ordered or caused by the government and that result in compensation to the contractor in the form of an extension of time to complete the work and, in some instances, recovery of additional costs caused by the work stoppage. Second, it discusses the contractor defense of "excusable delay" which functions primarily to protect the contractor from sanctions for late performance, such as default termination of the contract or assessment of liquidated damages.

§ 42.1   Compensable Delays—Supply and Service Contracts

(a) Ordered Suspensions of Work

In supply and service contracts, ordered suspensions are addressed by the "Stop-Work Order" clause, which is optional for use in negotiated supply, services, or research and development contracts. This clause provides that the Contracting Officer may require the contractor, by written order, to stop all or any part of the work.

If the stop-work order is later canceled, and the contractor submits a request for compensation, the Contracting Officer must make an equitable adjustment in the delivery schedule or contract price or both if the work stoppage resulted in demonstrable increased costs and performance time for the contractor. If the stop-work order is not canceled and the contract work is terminated for the convenience of the government or for default, the Contracting Officer must allow the reasonable costs resulting from the work stoppage.

(b) Constructive Suspensions of Work

The "Government Delay of Work" clause must be included in fixed-price contracts for most types of supplies. The use of the clause is optional in fixed-price contracts for services or for supplies that are commercial or modified-commercial items. This clause covers suspensions of work that are caused by the government but occur without an express order from the Contracting Officer—known as "constructive suspensions" of work. In the event of a government delay of the work, an adjustment in the contract price and schedule will be made for any increase in performance costs or time caused by the delay.

(c) Recovery for Constructive Suspensions

To recover additional money under the "Government Delay of Work" clause, the contractor must first prove that the delay was for an unreasonable period of time. The period of time that will be considered unreasonable varies depending on the circumstances of the particular case. Generally, if the government was the sole cause of the delay, any delay is unreasonable and the contractor can be compensated for the resulting extra costs arising during the additional time frame.

If the cause of the delay was due to the government's exercise of a contractual right, or if both parties contributed to the delay, the contractor will be compensated for only part of the delay period or may receive no price increase at all. By the terms of the contract, a delay of work caused by the government does not constitute a breach, even if the delay is for an unreasonable period of time.

In sum, to prevail on a claim of government-caused delay, the contractor must show that (a) the specific delays were attributable to government-responsible causes, (b) the delays caused a delay in the completion of the overall project, (c) the government-caused delays were not concurrent with delays within the contractor's control and (d) the contractor incurs extra costs as the result of the delay.

(d) Limitations on Recovery

The "Government Delay of Work" clause includes several specific limitations on a contractor's ability to obtain compensation for a delay. The clause provides that (1) no contract adjustment will be made for any delay to the extent that performance would have been delayed by any other cause (including the fault or negligence of the contractor), (2) no cost will be allowed that was incurred more than 20 days before the contractor notified the government in writing of the cause of the delay, (3) the contractor's claim must be asserted in a specific amount as soon as practicable after the delay in the work ends, and (4) no allowance for profit will be granted.

As just indicated, the clause disallows any claim for any costs incurred more than 20 days before the contractor shall have notified the Contracting Officer in writing of the act or failure to act involved. Courts and boards ordinarily do not strictly construe this type of requirement, however, unless the untimely notice prejudiced the government. Claims asserted later than the day of final payment will be barred under the clause unless the matter was pending or of which the government had constructive knowledge at the time of final payment.

Arguably, one other limitation in the "Government Delay of Work" clause—that no contract adjustment will be made "for which an adjustment is provided or excluded under any other term or condition of this contract"—indicates that where a delay claim for an equitable adjustment could be brought under the contract's "Changes" clause (or "Government Property" or other clause), then the use of these other clauses is preferred.

(e) Types of Constructive Delays—Delays Involving Changes

The largest number of government-caused delays occurs with changes in the work that are ordered under the authority of the standard "Changes" clause (see Chapter 43).

The government's ordering of changes can result in two types of delays. First, there may be a delay between the time the contractor is told that the government is planning to make a change and the time the contractor is finally given all the necessary technical information and told to proceed with the changed work. Second, even after the contractor receives the change, the change may so increase the volume of work or so disorganize the contractor's planned sequence of operations for accomplishing the original work that completion of the entire work is delayed.

The first type—government delays in ordering changes—is one for which an equitable adjustment can be made under the "Government Delay of Work" clause. The second type of delay in connection with changes—resulting from an increase in the volume of work or disruption and disorganization of the contractor's planned operations—is one for which a contract adjustment can be made under the "Changes" clause.

(f) Types of Constructive Delays—Delays Involving Faulty Specifications

Closely related to delays in connection with contract changes are interruptions in work that occur when the government gives the contractor inadequate or faulty plans or specifications governing the performance of work. The general rule in these situations is that the government is liable—under an "implied warranty" theory (see Chapter 11)—for excess time or expense caused to the contractor as a result of the defective specifications. Under the "Changes" clause, contractors also have recovered profit on unabsorbed overhead costs that resulted from delays caused by defective government specifications.

Even where the specifications are defective, a contractor may not recover for a delay where the defects were patent. In this instance, the contractor will be barred from recovery because of the failure to alert the Contracting Officer to the defects.

(g) Types of Constructive Delays—Delays in Furnishing Property

The government's untimely failure to furnish materials or equipment for a contractor's use in performing the work may delay the contractor's performance. This type of delay for which the government is responsible can result in an equitable adjustment under the "Government Property" clause as well.

(h) Types of Constructive Delays—Delays in Approval or Inspection of Work

When the contract provides that the contractor must obtain government approvals before proceeding with the work or some part of the work, or where the contract requires government inspection of the work, such approvals or inspections must occur within a reasonable time. An unreasonable delay in approval or inspection may be compensable.

(i) Types of Constructive Delays—Delays Caused by Government Interference

As discussed in Chapter 43, each contracting party has an implied duty to cooperate with the other contracting party. Delays that result from the government's interference with contractor performance or from the government's failure to cooperate with the contractor generally are compensable. For example, the government can be held liable for increased costs associated with delays in performance when it has the ability to provide the contractor with access to the work site but refuses to do so.

§ 42.2   Excusable Delays—Supply and Service Contracts

As noted at the beginning of this chapter, the contract typically allocates the risks of performance delays between the parties, depending on which party is responsible for the events that delay performance.

When the delays are beyond the contractor's control, the contractor is usually excused from nonperformance. The purpose of the "excusable delay" contract terms is to protect the contractor from being penalized for late performance in these situations. Such penalties typically include termination of the contract for default, assessment of the excess costs of reprocurement or completion, actual damages, or liquidated damages (see Chapter 11).

When the impediment to performance is removed, the contractor generally must continue performance. If the government constructively accelerates performance despite the existence of an excusable delay, the contractor may also be entitled to additional compensation (see Chapter 43). By definition, excusable delay must occur after the contract award.

(a) Standard "Default" Clause

The standard "Default (Fixed-Price Supply and Service)" clause (see Chapter 49) lists a number of causes of delay that—provided they are beyond the control and without the fault or negligence of the contractor—will excuse the contractor's failure to perform on time:

1.   Acts of God (also referred to as a *force majeure*) or of the public enemy;

2.   Acts of the government in either its sovereign or contractual capacity;

3.   Fires;

4.   Floods;

5.   Epidemics;

6.   Quarantine restrictions;

7.   Strikes;

8.   Freight embargoes;

9.   Unusually severe weather; and

10. Subcontractor or supplier delays at any tier arising from unforeseeable causes beyond the control and without the fault or negligence of both the contractor and the subcontractor or supplier.

An extension of time—but not a price increase—will generally be granted if a contractor's performance is delayed by one of these occurrences.

(b) Elements and Proof

The mere occurrence of an event that qualifies as an excusable delay does not automatically entitle the contractor to an extension of time. The contractor must establish that (a) the event that caused the delay was unforeseeable, beyond the contractor's control, and without its fault or negligence, (b) the delay prevented timely completion of the contract, and (c) the contractor took every reasonable precaution to avoid foreseeable causes of delay and to minimize their effect. The contractor must also specify the number of extra days to which it is entitled.

The contractor has the burden of showing not only that the cause of the delay was excusable but also that the delay was beyond the control and without the fault or negligence of the contractor. For example, a contractor may not claim a strike as an excusable delay when the strike resulted from the contractor's own unfair labor practices. The contractor must also establish the extent to which its job performance was delayed by the event and make reasonable efforts to mitigate the effect of a delay or prevent delay where possible.

(c) Government Sovereign Acts

A contractor is generally excused from a delay in performance caused by a sovereign act of the government—that is, by an act of the government that affects the public generally, such as a legislative or executive act, and is not specifically directed to the contractor.

Government avoidance of breach liability under the sovereign acts defense depends on a two-part analysis, including whether the Government act underlying the breach is a public and general act that only incidentally affects the contract.

Some examples of sovereign acts that have resulted in excusable delays for contractors are (1) cancellation of a government loan and increase in the minimum wage and (2) unforeseen use of railways by the government during the Vietnam War that caused a shortage of contract supplies. However, a contractor is generally not entitled to an excusable delay where a sovereign act merely increased the contractor's costs, or the contractor assumed the risk that contract performance could be delayed by a sovereign act.

The government may waive the sovereign act defense. In a similar vein, a government promise to compensate a contractor for damages resulting from a sovereign act can be implied from other contract terms, provided the contract must be read as a whole on this point.

(d) Government Contractual Acts

Acts of the government in its "contractual" capacity are also potential causes of excusable delay. Such acts of the government must be directed to the specific contractor and must be wrongful to excuse the contractor from any resulting delay.

The following are examples of government actions that have been found to be excusable delays: (a) failure to respond to the contractor's request for clarification, (b) payment delays, and (c) unreasonable delays in approving contractor drawings, equipment, materials, or subcontractors. Because many of these actions can also be treated as actual or constructive changes to the contract (see Chapter 43), if the contractor is granted an extension of time for these actions under the "Changes" clause, there is no need to rely on the contract's excusable delay clause.

(e) Weather

Although weather is obviously of greater concern to a construction contractor than to a supply contractor, weather can also cause delays in the performance of a supply contract. A severe storm, for example, can cause loss of electric power needed to perform or can damage a contractor's production facilities.

Note that the weather must be unusually severe to justify a time extension. "Unusually severe weather means adverse weather that at the time of year in which it occurred was unusual for the place in which it occurred. The unusually severe weather must also have an adverse impact on work on the critical path. For example, even where a contractor argues that it encountered delays because of unusually hot weather, the claim will be insufficient where the contractor has failed to document the impact the weather had on workforce production.

Like other causes of excusable delay, unusually severe weather only excuses delay—it does not generally excuse performance of the contract or entitle the contractor to extra monetary compensation. The proof also must establish the delay in the completion of the work arose from unforeseeable causes beyond the control and without the fault or negligence of the Contractor, as stated above in § 42.2(b). The general rule is that unusually severe weather only relieves the contractor from completing performance for a temporary period equivalent to the delay caused by the weather. Under *Broome Constr., Inc. v. United States,* 492 F.2d 829 (Ct. Cl.1974), and similar cases, the contractor is not entitled to an equitable adjustment under the "Suspension of Work" clause where the claimed delays were due to the acts of another contractor or to unusually severe bad weather.

(f) Subcontractor Delays

One of the most frequent causes of delayed performance by contractors is the failure of suppliers or subcontractors to deliver material or to perform in a timely manner.

However, the "Default" clause's excusable delay provisions strictly limit the extent to which such delays are excusable. To be excusable, a delay of a subcontractor or supplier at any tier must be beyond the control and without the fault or negligence of both the contractor and all the intervening subcontractors. Thus, a prime contractor cannot cite delay of a subcontractor as an excusable delay unless the subcontractor delay is itself excusable.

The failure of a designated sole source supplier to deliver is not by itself an excusable delay. On the other hand, under the "Default" clause for supply contracts, the contractor is obligated to attempt to obtain other sources when a subcontractor has been excusably delayed. For example, when an oil embargo prevented a contractor's supplier from delivering petroleum products, the contractor's default was held not excusable because the contractor neglected to seek out other potential suppliers.

(g) Unenumerated Causes of Excusable Delay

The causes of delay listed in the "Default" clause are not intended to be exclusive. A contractor can also rely on another unspecified event that was beyond its control and occurred without its fault or negligence as a ground for excusable delay. However, the courts and boards of contract appeals typically take a restrictive view of such contentions, tending to find that the event was foreseeable or within the contractor's control. For example, delays due to financial difficulties, breakdown of equipment, or shortage of material during performance are usually not excusable where unconnected to government action.

§ 42.3   Construction Delays and Suspensions of Work

The subject of delays is especially relevant for a construction contractor because construction projects can be prone to excusable delays that cause a contract to continue beyond the scheduled completion date. Usually, the government has few real alternatives other than to let the contractor finish the job. When a contractor remains on the site beyond the originally scheduled completion date, its overhead ordinarily rises and its profits may fall, which may lead to a claim for a compensable delay.

A wide range of conditions and circumstances causes delays. The government may suspend the contractor's work, the contractor may fail to meet the contract performance schedule, or events beyond the control of either party may delay the project's completion. The procurement regulations include Contract clauses to allocate the risks for these delays between the parties.

The "Suspension of Work" clause is designed to provide an expeditious and inexpensive method of compensating a contractor for government interruption, delay, or suspension of work. The clause provides for both government-ordered and constructive suspensions.

(a) Ordered Suspensions

The "Suspension of Work" clause states that the "Contracting Officer may order the contractor, in writing, to suspend, delay, or interrupt all or any part of the work of [the] contract for the period of time that the Contracting Officer determines appropriate for the convenience of the government." Such express suspensions are relatively rare. Generally, suspensions will be ordered only when (a) it is advisable to suspend work pending a decision by the government (e.g., regarding the removal of unforeseen hazardous waste or the resolution of a design deficiency), and (b) the execution of a supplemental agreement providing for a suspension is not feasible.

In certain circumstances, the suspension order may arise from a combination of communications from government officials. In one case, a memorandum from a government inspector strongly suggesting that a contractor suspend work—coupled with a threat by the Contracting Officer to withhold progress payments—was held to be a suspension order entitling the contractor to relief under the

"Suspension of Work" clause. Note that, except for the conjunction of the inspector's memorandum with the Contracting Officer's threat, a compensable actionable suspension probably would not have been found because inspectors generally do not have the authority to order suspensions of work.

(b) The Reasonableness Requirement

Whether the government's delay of the contractor's performance is compensable will depend on whether the delay was "unreasonable." Delays have been determined to be "unreasonable" (and thus compensable) where they were caused by defective specifications, or by the inclusion in the contract of incorrect labor standards. On the other hand, the contractor will be unable to recover for government-ordered suspensions where a temporary restraining order has directed that the work be stopped and where the delay resulted from the agency's agreement to stop construction pending review of a citizen's environmental complaint.

Obviously, if the reason for the work suspension is due to contractor fault, the suspension will not be compensable. Similarly, a situation caused by factors outside of the government's control will relieve the government of liability, "irrespective of its faulty specifications." For example, a work suspension will not be compensable where the contractor's performance did not conform to the specifications.

(c) Constructive Suspensions—in General

A constructive suspension of work occurs under the "Suspension of Work" clause if an act or "failure to act within the time specified in this contract (or within a reasonable time if not specified)" on the part of the Contracting Officer interferes with the contractor's performance but there is no express order from the government to stop work.

The purpose of the clause language is to establish a mechanism for a fair and speedy administrative settlement to compensate the contractor if its performance is suspended, delayed, or interrupted for an unreasonable period of time and relief is not available under any other contract provision, such as the "Changes" clause. To recover for constructive work suspensions, the contractor must demonstrate that (a) the delay was caused by the government's actions, (b) the delay was for an unreasonable length of time, and (3) the delay resulted in some injury to the contractor.

(d) Constructive Suspensions—Government Fault

Proof of government fault is a prerequisite to recovery in all constructive suspension cases. The contractor must show that the government did something it should not have done (or failed to do something it should have done) and that, as a direct result, adversely affected the contractor's performance.

Although there have been several decisions suggesting that inequitable delays not caused by government fault may also be compensable, this rationale has been narrowly applied. The prevailing rule remains that government fault must be the sole proximate cause of the delay for the contractor to be compensated under the clause. Thus, the contractor must be able to apportion any concurrent delay that was not the responsibility of the government and will be denied recovery if the concurrent delay extends for the entire period of government delay.

The following types of government-caused delays illustrate the factual situations that can be held to constitute constructive suspensions of work:

1.   *Delay in issuing notice to proceed*—Even where the contract does not provide the time for issuing the notice to the contractor to proceed with the work, the government's delay beyond a reasonable time after award of the contract may constitute a constructive suspension.

In some instances, government delays in issuing notices to proceed have been deemed reasonable (and non-compensable) because of the surrounding circumstances. In one case involving a contract for a road construction project, notice to proceed was given to the contractor at a time when there would likely be the least interference from tourists. However, in a matter of weeks the government ordered a seven-month work suspension that brought the work period squarely within the tourist season. In another case, the government-caused delay was "reasonable" primarily because it resulted from a citizen's environmental complaint. Here, the contractor assumed the risk of delays of this nature because it was "charged with knowledge that a citizen might protest the project."

2.   *Delay in making site available*—The government will be liable to a contractor for its unreasonable delay in making the construction site available to start the work, and for subsequent unreasonable work stoppages that were not the contractor's fault (such as the evaluation of a building foundation's archaeological significance).

But where the delay is caused by another contractor—rather than the government—the contractor will not be compensated unless the government has expressly promised that the site will be available by a certain date. However, approval by the government of another contractor's progress schedule with full knowledge that it would result in interference with the contractor's work has been held to be a compensable suspension. Similarly, where the government issued a notice to proceed knowing that the work site was unavailable because of a previous contractor's failure to clear the site, the contractor may be compensated under the clause. However, the contractor must make more than a nominal effort to gain access to the site.

On several occasions contractors, using a warranty theory, have been able to recover for an unreasonable unavailability of the jobsite, sometimes even in the absence of a "Suspension of Work" clause. The problem in these cases is distinguishing between a warranty or guarantee of site availability and a "mere representation" by the government.

3.   *Delays from issuing change orders, making multiple changes, or failing to investigate*—Where the government unreasonably delays in investigating a differing site condition (see Chapter 36) or in issuing a change order (see Chapter 43) under a construction contract, a contractor may recover under the "Suspension of Work" clause.

Recovery under this clause has also been permitted for the delay and disruption caused to a contractor's performance by a multiplicity of changes and for the unreasonable delay in issuing a change order despite the government's prior knowledge of the relevant circumstances.

4.   *Delay in responding to contractor requests*—Unreasonable government delay in responding to a contractor's request for a contract deviation may constitute a constructive suspension of work if the contractor's procurement of a required item is delayed as a result. Similarly, an unreasonable delay in responding to a contractor's request for the Contracting Officer's interpretation of a contract provision might entitle the contractor to recover under the "Suspension of Work" clause.

5.   *Delay in approval of shop drawings, samples, or models*—To recover for these delays, the contractor must establish the amount of time that reasonably would be necessary to consider its submission, taking into account the nature of the work involved and the status of the project. Where some element of contractor fault is, to some extent, responsible for the delay in approval, no recovery will be allowed. In an analogous situation, the government will not be liable for any alleged delay when the government refused to approve a site plan that failed to meet contractual requirements for the follow on effort.

6. *Delay caused by defective government specifications or drawings*—Any delay that results from defective drawings or specifications is *per se* unreasonable and thus compensable. On the other hand, inaccurate drawings alone are not sufficient to support delay damages if the contractor cannot quantify those costs.

(e) Constructive Suspensions—Unreasonable Delay

Recovery of costs under the "Suspension of Work" clause is granted only for delays of an "unreasonable" duration. Delays that result from government fault, such as those caused by defective government specifications, are always unreasonable and thus fully compensable under the "Suspension of Work" clause.

Profit is not an allowable element for a suspension of work. However, the "Changes" clause may be applicable, instead of the "Suspension of Work" clause, in which case profit is an allowable element of the contractor's recovery. In addition, the delays may be so great that the contractor may be able to argue they constitute a "cardinal delay," entitling contractor to breach of contract damages.

In many situations, the amount of delay for which the government is liable will depend on the reason for the government's interference with the contractor's work. The duration of the suspension is not the only factor to be considered but the relationship of what is unreasonable in light of all the other circumstances is also required to be considered, including the reason for the government's interference and whether the act of interference was itself unreasonable.

For example, if the delay arose from the government's exercise of a contractual right (such as the issuance of a change order), the contractor will be compensated only for the unreasonable portion of the delay, a determination of which is entirely dependent on the circumstances of the particular case.

Although the contractor usually has the burden of proving the unreasonableness of the delay period, if the government has exclusive knowledge of the facts relating to the suspension, the government is obligated to prove the reasonableness of the delay period. For example, the government had the burden of proof in one case where it had ordered all contractor personnel removed from the site during the movement of highly classified weapons.

(f) Recoverable Costs

The "Suspension of Work" clause provides for an adjustment in the contract price "for any increase in the cost of performance of this contract (excluding profit) necessarily caused by the unreasonable suspension, delay, or interruption." To recover its increased costs, the contractor must establish not only the amount of the costs, but that the costs would not have been incurred but for the unreasonable suspension.

Compensation for delays under the "Suspension of Work" clause may include both actual delay costs as well as the impact costs of the delay on the other parts of the contract work. Examples of recoverable costs are listed below:

1.   *Overhead*—The costs of both unabsorbed home office overhead and work site overhead during extended performance are recoverable unless the contract states otherwise. But if the contractor is able to perform suitable replacement work during the delay period, it will not be able to recover its extended or unabsorbed overhead. Similarly, overhead is allowable when tied to mitigation of damages efforts.

2.   *Idle time*—The unavoidable cost of equipment lying idle due to a suspension is recoverable.

3.   *Increased costs of labor and materials*—Where a suspension causes the contractor to perform a portion of the work in a later, more expensive time period—for example, after a wage increase has gone into effect—the amount of the cost increase is recoverable. The same is true for increases in material costs.

4.   *Insurance and bond premiums*—Additional bond and insurance premiums that must be paid in the extended performance period are recoverable.

5.   *Increased costs of performing during adverse weather conditions*—If the government delays the contract, and the contractor is foreseeably forced to perform under more difficult weather conditions, the increased cost of performance is recoverable. Such recovery may occur, for example, if performance is extended into seasons for rain, cold weather, or flooding. However, if the weather conditions would have been encountered regardless of the suspension, no recovery will be allowed. The contractor must demonstrate—through contemporaneous records if possible—the extent of the adverse weather and its impact on critical activities.

6.   *Loss of efficiency*—Although difficult to prove, if work is necessarily performed less efficiently in the extended period because of the delay, recovery is allowed. The contractor should, however, demonstrate the loss of efficiency through contemporaneous documents comparing the productivity differences between impacted and unimpacted periods.

7.   *Interest on borrowings*—If the contract contains a "Pricing of Adjustments" clause making the cost principles applicable to the

pricing of an equitable adjustment, there is little likelihood that interest on borrowings will be recoverable.

§ 42.4   Notice and Claim Requirements

The "Suspension of Work" clause provides that the contractor may not recover "for any costs incurred more than 20 days before the contractor shall have notified the Contracting Officer in writing of the act or failure to act involved." The purpose of the notice requirement is to alert the government to the conduct that the contractor believes constitutes a constructive suspension of the work. Note that the 20-day notice provision does not apply to an ordered suspension.

Despite the literal rigidity of this 20-day notice requirement, failure to give such notice will not bar a claim for suspension if the government knows or should have known that it was called upon to act. This outcome is in accord with the general rule that notice provisions should not be applied too strictly where the government is aware of the operative facts. However, if the absence or lateness of the contractor's notice prevents the agency from taking necessary remedial action, i.e., the government has been prejudiced by the tardy notice, the contractor's claim will likely be denied.

The clause also contains a separate limitation on the period within which the contractor can file its claim for increased costs. It provides that a claim stated in a definite amount must be presented in writing as soon as practicable after the end of the suspension period—but not later than the date of final payment under the contract.

§ 42.5   Concurrent Delays

The "Suspension of Work" clause precludes recovery if the delay is due to concurrent causes attributable to both the contractor and the government. In this instance, neither party is generally allowed to benefit. This means that the government cannot recover liquidated damages for the period of delay caused by the agency and the contractor cannot recover its delay costs under the "Suspension of Work" clause (or under the "Changes" clause, see Chapter 43).

For instance, a contractor's suspension-of-work claim was denied in one case because its failure to submit an approved safety plan was concurrent with the government's failure to provide necessary information. Each failure standing alone would have delayed commencement of the work.

Similarly, a contractor will not be allowed to recover where the government-caused delay is concurrent and intertwined with delay for which the government is not responsible—such as delay attributable to a third party. However, if the government was responsible for the third party's delay, the contractor may recover. If the contractor's delays can be separated from those of the government, and the extent of each delay apportioned between the two, the contractor may be allowed to recover the apportioned amount.

Courts and boards have, on occasion, taken a liberal view in determining liability in these matters. Thus, in one case where the overall delay in completing a contract was attributable not only to late delivery of government-furnished equipment but also partly to contractor inexperience and inefficiency, the contractor could recover to the extent that the government delay caused one-third of the extra expense incurred by the contractor because of the overall delay. In another case, where both parties were responsible, the delay was apportioned between them.

§ 42.6   Critical Path Method

Most of the planning and scheduling of construction projects—especially larger ones—is conducted with the use of Critical Path Method (CPM) analysis. CPM is a scheduling process in which the contractor identifies one or more "critical paths"—that is, tasks that must be completed before work on other tasks can proceed. CPM analysis frequently arises from use of commercially available project management software.

The "critical path" is the sequence of work on a project that will take the longest time to complete. Delays that occur in the critical path delay the entire project's completion, whereas delays on noncritical paths do not have this effect. CPM analysis plays a major role in the determination of the government's liability for delays. In the case of delays caused by both parties, if the government's delay occurred on the project's critical path and the contractor's delay was limited to noncritical path areas of the work, the delay will be considered to be nonconcurrent and the contractor will be allowed to recover under the "Suspension of Work" clause.

Simply put, under a CPM analysis, for any delay found on the critical path, a corresponding delay to project completion will be found. CPM has assumed such importance in determining liability in these cases that boards and courts will likely deny recovery if a CPM analysis cannot be made or will determine that a contractor's failure to produce its CPM schedule entitles the tribunal to infer that the schedule would be adverse to contractor's delay claim. In one case, the Court of Federal Claims stated in *Mega Const. Co., Inc. v. United States,* 29 Fed. Cl. 396 (1993), that it "cannot rely on the assertions of a contractor, not supported by critical path analysis of the project, to award critical path delay costs."

§ 42.7   Excusable Delays—Construction Contracts

(a) Guiding Principles

Under the standard "Default (Fixed-Price Construction)" clause, a contractor is excused from full compliance with the original contract schedule and the contract is not subject to termination for default when the delay in performance or failure to perform arises out of "unforeseeable causes beyond the control and without the fault or negligence of the contractor."

A contractor's failure to assert excusable delay in a claim to the contracting officer precluded excusable delay as a defense to a termination for default, the Armed Services Board of Contract Appeals has held in denying a challenge to a termination for default. *ECC CENTCOM Constr.*, ASBCA 60647, 18-1 BCA ¶ 37133.

"Foreseeable" in this context generally is interpreted in the context of normal commercial practices or business conditions. Thus, when a contractor is entitled to more time due to excusable delay, the Contracting Officer is obligated to extend the completion date before comparing it to the remaining work to determine whether a default termination for failure to make progress is proper.

The construction contract's "Default" clause is basically the same as the supply contract "Default" clause. The list of enumerated excusable delays for construction contracts includes, however, one cause of excusable delay in addition to those enumerated for supply contracts: "acts of another contractor in the performance of a contract with the government." In addition, the construction contract "Default" clause requires that the contractor notify the Contracting Officer in writing of the causes of delay within 10 days from the beginning of any delay. The supply and service contract "Default" clause does not contain a notice requirement.

Note that the examples of excusable delay enumerated in the "Default" clause are not exclusive—the test for determining if a delay is excusable is whether it is "beyond the control and without the fault or negligence" of the prime contractor, its subcontractors, and suppliers.

Under prior law, courts and boards held that when the tribunal is faced with a claim by a contractor for costs incurred as a result of a delay, and the government thereafter extended the period of contract performance, the tribunal would invoke a presumption, subject to rebuttal, that the government was at fault for the delay.

This presumption was especially strong where the time extensions are granted after the delay has occurred. The Federal Circuit has overruled this doctrine because it conflicts with the de novo review required by the Contract Disputes Act. *England v. Sherman R. Smoot Corp.*, 388 F.3d 844 (Fed. Cir. 2004).

Simply stated, if an event can be reasonably prevented from occurring by the contractor, it is not beyond the contractor's control. Furthermore, if the delay was caused by acts or omissions of the contractor, it may be deemed caused by its fault or negligence. The contractor must also demonstrate that the excusable delays were on the critical path (see § 42.6), not concurrent with other contractor-caused delays, and caused a delay in the overall project. If there is a concurrent delay, the contractor has the burden of apportioning the excusable and inexcusable delays.

With a constructive acceleration, each time the contractor incurs an excusable delay, it becomes entitled to a commensurate extension of the contract schedule. Excusable delay is difficult for the contractor to prove in litigation. The established rule is that causes under the contractor's control, such as financial inability or difficulty in obtaining necessary labor, unconnected to government action, will not suffice. Courts and boards have rejected contractor constructive acceleration claims where the delays were not excusable.

With the above factors in mind, the following sections focus on four major types of delay not caused by one of the contracting parties that are common in construction contracting—weather delays, labor delays, subcontractor delays, and delays arising from the acts of another contractor. It bears emphasis that the government does not characteristically battle its contractors on excusable delays. Generally, where the issue is excusable delay as opposed to compensable delay, the government accedes, because alternatives such as default termination are not feasible or otherwise not in the government's best interests.

(b) Weather Delays

One of the enumerated examples of excusable delay in the "Default" clauses—"unusually severe weather"—is more frequently involved in construction delays than in supply or service contract delays. "Unusually severe weather" has been defined as "adverse weather which at the time of year in which it occurred is unusual for the place in which it occurred." The theory behind this requirement is the contractor is expected to calculate the effect of normal weather in its bid or proposal estimate of the time needed to perform the contract.

To substantiate a claim of unusually severe weather, a contractor must present weather records of the same period in prior years to show that the weather it encountered surpassed in severity the weather usually encountered or reasonably expected in the particular locality during the time of year involved.

For example, in one case where precipitation over a two-month period was 9.44 inches and 6.98 inches, while normal totals for those months were 4.15 inches and 4.90 inches as shown by weather records, a construction contractor was given a time extension for the resulting floods that delayed the work. A contractor is also entitled to rely on the contract's weather data, not as a warranty of future weather but as a representation of past weather conditions at the work site, on which the contractor can base its prices and work schedule.

Even where a contractor could reasonably have expected a wet season, weather has been held to be unusually severe not only because more rain fell than normal but also because the rain occurred at such intervals that the area did not dry out to permit proper compaction. Other occurrences that have been held to be unusually severe weather excusing delays include (1) abnormally high humidity, (2) an abnormal amount of fog, and (3) an unusually heavy snowfall.

Unusually severe weather occurring before award of the contract can be the cause of an excusable delay. Thus, an excusable delay was found in one case where excavation could not be started promptly because the ground had been saturated by heavy rains prior to award.

The mere occurrence of unusually severe weather is not enough to justify a delay. The contractor must show that the bad weather actually prevented it from meeting the performance schedule. Thus, the key for unusually severe weather is not the cause *per se*, i.e., the weather, but the effect of the unforeseen weather on the work being performed.

(c) Strikes

Another excusable delay listed in the "Default" clause is "strikes." With a construction contract, a strike generally must be unforeseeable to excuse delay. In addition, the contractor must establish that the strike actually delayed the contractor's performance, and it must act reasonably to avoid the effects of the strike or to end the strike if possible.

The FAR makes the point that "[a] delay caused by a strike that the contractor or subcontractor could not reasonably prevent can be excused; however, it cannot be excused beyond the point at which a reasonably diligent contractor or subcontractor could have acted to end the strike." For example, when a steel strike began several months before the contractor submitted its bid and was still in progress at the time of bidding, the contractor was not allowed to cite the strike as an excusable cause of its delay.

(d) Labor Shortages

Hiring and retaining skilled workers to perform the contract is frequently difficult in construction contracting. Generally, the contractor is solely responsible for assuring an adequate labor force. Especially when a labor shortage was known to the contractor at the time the contract was executed, no extension of time will be granted based on a shortage of laborers during contract performance unless, for example, the labor shortage was caused by government action.

(e) Subcontractor Delays

The standard "Default" clauses provide that to be excusable, a delay or failure by a subcontractor at any tier must be beyond the control and without the fault or negligence of both the subcontractor and the contractor. This means that to be excusable, the delay must be excusable to the subcontractors at each tier—i.e., all intervening subcontractors between the contractor and the delayed subcontractor. This rule also applies to delays caused by sole-source subcontractors—even those that were designated by the government. The construction contract "Default" clause adds the requirement that subcontractor delays must arise from unforeseeable causes to be excusable.

(f) Acts of Another Contractor

The standard construction contract "Default" clause includes an enumerated cause of excusable delay not listed in the supply and service contract clause—"acts of another contractor in the performance of a contract with the government." This type of delay commonly arises in construction contracts where the government enters into agreements with several contractors for concurrent or sequential performance at the same site. In this situation, the delay of one contractor may affect the ability of another contractor to perform on time and thus entitle the affected contractor to additional time to perform.

Chapter 43

CHANGES AND EQUITABLE ADJUSTMENTS

Analysis

This chapter examines (a) the standard "Changes" clauses used in government contracts, (b) the authority of government representatives to order changes, (c) the contractor's duty to proceed with contract performance even though an adjustment for a change is in dispute, (d) formal change orders, (e) the constructive change doctrine, and (f) the principles of equitable adjustments.

The Federal Acquisition Regulation (FAR) sets forth several standard "Changes" clauses for use in government contracts. The choice of clause depends on the nature of the contract. For purposes of examining these standard clauses, it is best to treat those used in fixed price contracts separately from those used in cost reimbursement contracts—a distinction made in the FAR.

The FAR sets forth a clause more consistent with commercial terms and conditions for use in commercial item contracts. This clause contains a "Changes" term that replaces the "Changes" clauses typically found in government contracts. Although the term is described below, most of the material in this chapter relates to contracts incorporating the standard "Changes" clauses.

A. CHANGES

§ 43.1   Fixed Price Contracts

The standard "Changes-Fixed price" clause set forth in the FAR for fixed price contracts is designated for use in supply contracts. Alternate formulations for this clause are provided so that it can be tailored for use in other fixed price contracts.

Under the standard clause, the Contracting Officer may "at any time, by written order . . . make changes within the general scope of this contract" in the (1) drawings, designs, or specifications, (2) method of shipment or packing, or (3) place of delivery. If such changes increase the contractor's costs, the contractor is entitled to a contract price increase, and if they delay the contractor's performance, the contractor is entitled to an extension of the contract completion date. On the other hand, if the change revises the work or decreases the cost of or time for performance, the government could be entitled to a price decrease and a shortened completion time.

Where the change and any equitable adjustment are not combined in the same process, the clause requires the contractor to submit a request for an adjustment to the Contracting Officer within 30 days of the date of receipt of the change order. This requirement will usually be dispensed with when the government is not prejudiced by the contractor's failure to give timely notice, for example, when it is reasonably certain that the government would not have acted differently if notice had been given.

Indeed, the clause provides that the Contracting Officer may receive and act on a change proposal asserted at any time before final payment. But a proposal asserted after the government has made its final payment under the contract will almost always be barred. Final payment occurs after the contractor has completed performance. The last payment check is usually accompanied by a voucher marked "Final Payment."

The standard "Changes" clause set forth in the FAR for use in certain fixed price construction contracts is even broader in scope than the supply contract clause. For example, the construction contract "Changes" clause gives the Contracting Officer the right to order a change within the general scope of the contract that accelerates the performance of the work. The construction contract clause contains a term similar to that discussed above relating to the time within which the contractor must assert a changes claim after receipt of a change order.

§ 43.2   Cost Reimbursement Contracts

A distinctive feature of most cost reimbursement contracts (see Chapter 16) is that the contractor's primary obligation is not to complete the contract but rather to work until the funds allotted to the contract have been expended. Thus, the contractor in this circumstance has no obligation to proceed with contract performance until the government furnishes additional funds. To the same end, an adjustment for additional compensation under the "Changes" clause is essentially only as an adjustment for additional fees or costs subject to sharing under a cost plus incentive fee contract.

The government sometimes provides for cost ceilings (also known as a cost cap) in cost reimbursement contracts (as distinguished from the contract's cost estimate or cost limitation) (see below). Because the ceilings apply only to work called for by the original contract, any additional work ordered should fall under the "Changes" clause, entitling the contractor to the normal equitable adjustment, unless the contract specifically provides otherwise.

A problem that often arises in a cost reimbursement contract is defining what constitutes a "change." This is because the government frequently awards cost reimbursement contracts for projects in which it is difficult to describe the work with a high degree of precision. For example, the work statement might only describe the end objective that the contractor must achieve. In such cases, the best measurement for determining whether a change has occurred is to examine the work contemplated by the parties when they negotiated the estimated costs of the contract.

§ 43.3   Commercial Item Contracts

Unlike the standard "Changes" clauses described in various sections above, changes to commercial item contracts, at least with respect to the contract's terms and conditions, would require the written agreement of the government and the contractor. A qualification is that FAR permits this clause to be tailored by the parties, but only where consistent with customary commercial practice unless a waiver is approved in accordance with agency procedures. In such instances, therefore, the government might be able to bargain for a unilateral "Changes" clause as exists in standard FAR practice.

§ 43.4   Changes Outside Contract's "Scope"

A Contracting Officer has no authority to order what are called "cardinal changes"—that is, changes that have the effect of making the work as performed not essentially the same work the parties bargained for when the contract was awarded. These out of scope actions are actually separate procurements that are vulnerable to sustained protests by third parties who desire the work at issue. Furthermore, such cardinal changes can be a material breach of the contract by the government that can free the contractor of all remaining obligations under the agreement.

In determining whether a change is "within the general scope of the contract," the character of the change is more important than the amount by which the change increases performance costs, although the latter issue will be relevant to the determination. The number of contract changes does not necessarily determine whether the contract has been altered beyond its scope. Multiple changes to a hospital construction contract, for instance, which altered many of the materials used, were found in one case to be within the scope of the contract because the hospital was not different in size or design after the contractor performed the changes.

Many difficulties in determining whether a change is in scope can be resolved by the following guiding principle. The broader the scope of the original contract, the more leeway the agency will have to issue an in scope change, especially where the existing scope contemplates the type of change at issue. Conversely, the more restricted the scope of work, the government would have less leeway to make the change under the existing scope.

§ 43.5 Contractor's Duty to Proceed

The typical "Changes" clause specifically provides that although a contractor may dispute an adjustment for a change, "nothing in this clause shall excuse the contractor from proceeding with the contract as changed." Moreover, the standard "Disputes" clause prescribed by the FAR requires the contractor to "proceed diligently with performance of this contract, pending final resolution of any request for relief, claim, appeal, or action arising under the contract, and comply with any decision of the Contracting Officer."

(a) General Coverage

The contractor's duty to proceed with the work in the face of a dispute does not apply to orders to perform cardinal changes, i.e., changes that alter the fundamental nature of the work. This duty to continue performance applies only to claims "arising under" a contract—for example, claims for equitable adjustments based on contract changes. Contracting agencies are authorized, in unusual circumstances, to require a contractor to continue performance pending final resolution on a claim "relating to" the contract—that is, pending resolution of a claim for breach of contract.

The irony here is that where the contract contains such a term to continue the work, the contractor must proceed as directed even though the change ordered could be a cardinal change or another type of breach of contract. It should be re-emphasized, however, that a contractor runs a risk in not proceeding with performance merely because it believes that a government representative has issued an order beyond his or her authority. The risk for the contractor is that if the contractor refuses to continue because it believes the government has materially breached the contract, the contractor could find itself on the outside looking in if a board or court agrees with the government that it was the contractor that committed the first uncured material breach by refusing the Contracting Officer's order to perform, thereby leaving the contractor open to a default proceeding (discussed further below).

A more important exception to the contractor's duty to proceed arises when the Contracting Officer fails to provide the contractor with clear direction regarding the course of action the government wants the contractor to follow. For example, when the contractor discovers that the specifications are defective and informs the government of the problem, the contractor is entitled to withhold performance until it receives a meaningful response to its reasonable request. In this situation, the contractor should make sure to provide the government with timely notice of the problem.

Another exception to the duty to proceed is when the government's action leaves the contractor in an untenable position. For example, one contractor was excused from continuing performance after the government used faulty testing methods in rejecting the items delivered by the contractor.

(b) Effect of Failure to Proceed

The government's remedy is drastic when a contractor refuses to perform pending resolution of a disputed changes claim (assuming the government had authority to direct the contractor to proceed). If the contractor refuses to follow the directions of the Contracting Officer, the contract might be terminated for default (see Chapter 49).

In one case, a contractor refused to follow the Contracting Officer's directive to remove and replace a tile floor and instead abandoned the work and refused to proceed except at government expense and by a method of installation specified by the government. Here, such an election was "not open" to the contractor under the "Disputes" clause.

The wisest course for a contractor to follow, if it believes the Contracting Officer's directive is improper, is immediately to submit a written notice describing its disagreement and preserving its rights to file an equitable adjustment request later while continuing to work "diligently." If the contractor follows the Contracting Officer's directive, it will not lose its rights to an equitable adjustment or a subsequent claim.

§ 43.6   Formal Change Orders

The impetus for a change can originate with either the government or the contractor, depending on the circumstances. Changes may arise based on either revised contract requirements or a better (or different) way to perform the work. In both instances, an exchange of information between the government and the contractor will be necessary before the change is adopted.

The agency has great flexibility regarding the period a change can be ordered. The standard "Changes" clauses state that a change can be made "at any time"—i.e., at any time after the contract is signed and before final payment. When a decision has been made to change contract work, the Contracting Officer is responsible for preparing and issuing the necessary documents to the contractor. The Contracting Officer ordinarily uses Standard Form 30, "Amendment of Solicitation/Modification of Contract." Case law conflicts on whether the government must use the SF 30 to accomplish the modification.

The Contracting Officer also must decide whether the change can be issued in bilateral form, in which both government and contractor agree to all the terms of the changes, or unilateral form, in which the Contracting Officer issues orders to modify the contract without the agreement of the contractor.

Although the "Changes" clause speaks in terms of unilateral orders of the Contracting Officer, most government agencies try to avoid the use of unilateral changes (which by definition is not finalized and could be disputed). The reason is that agencies have found that a contractor's original estimate of the eventual cost of the change is frequently too high, with the result that the actual cost of the change might eventually be greater than anticipated by the Contracting Officer if this official were to proceed unilaterally and the government later encounters difficulty in negotiating the pricing. Thus, the government's general policy is to make every effort to negotiate the price of a proposed change at the time it is being considered and to issue the change as a bilateral modification to the contract.

It is not always possible to enter into a bilateral agreement on a change, with such factors as time or the difficulty of the subject matter precluding a satisfactory settlement. Another issue is that additional work may be necessary—such as prototype manufacturing—to determine the specific nature of the change and its price impact. In these relatively rare circumstances, the Contracting Officer may have little choice but to issue a unilateral change order. When it is too soon to know the ramifications of the change, the unilateral order might not mention the price or time impact of the change, and the contractor would be free later to submit a proposal for an equitable adjustment.

Note that the standard "Changes" term used in commercial item contracts precludes unilateral changes to the contract's terms and conditions by the Contracting Officer. Instead, the term provides that changes may only be made "by written agreement of the parties." As stated above, however, the parties might be able to bargain for unilateral change authority.

§ 43.7   Constructive Changes

A "constructive change" occurs "where a contractor performs work beyond the contract requirements, without a formal order under the Changes Clause, either due to an informal order from, or through the fault of, the government." Although the government may believe that the action was proper under the terms of the contract, if the contractor's view that the extra work was not required by the contract ultimately prevails, the action will be construed as a constructive change (or a breach of contract), and the contractor will be entitled to compensation for the extra reasonable costs it incurred.

Regardless of the type of government conduct that forms the basis for a constructive changes claim, for the government to be held liable for the cost of the extra work, the contractor must establish the following three elements: (1) the government's act can be traced, in some way, to a government employee with authority to order the additional work, (2) the "extra" work exceeded the requirements of the contract, and (3) depending on the specific contract involved, the contractor gave the proper notice to the government of the government action that the contractor believed constituted a constructive change.

Examined below are the five major types of government conduct that may result in constructive changes.

(a)   Contract Interpretation

A common type of constructive change occurs when the government, during contract administration, interprets the contract to require work that is more extensive than the work contemplated by the contract. There are two fundamental steps in interpreting a contract: (a) determining the meaning of contract language when the contractor's and the government's interpretations differ and (b) determining which party should bear the risk of misinterpretation of the contract when the rules of interpretation provide no clear solution to the problem.

To accomplish the first step, the court or board will attempt to ascertain the intent of the parties at the time they entered into the contract. Because, in most litigated cases, the parties are not of a single subjective state of mind when they agree to the contract, it will be necessary to use principles of contract interpretation to resolve the issue.

The second step—which party should bear the risk of misinterpretation when the intent of the parties cannot be ascertained—will require the board or court to apply risk allocation principles. For example, the legal doctrine of *contra proferentem* requires that after all other principles of contract interpretation are examined and do not resolve the issue, an ambiguity in a contract generally must be reasonably construed against the party that drafted the contract language—in government contracts, that is typically the government. Also, even where a contractor's interpretation of disputed contract language is within the zone of reasonableness, it must also provide evidence of how it construed those terms during its offer preparation process.

(b) Interference and Failure to Cooperate

A constructive change can also arise when the government increases the contractor's cost of performance by actively interfering with the progress of the work or by failing to cooperate with the contractor. Each contracting party has an implied duty to cooperate with the other contracting party. Thus, for example, relief on the basis of constructive change has been granted to contractors where the government (1) improperly disapproved first articles, (2) inspected performance in an overly restrictive manner, thereby causing extra work, and (3) restricted the contractor to two methods of performance even though the contract provided for three or even more methods.

(c) Defective Specifications

The constructive change theory also has been applied where the specifications are defective or call for performance that cannot be attained (see Chapter 11) and the contractor incurs additional expense in attempting to comply with the specifications. Equitable adjustments have frequently been granted in such cases. Indeed, the defective specifications-type of constructive change is implicitly incorporated in the "Changes" clause used mainly in construction contracts.

In one case, a contractor was allowed to recover its costs of trying to perform under an impossible specification—even though it inexcusably failed to perform the contract (to deliver supplies) after the specification was corrected. To recover under this theory, the contractor must show both that the specifications are defective and that the defects caused the additional work claimed.

(d) Nondisclosure of Vital Information

The fourth type of constructive change occurs with government "superior knowledge," i.e., when the government has information that it knows the contractor will need to achieve satisfactory performance but fails to disclose it, resulting in extra effort and expense by the contractor. The nondisclosure of that vital information is a contract "change" in the sense that it should have been given to the contractor at the outset. It follows that the equitable adjustment for this type of constructive change should cover all costs resulting from nondisclosure of the information.

A contractor pursuing a superior knowledge contention must show: (1) it undertook to perform without vital knowledge of a fact that affects performance costs or direction, (2) the government was aware the contractor had no knowledge of and had no reason to obtain such information, (3) any contract specification supplied misled the contractor, or did not put it on notice to inquire, and (4) the government failed to provide the relevant information.

The leading case on the subject of duty to disclose arose when the government issued a competitive solicitation for the production of a chemical compound without revealing the production method found by a recently completed research and development contract. The Court of Claims held in *Helene Curtis Industries, Inc. v. United States*, 312 F.2d 774 (Ct. Cl. 1963), that the government had a duty to share the information with prospective contractors rather than let them "flounder on their own" because the balance of knowledge was so clearly on the government's side.

The information that the government must disclose usually relates to the work to be performed. Such information is often technical in nature—for example, that prior contractors had encountered the same difficulties, or that the roads at a facility had load limitations.

(e) Acceleration

The fifth type of constructive change occurs when the contractor is ordered or induced to incur additional costs to accelerate the work to complete performance before the time required by the contract. The most common formulation of this doctrine contains five elements:

1.   The contractor encountered a delay that is excusable under the contract;

2.   The contractor made a timely and sufficient request for an extension of the contract schedule;

3.   The government denied the contractor's request for an extension or failed to act on it within a reasonable time;

4.   The government insisted on completion of the contract within a period shorter than the period to which the contractor would be entitled by taking into account the period of excusable delay, after which the contractor notified the government that it regarded the alleged order to accelerate as a constructive change in the contract; and

5.   The contractor was required to expend extra resources to compensate for the lost time and remain on schedule.

The essence of constructive acceleration is an act or order of the Contracting Officer that forces the contractor to perform earlier than it would have been required to perform had the contract schedule been properly adjusted to reflect excusable delays (see Chapter 42). The theory is that each time a contractor incurs an excusable delay, it becomes entitled to a commensurate extension of the contract schedule. Therefore, if the Contracting Officer does not recognize these schedule changes but instead demands performance in accordance with the original or any shorter schedule, his action will be treated as a constructive acceleration.

The Government can have a procedural defense to claims based on a constructive change. Thus, a valid release covering the costs in question would bar such a claim. An example would be an unambiguous, consensual "Bilateral Settlement Agreement" previously signed by the parties served to bar the appellant's claim.

B.   EQUITABLE ADJUSTMENTS

§ 43.8   Equitable Adjustments—Basic Rules of Computation

With respect to the negotiations and agreements concerning equitable adjustment proposals, the "Changes" clause does not use the term "claim." Instead it references "proposals" that seek a "right to an adjustment." This usage clarifies that contractors are not entitled to Contract Disputes Act interest by the mere filing of a request for an equitable adjustment. Of course, where the parties disagree on the merits of the equitable adjustment proposal, the contractor may submit a "claim" by authority of the Disputes Clause (see Chapter 33). The same principles of compensation govern the adjudication of claims.

Although there are variations depending on the type of contract, the typical "Changes" clause does not offer precise guidance on how to compute an allowable equitable adjustment. For example, the "Changes" clause set forth in the FAR for fixed price supply contracts states that the following is to take place if a change occurs:

> If any such change causes an increase or decrease in the cost of, or the time required for, performance of any part of the work under this contract, whether or not changed by the order, the Contracting Officer shall make an equitable adjustment in the contract price, the delivery schedule, or both, and shall modify the contract.

A basic rule of repricing changed work, however, is that the economic positions of both parties must be considered. That is, (1) the contractor must be "kept whole" when the government modifies a contract, and (2) the government's pricing position must be preserved in the portion of the work not affected by the change. To achieve these goals, the adjustment process can be viewed as having three components. First, the proper amount of costs attributable to work added by the change order must be ascertained. Second, deductions must be made for any costs directly attributable to work deleted by the change order. Third, overhead and profit increments must be applied to the costs directly attributable to the change.

Thus, an equitable adjustment is not based upon market prices, but upon the contractor's reasonable incurred costs. In sum, an equitable adjustment reflects "a particular contractor's costs," and "not the universal, objective determination of what the cost would have been to other contractors at large." *Kellogg Brown & Root Services*, ASBCA No. 57530, 19-1 BCA ¶ 37,205 (good discussion).

The burden for establishing the amount of a total equitable adjustment is allocated to the party claiming the benefit of the adjustment. In fulfilling this burden of proof, the party must establish both the reasonableness of the costs claimed and their causal connection to the event on which the claim is based. As in other civil actions, the standard used to determine whether the burden has been met is the "preponderance of the evidence" test.

(a) Added Work

When a contractor is able to prove that it is entitled to an equitable adjustment because of additional work, the new work is normally priced at its reasonable cost to the contractor. This general rule is subject to two considerations: (a) the timing of the pricing, and (b) determining what are the reasonable costs. The FAR cost principles typically apply to the pricing of equitable adjustments.

Timing is important because equitable adjustment negotiations can occur before the costs are actually incurred. The general rule, consistently applied in these cases, is that estimated costs are a proper source of determining the reasonable amount of an adjustment if they constitute the most accurate information existing at the time of the pricing action. If the pricing negotiations take place after some (or all) of the additional costs have already been incurred, the actual cost information that the contractor has accumulated may be used for determining the value of the new work performed.

Actual costs may be used in testing what are "reasonable" costs for the additional work. These costs, as opposed to the "reasonable value" of the additional work to the government, will be presumed to be the proper measure of recovery for the contractor. Because the purpose underlying such adjustments is to safeguard the contractor against increased costs engendered by the modification, the measure of compensation cannot be the value received by the government. Instead, it must be more closely related to and contingent upon the altered position in which the contractor finds himself by reason of the modification.

(b) Deleted Work

When the government deletes work from the contract—and the contractor has not yet performed the work—the government is generally entitled to a downward adjustment in the contract price equal to the amount of cost the contractor would have incurred had the work been performed. Under that rule, downward adjustments under the Changes clause are measured by the difference between the reasonable cost of performing without the deletion and the reasonable cost of performing with the deletion.

If possible, cost information current at the time the change is ordered (as opposed to the contractor's original estimate of the cost of the deleted work) will be used to ascertain the costs. Other measures may be used if appropriate. Where the contract is not severable, the "would have cost" rule is the proper method for pricing the deduction.

Note also that, if the contractor is in a loss position because its original estimate was erroneously low, it will be forced to bear the loss that it would have borne had the change not been issued. The government has the obligation of proving the amount of the deduction to which it is entitled in these situations.

§ 43.9   Overhead and Profit

(a) Overhead

A contractor is entitled to overhead as part of an equitable adjustment that increases the contract price. The normal rules governing contract costs apply to determining how a contractor's overhead rate—and the types and amounts of costs included—will be determined. In normal accounting practice, indirect costs are charged as a percentage of direct costs, reflecting the contractor's cost experience over a period of time. In many cases, therefore—especially where the change can be easily factored into the contractor's performance—a board or court may determine that the direct costs in an equitable adjustment bear the standard amount of overhead

The mandatory *Eichleay* formula equitably determines the allocation of unabsorbed home office overhead to compensate a contractor for government-caused delay. The formula, which was originally set forth by the Armed Services Board of Contract Appeals in *Eichleay Corp.*, A.S.B.C.A. No. 5183, 60-2 B.C.A. (CCH) ¶ 2688, establishes a contractor's damages for unabsorbed home office overhead using three steps:

1.   Contract billings/Total billings for contract period) × Total overhead for contract period = Overhead allocable to the contract

2.   Allocable overhead/Days of performance = Daily contract overhead

3.   Daily contract overhead × Days of delay = Amount recoverable

The contractor must meet three strict prerequisites for the application of the *Eichleay* formula (discussed and refined in numerous subsequent cases). First, the occurrence of government-caused delay of an uncertain duration. Second, the delay extended the original time for performance or that, even though the contract was finished within the required time period, the contractor incurred additional costs because he had planned to finish earlier. Finally, the contractor must have been on standby and unable to take on other work during the delay period. A contractor will not be entitled to recover unabsorbed overhead under the *Eichleay* formula where that method of calculating unabsorbed overhead is not available if the delay occurs before the contractor starts work.

In an off-shoot of the *Eichleay* doctrine, the ASBCA has allowed an equitable adjustment for extended field overhead, additional direct costs and certain unabsorbed overhead for project delays where the government failed to compensate contractor adequately for a differing site condition and other reasonably unforeseeable circumstances.

(b) Profit

Profit is also an integral part of the equitable adjustment where the contractor establishes this part of the entitlement. The type of work required to be performed under the change, as well as the risks involved in the changed work, must be considered in determining the amount of profit to which a contractor is entitled in the equitable adjustment.

The FAR provides direction for profit analysis through the consideration of specific factors in computing the profit to which a contractor may be entitled—called the "weighted guidelines" method in the Department of Defense FAR Supplement. The FAR also provides that if a change involves a relatively small dollar amount and the same type and mix of work as the basic contract, the basic contract's profit rate may be applied.

§ 43.10 Proving the Equitable Adjustment Amount

Agency boards of contract appeals and the courts have set forth some basic principles as to the type of information that is acceptable to prove the amount of the equitable adjustment.

A contractor must prove its costs using the best evidence available under the circumstances. The preferred method is through the submission of actual cost data. In maintaining cost data, a contractor should segregate costs associated with the change where it is feasible to do so, and especially where the contractor can anticipate submitting a large claim. Where actual cost data are not available, estimates of the costs may be used. Such estimates should be prepared by competent individuals with adequate knowledge of the facts and circumstances. Estimates should also be supported with detailed substantiating data. The expert testimony of individuals familiar with the facts is admissible in verifying the validity of estimates.

(a) Actual Cost Data

As indicated above, the preferred way for a contractor to prove increased costs is to submit actual cost data. This method provides a board or court, or the Contracting Officer, with documented underlying expenses, ensuring that the final amount of the equitable adjustment will not be a windfall for either the government or the contractor. The parties can negotiate the reasonableness of the actual costs.

Actual costs are more likely to be available where (a) a formal change order has been issued, (b) the contractor initiated the accounting procedures necessary to identify all costs that causally relate to the change, and (c) the changed work has been completed. Where it is impractical for a contractor to prove its actual costs because it failed to keep accurate records, when such records could have been kept, and where the contractor does not provide a legitimate reason for its failure to keep the records, the total cost method of recovery, mentioned below, is not available to the contractor.

For other reasons, this actual cost data method cannot always be used. For example, as noted above, where the change is "constructive" in nature, the contractor typically does not recognize the existence of the change until after a number or even all of the costs related to it have been incurred without being segregated by the contractor's accounting system. In these other situations, alternative methods of proving the equitable adjustment amount must be used, because it will be impracticable for the contractor to maintain detailed cost records of actual costs.

(b) "Total Cost" Method

The "total cost" method of computing the amount of an equitable adjustment is used, with some reluctance, where no alternative method of computation is available. Under the total cost method, the total cost of the work performed is used as a base, and from it is subtracted the original estimate of the work the contractor made during the bidding or negotiation of the contract. The remainder represents the amount of the equitable adjustment (i.e., the amount attributable to the change).

The validity of this method of determining the amount of an equitable adjustment is inherently suspect because it assumes that (1) the costs in excess of the original estimate were caused by the changes, (2) the contractor's original estimate is a fair indication of what it would have cost to perform the work absent the changes that occurred, and (3) all the extra costs incurred by the contractor are related to the change. For these reasons, courts and boards use the total cost basis only as a last resort or reject its use outright.

Before a contractor can obtain the benefit of the total cost method, it must prove: (1) the impracticability of proving its actual losses directly; (2) the reasonableness of its bid; (3) the reasonableness of its actual costs; and (4) lack of responsibility for the added costs. It bears repeating, however, the use of the total cost method is only appropriate if there is no other method of proof available to the parties.

In a related doctrine, the courts and boards have rejected the "total time" approach to compute a non-price issue, which is the amount of delay caused by government action. The calculation under this approach is to compute the delay by subtracting the estimated or scheduled time from the time actually used in performance to determine the amount of delay attributable to the government. The logic of this method and the attendant difficulties are the same as with the total cost method.

Under some circumstances, a modified total cost method may be used to determine the proper amount of an equitable adjustment for a contract change. Under the modified method, the amounts that could be attributed to underbidding, contractor inefficiency, or unrelated contractor costs (i.e., costs not incurred because of the change) are excluded from the equitable adjustment, and whatever available evidence the contractor has of the specific costs incurred is examined. This method does not turn on whether additional work that was performed was identified as such before or after the fact; to the contrary, it entails not identifying the direct costs of the additional work. In all likelihood, an expert witness would be required in complex cases to estimate the amount of the costs for which the government should be responsible.

The former Court of Claims in *Boyajian v. United States,* 423 F.2d 1231 (Ct. Cl. 1970), commented favorably on this computation method because, when properly used, it minimizes a number of dangers inherent in the total cost approach.

(c) "Jury Verdict" Method

The third major method for computing the amount of an adjustment is popularly known as the "jury verdict" method.

Under this method, after the board or court considers the evidence of the actual costs the contractor expended, the opinions of any experts, and other evidence in the case, much as a jury does, the board or court determines the amount to which the contractor is entitled. The court may adopt the jury verdict approach where, (1) there is clear proof that the contractor was injured, (2) there is no more reliable method for computing damages, and (3) the evidence adduced is sufficient for the court to make a fair and reasonable approximation of the damages.

Although the jury verdict method attempts to consider the costs that causally relate to a change, it can involve a considerable amount of subjectivity and speculation. For this reason, it is not a preferred method for determining equitable adjustment amounts. Indeed, the U.S. Court of Appeals for the Federal Circuit indicated in *Dawco Const., Inc. v. United States*, 930 F.2d 872 (Fed. Cir. 1991), that the jury verdict method should not be used unless the contractor can prove that it could not have accumulated cost data on the changed work. Note that in no event will the jury verdict method be used when substantial evidence of the validity of the contractor's claim is lacking.

§ 43.11 Claim Preparation Costs

As with equitable adjustments, formal contract claims require preparation. In some instances, this process may amount to little more than a brief review of the cost records that relate to the changed work. In complicated cases, however, a significant amount of effort— on the part of the contractor's administrative staff as well as any attorneys, engineers, and other consultants—may be required to prepare and present a complete claim to the Contracting Officer. If the Contracting Officer denies the claim, the contractor will incur additional costs in litigating the claim before a board or court.

The FAR cost principles state that the costs of attorney's fees— and those of other experts—are not allowable when they are incurred in connection with the "prosecution of claims or appeals against the federal government" or in "[d]efense against federal government claims or appeals." However, the U.S. Court of Appeals for the Federal Circuit concluded in *Bill Strong Enterprises, Inc. v. Shannon*, 49 F.3d 1541 (Fed. Cir. 1995), that if the costs were incurred with the genuine purpose of "materially furthering" settlement negotiations, they should normally be treated as allowable contract administration costs even if the matter eventually ripens into litigation.

The costs of converting a request for equitable adjustment into a CDA claim, however, will be an unallowable claim prosecution cost, as will be true for costs incurred after a CDA claim has been submitted. Therefore, in determining allowability, the court or board will generally look to the objective reason why the contractor incurred a particular cost.

In connection with claim preparation costs, the Equal Access to Justice Act provides for the award of attorney's fees and expenses to eligible individuals and small businesses that prevail in civil suits involving the government, unless the government can show that its position was "substantially justified."

§ 43.12 Interest

(a) Claims

If negotiations between the contractor and the Contracting Officer over the amount of the equitable adjustment fail, the contractor must decide whether to submit a claim under the

"Disputes" clause of the contract. In the claims process, the contractor will seek the Contracting Officer's final decision on the claim and then litigate any denied claim before a board of contract appeals or the Court of Federal Claims (see Chapter 33).

Under the Contract Disputes Act (CDA), if the contractor is successful, it is entitled to interest on the claim from the date a proper claim is submitted to the Contracting Officer until payment pursuant to order of a court or board. Even if the Contracting Officer agrees—after receipt of a claim conforming to the requirements of the Act—that all or part of the claimed amount is payable, the contractor is still entitled to interest. Also, the CDA contemplates interest payments only to those contractors that incur additional costs in continuing performance under a government contract.

Interest accrues under the CDA even if the claim is finally settled by the Contracting Officer with the result that no final decision is ever issued. Interest under the CDA in all instances is simple interest that accrues at a variable rate specified by the Secretary of the Treasury for each six-month period during which the claim was pending. However, if interest is not mentioned in the settlement negotiations or agreement, the contractor may be considered to have waived or abandoned its interest claim.

(b) Borrowings

The FAR cost principles specifically disallow the recovery of interest on monetary borrowings (however represented). Also, the Federal Circuit in *England v. Contel Advanced Systems, Inc.*, 384 F.3d 1372 (Fed. Cir. 2004), strongly reaffirmed the principle that the government is not liable for interest except where the United States has waived its sovereign immunity protections. In *Sys. Fuels, Inc. v. United States*, 666 F.3d 1306 (Fed. Cir. 2012), the Federal Circuit has reaffirmed the strong policy against allowing contractors interest on borrowings even when incurred as a result of a government breach.

§ 43.13 Notice of Right to Adjustment

A contractor has an obligation, under almost all versions of the standard "Changes" clause, to notify the Contracting Officer of any request for an equitable adjustment in the contract price or schedule. Specifically, the contractor must "assert its right to an adjustment" within 30 days of the receipt of a change order. In addition, the construction contract "Changes" clause implicitly requires notice of constructive changes.

The "Changes" clause notice requirements have never been strictly enforced. The government in arguing for a strict timeliness interpretation must demonstrate that it was prejudiced by the untimely notice, such as the loss of the ability to mitigate its costs.

Notice to the contractor of a proposal by the government for a downward equitable adjustment in the contract price is not governed by any "Changes" clause language, but such proposals may be considered untimely if not asserted within a "reasonable" time. In addition, under the Contract Disputes Act, government claims under the Act must be submitted within six years after the accrual of a claim unless the claim is based on a claim by the contractor involving fraud.

Chapter 44

SUBCONTRACTING

Analysis

The complexity of government contracts often makes it necessary for prime contractors to seek assistance during the course of their performance. Although the contractual arrangements may vary—one alternative being a joint venture—the most common manner for providing this assistance is through subcontracts.

Because subcontracting is an important part of government contracting, it is treated as a separate part of this Hornbook. This chapter discusses (1) the basic matters involving subcontracts as they pertain to government contracts, and (2) subcontract terms and conditions.

§ 44.1   "Subcontracts" Defined

The term "subcontractor" refers generally to any firm that supplies materials or performs services for a prime contractor or for a higher tier subcontractor. Pub. L. No. 115–91, § 820, adds the following information to the definition of "subcontract" in 41 U.S.C.A. § 1906(c)(1).

In this subsection [which lists laws inapplicable to procurements of commercial items], the term "subcontract" includes a transfer of commercial items between divisions, subsidiaries, or affiliates of a contractor or subcontractor. The term does not include agreements entered into by a contractor for the supply of commodities that are intended for use in the performance of multiple contracts with the Federal Government and other parties and are not identifiable to any particular contract.

Government subcontracts have a dual character. On the one hand, the government disclaims any direct responsibility for the subcontract or to the subcontracting parties—because of the lack of

461

"privity of contract" (a direct contractual relationship between the subcontractor and the government). On the other hand, the government seeks to retain a large measure of control over the parties by, for example, requiring that certain clauses be included in subcontracts and maintaining the right to approve certain subcontracts. A prime-subcontractor relationship is one form of a teaming agreement.

Thus, subcontracts under government prime contracts are, in a sense, hybrid documents. They include many of the characteristics of contracts between purely commercial entities (the prime contractor/ higher tier subcontractor and the subcontractor), while imposing on the subcontractor a number of the government-unique duties and controls imposed on the prime contractor/higher tier subcontractor.

The "sales" article—Article 2—of the Uniform Commercial Code (UCC) sets forth the basic rules for contracts for the sale of goods throughout most jurisdictions in the United States. It is intended to be the sole statement of sales law for the points it covers. Therefore, government subcontracts for such sales—to the extent that a particular point is not preempted by the federal statute or the procurement regulations—will be interpreted and enforced in accordance with the UCC, except that subcontractor disputes by private parties could be controlled by federal law when the litigation touches the rights and duties of the United States and a uniform national approach is needed.

The courts and agency boards of contract appeals have also been quite willing to apply UCC Article 2 concepts as persuasive authority in appropriate circumstances, particularly in the areas of implied warranty and unconscionability. As a result, where subcontracts are in use on a government prime contract for supplies, the parties must be aware of the FAR and of the Article 2 provisions of the UCC as well. The UCC, however, is not a formal part of the Federal Acquisition Regulation system and does not supersede express language in a prime government contract.

§ 44.2 The Privity Rule

To enforce contractual rights against a party, there must be a direct contractual relationship with that party (i.e., there must be "privity of contract"). Thus, there are situations where, although the ultimate responsibility for a contract problem (such as defective drawings) can be readily traced to the government, a subcontractor is unable to seek a remedy directly from the government—unless the subcontractor is otherwise in privity with the government through a direct contractual tie. Similarly, although the government may ultimately provide the entire contract funding, it is not liable to a subcontractor for problems caused by the prime contractor/higher tier subcontractor.

As a federal circuit court of appeals stated the long-standing privity rule in *Nickel v. Pollia*, 179 F.2d 160 (10th Cir. 1950):

> [T]he fact that the entire cost of the project came from the government did not create a contractual obligation between the government and the subcontractors under contracts to which the government was not a party. The subcontractor perforce was required to look to the one who promised to pay him for his work and to him alone. There being no privity of contract between [the subcontractor] and the government, [the subcontractor] could not maintain an action against the government for money due him from [the prime contractor] alone.

The rationale of the privity rule has merit because the government normally deals only with the prime contractor. The manner in which the prime has obligated itself to produce is the prime's concern. Thus, if government activities cause damage to a subcontractor in the course of performance, it should be the prime's responsibility to seek compensation from the government and, in turn, to pass the recovery on to the subcontractor. Similarly, the government will hold the prime contractor responsible for the actions of its subcontractor under the contract.

As explained below, the most common technique in which subcontractors may acquire an indirect right to recovery against the government is when the prime contractor sponsors a claim against the government or where the subcontractor uses the prime's name with the prime contractor's permission. One other possible way for the subcontractor to acquire (direct) rights against the government is to qualify as a third party beneficiary under the prime contract, but successful challenges on this basis are rare.

While most of this chapter covers subcontract disputes, privity issues also arise in protests against awards. The most prominent is the general rule that a disappointed bidder lacks judicial and administrative standing to challenge a procurement as a subcontractor.

FAR 42.202(e)(2) states generally that prime contractors are responsible for managing their subcontractors. The contract administration office's review of subcontracts is normally limited to evaluating the prime contractor's management of the subcontracts (see Part 44). Therefore, supporting contract administration shall not be used for subcontracts unless—

(i)   The Government otherwise would incur undue cost;

(ii)   Successful completion of the prime contract is threatened; or

(iii) It is authorized under paragraph (f) of this section or elsewhere in this regulation.

In determining whether FAR 42.202(e)(2) imposed a requirement on the prime contractor to form a basis for a government claim, the analysis has focused on whether the FAR term was incorporated into the contract. Where the term was not part of the contract, it would not impose the responsibility to manage subcontractors that could enable Government to assert that inefficient subcontract costs were not allowable. *Lockheed Martin Integrated Sys., Inc.*, ASBCA 59508 et al., 17-1 BCA ¶ 36597.

§ 44.3   Indirect Subcontractor Appeals

A key consequence of the privity requirement is the prime contractor has no basis for permitting or sponsoring the subcontractor's suit. A qualification will be present where the prime has paid the subcontractor or remains liable to reimburse it in the future. The former Court of Claims established this rule in *Severin v. United States*, 99 Ct. Cl. 435 (1943).

In that case, the court barred a prime contractor from recovering on a breach of contract claim made on behalf of its subcontractors where the subcontractor had fully relieved the prime contractor from liability for costs incurred by the subcontractor resulting from the government act on which the claim was based. Courts and boards of contract appeals have recognized the harshness of the rule and have allowed the prime contractor to bring claims on behalf of subcontractors even if the subcontracts contained a "hold-harmless" clause similar to the one in the *Severin* case.

The FAR specifically states—with respect to disputes procedures—that the Contracting Officer may not give his approval to any subcontract clause that purports to give a subcontractor the right to obtain a direct decision of the Contracting Officer on a claim against the government or the right of direct appeal to a board of contract appeals.

Even if a Contracting Officer erroneously approved such a clause, the board would deny a direct appeal. Along similar lines, the U.S. Court of Federal Claims lacks jurisdiction over a subcontractor's breach action against its prime. However, the subcontractor can obtain relief against the government indirectly because it is common for a subcontractor's claim to be prosecuted by either (a) the prime contractor on behalf of the subcontractor, or (b) (more typically) the subcontractor using the prime contractor's name with the prime's permission.

Thus, the requirement that the prime contractor constantly act as a buffer between the government and a subcontractor has been significantly modified in actual practice. Sponsorship of subcontractor appeals by prime contractors is mainly a matter of form because the prime contractor need not be actively involved in prosecuting the subcontractor's claim. The prime contractor, however, must certify the accuracy of subcontractor claims over $100,000 (see Chapter 33), although the prime need only believe that there is "good ground" to support the subcontractor's claim.

The FAR permits such indirect appeals but also provides that subcontracts granting such rights of appeal to subcontractors may not attempt to obligate the Contracting Officer or a board to (1) decide questions that do not arise between the government and the prime contractor or (2) deal directly with the subcontractor. Thus, the government must also have a financial interest in the subcontractor's appeal for a board to retain jurisdiction.

Claim certification issues have arisen with sponsored claims. Under the Contract Disputes Act (CDA), the contractor's ability to correct defects in a claim certification is not limited to "technical" defects. *Dai Global v. Administrator of the United States Agency for International Development*, 945 F.3d 1196 (Fed. Cir. 2019).

Because the subcontractor must proceed in the name of the prime, it is important that the prime not take any actions that could jeopardize the subcontractor's position. For example, if the prime contractor executes a release of the government from further liability, the subcontractor's indirect appeal rights would be extinguished. Similarly, if the prime contractor fails to give timely notice of appeal, the subcontractor would be barred from taking an indirect appeal, even though the prime was at fault in not giving the required notice. However, a subcontractor that erroneously files an appeal in its own name may be allowed to substitute the name of the prime contractor if the prime contractor had agreed to sponsor the appeal.

Based on the foregoing, the ASBCA has held that it lacks jurisdiction over a subcontractor appeal where the prime contractor did not sponsor the claim and where a subcontract clause cited by the subcontractor did not otherwise create a right to sponsorship.

Generally, agreements between prime contractors and subcontractors are private contracts governed by local law. Where a dispute between them implicates the interpretation of a federal statute, regulation, contract clause, or other federal policy, the controversy will be controlled by federal law where the litigation touches the rights and duties of the United States and where a uniform national approach is necessary.

Sometimes, the government encourages or even directs a prime contractor to subcontract with a particular subcontractor. Such arrangements, however, have the potential to relieve the prime contractor of responsibility for subcontractor performance and may increase the agency's financial liability in cases of substandard contractor performance. It also may create privity of contract between the agency and the subcontractor under the sponsorship theory.

Extraordinary contractual relief under Public Law 85–804 is available to subcontractors as well as prime contractors (see Chapter 33). The prime contractor on behalf of the subcontractor may file a petition for such relief. Ordinarily, the relief, if granted, is passed through the prime by amending the prime contractor's contract with the government.

§ 44.4   Prime Contractor/Subcontractor Litigation

In many cases, the government has no liability for the problem encountered by either the prime contractor or the subcontractor. If government liability is not in question—as where the prime contractor prepares and furnishes defective specifications to the subcontractor—the subcontracting parties are free to pursue the same remedies as between them that would be available under any commercial contract. Depending on the location of the parties, where the contract was entered into, and where the work was performed, lawsuits may be filed in state or federal courts or (if international subcontracts are involved) in foreign tribunals.

Alternative dispute resolution (ADR) is another avenue that is sometimes used to resolve disputes between the prime contractor and subcontractor. The parties may include a clause in their subcontract providing for arbitration or mediation of disputes by the American Arbitration Association or some similar organization. The results of any arbitration, judicial determination, or voluntary settlement of the dispute between the prime contractor and the subcontractor are not binding on the government. However, the government generally recognizes such decisions unless there is a substantial reason for not doing so.

§ 44.5   Government Control over Subcontractors

Although there is no direct contractual relationship between the government and subcontractors, the government nevertheless exercises considerable control over subcontracts and subcontractors.

This control is manifested in several notable ways: (a) a requirement in various instances for government review of a contractor's purchasing system, (b) the requirement that the government consent to certain subcontracts, (c) the requirement that certain contract clauses in the prime contract be passed on ("flowed down") by the prime contractor to the subcontractor, (d) the government's policy of encouraging subcontracting with disadvantaged social groups, and (e) terms protecting subcontractors from late payment from prime contractors.

Pub. L. No. 115–232, § 852, amends 10 U.S.C.A. § 2307(a) to restore accelerated payments to small business subcontractors.

(a) Contractor Purchasing System Review

The purpose of a Contractor Purchasing System Review (CPSR) by the government "is to evaluate the efficiency and effectiveness with which the contractor spends government funds and complies with government policy when subcontracting." The FAR requires a CPSR for each contractor whose sales to the government (under prime contracts or subcontracts, excluding competitively awarded firm, fixed-price contracts, fixed-price contracts with economic price adjustment provisions, and sales of commercial items pursuant to FAR Part 12) are expected to exceed $25 million during the next 12 months. The $25 million threshold can be raised or lowered by agency heads if this is considered to be in the government's best interest.

To this end, the Department of Defense has issued a Defense Federal Acquisition Regulation Supplement final rule to double to $50 million the FAR 44.302(a) threshold for contractor purchasing system reviews. According to DOD, the change allows DOD to focus its personnel and resources on "other essential priorities and missions of greater contractual risk, while reducing regulatory impact on contractors." See 84 Fed. Reg. 72247 (Dec. 31, 2019). Competitive firm-fixed-price contracts, competitive fixed-price contracts with economic price adjustment and commercial item contracts are not subject to FAR CPSR requirements. The review provides the Contracting Officer "a basis for granting, withholding, or withdrawing approval of the contractor's purchasing system."

The government's review procedures are designed to evaluate how the prime contractor selects subcontractors and administers its subcontracts. Specifically, the Federal Acquisition Regulation (FAR) requires that special attention be given to (1) the degree of price competition achieved, (2) pricing policies and techniques, (3) methods of evaluating subcontractor responsibility, (4) treatment accorded affiliates, (5) practices pertaining to small businesses, including small disadvantaged and women-owned businesses, (6) planning, award, and management of major subcontract programs, (7) compliance with the applicable Cost Accounting Standards in awarding subcontracts, (8) appropriateness of the types of contracts used, and (9) management control systems and internal audit procedures to administer progress payments to subcontractors.

Approval of a prime contractor's purchasing system facilitates the contractor's ability to place subsequent subcontracts. The Administrative Contracting Officer will approve a contractor's purchasing system when satisfied that the contractor's practices and policies are efficient and adequately protect the government's interests. Approval will be withheld where the system has major weaknesses. At least every three years, the Administrative Contracting Officer must determine whether another purchasing system review is necessary

(b) Consent to Subcontracts

The government also exercises control over subcontracts when it includes a clause in certain types of prime contracts requiring the consent of the government to subcontract. If the prime contractor has an approved purchasing system, agency consent generally will only be required for subcontracts specifically identified by the Contracting Officer in the "Subcontracts" clause of the contract.

Typically, these would be subcontracts of a critical nature or high-dollar value (e.g., those for critical systems, subsystems, or components). In addition, the Contracting Officer may require consent to subcontract when necessary to protect the government's interests. If the prime contractor does not have an approved purchasing system, the FAR provides that consent to subcontract is required under cost reimbursement, time and materials, labor hour, or letter contracts, and also under certain unpriced actions that exceed the simplified acquisition threshold. Consent may also be required for subcontracts under prime contracts for architect-engineer services.

The subcontract approval clauses provide for consideration of various factors before they become operative. When operative, they require the prime contractor to notify the Contracting Officer in advance of entering into any described subcontract. The notice must include, for example, (1) a description of the work to be performed by the subcontractor, (2) identification of the type of subcontract to be used and the proposed subcontractor, (3) the proposed subcontract price, (4) the subcontractor's cost or pricing data, if required by other contract terms, and Cost Accounting Standards Disclosure Statement, if required by other terms, and (5) the subcontract price negotiation memorandum.

The FAR lists 13 separate criteria for the Contracting Officer to consider in determining whether to give required consent to a subcontract. They include consideration of (a) the prime contractor's basis for selecting the subcontractor, (b) whether adequate price competition was obtained, (c) the appropriateness of the type of subcontract used, and (d) whether the prime contractor has adequately translated prime contract technical requirements into subcontract requirements. The FAR instructs the Contracting Officer to exercise particular diligence where:

1.   The prime contractor's purchasing system or performance is inadequate;

2.   Close working relationships or ownership affiliations between the prime contractor and subcontractor may preclude free competition or result in higher prices;

3.   Subcontracts are proposed for award on a noncompetitive basis, at prices that appear unreasonable, or at prices higher than those offered to the government in comparable circumstance; or

4.   Subcontracts are proposed on a cost-reimbursement, time-and-materials, or labor-hour basis.

Despite the control over subcontract selection that the contracting agency enjoys, the Contracting Officer's consent to a subcontract does not constitute approval of the terms and price of the subcontract.

The prime contractor's failure to obtain the requisite consent for subcontracts could result in a partial termination of the prime contract for default, although such a circumstance would be rare except for an egregious violation of the rules. Termination for default is discussed in detail in Chapter 49.

(c) Flow-Down Contract Clauses

Flow-down clauses are clauses from a prime contractor's contract that are to be incorporated into the prime's subcontracts. They are designed to protect the government's rights and interests and to otherwise promote its procurement and socioeconomic policies.

Some flow-down clauses are mandatory; that is, they are required to be included in a particular subcontract by statute, Executive Order, the procurement regulations, or the terms of the clause itself. The Contracting Officer may require other clauses, although not mandatory, to be flowed-down if necessary to protect the government's interests. The type of work to be performed, the dollar amount of the contract, and the contract type normally determine which clauses must be flowed-down.

(d) Policies Favoring Special Groups

Another way in which the government exerts control over subcontracts is through requirements that encourage subcontracts with special groups. Several of these requirements were discussed in Chapter 19.

Notable among the various government policies favoring special groups is the Small Business Act of 1958, as amended, which requires the utilization of small and socially or economically disadvantaged businesses in many government contracts. Under the law, certain prime contracts must include clauses that encourage subcontracting with small business concerns and small business concerns owned by socially and economically disadvantaged individuals.

The requirement is implemented primarily through the use of two FAR contract clauses. The first, required in government contracts expected to exceed the simplified acquisition threshold (except contracts for personal services or contracts that will be performed entirely outside of the United States), is the "Utilization of Small Business Concerns" clause. This clause obligates prime contractors to provide small and small disadvantaged businesses, women-and veteran-owned small businesses, and small businesses located in historically underutilized business zones (HUBZones) with a "maximum practicable opportunity" to participate in contract performance. A pending FAR change could make this clause applicable outside the United States. See Chapter 10, Introductory paragraph.

The second clause, required in contracts that exceed $700,000 ($1.5 million for construction contracts involving public facilities), is the "Small Business Subcontracting Plan" clause. Under this clause, prime contractors must prepare subcontracting plans detailing the efforts the contractor will take to ensure that small and small disadvantaged businesses, women-and veteran-owned small businesses, and HUBZone small businesses have an equitable opportunity to compete for subcontracts. Contracting Officers are instructed to take action to enforce the subcontracting plan (including the assessment of liquidated damages) after the prime contract is awarded. A prospective prime contractor's compliance with small business subcontracting plans under prior contracts is a factor in determining the contractor's responsibility (see Chapter 9).

(e) Payment

The government encourages prime contractors to pay their subcontractors, where due and owing, without delay. To help achieve this goal, the FAR 32.112, "Nonpayment of subcontractors under contracts for noncommercial items," provides that upon a subcontractor's or supplier's assertion that it has not been paid in accordance with the payment terms of the subcontract or other type of agreement, the Contracting Officer may determine whether the contractor has made progress payments or final payments to the subcontractor/supplier.

The Contracting Officer also may determine the accuracy of a prime contractor's certification of payment to a subcontractor/supplier accompanying the prime's payment request to the government. If the prime contractor is found not to be in compliance with the subcontract's payment terms, the Contracting Officer may encourage the prime to make timely payments and, if authorized by the applicable payment clauses, reduce or suspend progress payments to the prime. Such a false certification could lead to civil or criminal False Claims Act liability (see Chapter 3). The Contracting Officer must also initiate appropriate administrative or other remedial action if the prime contractor's certifications are inaccurate in any material respect.

§ 44.6   Subcontract Terms and Conditions

The general terms of government prime contracts (the "boilerplate") have, over the years, assumed a standard form. Thus, although there are some variations, most contracts—whether they are for supplies, services, construction, etc.—contain the same basic clauses. This concept of standard general terms is a good one. The various clauses, their operation, and their interpretation become familiar to the parties. Also, to some extent at least, these standard terms minimize unexpected occurrences and allocate risks equitably. Moreover, their use saves time and effort because it reduces the need to negotiate specific and new contract language for each procurement.

Much of this standardization has also become a part of government subcontract terms and conditions. The next sections of this chapter discuss subcontract terms and conditions in general and review some of the more significant individual subcontract clauses that are important in government contracting.

(a) Standard Government Contract Clauses

Just as the government has issued standard clauses for inclusion in its prime contracts, the FAR prescribes that many of these prime contracts, in turn, require standard clauses be "flowed down" by the prime contractor to its subcontractors. These flow-down terms and conditions will vary depending on the specific desires and interests of the prime contractor that issues them, consistent with regulatory constraints.

As the discussion below demonstrates, the prime contract clauses that must be "flowed down" to a subcontractor sometimes need not necessarily be passed down verbatim. Therefore, a prime contractor is sometimes free to propose modified mandatory flow-down clauses that secure more or varying rights for the prime (perhaps at the subcontractor's expense), so long as the minimum government requirements remain in effect.

The Contracting Officer is normally not directly concerned with the terms that a prime contractor attempts to impose on its subcontractor, provided (a) that the essence or requirements of the flow-down clauses have been passed down, and (b) no prohibited language is included in the subcontract clauses by the prime contractor, such as language giving the subcontractor the right of direct appeal to an agency board of contract appeals. Thus, subcontractors on government prime contracts cannot rely on the government to intercede on their behalf; they must carefully review each of the prime's proposed terms and conditions before accepting them.

Consider, for example, the government's right to terminate a prime contract for the government's convenience. A number of clauses give the government power to terminate prime contracts "in whole or, from time to time, in part if the Contracting Officer determines that a termination is in the government's interest" (see Chapter 49). The concept of a termination for convenience is not always found in commercial contracts, and the "Termination for Convenience of the Government" clause is not a mandatory flow-down to government subcontracts, although the FAR does contain convenience termination clauses that it suggests for use (together with appropriate modifications) in fixed-price and cost-reimbursement subcontracts.

Experienced prime contractors realize that they must reserve the right to terminate their subcontracts for convenience in the event that the government terminates their prime contracts in that manner. For this reason, a "Termination for Convenience" clause almost always appears in government subcontracts to protect a legitimate prime contractor right. But many prime contractors do not limit their right to terminate their subcontracts solely to where the prime contract is terminated; they also frequently provide an additional right to terminate their subcontracts at their own option unrelated to the government's actions. Subcontractors would be well advised to question this broader termination right and to seek to limit the clause's application to where the government has terminated the prime contract.

(b) Flow-Down Contract Clauses

There are few limits on the standard clauses or variations of standard clauses that government prime contractors can include in their subcontracts. Four different general categories of clauses are listed below:

1. Prime contract clauses directing that they should be incorporated in subcontracts exactly as written ("mandatory" flow-down clauses);

2. Prime contract clauses requiring that their "substance" be incorporated in subcontracts;

3. Clauses "automatically" applicable to subcontracts by operation of law; and

4. Prime contract clauses that, although not mandatory flow-downs, impose obligations on prime contractors that cannot be effectively fulfilled unless similar terms are incorporated into the primes' subcontracts.

(c) Typical Flow-Down Contract Clauses

Set forth below are examples of some typical FAR and Department of Defense FAR Supplement (DFARS) prime contract clauses that may or may not be flowed down to subcontracts. Note that not all clauses found in the procurement regulations are discussed below; the list is illustrative rather than comprehensive. Note also that the FAR lists a series of statutes that are inapplicable to subcontracts at any tier for the acquisition of commercial items or to subcontracts at or below the usual simplified acquisition threshold (see Chapter 13).

"Changes" clauses—It is not mandatory to flow down the "Changes" clause to subcontracts. However, because the prime contractor cannot effectively perform changed work unless it can require its subcontractors to perform changed work, most subcontracts contain a "Changes" clause.

The "Notification of Changes" clause also is not a mandatory flow-down. Because it imposes strict reporting and notification requirements on prime contractors, however, its substance should be passed on to subcontractors when it is included in prime contracts. Similarly, the "Change Order Accounting" clause, which permits the Contracting Officer to require change order accounting when a change or series of changes exceeds $100,000, is not a mandatory flow-down, but its substance should be included in subcontracts where it is likely that subcontractor cooperation will be required.

"Inspection" clauses—These clauses are not mandatory flow-downs. Because they (a) provide the government with the right to inspect all work (including subcontracted work) at the place where it is being performed, and (b) instruct the prime contractor to require subcontractors to cooperate with government inspectors, an "Inspection" clause covering at least these points will be found in most subcontracts.

"Assignment of Claims" clause—This is not a mandatory flow-down clause. Many prime contractors, however, require that subcontractors obtain prior consent before assigning either the subcontract work or monies due (or to become due) from the prime contractor.

"Termination" clauses—Here again, although prime contract "Default" clauses and "Termination for Convenience" clauses are not mandatory flow-downs, the prime contractor will undoubtedly wish to retain the right to terminate its subcontracts in the event that the government terminates the prime contract for default or convenience.

"Disputes" clause—The prime contract "Disputes" clause is not a mandatory flow-down, and subcontracts that contain clauses purporting to give a subcontractor a right to directly appeal a claim should not be approved by the Contracting Officer. Subcontractors should consider negotiating a clause giving them the right to pursue appeals indirectly, in the name of the prime contractor.

"Labor Standards" clauses—The "Walsh-Healey Public Contracts Act clause," providing for overtime compensation in supply contracts, is not a mandatory flow-down, but prime contractors frequently pass down a similar clause to subcontractors. The "Service Contract Labor Standards Act" clause ensuring minimum wages and fringe benefits for service employees must be flowed down to all subcontracts subject to the Act. Note that the FAR exempts subcontracts at any tier for the acquisition of commercial items from both the Walsh-Healey and Service Contract Labor Standards Act requirements. The "Equal Opportunity" clause, which implements the policy of equal employment opportunity in government contracts, must be incorporated in all government prime and subcontracts over $10,000.

"Patents & Data Rights" clauses—The "Authorization and Consent" clause is a mandatory flow-down in subcontracts at any tier that exceed the simplified acquisition threshold (and optional below the threshold. It is prohibited when both complete performance and delivery are outside the United States. Its provisions automatically

apply to subcontractors if the clause appears in a prime contract. The "Notice and Assistance Regarding Patent and Copyright Infringement" clause is also a mandatory flow-down to subcontractors if it is included in a prime contract. The "Patent Indemnity" clause and "Waiver of Indemnity" clause are not mandatory flow-downs, but if they are contained in the prime contract, their substance should be passed on to subcontractors.

The "Filing of Patent Applications—Classified Subject Matter" clause is a mandatory flow-down in all subcontracts that cover—or are likely to cover—classified subject matter. Prime contract "Rights in Data" clauses place the burden on prime contractors to obtain the necessary data rights from their subcontractors by including similar clauses in their subcontracts.

"Insurance-Work on a Government Installation" clause—This clause requires the prime contractor to maintain, for the period of performance, the minimum insurance coverage called for by the contract. Its substance must be flowed down when subcontractors must work on a government installation.

"Notice to the Government of Labor Disputes" clause—This clause is not a mandatory flow-down, but it should be imposed on subcontractors as a protection to prime contractors that must notify the government when a labor dispute may delay timely performance of the contract.

"Security Requirements" clause—All classified prime contracts must contain this clause. Its substance must be included in all subcontracts that involve access to classified information.

"Superintendence by the Contractor" clause—Although not a mandatory flow-down, the substance of this clause is generally passed on to appropriate subcontractors.

"Material and Workmanship" clause—This clause is not a mandatory flow-down but one that a prime construction contractor should pass down to subcontractors.

"Preference for Privately Owned U.S.-Flag Commercial Vessels" clause—This clause is required in many prime contracts that stipulate the transport of supplies, materials, or equipment on privately owned U.S. vessels. Where it appears in a prime contract, a similar clause should be included in subcontracts.

"Subcontracts" clause—This clause is designed for use in most types of prime contracts. When used in subcontracts, it should include a prohibition against the use of cost-plus-percentage-of-cost payments. Also, when used in the prime contract, specific clauses

(e.g., the "Limitation on Payments to Influence Certain Federal Transactions" clause) must appear in certain types of subcontracts.

"Government Property Furnished 'As Is' " clause—This is not a mandatory flow-down clause, but since it eliminates any warranties with regard to government-furnished property, a similar clause is usually included in subcontracts where the prime contractor proposes to transfer any property "as is" to subcontractors.

"Contractor Code of Business Ethics and Conduct" clause—This clause requires certain subcontractors to institute a code of business ethics and conduct, along with an awareness program and internal control system for other than small business concerns. The clause is required in subcontracts that are expected to have a value in excess of $5,500,000 and a performance period of more than 120 days, except when the contract is for the acquisition of a commercial item or is performed outside the United States.

"Special Tooling" clause—This clause must be included in all negotiated prime contracts where the government is to acquire full rights to special tooling in addition to the specific end products required under the contract. Any subcontracts that involve the use of special tooling, the full cost of which is charged to such subcontracts, must include appropriate provisions to obtain rights comparable to those granted to the government by the prime contract clause. The only exception to this requirement occurs when the government determines—on the prime contractor's request—that such rights are not of substantial interest to the government.

"Special Test Equipment" clause—This clause must be included in negotiated prime contracts that provide that the contractor will acquire or fabricate special test equipment for the government but do not specify the items to be acquired or fabricated. The prime contractor is required to include the clause's substance in all subcontracts where special test equipment may be acquired or fabricated for the government.

"Audit and Records-Negotiation" clause—This clause is required in virtually all competitively negotiated prime contracts exceeding the simplified acquisition threshold. It must be flowed down to certain types of subcontracts that exceed the simplified acquisition threshold (see Chapter 13), except those for commercial items where the subcontractor is not required to provide cost or pricing data.

"Progress Payments" clause—This clause must be included in prime contracts under which the government will provide progress payments based on costs. Its substance should be included in subcontracts where progress payments based on costs are contemplated.

"Advance Payments" clause—This clause must appear in prime contracts where the government will provide advance payments. It is not a mandatory flow-down. However, the prime contractor's obligations cannot be fully discharged unless subcontracts providing for advance payments also provide for a government lien paramount to all other liens and impose on the subcontractor and the depository bank substantially the same duties and give the government the same rights provided by the prime contract clause.

"Audit and Records-Sealed Bidding" clause—This clause must be included in all prime contracts that result from sealed bidding and are expected to exceed the threshold for submission of cost or pricing data (see Chapters 13 & 15). The provisions of the clause must be passed down to all subcontracts exceeding the threshold for submission of cost or pricing data.

"Limitation of Liability" clause—This clause is required in most prime contracts exceeding the simplified acquisition threshold. It is not a mandatory flow-down.

"Permits and Responsibilities" clause—This clause must be included in most prime construction contracts. Although not a mandatory flow down, a prime contractor should include its substance in all substantial subcontracts.

"Cleaning Up" clause—This clause, which requires that fixed-price demolition contractors leave the job site in a clean, neat, and orderly condition, is not a mandatory flow-down. However, its substance should be extended to appropriate subcontracts.

"Government Delay of Work" clause—This clause is required in all prime fixed-price supply contracts, except contracts for commercial items or modified commercial items. It is not a mandatory flow-down, but its substance may be included in appropriate subcontracts.

"Cost Accounting Standards" clauses—The "Cost Accounting Standards" (CAS) clause must be included in all negotiated prime contracts unless the contract is exempt or is subject to modified CAS coverage. The substance of the clause is a mandatory flow-down to all nonexempt negotiated subcontracts at any tier.

The clause provides for modified CAS coverage, and its substance must be included in subcontracts. The "Administration of Cost Accounting Standards" clause must be included in negotiated prime contracts on the same basis as the "CAS" clause or "Disclosure and Consistency" clause, and its substance must also be included in negotiated subcontracts. Note that prime contracts and subcontracts for the acquisition of commercial items are not subject to the CAS.

"Engineering Change Proposals" clause—This clause is not a mandatory flow-down. However, where it appears in a defense prime contract, its substance should be passed on to those subcontractors whose cooperation would be required to prepare engineering change proposals.

"Privacy Act" clause—This clause must be included in all prime contracts that require the design, development, or operation of a system of personal records to accomplish an agency function. It is a mandatory flow-down to all subcontracts containing the same requirement.

"Stop-Work Order" clause—This clause is authorized for use in all negotiated contracts for supplies, services, or research and development. It is not a mandatory flow-down, but its substance will generally be passed on to subcontractors.

"Warranty" clauses—These clauses are not mandatory flow-downs, but where they are included in prime contracts, it is typical for their substance to be included in major subcontracts.

"Limitation of Cost" clause—This clause is required for fully funded cost-reimbursement prime contracts. It is not a mandatory flow-down. However, where it is included in a prime contract, it will usually be included in appropriate subcontracts.

"Allowable Cost and Payment" clause—This clause for cost-reimbursement prime contracts is generally passed on in cost-reimbursement-type subcontracts, although it is not a mandatory flow-down.

"Excusable Delays" clause—This clause is included in virtually all cost-reimbursement prime contracts. Although it is not a mandatory flow-down, its substance is generally included in appropriate subcontracts.

Prime contractors often cause confusion by flowing down to the subcontract level in wholesale manner all the prime contract terms. This practice can be confusing because many prime contract terms have no application to subcontracts and would otherwise cause subcontractors undue burden. For example, FAR 52.219–9 requires prime contractors for most agreements exceeding $700,000 ($1.5 million for construction) to submit a subcontracting plan to the Government prior to the award.

Such a practice can only lead to a needles prime/sub dispute if these parties cannot resolve such an issue. For one, no federal policy exists for subcontractors to submit such a plan to the prime contractor. Another possible source of difficulty is when the prime contractor includes boilerplate commercial terms in the subcontract along with the FAR flow downs from the prime contract on the same subject. An example would be where the prime contractor includes a standard changes clause from the commercial world and also flows down the prime contract's FAR changes clause. The confusion here is that the clauses will inevitably conflict, which creates a recipe for ambiguity, claims and disputes, all to the detriment of the government's project.

Chapter 46

INSPECTION AND WARRANTY

Analysis

———

As with any other buyer, the government is entitled to receive what it bargains for when it makes a purchase under a contract. A major mechanism for ensuring this bargain occurs is through quality assurance measures—the inspection and warranty clauses that are included in government contracts.

With regard to inspection, this chapter discusses (a) the government's inspection rights under the regulations and contract clauses dealing with inspection, (b) inspection procedures, (c) government rejection and contractor correction of defective work, and (d) the effect, methods, and limits on the government's final acceptance of the contract work. In addition, this chapter briefly examines warranty coverage under government contracts.

§ 46.1   Government Inspection Rights

In a part titled "Quality Assurance," the Federal Acquisition Regulation (FAR) provides specific guidance on the inspection of contractor supplies and services. The FAR indicates that inspection is the primary means of assuring quality and that the intensity of the inspection process may vary considerably depending on the contractor involved in the procurement and the nature of the supplies or services being procured. Thus, quality assurance requirements may range from inspection at the time of acceptance to a requirement that the contractor establish a comprehensive program for controlling quality.

The extent of contract quality requirements, including contractor inspection, ordinarily will be based on the classification of the contract item, be it supply or service, as determined from its technical description, its complexity, and its criticality. For example,

FAR provides that a critical application of an item is one in which the failure of the item could injure personnel or jeopardize a vital agency mission. Critical application items frequently must carry with them the assurance of superior quality and reliability.

The FAR's emphasis on purchasing commercial items wherever possible (see Chapter 12), has had a significant impact on the government's inspection and acceptance process. The FAR instructs that contracts for commercial items must rely on contractors' existing inspection systems as a substitute for government inspection and testing before tender for acceptance, unless customary market practices for the commercial item being acquired include in-process inspection.

FAR Part 12 further requires that "[a]ny in-process inspection by the government shall be conducted in a manner consistent with commercial practice." Because of this emphasis on following commercial practices, the standard inspection clause used in commercial item contracts differs from the other standard clauses referenced in this chapter.

Even with respect to the acquisition of noncommercial items, the FAR demonstrates a policy of relying on contractors for the inspection of the contract work. For example, it states that in most cases the government must rely on contractors to accomplish all necessary inspection and testing for supplies or services acquired at or below the simplified acquisition threshold. The FAR also establishes standard inspection requirements in contract clauses as a means of assuring quality. Moreover, it recognizes that "higher-level" contract quality requirements apply to contracts for complex and critical items or when needed by technical requirements of the contract.

Note that the government has the right but not the duty to inspect contractor supplies and services. As the Court of Claims explained in *Kaminer Const. Corp. v. United States,* 488 F.2d 980 (Ct. Cl. 1973), the "Inspection" clause is intended for the government's benefit and thus does not "impose upon the government a duty to inspect."

§ 46.2 Standard Inspection Clauses

The standard FAR "Inspection" clauses set forth the basic rules and procedures for quality assurance, acceptance of the contract work by the government, and the parties' rights and obligations regarding inspection. Separate clauses are prescribed in the FAR for different categories of contracts.

The "Inspection of Supplies—Fixed-Price" clause contains the following four important elements: (1) a requirement that the contractor provide and maintain an inspection system acceptable to the government, (2) a reservation of the government's right to inspect the contractor's work during the course of contract performance or before acceptance, (3) a reservation of the government's right to require the contractor to correct or replace nonconforming work or to reduce the contract price to reflect the decreased value of the nonconforming work, and (4) a reservation of the government's right to correct or replace nonconforming work at the contractor's expense or to terminate the contract for default if the contractor fails to correct the work as directed.

This clause, which contains provisions similar to those found in almost all of the various "Inspection" clauses, provides the framework for the discussion in this chapter.

(a) Contractor Inspection

The "Inspection of Supplies—Fixed-Price" clause requires the contractor to "provide and maintain an inspection system acceptable to the government."

This contract requirement is supplemented by a FAR term emphasizing that the contractor retains the principal obligation for product quality and must (1) control the quality of the supplies tendered, (2) offer to the government only supplies that conform to the contract specifications, (3) ensure that its suppliers and subcontractors have adequate quality control systems, and (4) in some instances maintain substantiating evidence of conformance.

The above clause specifically requires the contractor to "prepare records evidencing all inspections made under the system and the outcome." It further directs that such records must be "kept complete and made available to the government during contract performance and for as long afterwards as the contract requires."

The FAR sets forth three levels of inspection: (1) inspection only by the contractor, (2) standard inspection (as prescribed by the standard "Inspection" clauses), and (3) higher-level quality inspection. The level of inspection that applies depends on the extent of quality assurance needed by the government for the acquisition involved.

For example, the government relies on inspection only by the contractor when purchasing commercial, noncritical items. Higher-level quality inspection requirements (which are imposed through a special contract clause, the "Higher-Level Contract Quality Requirement (Government Specification)" clause typically apply to complex and critical items and require the contractor to comply with a government-specified inspection or quality control system.

(b) Time of Inspection

Under the standard inspection clause, referenced above, the government reserves the right to inspect and test the contract supplies "at all places and times, including the period of manufacture, and in any event before acceptance." This gives the government flexibility in terms of when it may conduct inspections, but its discretion in this regard is not unlimited. Thus, the agency must inspect the items during the period specified in the contract, or else risk a deemed acceptance. The clause also states that the government "shall perform inspections and tests in a manner that will not unduly delay the work."

Note that not all government inspection delay is unreasonable; a contractor should expect to experience some delay in any system of inspection. Indeed, the government may conduct repeated inspections provided they are conducted at reasonable times and do not unduly delay performance. Moreover, if the contractor is already experiencing production difficulties at the time the government inspection is conducted, the contractor cannot place the blame for its delay on the government's inspection procedures. However, if the government unreasonably delays the contract work, the contractor may be entitled to an extension of time in the contract schedule (excusable delay) and the recovery of delay costs (see Chapter 42).

Although the clause contemplates that the government will generally inspect supplies before acceptance, the FAR provides for the use of a "Certificate of Conformance" (certification by the contractor that the supplies comply with the contract's requirements) as the sole basis for government acceptance of the supplies when (1) small losses would be incurred in the event of a defect, or (2) the contractor's reputation or past performance provides assurance that the supplies or services will be acceptable and any defective work will be corrected without contest. However, even where this procedure is followed, the government retains its right to conduct inspections if it wishes to do so.

(c) Place of Inspection

The standard inspection clause states that government inspection may be conducted "at all places." The FAR is more specific in that it requires each contract to designate the place or places (including subcontractors' plants) where the government reserves the right to perform the inspections it considers necessary to determine that the supplies conform to the contract requirements.

The FAR further requires that inspection be performed "at source" if (a) inspection at any other place would require uneconomical disassembly or destructive testing, (b) considerable loss would result from the manufacture and shipment of unacceptable supplies or delay in making corrections, (c) special required instruments, gauges, or facilities are available only "at source," (d) performance at any other place would destroy or require replacement of costly packing and packaging, (e) government inspection during contract performance is essential, or (f) it is otherwise in the government's interest.

In discussing subcontracts, the FAR provides that "when required in the government's interest," inspections may be conducted at a subcontractor's facility. Conversely, inspection "at destination" is usually appropriate, for example, for off-the-shelf items that require no technical testing or when necessary testing equipment is available only at the government destination.

(d) Costs of Inspection

The "Inspection of Supplies—Fixed-Price" clause requires that, if the government inspects on the premises of the contractor or a subcontractor, the contractor or subcontractor shall furnish "at no increase in contract price, all reasonable facilities and assistance for the safe and convenient performance of these duties." If inspection is conducted at a location other than the premises of the contractor or a subcontractor, "the government shall bear the expense." A contractor would be entitled to reimbursement (regardless of where the inspection was conducted) if it incurred additional costs in furnishing the government with special inspection equipment.

(e) Manner of Inspection

As noted above, the government must conduct its inspections so as to avoid undue delay in the contract work. There are other limitations on the government's inspection rights. The government may not inspect in a way that interferes with the contractor's performance—for example, by excessive supervision or undue numbers of inspectors or by impeding the contractor's employees' ability to accomplish their tasks. Similarly, inspection and test procedures used by the government must be consistent with the contract specifications. For example, the government may not use an unspecified test that does not reasonably measure contract compliance or use a test that increases the level of performance.

On the other hand, the government may use unspecified tests in place of those mentioned in the contract, provided that doing so does not impose any higher standards of performance on the contractor. Where inspection is by sampling and not all the testing procedures are set forth in the contract, the government is held to a "reasonableness" standard.

§ 46.3   Rejection and Correction

As noted in Chapter 11, the government has the right to insist on strict compliance by the contractor with the specifications and may reject non-compliant work. The "Inspection of Supplies—Fixed-Price" clause provides the government with alternative remedies in the event that supplies are found to be defective. The government may either (1) reject the nonconforming contract items or (2) direct the contractor to correct the defect.

(a) Nonconforming Supplies or Services

Nonconforming supplies or services under the inspection clauses are those that "are defective in material or workmanship" or otherwise do not conform in all respects to the contract's requirements. The FAR directs Contracting Officers to reject supplies or services when the nonconformance "is critical or major or the supplies or services are otherwise incomplete"—unless reasons of economy or urgency suggest that acceptance or conditional acceptance is in the government's best interest. If it can be accomplished within the delivery schedule, the Contracting Officer "ordinarily" should give the contractor "an opportunity to correct or replace" the nonconforming supplies or services.

Where a contract unambiguously provides that re-performance of any late or defective work will be at the sole election of the Government, a tribunal will not rewrite the agreement to provide that the contractor has the right to perform late or to reperform defective work, or that that such a right is dependent upon notice from the Government.

In one case involving a contract for ground maintenance services, the government's rejection of the work and use of an alternate contractor to make repairs was deemed improper because the government failed to furnish the contractor with a list of deficient items as required by the "Inspection of Services" clause, which also provided that the contractor must be given prompt opportunity to correct deficiencies.

(b) Rejection Notice Timing

Notice of rejection must "be furnished promptly to the contractor." If the government does not provide timely notice, acceptance of the contract work may be implied as a matter of law. Thus, in one case it was held that the government had—by implication—accepted almost 3,000 dozen eggs when it retained them for more than two months after inspection without communication of rejection to the contractor.

In a second case, a five-month delay in notice was deemed unreasonable (and hence the equivalent of acceptance) where the government knew of a defect shortly after the item's receipt, and its failure promptly to reject the item prejudiced the contractor. On the other hand, lengthy delays in notice may be reasonable where the delay is necessary and there is no prejudice to the contractor.

(c) Rejection Notice Form

The FAR does not set forth any specific format for a notice of rejection except to require that the notice include the reasons for rejection. Nor is it necessary for the notice to be in writing unless (a) rejection has occurred at a place other than the contractor's plant, (b) the contractor continues to offer nonconforming supplies or services, or (c) performance is inexcusably overdue.

Although the rejection notice may state the nature of the defect in general terms, the notice under the analogous authority of the Uniform Commercial Code (U.C.C.) should (1) fairly apprise the contractor of the defect, (2) repel any inference of government waiver of the defect, and (3) assert—at least by implication—that the government's rights have been violated. The notice of rejection may be found improper if the government does not inform the contractor of the defects that caused the rejection and there is time remaining in the contract delivery schedule for the contractor to correct the defects.

(d) Contractor Correction

As noted above, if the Contracting Officer elects to reject the tender, the contractor "ordinarily" must have an opportunity to correct the defects if that can be accomplished within the contract delivery schedule. Conversely, where it is evident that the corrections cannot be properly made within the contract period, the government does not have to offer the contractor the opportunity to do so.

If the Contracting Officer orders correction instead of issuing a rejection notice, however, the contractor is entitled to a reasonable time within which to make the correction without regard to the original delivery schedule. In any event, under the rule of "substantial compliance" if (a) the defects are relatively minor and can be corrected within a reasonable time, (b) the contractor reasonably believed that the supplies would be accepted, and (c) they were delivered before the contract delivery date, the contractor must be given a reasonable period of time beyond the delivery date to make the corrections.

Under the standard "Inspection" clause, if the contractor fails "promptly" to correct or replace rejected work, the government may either (1) remove, replace, or correct the rejected supplies at the contractor's expense, (2) terminate the contract for default and reprocure the supplies at the contractor's expense pursuant to its rights under the contract's "Default" clause (see Chapter 49), or (3) retain the nonconforming items and reduce the contract price based on the difference in value between the work as delivered and the work contemplated by the contract.

§ 46.4   Acceptance

"Acceptance," as defined by the FAR, "constitutes acknowledgement that the supplies or services conform with applicable contract quality and quantity requirements."

Consistent with the doctrine of economic waste, i.e., the principle protecting the contractor from excessive damages for the repair of non-conforming items, the government is entitled to strict compliance with the technical requirements. Depending on the terms of the particular contract, acceptance of contractor supplies may occur before, at the time of, or after delivery. Where acceptance takes place at a point other than destination, the supplies cannot be reinspected at destination for acceptance purposes but may be examined at destination for quantity, damage in transit, and possible substitution or fraud.

(a) Effect of Acceptance

The "Inspection of Supplies—Fixed-Price" clause expressly provides that acceptance of the contract work by the government is conclusive "except for latent defects, fraud, gross mistakes amounting to fraud, or as otherwise provided in the contract." Thus, in the absence of one of the exceptions, mentioned below, the government is bound by its acceptance whether it was made with actual knowledge of the defects in the supplies or without such knowledge.

Because acceptance is an acknowledgment of conformity to contract requirements, it (a) limits the government's rights against the contractor with respect to patent (obvious) defects in the work, (b) entitles the contractor to payment of the contract price, (c) usually transfers the risk of loss of the work from the contractor to the government, and (d) unless otherwise provided, starts the running of any warranty period.

Although the government always has the initial right to insist upon strict compliance with contract requirements, as mentioned above, the FAR permits acceptance of nonconforming supplies or services if there are "circumstances (e.g., reasons of economy or urgency)" when acceptance is "in the best interest of the government." If the government accepts nonconforming supplies or services on this basis, the contract (except in the case of extremely minor defects) must be modified to provide for an equitable price reduction or other consideration.

(b) Method of Acceptance

The method of acceptance is not specified in the FAR "Inspection" clause. Although government agencies typically prescribe the use of standard forms to document formal acceptance by the agency, acceptance can also be implied. One form of implied acceptance—untimely rejection—was discussed above.

Implied acceptance may also occur where the government does anything substantially inconsistent with the idea of the contractor's continued ownership of the supplies. This most frequently occurs through the government's retention or use of the goods. In one case, the government was found to have impliedly accepted a boiler where, among other things, it operated the boiler for its own purposes for more than 80 days, selected the employees to operate the boiler, and controlled when the boiler would be operated.

Implied acceptance has also been found where the government lost the items delivered to it, altered the nature of the supplies, and merely used the items without altering their nature. The contractor must usually show implied acceptance by the totality of the circumstances rather than through just one event. That is, in determining whether an implied acceptance has taken place, all the relevant facts and circumstances must be considered. Thus, a contractor's contention that daily inspections amounted to acceptance was rejected because such inspections were for the government's benefit and did not alter its rights under the contract.

In construction contracts, the situation is different because of the "Use and Possession Prior to Completion" clause, which provides that, with respect to any completed or partially completed work, the government's "possession or use shall not be deemed an acceptance of any work under the contract." This language has shielded the government from implied acceptance where it takes possession before work is completed.

§ 46.5   Government's Post-Acceptance Rights

As stated above, the government's acceptance of contractor supplies is final and the government has no rights against the contractor for defective work unless one of the four following circumstances is present: (1) the particular defect was latent, (2) fraud was involved, (3) there were gross mistakes amounting to fraud, or (4) a contract term specifically provides otherwise. The presence of one of these circumstances gives the government broad post-acceptance rights, including the right to revoke its acceptance.

(a) Latent Defects

A "latent" defect is one that existed at the time of acceptance but could not be discovered by ordinary and reasonable care or by a reasonable inspection. A defect that can be readily discovered by an ordinary examination or test is patent, not latent, and a failure to conduct the examination or test properly does not make the defect latent. Similarly, if the government knows of the defects at the time of acceptance—even if the defects might not have been discovered by a reasonable inspection—the defects are not latent. However, the government is entitled to rely on the testing and inspection obligations imposed on the contractor.

The government must prove that the defect was latent, and this is a heavy burden. The government must demonstrate (a) that the defect was in existence at the time of delivery, (b) the nature of the examination or test that would have revealed the defect, and (c) whether the government could reasonably be expected to use that type of inspection. Expert testimony frequently is crucial in these respects. Thus, dimensional defects, readily discoverable by measurements, were determined not to be latent, and the lack of specified hardness of a grinding wheel was held not latent because a simple test would have revealed it.

The difficulty in conducting the inspection is also a matter for consideration—thus, sixteen undersized bolts holding a derrick that could have been discovered by turning the bolts with a special torque wrench were deemed to constitute a latent defect where there were 11,967 bolts in the structure.

Unless the contract provides otherwise, the contractor is liable for latent defects discovered at any time after final acceptance—even after expiration of a separate warranty period. However, if the government continues to use contract items after it discovers—or should have discovered—a latent defect, it may be held to have impliedly reaccepted those items. The government must assert latent defect claims in a timely fashion. Thus, contractors were presumed to have been prejudiced—and the revocation of acceptance was not permitted—where the government's assertions of latent defects were not made until three years and nine years after acceptance.

(b) Fraud and Gross Mistakes

The government may also revoke acceptance if the contractor, with the intent to deceive the government, makes a statement or representation it knows to be untrue, and the government accepts the contract items in reliance on that misstatement or misrepresentation.

In addition to revoking its acceptance of the contractor's supplies, such fraud on the part of the contractor might entitle the government to prosecute the contractor under the civil or criminal fraud statutes (see Chapter 3). Note that proof of contractor fraud by a preponderance of the evidence is sufficient to revoke the government's acceptance, and that a Contracting Officer has the right to revoke acceptance even if the contractor's fraudulent acts were not fully known at the time of acceptance.

Similarly, the government may revoke acceptance for "gross mistakes amounting to fraud," except that it does not have to prove that the contractor specifically intended to deceive. A "gross mistake amounting to fraud" has been described as "a mistake so serious or uncalled for as not to be reasonably expected, or justifiable, in the case of a responsible contractor for the items concerned." The test here is essentially whether the contractor acted in wanton disregard of the facts.

The government has used this "gross mistake" concept more frequently than the fraud theory to revoke acceptance, probably because it is easier for the government to prove its case and because the government is more likely to seek remedies for contractor fraud under the civil or criminal fraud statutes. The gross mistake theory was successfully invoked by the government where a contractor failed to tell the Contracting Officer and a government inspector of a change in material in a previously approved component, and where a contractor incorrectly certified that certain contract items were identical to ones previously tested and approved by the government.

However, gross mistake was not found in a case where the contractor failed to conform precisely to the specifications but did not suspect that the change would have any adverse effect on the product being furnished to the government.

(c) Other Contract Terms

The last exception to the finality of government acceptance is if the contract separately provides that the contractor will be liable for any defects discovered after acceptance. A "Certificate of Conformance" clause or a "Warranty" clause, for example, usually extends the contractor's liability for defects beyond acceptance.

In one case where the standard "Inspection" clause was supplemented by a special clause that stated that final acceptance of the work would not be binding or conclusive if the contractor "has otherwise departed from the terms of the contract," it was held that the contractor's failure to provide a particular hoist was such a departure and that the Contracting Officer could order correction of the item after accepting it.

§ 46.6 Warranties

Warranties—another means of assuring the quality of contract performance—can, under some circumstances, increase the scope and the duration of a contractor's liability for the goods it provides the government. The FAR defines a "warranty" as "a promise or affirmation given by a contractor to the government regarding the nature, usefulness, or condition of the supplies or performance of services furnished under the contract." Warranties are closely related to, but distinct from, disclosures or disclaimers.

There are two types of warranties—express and implied—that may apply to government contracts. A general description of each and a discussion of their effect are given below.

(a) Express Warranties—FAR Clauses

The FAR states that the "principal purposes of a warranty in a government contract are—(1) to delineate the rights and obligations of the contractor and the government for defective items and services and (2) to foster quality performance." The FAR sets forth five factors that must be considered by the government in determining whether to include a warranty clause in a given contract:

1.   Nature and use of the supplies or services—their complexity and function, the difficulty of detecting defects before acceptance, and the potential harm to the government that could result if there are defects;

2.   Cost—the contractor's charge for accepting deferred liability and the cost of government administration and enforcement;

3.   Administration and enforcement—the government's ability to enforce the warranty;

4.   Trade practice—whether the contract item is customarily warranted in the trade; and

5.   Reduced requirements—the possibility of reducing government inspection in light of the warranty.

The FAR also instructs that a warranty should (a) survive acceptance, (b) provide a stated period of time or use or the occurrence of a specified event after acceptance for the correction of defects, and (c) provide benefits commensurate with the cost of the warranty to the government.

The FAR provides that the duration of the warranty must be clearly specified, and that factors such as the nature of the item, its shelf life and estimated useful life, and trade practice must all be considered in establishing the warranty period. The period specified, however, should not extend the contractor's liability for defects beyond a reasonable time after acceptance by the government.

The FAR also provides that the warranty clause shall specify a reasonable time for furnishing notice to the contractor regarding the discovery of defects. This time period should be determined after considering the time period that is likely to be required for the government to discover and report to the contractor the existence of the defect, as well as the time required to discover and report defective replacements. Where the government fails to provide such notice, a board or court may reject a warranty claim.

(b) Express Warranties—Government's Remedies

The FAR contains several "Warranty" clauses for inclusion in various kinds of contracts at the option of the Contracting Officer. If there is a breach of warranty, the Contracting Officer has alternative remedies available under the "Warranty" clauses for supply contracts. The Contracting Officer may either (a) require the contractor to correct or replace the nonconforming supplies (or parts) or (b) retain the nonconforming supplies and reduce the contract price (see, e.g., Paragraph (c) of the clause).

Moreover, the FAR provides that, when appropriate, the Contracting Officer can include in the warranty's terms other remedies for breach of warranty, such as repair or replacement of the defective item by the government at the contractor's expense. Where the contractor is not liable under the warranty, however, such as where a subcontractor makes the warranty to the owner, the government must proceed against the party responsible under the warranty. If the contract simply requires the contractor to provide a conforming warranty, the contractor's obligations will be fulfilled.

The remedies available to the government under the "Warranty" and "Inspection" clauses are cumulative. Unless the contract specifications provide otherwise, a contractor's liability for latent defects and defects resulting from fraud and gross mistake (under the contract's "Inspection" clause) will continue to apply after the expiration of the time period set forth in the contract's "Warranty" clause.

Additionally, most "Warranty" clauses contain language specifying that they override the finality of acceptance under the "Inspection" clause. Thus, the standard warranty clause for noncomplex supply items states that the "rights and remedies of the government provided in this clause are in addition to and do not limit any rights afforded to the government by any other clause of this contract."

(c) Express Warranties—Burden of Proof

The government has the burden of proving a contractor's warranty breach. When asserting a breach of warranty claim, the government has the initial burden of demonstrating that "the most probable cause" of the defective material or workmanship was the failure of the contractor's performance. Once this has been accomplished, the burden shifts to the contractor to prove either that the defect was not its responsibility or that there are, in fact, no defects.

(d) Implied Warranties

The U.C.C. provides the two implied warranties of quality that apply to the sale of supplies: (1) the implied warranty of merchantability—that is, that the supplies will be fit for the ordinary and usual purposes for which such goods are sold and (2) the implied warranty of fitness for a particular purpose. The U.C.C. also permits the exclusion of these warranties by clear language in the contract.

The U.C.C. is not part of the federal procurement statutes and regulations. To the extent that the U.C.C. is not inconsistent with federal law, however, courts and boards commonly use it for permissive guidance in determining the rights and liabilities of the parties to a public contract.

The FAR states that where express warranties are included in a contract (except contracts for commercial items), all implied warranties of merchantability and fitness for a particular purpose "shall be negated." Moreover, because the "Inspection of Supplies—Fixed-Price" clause provides that acceptance is conclusive unless "otherwise provided in the contract," courts and boards of contract appeals have held that where contracts contain such language, final acceptance by the government bars government claims based on the implied warranties since they are not "contained" in the contract. On the other hand, if no such language is included in the contract, there is nothing to bar the government from taking advantage of implied warranties—and it has done so.

(e) Commercial Item Contracts

The FAR prescribes a different warranty policy for government acquisitions of commercial items. First, the implied warranties are not negated. Instead, the Contracting Officer is instructed to consult with legal counsel prior to asserting any claim for breach of the implied warranties. Express commercial warranties must be used by the Contracting Officer "to the maximum extent practicable," and solicitations for commercial items must require offerors to offer the government at least the same warranty terms offered to the general public in customary commercial practice. Finally, the Contracting Officer is required to analyze any express commercial warranty to determine if (1) the warranty is adequate to meet the needs of the government, (2) the warranty terms allow the government effective post-award administration, and (3) the warranty is cost effective.

Chapter 48

VALUE ENGINEERING

Analysis

---

§ 48.1   In General

Under the typical government contract "Changes" clause, a contractor has little monetary incentive to submit a change proposal suggesting a method of reducing the cost of performance. If such a change is ordered, the contract price will be reduced by the full cost saved, plus the contractor's profit on such cost. As a result, the contractor is "penalized" by a reduction in profit for suggesting a method of saving the government money.

To avoid this potentially unfair result, and to encourage contractors to come up with new ways of performing contracts more economically, the government developed the concept of "value engineering," which permits contractors to share in savings resulting from their suggestions. The government encourages the use of value engineering through its regulations, contract clauses, and even in its implied contract requirements.

In fact, the use of "Value Engineering" clauses is mandatory in a great number of government contracts. The most widely used clauses for implementing the concept are the "Value Engineering" clause for supply and service contracts, and the "Value Engineering-Construction" clause, which is used in most construction contracts.

§ 48.2   Value Engineering Change Proposals

"Value Engineering" clauses contemplate the use of value engineering change proposals (VECPs). Submission of these cost saving proposals under the clauses is generally left entirely up to the contractor. However, if a contractor's VECP is submitted and accepted, the "Value Engineering" clause provides for the contractor to share in (a) the savings generated on the contract being performed ("instant contract savings"), (b) savings on concurrent contracts for essentially the same items ("concurrent contract savings"), (c) savings on future contracts ("future contract savings"), and (d) savings by the government in operation, maintenance, or logistic support, or property resulting from the value engineering change ("collateral savings").

Note that for "concurrent contract savings" and "future contract savings" under the "Value Engineering" clause used in supply and service contracts, the contractor may share in savings generated under contracts awarded to other contractors as well as under additional contracts it performs itself. The "Value Engineering-Construction" clause provides for contractor sharing only in "instant contract savings." Both clauses specify the contractor's share of the net savings. Under the supply and service clause, the contractor's share ranges from 15% to 50%. Under the construction clause, it ranges from 45% to 75%.

The most common VECPs submitted by contractors are suggestions for reducing costs by modifying the specifications or drawings to allow the use of simpler methods, less expensive materials or components, or other changes to the work that will not adversely affect the final product or construction. The government may not defeat a value engineering claim by arguing that the contract already required the contractor to use the cheapest method available.

Entitlement to a VECP can be dependent upon the interpretation of what constitutes the contractor's product. In a 2006 Federal Circuit decision, *Applied Companies v. Harvey*, 456 F.3d 1380 (Fed. Cir. 2006), the court considered a VECP covering cost savings resulting from the use of commercial parts in a specific air conditioning unit. This VECP unambiguously limited cost savings to the single unit. Thus, the Army's decision to commercialize all air conditioning units did not entitle the contractor to a share of the overall savings, even though the savings concept was similar. A contractor will have no entitlement to any cost savings, however, where an insufficient nexus exists between the proposed and actual savings.

§ 48.3   Administration

A contractor acting in good faith should always identify its proposal as a VECP—so that the proposal is not considered merely a gratuitous suggestion for which the contractor expects no reward. Many disputes have arisen over whether a Contracting Officer accepted a VECP from the contractor or issued a change order independent of the proposal. Clearly, if the change order is issued after submission of the proposal, there is a presumption that the two are connected—and the government will have a difficult task to overcome this presumption. On the other hand, the contractor may not receive a value engineering change share for what is, in essence, a government concept.

The VECP must relate directly to the work required under the contract. Government officials have no authority to purchase unsolicited suggestions that are not submitted under an existing contract. Furthermore, a contractor cannot enforce a "Value Engineering" clause that was improperly included in its contract.

The Contracting Officer's decision to adopt or reject a contractor's VECP has traditionally not been subject to review under the Contract Disputes Act (CDA), and former versions of the "Value Engineering" clauses specifically provided that VECP decisions were not subject to the "Disputes" clause of a contract. The "Value Engineering" clause was modified, however, to delete the CDA exemption after the U.S. Court of Federal Claims ruled in *Rig Masters, Inc. v. United States*, 42 Fed. Cl. 369 (1998), that the clause's attempt entirely to exempt VECP decisions from CDA coverage was invalid. The clause now provides that the decision to accept or reject a VECP "is a unilateral decision made solely at the discretion of the Contracting Officer." Thus, courts and agency boards of contract appeals may review a Contracting Officer's VECP decision under the CDA to determine whether there has been an abuse of discretion.

Other disputes arising under the "Value Engineering" clause routinely have been appealed by contractors. For example, contractors have appealed the Contracting Officer's determination that (1) the contractor was not entitled to "future contract" royalties for merchandise delivered under a subsequent contract, (2) a contractor that suggested a VECP was not owed royalties when the government inadvertently omitted the proposal from a subsequent contract, and (3) a time extension granted by the Contracting Officer to another contractor deprived the protester of royalties it would have earned under a VECP. Whether a VECP can be "constructively accepted" by the government after the contract has been completed also has been the subject of appeals.

Chapter 49

TERMINATIONS FOR DEFAULT AND CONVENIENCE

Analysis

This chapter first explores the subject of default termination as provided for under standard government contract "Default" clauses. Specifically, it examines (a) the standard "Default" clauses for fixed-price contracts, (b) contractor actions that can lead to default termination, (c) the government's termination decision, (d) contractor defenses to default termination, such as excusable delay or waiver by the government, (e) the government's remedies after a valid default termination, and (f) how contractors can contest default terminations.

A.   DEFAULT TERMINATIONS

§ 49.1   Standard "Default" Clauses

Default terminations are provided for in government contracts under standard Federal Acquisition Regulation (FAR) clauses. The major clauses are the "Default (Fixed-Price Supply and Service)" clause used for most fixed-price supply and service contracts, the

"Default (Fixed-Price Construction)" clause used for most construction contracts, and the "Termination for Cause" term used in commercial item contracts. The "Termination for Cause" term replaces, in government commercial item contracts, the "Default" clause typically used in standard government supply and service contracts.

A contractor that believes its contract has been improperly terminated for default may appeal this government action to the appropriate agency board of contract appeals or file suit in the Court of Federal Claims. The procedures used in these forums are explained in detail in Chapter 33.

The "Default" clause for fixed-price supply and service contracts provides that when a contractor fails to deliver required supplies or to perform services within the time set forth in the contract, the government may terminate the contract immediately. However, for any other default of a fixed-price supply or service contract, the Contracting Officer must notify the contractor in writing of its deficiencies and give the contractor 10 days to correct them, or a longer period as authorized by the Contracting Officer. This is called a "cure notice," and it is required where the contract schedule has not expired and more than 10 days remain before the contract's due date.

In practice, however, the government rarely issues a default notice on any contract without first using a cure notice or other expression of concern with the contractor's performance. Before using this notice, the Contracting Officer must ascertain that an amount of time equal to or greater than the cure remains in the contract schedule. Only if the contractor fails to cure the problems delineated in the cure notice can the Contracting Officer properly terminate the contract for default.

In contrast, the "Default" clause for construction contracts makes no provision for pre-termination cure notices, but they (or another form of delinquency notification) are often used nonetheless.

A termination for default is a government claim under the Contract Disputes Act. The government issues it by a final CO decision. It is both adverse to the contractor and relates to the contract because it involves a determination that the contractor has failed to fulfill its contractual duties. The Contract Disputes Act states that contractor may appeal a Government claim to an appropriate board of contract appeals without having to submit monetary claim of its own to the contracting officer. *Malone v. United States*, 849 F.2d 1441 (Fed. Cir. 1988). In the alternative, the contractor in the same way may appeal this government claim to the Court of Federal Claims.

The Government cannot convert a termination for convenience to a termination for default. *Phoenix Data Solutions LLC*, ASBCA 60207, 18-1 BCA ¶ 37164.

§ 49.2   Bases for Termination

Terminations for default are much more common in supply and service contracts than in construction contracts. Reflecting this fact, the "Default" clause for supply and service contracts is more specific in stating the bases for default termination than is the clause for construction contracts. The standard clause used in supply and service contracts recites that the government has the right to terminate for default if the contractor fails to (1) deliver the contract supplies or perform the services on time, (2) make progress so as to endanger performance of the contract, or (3) perform any of the other provisions of the contract.

The "Termination for Cause" term also names three bases for terminating a commercial item contract for default: (a) "any default" by the contractor, (b) failure by the contractor "to comply with any contract terms or conditions," and (c) failure by the contractor to provide the government, on request, with "adequate assurances of future performance."

By contrast, the standard construction contract "Default" clause merely states that the government may terminate the contract if the contractor "refuses or fails to prosecute the work or any separable part, with the diligence that will insure its completion within the time specified in [the] contract including any extension, or fails to complete the work within this time."

In addition, although not explicitly set forth in either the "Default" clauses or the commercial item contract "Termination for Cause" term, express or implied repudiation of the contract also constitutes a basis for default termination. The government's right to terminate is not limited by standard inspection clauses, because they permit the government to exercise any other rights and remedies allowed by the contract.

A court or board may sustain a default termination relying on circumstances that existed at the time even if the Government had made its termination relying on another ground. Query whether this doctrine encourages contracting officials to engage in post-hoc rationalizations—and whether those new rationales likely reflect the agency attorney's input and not the considered views of the contracting officer. In bid protests, the rule is the opposite that post-hoc rationales are inadmissible This approach serves to re-enforce the agency's obligation to examine the relevant data and articulate a satisfactory explanation for its action including a rational connection between the facts found and the choice made.

This permissive stance in disputes allowing post-hoc rationales arose with a 1925 Supreme Court decision, *College Point Boat Corporation v. United States*, 267 U.S. 12 (1925), that pre-dates the Contract Disputes Act of 1978 and its requirement for a Contracting Officer decision on the contractor's claims. To this extent, Congress with the enactment of the Disputes Act has effectively disregarded the decision but the case has not been formally overruled. Nonetheless, the agency has a major obligation in disputes to ensure full and fair consideration of the claim in light of all the facts and circumstances. The argument should be that unless the Contracting Officer ruled on the Government's theory for the default in the Final Decision, a board or court should remand the action to the Contracting Office for consideration.

(a) Failure to Deliver or Perform—General Policy

The standard default clause for supply and service contracts provides that a contract may be terminated for default if the contractor fails to "[d]eliver the supplies or perform the services within the time specified in [the] contract or any extension."

This term has traditionally been viewed as giving the government the right to terminate a contract if (1) the contractor fails to deliver on the date specified, or (2) the contractor fails to comply with the specifications set forth in the contract. Thus, if the contractor fully complies with the specifications but fails to deliver on the date required, the contract may be terminated for default. Conversely, if the contractor delivers the items specified or performs the services required on time, but fails to comply with the specifications, the contract may also be terminated.

Contractors are expected to perform in strict conformance with contract delivery schedules and contract specifications, even if the original bid or proposal failed to comply with the solicitation. Rarely, however, will the government default for a technical breach alone; as will be explained below, the government commonly factors the attendant business realities into the determination.

No contract is perfect and no contractor performs in perfect compliance with all contract terms. Consistent with this pragmatic viewpoint, the case law states that whether considered individually or collectively, isolated instances of contract violations do not constitute substantial evidence of a sufficient disregard of contract terms for purposes of supporting a termination for default.

(b) Failure to Deliver or Perform—Timely Delivery

Time is of the essence in any contract containing a fixed date for performance, provided the government has not "waived" the delivery date (or otherwise has foregone its rights). When a contractor fails to make timely delivery, the government ordinarily may terminate the contract for default immediately and without notice after the close of business on the exact day specified in the delivery schedule.

Thus, a supply or service contractor is in danger of having its contract terminated for default as soon as the scheduled date for delivery has passed. In fact, even an untimely delivery made before the government had a reasonable opportunity to issue a termination notice has been found not to bar a default termination action. However, a mere untimely delivery will rarely prompt the government to proceed to a default action.

Once the government has met its burden in terminating a contract for default of proving that timely performance is beyond the contractor's reach, the contractor has the evidentiary burden of going forward to prove either that it was making progress such that timely completion of the contract was not endangered or that there was excusable delay.

It will frequently occur that the agency has foregone the original contractual delivery date for the goods but does not formally reset a new date by the time of actual delivery. In this circumstance, when delivery does eventually occur, the agency's acceptance effectively established a new enforceable delivery date. Therefore, the contractor here remains obligated to provide conforming supplies as of the actual delivery date. See also § 49.4.

(c) Failure to Deliver or Perform—Compliance with Specifications

As noted in Chapter 11, the government is entitled to insist on strict compliance with the contract specifications. Nevertheless, the government rarely defaults for technical non-compliance alone with the specifications.

The government may not terminate the contract in the absence of objective, non-defective and enforceable performance standards. Furthermore, termination of a contract for default may not be upheld if the contractor's performance is deemed substantially complete (see Chapter 11). Even though a contract has been substantially completed, however, a contractor must complete or correct work that is practicable to perform. The government may terminate a contract for default on the basis of a contractor's refusal to perform as required.

(d) Failure to Make Progress

A termination for failure to make progress may occur when the contractor fails to progress satisfactorily toward completion of performance—even though the final performance date has not yet arrived. This basis for default termination is recognized in standard fixed price supply/service contracts and construction contracts. The rationale also appears in the "Termination for Cause" clause used in commercial item contracts. The commercial item "Termination for Cause" term also includes a different basis for default termination: the contractor's failure to "provide the government, upon request, with adequate assurances of future performance."

The "Default" clause for fixed-price supply and service contracts lists failure to make progress so as to endanger contract performance as a separate basis for default. Unlike default terminations for untimely delivery, however, a contractor is entitled under the clause, to receive notice and 10 days—or longer as the Contracting Officer authorizes in writing—to cure the default before the government may terminate the contract.

Termination for default for failure to make progress does not require government proof that it was impossible for the contractor to finish the job; instead, it means only that the contractor's demonstrated lack of diligence indicates a lack of adequate assurance that the contractor could achieve timely completion. Where the contractor has failed to meet the requisite delivery date, the Government need only show that the termination was justified and then the burden shifts to the contractor to prove that its late delivery was excusable. The ASBCA has held, however, that an attempt to terminate a contract for failure to make progress would be unsuccessful in the absence of an effective delivery date.

The fixed-price construction contract clause does not require the government to give the contractor any notice before terminating the contract for failure to "prosecute the work . . . with the diligence that will insure its completion within the time specified." But if a cure notice is issued to the construction contractor, the contractor's failure to provide reasonable notice that the project will be completed on time constitutes a possible repudiation of the contract, potentially justifying a default termination.

The agency's failure to issue a cure notice sometimes becomes a key issue in CDA litigation. The rule is that a cure notice is not required when the termination is for failure to meet a delivery date as opposed to for failure to make progress toward meeting a delivery date that has not yet arrived.

As mentioned earlier, the commercial item contract "Termination for Cause" term also does not contain a warning notice requirement; however, the FAR termination procedures for commercial item contracts do require the Contracting Officer to "send a cure notice prior to terminating a contract for a reason other than late delivery."

A termination for failure to make progress will be upheld only if the government is able to provide convincing proof that it is reasonably certain that the contractor, on the date of termination, was incapable of completing the contract within the time prescribed. For example, in a case where 60% of the scheduled time had elapsed but only 15% of the work had been completed, it was held that a termination for failure to make progress was proper.

But where the contractor was able to demonstrate that the government had not adequately considered schedule extensions and concurrent delays, a default termination was overturned. Similarly, if the Contracting Officer relied on materially inaccurate information or if the government's failure to cooperate created the problems that prevented timely performance, default termination is improper.

The Federal Circuit has reaffirmed that *Lisbon Contractors, Inc. v. United States,* 828 F.2d 759 (Fed. Cir. 1987), sets out the proper standard for review of a default termination for failure to make progress. Under *Lisbon,* the Contracting Officer must have a reasonable belief that there was no reasonable likelihood of timely completion.

(e) *Failure to Perform Other Contract Terms*

The "Default" clause for fixed-price supply and service contracts provides, as a third specific ground for default termination, the contractor's failure to perform "any of the other provisions of [the] contract." As with terminations for failure to make progress, the "Default" clause requires that a cure notice be given before a termination on this ground.

As a basis for default, the other provision must constitute a significant requirement of the contract. Default termination based on a contractor's breach of other contract provisions has occurred where a contractor refused to provide cost records, submitted fraudulent test reports, did not furnish required payment bonds, submitted first articles that did not meet design and quality requirements, failed several food service public health inspections, delivered supplies that did not comply with Buy American Act requirements, failed to obtain necessary approvals from local authorities, or failed to provide required documentation.

In still another example, after the Small Business Administration determined that a contractor was not a small business as a result of its failure to comply with the nonmanufacturer rule (see Chapter 19), the applicable regulations required the termination of the contract for cause. *Third Coast Fresh Distribution, L.L.C.*, ASBCA 59696, 16-1 BCA ¶ 36340.

(f) Anticipatory Breach of Contract

Although not expressly set forth in the supply and service contract or the construction contract "Default" clauses or in the commercial item contract "Termination for Cause" term, a contractor's repudiation of the contract, whether express or implied, may also be a basis for default termination.

The government retains this common-law right under the standard clauses, and the "Termination for Cause," which state that the contractor is "liable to the government for any and all rights and remedies provided by law." An "anticipatory breach" occurs whenever there is "a positive, definite, unconditional, and unequivocal manifestation of intent . . . on the part of a contractor . . . not to render the promised performance when the time fixed by the contract shall arrive."

A termination for anticipatory breach or repudiation of the contract will be found in two situations: (a) actual, inexcusable abandonment of performance or (b) where the contractor, before performance is due, makes a positive, definite, unconditional, and unequivocal statement that the contractor will not perform in accordance with the contract's terms.

A contractor's refusal to continue performance of the contract because of disagreement with the agency's reasonable interpretation can be an anticipatory repudiation supporting a termination for default. Similarly, a contractor's unwarranted demand for an additional payment on a fixed price contract has been found to be an anticipatory repudiation of a contract. The COFC has upheld a termination for default upheld on the basis of the contractor's anticipatory repudiation even though government had forfeited the completion date and had not established a new one.

§ 49.3 The Termination Decision

(a) Contracting Officer Discretion

Although the government has the right under the "Default" clause to terminate the contract when the contractor fails to perform, the government does not have to exercise that right.

FAR 49.402–3(f) requires Contracting Officers to consider various factors in arriving at a default termination decision—such as the contractor's explanation for its failure, the availability of the supplies or services from other sources, the need for the supplies or services balanced against the time it would take to obtain them from another source, and the effect a termination would have on the contractor's other contracts. Although the Contracting Officer has an affirmative obligation to assess all of the relevant circumstances of the contract, consideration of each of the FAR factors in 49.402–3(f) is not a prerequisite to a valid termination.

If the Contracting Officer bases a termination decision on materially erroneous information (even if unknowingly), the decision represents an abuse of discretion. In that setting, a court or board under standard default clauses could convert the default into a convenience termination. On the other hand, as explained below, an otherwise proper decision is likely to stand on appeal despite the agency's failure to consider the above FAR criteria.

The FAR factors need not be considered before default terminating a commercial item contract. However, the former General Services Administration Board of Contract Appeals has held that the government has the same burden to prove the propriety of a termination for cause in a commercial item contract as it would a default termination under any of the standard clauses.

Although the "Default" clauses refer to an action by the "Government," rather than by the "Contracting Officer," the FAR and the case law make it clear that the Contracting Officer must exercise independent, sound discretion to ensure that termination is in the agency's best interests. Indeed, a Contracting Officer may reasonably decide to terminate a contract for default after consulting legal counsel and other agency experts. But the procuring agency official must exercise the independent discretion granted to him or her in deciding whether to terminate a contract. For example, termination based on acceding to the instructions of a U.S. Senator has been deemed improper.

(b) Improper Motive or Grounds

Courts and boards commonly say that a default termination is a drastic sanction that requires strict accountability by the government. The default proceeding is often said to be essentially a forfeiture so that every reasonable presumption is against the forfeiture. But see Steven W. Feldman, *The Rhetoric and Reality of Termination for Default,* 53 Procurement Lawyer 5 (Spring 2018) (challenging these statements). Thus, the government has the ultimate burden of sustaining its contention that there was a basis for the termination for default.

A default termination that is unrelated to contract performance is arbitrary and capricious and thus an abuse of the Contracting Officer's discretion. In this respect, the government has the duty to act in good faith and to cooperate in the contractor's performance.

The matter of government bad faith is a frequent issue in termination for default litigation. A contractor alleging a breach of the duty of good faith and fair dealing need not prove in all cases that the Government took action specifically targeted to re-appropriate the benefits the other party expected to obtain from the contract. Instead, precedents stating a broader duty of good faith and fair dealing apply. Thus, the duty of good faith and fair dealing includes the duty not to interfere with the other party's performance and not to act so as to destroy the reasonable expectations of the other party regarding the fruits of the contract.

Sometimes the basis of the termination for default referenced in the government's termination notice or the cure notice is not legally supportable but other grounds for default could exist at the same time and save the default. For example, a particular defect in a contractor's product—cited in the termination notice—may be found not to exist, but the product was still defective in other respects and could have justified a default action. In such a situation, the termination will usually be upheld unless the government's error in incorrectly specifying the basis for the default action has prejudiced the contractor. This principle is well settled. See § 49.2, supra.

(c) Notices

The government's failure to issue the notices required by the "Default" clause or other relevant regulations may also invalidate the government's termination decision. Under the standard supply/service clause (but not the construction clause), a 10-day "cure notice" demanding that the contractor cure the failure is only required when the government seeks to terminate a contract before the scheduled date of delivery or performance. A cure notice is not required if the delivery or performance schedule has expired, the contractor has repudiated performance, or less than 10 days remain before performance is due. Failure to issue a "cure notice" when required can invalidate the default termination. Even so, the government will rarely wait that long before issuing the cure notice.

Another notice will usually be employed. When a termination for default "appears appropriate," the Contracting Officer "should, if practicable," notify the contractor of the possibility of termination and ask the contractor to "show cause" why the contract should not be terminated for default. Although "show cause notices" are often sent to tardy contractors, the government is not legally obligated to send such a notice or to wait the entire 10 days (or other period specified) before terminating the contract for default. As indicated above, the government will normally be cautious and will issue the show cause notice to protect its rights (and not incidentally) the contractor's) rights.

After complying with all the procedures set forth in the FAR and determining that termination is proper, the Contracting Officer must notify the contractor of a possible default in writing. Although the FAR lists the information that should be included in a "termination notice," the government's omission of some of the required information will not invalidate a termination decision unless the omission prejudices the contractor.

§ 49.4   Contractor Defenses

When faced with termination of a contract for default, and the ground is late delivery, the contractor may be able to avoid the termination if it can show either (1) that contract performance is not late because the contractor encountered an excusable delay that extended the contract's schedule or (2) performance is late but the government nevertheless waived the contract's due date.

The contractor's financial incapability generally is not a defense, with exceptions for where the government fails to pay invoices in a timely manner and the late payment renders the contractor financially incapable of continuing performance, or the government's action was the primary or controlling cause of the default, or the government's action was a material breach of contract.

The contractor's status as a small business concern does not merit special treatment in litigation concerning default termination.

(a)   Excusable Delays

Both the supply/service contract "Default" clause and the construction contract "Default" clause provide examples of some recognized causes of delay that may excuse a contractor's failure to perform on time.

Note that excusable causes of delay are not enumerated in the commercial item contract "Termination for Cause" clause. Instead, the "Contract Terms and Conditions-Commercial Items" clause contains a separate "Excusable Delay" term, which includes examples of excusable causes of delay similar to those enumerated in the "Default" clauses. The commercial item contract "Excusable

Delay" term also requires the contractor to notify the government, in writing, of any excusable delay "as soon as it is reasonably possible."

In addition to the delaying events enumerated in the "Default" clauses, other events may also be grounds for excusing a contractor's failure to deliver or perform on time. Perhaps the most common of these are constructive changes (see Chapter 43) in the scope or nature of performance brought about by the government's action or inaction.

A contractor's failure to assert excusable delay precluded excusable delay as a defense to a termination for default, the Armed Services Board of Contract Appeals has held in denying a challenge to a termination for default *ECC CENTCOM Constr.*, ASBCA 60647, 18-1 BCA ¶ 37133.

(b) Waiver of Due Date

The issue can arise whether the government can waive (better stated as "forfeit") the right to issue a default when the contractor is late. Normally the agency's inaction is not an intentional relinquishment as would be applicable for a true waiver. Thus, the government would lose its right to terminate the contract for default if (1) it fails to terminate within a reasonable time after the default, and (2) the contractor continues to perform the contract in reliance on the government's failure to terminate. The key is the "contractor's reliance . . . rather than the government's failure to have insisted upon strict adherence to the terms of the delivery schedule."

If the contractor fails to perform on or before the due date, the government thereafter must—within a reasonable time—elect whether to terminate the contract for default or permit performance to continue. The government is entitled to a period of "forbearance"— that is, a sufficient time in which to determine what to do. However, if the government does not exercise its right to terminate within a reasonable time, and if the contractor relies on the government's inaction and continues to perform the contract and incur costs, the government may lose its right to terminate the contract.

The erosion of the rule that "waiver" of the delivery date is not applicable to construction contracts has continued even as such waivers have been denied. In an ASBCA case, the Board stated the applicable rule as being that "absent unusual circumstances," a reasonable time for forbearance is permitted in construction contracts, which is far short of saying that waiver could never occur.

(c) Termination After "Waiver"

After "waiving" the delivery date, the government can revive its right to terminate for default by establishing a new delivery schedule either unilaterally or by agreement with the contractor. If the contractor agrees to a new delivery schedule, it will not be permitted to complain later that the new schedule allowed it less than a reasonable time to perform. However, when the government unilaterally establishes a new delivery schedule, it must set a specific date and notify the contractor. The new performance date must take into consideration the capabilities of the particular contractor and be reasonably possible for the contractor to meet.

§ 49.5 Government Remedies

The principal remedies for the government on default termination of a contract are provided in the standard "Default" clauses for fixed-price contracts. Where the government properly terminates a contract for default, it is entitled under the standard clauses to charge the contractor the "excess costs" of reprocurement.

This remedy provides the government with a shortcut method of obtaining the contract work or items from a new source and charging the defaulted contractor for any increase in the cost of the reprocured work or items. To recover excess reprocurement costs, the government must establish not only that the contract was properly terminated for default but also that the reprocurement contract was for similar services.

Courts and boards have denied the Government its entitlement to excess reprocurement costs because the agency failed to show that the substitute was comparable and that the amount it sought was the precise amount that it had spent in reprocurement. Even when an agency claim for excess costs of reprocurement fails for the government's lack of due diligence in conducting the follow-on acquisition, the Government after a default may proceed under a general breach of contract theory, but it must shoulder the heavier burden of proving actual damages versus just relying on the costs of reprocurement.

The standard "Default" clauses also provide that the government's right to recover the excess costs of reprocurement is "in addition to any other rights and remedies provided by law or under this contract." Thus, the government may recover its actual damages, recoup unliquidated progress payments, or confiscate project-related inventory in addition to or instead of excess reprocurement costs. Because most defaulted contractors will be insolvent, however, this right to excess costs often exists in name only.

Liquidated damages may also be assessed against the defaulted contractor if the contract contains a "Liquidated Damages" clause that meets the requirements of enforceability. The government may assess liquidated damages as an alternative to termination in the case of default by the contractor or as a substitute for actual damages for delayed or incomplete work. Again, recovery of these damages could be problematic if the defaulted contractor is insolvent.

The commercial item contract "Termination for Cause" term states only that the contractor "shall be liable to the government for any and all rights and remedies provided by law." The FAR provides, however, that the government's rights after a terminating a commercial item contract for cause "shall include all the remedies available to any buyer in the marketplace," noting that the government's "preferred remedy" will be to acquire similar items from another contractor and to charge the defaulted contractor with any excess reprocurement costs together with any incidental or consequential damages incurred because of the termination.

In addition to the difference in price between the terminated contract and the reprocured contract, excess reprocurement cost assessments may include the additional costs necessary for contract completion, such as (1) the cost to the government of installing and then removing defective items, (2) recovery of interest, (3) the administrative costs of reprocuring the supplies or services, and (4) necessary costs unique to a particular procurement.

An agency may properly exclude a defaulted contractor from a reprocurement for the remaining work in the defaulted contract; to the extent that prior cases state that a contracting officer may not automatically exclude a defaulted contractor from the competition for a reprocurement, the GAO has overruled those decisions. See *Montage, Inc.*, B-277923.2, 97-2 CPD ¶ 176.

The government may also pursue other remedies provided by law, such as maintaining an action for breach of contract on the contractor's default. Common law damages for breach of contract are available in addition to or instead of the excess costs of reprocurement. The breach of contract damages available to the government in the case of default are the same as those available to the government following a contractor's delay (although the damages may be limited to the extent the contract contains a "Liquidated Damages" clause that covers such damages). Remedies apart from those provided under the "Default" clauses are only infrequently pursued—probably because the measure of proof required tends to be greater than it would be under the clause.

§ 49.6   Relation to Termination for Convenience

If a board or court determines that the contractor was not actually in default or the default was excusable, the termination for default, under the standard clauses, will be converted into a termination for convenience. Similarly, before the appeal is even decided, the Contracting Officer can convert the termination for default into one for the government's convenience.

The contractor's recovery under a convenience termination may be significant. For example, under a convenience termination, the contractor is eligible to recover its costs of performance, some "continuing costs," settlement expenses, and a reasonable profit on completed work. This chapter will provide below a more detailed discussion of the contractor's rights when a termination for default is converted into a termination for convenience.

B. CONVENIENCE TERMINATIONS

§ 49.7 Standard "Termination for Convenience" Clauses

The "Termination for Convenience" clause permits the government to cancel a contract without cause—that is, to halt a contractor's right to continue with performance regardless of fault simply because it is in the government's best interest—which differs from whether a termination is in the contractor's interests.

The following sections review the government's rights under the "Termination for Convenience" clause. Specifically, they examine (1) the standard "Termination for Convenience" contract clauses and the scope of the government's right under those clauses, (2) the termination procedures set forth in the clause and the regulations that apply to both the government and the contractor, (3) constructive terminations for convenience, (4) what a contractor can expect to recover in the termination settlement, and (5) partial terminations.

§ 49.8 Government's Convenience Termination Right

The government's reservation in its contracts of the right to terminate contracts for convenience is extremely broad. It is not limited to a cardinal change in government requirements or a decrease in the need for the purchase items.

Thus, in exchange for the privilege of being able to terminate a contract with relative ease, the government agrees to make the contractor "whole;" that is, to reimburse the contractor for all reasonable, allowable, and allocable costs incurred in connection with performance, as well as a reasonable profit on work done. The contractor may also recover certain post-termination costs and settlement expenses. The contractor may not, however, recover its anticipated profits, i.e., profits it had reasonably expected to earn on the terminated portion of the contract. The reason is that the government does not breach the contract when it exercises this right, and recovery for lost profits is only available for actions in breach.

The right of the government to terminate a contract for its own convenience is embodied in standard "Termination for Convenience of the Government" clauses. Typical of these clauses is the FAR's "Termination for Convenience of the Government (Fixed-Price)" clause, designated for use in fixed-price contracts expected to exceed the simplified acquisition threshold (see Chapter 13). Another important clause is the "Termination for the Government's Convenience" term in the "Commercial Items" clause that is a part of the standard terms for commercial item contracts, even though the right to terminate contracts without cause is generally inconsistent with standard commercial practices.

So important is the government's right of convenience termination that even when a contracting agency neglects to include a convenience termination clause, it will be incorporated into the contract as a matter of law under the *Christian* doctrine (see Chapter 1), absent countervailing reasons.

§ 49.9   Scope of Discretion

In a leading case, the U.S. Court of Appeals for the Federal Circuit held in *Krygoski Cont. Co., Inc. v. United States*, 94 F.3d 1537 (Fed. Cir. 1996), that the government's decision to terminate a contract for convenience is conclusive and will not be disturbed by the courts unless the contractor can prove that the government acted in bad faith—which the contractor must demonstrate by clear and convincing evidence that the government acted with specific intent to injure the contractor—or that the government abused its discretion (i.e., its decision to terminate had no reasonable relation to the government's best interest). The court listed the following as factors to consider in determining whether the government abused its discretion: (1) the procurement official's bad faith, (2) the reasonableness of the decision, and (3) the amount of discretion delegated to the procurement official.

As indicated above, an improper termination for convenience may give rise to a breach of contract claim if the agency (1) terminates the contract in bad faith or (2) abuses its discretion in terminating the contract. If the contractor's theory is that the Government entered into the contract with no intention of performing, then the contractor may be able to overturn a termination for convenience without proving intent to injure the contractor.

Occasionally, the government may seek to rescind a convenience termination. The agency may reinstate the terminated portion of the contract, with the contractor's written consent, when the Contracting

Officer determines a requirement exists for the terminated items, and where the reinstatement is advantageous to the government.

§ 49.10 Termination Procedures

The FAR sets forth procedures to be followed by the Contracting Officer when terminating a contract for convenience. It also describes the duties of the contractor after receiving a notice of termination from the government.

In addition to terminations for convenience that are effected by written notice to the contractor from the Contracting Officer, a convenience termination may be deemed to have taken place by operation of law. These so-called "constructive terminations" can come about either by (1) conversion of an improper termination for default into a termination for convenience or (2) cancellation of a contract, an award, or work.

(a) Written Notice

The FAR directs the Contracting Officer to issue a detailed, written notice to terminate a contract for convenience. Under the FAR, the termination notice should include the following:

1.   A statement that the contract is being terminated for the convenience of the government;

2.   The effective date of the termination;

3.   The extent of the termination (i.e., whether the entire contract—or only a designated portion—is being terminated);

4.   Any special instructions regarding work-in-process or other matters; and

5.   Steps the contractor should take to minimize the impact of the termination on personnel, especially if the termination will result in a significant reduction in the contractor's work force.

(b) Contractor's Obligations

The written notice from the government to the contractor that the contract is being terminated for the government's convenience usually includes detailed and specific procedures for the contractor to follow, including direction to follow the procedures contained in the "Termination for Convenience of the government" clause in the contract. Failure of the contractor to follow these instructions exactly might result in disallowance of at least some of the costs incurred.

The notice and clause generally require that the contractor—

1.   Stop work immediately on the terminated portion of the contract and stop placing subcontracts;

2.   Terminate all subcontracts related to the terminated portion of the prime contract;

3.   Immediately advise the Terminating Contracting Officer (TCO) of any special circumstances precluding stoppage of work;

4.   Perform the continued portion of the contract if the termination is partial and submit any request for equitable adjustment promptly;

5.   Take any action necessary to protect property in the contractor's possession in which the government has or may acquire an interest;

6.   Promptly notify the TCO of any legal proceedings growing out of any subcontract or other commitment related to the terminated portion of the contract;

7.   Settle subcontractors' claims arising out of the termination, obtaining any required approvals and ratifications from the TCO;

8.   Promptly submit (within one year from the effective date of the termination) a settlement proposal to the government, supported by appropriate schedules; and

9.   Dispose of termination inventory, as directed and authorized by the TCO.

§ 49.11 Commercial Item Contracts

The standard FAR government contract termination rules do not apply to the termination, either for convenience or for cause, of contracts for commercial items. Instead, the FAR requires Contracting Officers to follow the standard termination procedures as "guidance" only to the extent that standard rules do not conflict with FAR commercial item policy and the "Commercial Items" contract clause. Where the costs of additional work for a commercial item convenience termination cannot be readily separated from the cost of the basic contract, a cost based approach is an appropriate measure of the percentage of work completed.

A final FAR rule clarifies that FAR Part 49, Termination of Contracts, does not necessarily apply to the acquisition of commercial items if FAR Part 12 procedures are used. However, Contracting Officers may consult FAR Part 49 in terminating a FAR Part 12 contract for convenience where to do so is commercially reasonable.

§ 49.12 Contractor Settlements

When a contract is terminated for convenience, the general rule is the contractor may recover (1) the costs of performance incurred up to the time of termination, (2) certain "continuing costs" (post-termination costs), (3) settlement expenses, and (4) under a fixed-price contract, an allowance for profit for work performed (unless the contract would have been performed at a loss) or, under a cost-reimbursement contract, the earned portion of the fee.

With a convenience termination, the contractor's recovery for incurred allowable direct costs will be capped at the contract price. However, the government's "overriding objective" in a termination settlement should be to make the contractor "financially whole for all the direct consequences" of the termination.

One exception exists to the general rule mentioned above. Where the government and the contractor are both responsible for the causes resulting in contract termination, the contractor should be denied full recovery of termination costs. Termination for convenience recovery must be based on contract unit rates rather than the contractor's costs as would be applicable under the changes clause.

(a) Settlement Basis

In addition to the general guidance in the FAR regarding settlement agreements, the FAR provides special principles for settlements involving fixed-price contracts and cost-reimbursement contracts. The principles for fixed-price contracts are the more detailed and are particularly noteworthy for describing two major bases for settlement proposals: the "inventory basis," which is preferred, and the "total cost" basis.

Under the inventory method, the contractor's costs are allocated to inventory items such as raw materials, purchased parts, work-in-process, and tooling. Other appropriate charges—such as initial and administrative costs and the costs of settling with subcontractors—are added. The aggregate costs are then augmented by profit (or adjusted for loss), and any credits owing to the government—for example, unliquidated progress payments—are deducted to arrive at a net settlement amount.

The total cost method measures total costs incurred without allocating costs to particular items of inventory. This method is appropriate for use only when the inventory method is not practical or will unduly delay settlement—for example, when the contractor's accounting system does not adequately establish the unit costs of work-in-process and finished products. Settlement expenses, profit, loss, and credits are handled in the same manner as in the inventory method.

(b) No-Cost Settlement

If the contractor has incurred no costs pertaining to the terminated portion of the contract—and no credits owing to the government—the parties may execute a no-cost settlement agreement. Use of such agreements is also, on occasion, the only practicable way in which disputes involving settlements can be resolved.

(c) Settlement Principles and Limitations

The FAR provides that the usual cost principles are to be used in determining termination settlement costs "subject to the general principles" in the FAR regarding the TCO's negotiation of settlement agreements. These "general principles" emphasize that the overriding aim is the TCO should exercise "business judgment" to achieve the general goal of "fair compensation" to the contractor.

(d) Special Termination Costs

When a contract is terminated for convenience, the recovery of some types of costs often proves problematic for the contractor, even with the guidance of the FAR cost principles. For example, "startup" or precontract costs are frequently disproportionate to the number of items completed at the time of termination, and equipment and facilities may be rendered useless on termination.

(e) Settlement Expenses

Settlement expenses are direct charges for the contractor's preparation of the termination settlement claim. Normally, such expenses would be considered indirect or overhead costs, but the FAR requires that they be removed from the indirect cost category and charged directly to the settlement claim. Examples of settlement expenses that are generally allowable include the following:

1.   Accounting, legal, clerical, and similar costs reasonably necessary for (1) preparing and presenting to the TCO settlement claims and supporting data and (2) the termination and settlement of subcontracts;

2.   Reasonable costs for the storage, transportation, protection, and disposition of property acquired or produced for the contract; and

3.   Indirect costs related to salary and wages incurred in connection with settlement—normally limited to payroll taxes, fringe benefits, occupancy costs, and immediate supervision costs.

Although FAR 49.207 caps termination settlements at the contract price, the FAR does not limit the size of the contractor's settlement proposal. A contractor may not, however, recover anticipatory or consequential damages for a termination for convenience. Instead, the Government is liable only for the contract awardee's performance up to the time of the termination for convenience, and certain other costs.

(f) Subcontractor Proposals

Prime contractors are responsible for reviewing, negotiating, and settling—subject to government approval or ratification—proposals of their immediate (first-tier) subcontractors. The FAR states that prime contractors "should" include a "Termination for Convenience" clause in their subcontracts "for their own protection" and provides a suggested clause.

A subcontractor proposal that is negotiated and approved by the government is a proper cost to be included in the prime contractor's settlement proposal. Subcontractor settlements resulting from arm's-length negotiations between the prime and subcontractor will likely readily be approved by the government for purposes of cost recovery after a termination for convenience. Thus, the government cannot question a contractor's sound business judgment or negotiating tactics but may resist compensation based on evidence of bad faith, self-dealing, absence of proof, or willful neglect or wrongdoing.

Allowability of a settlement with a subcontractor after initiation of litigation between the prime contractor and subcontractor depends on a determination whether the risk and expense of the litigation justified the prime contractor's decision to settle. Judgments or arbitration awards obtained by subcontractors against the prime contractor will be allowed if the prime contractor's actions in connection with the subcontracts and the defense of the subcontractors' suits were reasonable.

(g) Profit

Unless completion of a fixed-price contract would have resulted in a loss, a contractor may recover a "reasonable allowance for profit on work done (and not terminated work)." The FAR specifies various factors to be considered in determining a fair profit, such as the difficulty of the work and the efficiency of the contractor. However, the contractor's usual rate of profit may be the standard used for measuring allowable profit.

Because the determination of an appropriate profit factor is judgmental and speculative, it is important for a contractor to present convincing proof that (1) the contractor was not performing the contract at a loss, and (2) the contractor's expected profit was realistic in light of past experience and the peculiarities of the contract. Profit will not be denied in a convenience settlement when the Government substantially contributed to the increased costs and it is not possible to separate the Government portion of the loss from the possible losses caused by the contractor.

As indicated above, if completion of a fixed-price contract would have resulted in a loss, a contractor cannot recover a profit in a termination settlement. Indeed, the FAR requires that the contractor's recovery—exclusive of settlement expenses—be reduced by a percentage equal to the percentage of loss the contractor would have suffered on the entire contract if it had been completed, and the FAR spells out a detailed procedure for applying this "loss formula."

The theory behind this policy is that a contractor should not be financially better off as a result of a termination for convenience than the contractor would have been had the contract been completely performed. The Government has the burden of proof to show that the contractor was in a loss position and thereby not entitled to profit with a convenience termination.

§ 49.13 Commercial Item Contracts

When a commercial item contract is terminated for the government's convenience, the contractor is entitled to (1) a percentage of the contract price reflecting the percentage of the work performed before notice of the termination and (2) any charges that the contractor can demonstrate resulted directly from the termination.

In keeping with the goal stated in the FAR of "having a simple and expeditious settlement" of a convenience termination, the contractor may demonstrate these charges using its standard recordkeeping system. The government does not have a right to audit the contractor's records solely because of the termination for convenience.

§ 49.14 Partial Terminations

A termination for convenience need not terminate the entire contract. Partial terminations are possible. On receipt of a notice of a partial termination—which should specify the extent of the termination—the contractor is required to take similar actions with regard to the terminated portion of the contract as in the case of a complete termination. Of course, if the termination is only partial, the contractor must continue performance on the work that has not been terminated. Furthermore, the contractor may request an equitable adjustment for the continued portion of the contract.

(a) Partial Termination vs. Deductive Change

Both the "Termination for Convenience of the Government" clause and the "Changes" clause in the contract permit the government to delete work. The procedure the government elects to use is important where the contract is for a fixed price because the different pricing formulas used by the two clauses may have a significant effect on the amount of compensation allowed the contractor.

As indicated in Chapter 43, use of the "Changes" clause is appropriate only when the change ordered by the government is within the scope of the contract. Generally, a major deletion of the work called for by the contract should be effected by a partial termination, while a minor deletion should be accomplished by a deductive change. Thus, where major portions of the work are deleted and no additional work is substituted thereby, the termination for convenience clause must be used. By contrast, the deletion of relatively minor and segregable work items will be a deductive change. However, deletion of as little as 5% of the work has been held to require application of partial termination procedures.

(b) Contractor Recovery

The standard "Termination for Convenience" clause provides that, in case of a partial termination, the contractor is to be paid the contract price for work not terminated, except that the contractor may request an equitable adjustment in the price of the non-terminated work. As in the case of a complete termination, anticipated profits on the terminated portion or consequential damages are not recoverable in a partial termination.

The equitable adjustment provided for by the clause is supposed to compensate for any additional costs incurred by the contractor in performing the work not terminated as a result of the partial termination. Usually, actual costs incurred are used as the basis for the equitable adjustment, subject to a loss adjustment if the contractor would have lost money in performing the entire contract. The adjustment should not increase the contractor's profit margin or reverse a loss position. For further explanation of this general area, see Chapter 43.

Table of Cases

Index

References are to Pages

Payment, 470
Prime contractor/subcontractor
    litigation, 466
Privity rule, 462
Small business preferences, 470
Terms and conditions, 471

SUPPLY CONTRACTS
Commercial items acquisitions,
    service/product distinctions,
    140
Construction contracts compared
        Generally, 403 et seq.
        See also Construction and
            Architect-Engineer
            Contracts, this index
Delays and Suspensions of Work, this
    index
Required or Authorized Sources of
    Supplies and Services, this
    index

SUSPENSION
Delays and Suspensions of Work, this
    index
Qualifications of contractors, 107,
    114

**SYSTEM FOR AWARD
MANAGEMENT,** 49

TASK ORDERS
Delivery orders distinguished, 82

TAXES, 311

TERMINATIONS
        Generally, 501 et seq.
Anticipatory breach of contract
        Generally, 508
        Convenience terminations,
        below
Cause terminations, 503
Commercial item contracts
        Generally, 518
        Settlements, 522
Construction contracts, 407
Contracting officer discretion, 508
Contractor defenses, 511
Contractor obligations, 517
Convenience terminations
        Generally, 515 et seq.
        Commercial item contracts
            Generally, 518
            Settlements, 522
        Contractor obligations, 517
        Contractor recovery, 523
        Costs, 520
        Default terminations
            distinguished, 514
        Discretion of government, 516
        Government rights, 515
        Partial terminations, 522

Procedure, 517
Settlements
        Generally, 518
        Commercial item
            settlements, 522
        Subcontractor proposals, 521
Costs, convenience terminations, 520
Cure notices, 502
Deductive charges, partial
    terminations compared, 522
Default terminations
        Generally, 501 et seq.
        Anticipatory breach of contract,
        508
        Construction contracts, 407
        Contracting officer discretion,
        508
        Contractor defenses, 511
        Convenience terminations
            distinguished, 514
        Cure notices, 502
        Excusable delays, 511
        Government remedies, 513
        Notices, 510
        Specification failures, 505
        Timely delivery
            Generally, 505
            Waivers, 512
Discretion of government, 516
Excusable delays, 511
Government remedies, default
    terminations, 513
Government rights, convenience
    terminations, 515
Notices, default terminations, 510
Procedure, convenience terminations,
    517
Settlements
        Generally, 518
        Commercial item settlements,
        522
Specification failures, 505
Subcontractor proposals, 521
Timely delivery
        Generally, 505
        Waivers, 512

TIMING MATTERS
Contracting by negotiation, 190
Cost accounting standards
    disclosures, 321
Decisions, time for issuance, 374
Delivery requirements
        Generally, 505
        Waivers, 512
GAO level protests, 347
Option exercises, 251
Sealed bidding, 170

TRADEOFF PROCESS, 215

TUCKER ACT, 4